Romantic Marks and Measures

Romantic
Marks and Measures

Wordsworth's Poetry
in Fields of Print

Julia S. Carlson

PENN

UNIVERSITY OF PENNSYLVANIA PRESS

PHILADELPHIA

Published by
University of Pennsylvania Press
Philadelphia, Pennsylvania 19104–4112
www.upenn.edu/pennpress

Printed in the United States of America on acid-free paper
1 3 5 7 9 10 8 6 4 2

Cataloging-in-Publication Data for this book is available
from the Library of Congress.
ISBN 978-0-8122-4787-9

For my parents

Even though we navigate daily through a perceptual world of three spatial dimensions and reason occasionally about higher dimensional arenas with mathematical ease, the world portrayed on our information displays is caught up in the two-dimensionality of the endless flatlands of paper and video screen. . . . *Escaping this flatland is the essential task of envisioning information—for all the interesting worlds (physical, biological, imaginary, human) that we seek to understand are inevitably and happily multivariate in nature. Not flatlands.* . . . Even our language, like our paper, often lacks immediate capacity to communicate a sense of dimensional complexity.

—Edward Tufte, *Envisioning Information*

I have the whole punctuation to settle; which in blank-verse is of the last importance, and of a species, peculiar to that composition; for I know no use of points, unless to direct the voice, the management of which, in the reading of blank-verse, being more difficult than in the reading of any other poetry, requires perpetual hints, and notices, to regulate the inflexions, cadences and pauses. This however is an affair, that in spite of grammarians, must be left pretty much *ad libitum scriptoris* [to the discretion of the writer]. For (I suppose) every author points according to his own reading.

—William Cowper to William Unwin, 2 October 1784

A British man, speaking French . . . discovers his country as much by the emphasis he lays upon particular syllables, as by any other mark.

—James Burnett Monboddo,
Of the Origin and Progress of Language

Contents

Illustrations

Abbreviations

1799   William Wordsworth, *The Prelude, 1798–1799*, ed. Stephen Parrish (Ithaca: Cornell University Press, 1977)

1805   William Wordsworth, *The Thirteen-Book Prelude*, ed. Mark L. Reed, 2 vols. (Ithaca: Cornell University Press, 1991). All citations are from volume I unless otherwise stated.

1850   William Wordsworth, *The Fourteen-Book Prelude,* ed. W. J. B. Owen (Ithaca: Cornell University Press, 1985)

BL   Samuel Taylor Coleridge, *Biographia Literaria*, ed. James Engell and W. Jackson Bate, 2 vols. (Princeton: Princeton University Press, 1983)

CL   *Collected Letters of Samuel Taylor Coleridge*, ed. E. L. Griggs, 6 vols. (Oxford: Clarendon Press, 1956–71)

Excursion   William Wordsworth, *The Excursion*, ed. Sally Bushell, James A. Butler, and Michael Jaye (Ithaca: Cornell University Press, 2007). Internal quotation marks are supplied for speech in block quotations and where relevant to argument.

EY   *The Letters of William and Dorothy Wordsworth: The Early Years, 1787–1805*, 2nd ed., ed. Ernest De Selincourt, rev. Chester L. Shaver, 2 vols. (Oxford: Clarendon Press, 1967), vol. I

HC   John Thelwall, *Letter to Henry Cline, Esq. on Imperfect Developments of the Faculties, Mental and Moral, as well as*

Constitutional and Organic; and on the Treatment of Impediments of Speech (London, 1810)

LB   Lyrical Ballads, *and Other Poems, 1797–1800*, ed. James Butler and Karen Green (Ithaca: Cornell University Press, 1992)

PW   *The Poetical Works of S. T. Coleridge*, ed. J. C. C. Mays, 3 vols. (Princeton: Princeton University Press, 2001)

W Prose   *The Prose Works of William Wordsworth*, ed. W. J. B. Owen and J. W. Smyser, 3 vols. (Oxford: Clarendon Press, 1974)

Introduction

When Francis Jeffrey reviewed *Thalaba* in 1802, he made Robert Southey's poem a test case of all that was wrong with the new, revolutionary school of poetry. One of his strongest criticisms concerned the poem's measures: Southey's predilection for experimental, unrhymed verse-forms was, he said, untraditional and un-English: "Blank odes have been known in this country about as long as English sapphics and dactylics; and both have been considered, we believe, as a species of monsters, or exotics, that were not very likely to propagate, or thrive, in so unpropitious a climate."[1] Here Jeffrey echoed the satire of Gillray whose 1798 print "The New Morality" portrayed Southey as an unpatriotic worshipper at the shrine of revolutionary France on the basis of his unrhymed experimental forms (Figure 1). Southey is pictured as an ass braying out "Sapphics" as radical print spills round his knees from a "cornucopia of ignorance," the blank verse *Joan of Arc* stuffed in his pocket. His collaborators Lamb and Lloyd are depicted as frog and toad croaking blank verse from their volume by that name, while Coleridge, also pictured as an ass, counts out dactyls on his fingers. Blanks were not musical but mechanical, dissonant, and dangerous: the vehicle of foreign and Jacobinical ideas.[2]

Southey's attempt to naturalize sapphics had failed, Jeffrey asserted, and he predicted a no better fate for *Thalaba*—"a jumble of all the measures that are known in English poetry, (and a few more), without rhyme, and without any sort of regularity in their arrangement." Strange combinations exercised the mind, and rather than being "repeated with any degree of uniformity were multiplied, through the whole composition, with an unfounded licence of variation." *Thalaba*'s cadences were not merely unprecedented but failed to set precedents within the poem.[3] Readers, in effect, were presented with a trick of print—"the greater part of the book," Jeffrey declared, "is mere prose, written out into the form of verse" (70). He excerpted various passages, defying readers to discover in the clusters of indented lines the melodies that Southey claimed were there. The voice of the "dullest reader," Southey asserted in the preface, could not fail to make them "perceptible."[4]

Figure 1. James Gillray, "New Morality; — or — the promis'd instalment
of the high-priest of the Theophilanthropes, with the homage of Leviathan
and his suite" (London, 1798), detail. © Trustees of the British Museum.
Reproduced by permission of the British Museum.

Cut away to the year 1812: another critic was printing excerpts from a
Southey epic and inviting readers to discover their measure. In his *Selections for
the Illustration of a Course of Instruction on the Rhythmus and Utterance of the
English Language,* John Thelwall reproduced a passage from *The Curse of Ke-
hama* (1810), extolling its "beautiful variety of lyrical measure, well worthy of
elocutionary analysis."[5] What was a monstrous jumble to Jeffrey the tradition-
alist was a beautiful variety to Thelwall the radical. However, beyond their
opposition over politics and the politics of literature, the two men's responses
to Southey's poetry display an underlying similarity, for both hinged on the
voicing of print. How could Southey's unrhymed lines be construed into melody from the page? Jeffrey thought they could not be, and so condemned
them; Thelwall disseminated a system of "elocutionary analysis" that would
help readers to reveal the poet's "rhythmus," release their constrained tongues,
and encourage the development of their intellects and feelings. If Gillray pictured Thelwall in 1798 declaiming his politics and bearing the mud slung by
disaffected crowds (Figure 1, left), Thelwall's 1812 *Selections* promised to reform
the affections of his readers—and to empower them—by engaging them actively in the exercise of scanning and voicing poetic texts. In this, he radicalized

the project of elocution and the interactions with print shaped by his prede-
cessors in liberal prosody, who had worked to reveal the accentual nature of
English in order to renovate the culture and to prove, in the words of Thomas
Sheridan, that the "*English tongue* is as capable of all the Art and Elegancies of
Grammar and *Rhetorick*, as *Greek* or *Latin*, or any other Language in the
World."[6]

When Jeffrey unmasked *Thalaba* as "mere prose, written out into the form
of verse" and when a reviewer for the *British Critic* jeered "were not the lines
divided by the printer, no living creature would suspect them to be even intended for verse,"[7] they mobilized eighteenth-century aesthetic hierarchies and
suspicions of print to attack the leveling tendencies of the new Lake School of
poets. In fact, Jeffrey's review of *Thalaba* was as much an attack on *Lyrical
Ballads* and particularly Wordsworth's Preface as it was on Southey. In turn,
Thelwall applied his "elocutionary analysis" not just to Southey's poetry but
also to Wordsworth's. Thelwall had discussed prosody with Wordsworth and
Coleridge when he visited Alfoxden in the summer of 1797. The following year
poetry was again discussed when Wordsworth and Coleridge traveled to Wales
to meet Thelwall at his Llyswen retreat. But it was in 1803, when Thelwall came
to the Lakes to give a course of lectures on elocution—lectures in which the
recitation of verse was crucial—that the conversation was renewed in greater
detail. Thelwall sent an outline of his lectures to the poets in Grasmere and
Keswick. Coleridge excused himself; Southey made the journey; Wordsworth
stayed home but wrote a cordial letter that constitutes one of his most detailed
discussions of prosody.[8]

Yet it seems this letter was not followed up by further discussions. The
poets diverged—not least politically. Thelwall remained a republican, channeling his energies into his elocutionary project; the other poets made their ac-
commodations with the Regency—Southey became Laureate, Wordsworth a
sinecurist of Lord Lonsdale, one of the most powerful conservative political
magnates; Coleridge wrote for the Tory press and disavowed his Jacobinism.
When, in the *Biographia Literaria* (1817), Coleridge played down his radical
politics and turned the Alfoxden visit into bucolic comedy, Thelwall annotated
his copy incredulously. And when in 1814 Wordsworth published his magnum
opus of blank verse nature poetry *The Excursion* (part of the *Recluse* project
conceived at Alfoxden in 1797–98), Thelwall scanned the entire volume, marking cadence, stress, and occasional marginalia in his copy of the book.

At issue as Thelwall marked up *The Excursion* was the nature of blank verse
and democratic access to its measures. Is it iambic and decasyllabic, as critics

generally held and as printers represented it, or is it made of "metrical cadences + rhythmical clauses,"[9] as Thelwall's scansion implied? For Jeffrey when reviewing *Thalaba* and *Lyrical Ballads,* it was the very legitimacy of blank verse that was at stake. Dryden and Johnson had implied that the unrhymed, ten-syllable line merely posed as verse. The spatial organization of "*prose mesurée*" made it appear to the eye as poetry—an effect that was supported by print.[10] To some critics wedded to neoclassical aesthetic strictures—closed, rhyming couplets, strict iambic alternation, medial caesuras—and to their regulation of the mind and morals, blank verse was merely the visual effect of print: formal laxity in disguise.[11] In an ironic turn, however, Thelwall's prosodic precursors, including Samuel Say, John Rice, Joshua Steele, and Richard Roe, seized upon the technology of print to erode neoclassical theories of meter and the line. What figured in conservative criticism as a tool of deception and symbol of cultural, social, and political anxiety was recruited as a technology of illustration and as an agent not merely of linguistic revelation but also of social, cultural, and individual renovation. Thus when Rice invoked the trope of the anarchic "Printing-House," in which "a Compositor can convert Prose into Verse at Pleasure, by printing it in detached Lines of ten Syllables,"[12] he did so not to join critics in discrediting blank verse but rather to expose the arbitrariness of its conventional pentameter division and to propose reforms in printing that would make its harmony more apparent to the "Generality of readers" (179). Divided into "Periods," or "the quick succession of a few flowing Syllables," a reformed *Paradise Lost* would contain lines such as these:

> And round skirted his Loins and Thighs with downy Gold
> And Colours dipt in Heaven.
> The third his Feet shadow'd from either Heel with feather'd Mail,
> Sky tinctur'd Grain. (177)

Richard Roe went further: alluding to the impulse for "accuracy" in contemporary cartographic culture, he employed "rule and compasses" to demonstrate the isochrony of English metrical units. Converting time of utterance into spatial extent, he charted the quantities of prose and verse cadences, mostly blank, along scale bars marked to show the "equidistance" of accent from foot to foot—and he invited the reader, "while perusing the examples, to carry the point of a pin, by way of index, with an equable motion over the spaces marked on the lines."[13] Thelwall's scansion of *The Excursion* and his broader project to energize Britons by their own marking and voicing of his literary *Selections* enacted a democratic and patriotic extension of such efforts to reveal in print the unrecognized "measures" and "melodies" that organized English speech, verse, and prose.[14]

Thelwall was not the only contemporary to subject Wordsworth's poetry to a system of measuring and marking that effected a revisualization and rearticulation of his printed pages. Consider, for example, the popular Victorian travel book *Black's Picturesque Guide to the English Lakes, with a Copious Itinerary, a Map, and Four Charts of the Lake District; and Engraved Views of the Scenery*, which quoted copiously from local writers to "illustrate the scenery through which [the tourist] will pass."[15] Wordsworth's verse pervades the *Guide*, and the quoting of one of his two "best specimens" of blank verse, particularly in the fifth and following editions, is suggestive.[16] In guiding tourists from Borrowdale toward Buttermere, Crummock, and Loweswater, *Black's* asks them to turn from the main road to observe the "four yew trees of extraordinary size" that Wordsworth "commemorates," directing their eyes with lines from the middle of "Yew-Trees"—

———"But worthier still of note
Are those fraternal four of Borrowdale,
Join'd in one solemn and capacious grove;
Huge trunks!—and each particular trunk a growth
Of intertwisted fibres, serpentine,
Upcoiling and inveterately convolved,
Nor uninform'd with phantasy, and looks
That threaten the profane; a pillar'd shade,
Upon whose grassless floor of red-brown hue,
By sheddings from the pining umbrage tinged"[17]

—before a full-page topographical map intervenes, presenting a detailed view from above of Buttermere, Crummock, and Loweswater, their tributaries, and surrounding hills, tarns, and mountains. Resuming on the next page, the sweeping blank-verse sentence brings into hazy, partial focus the haunted interior of that "capacious grove":

"Perennially—beneath whose sable roof
Of boughs, as if for festal purpose deck'd
With unrejoicing berries—ghastly shapes
May meet at noontide, there to celebrate

As in a natural temple, scatter'd o'er
With altars undisturb'd of mossy stone,
United worship." (83)

A second sudden shift in scale attends the poem, when, following another page of prose, two "Outline Views of Mountain Groups" ask readers to scan the "MOUNTAINS AS SEEN FROM THE KNOTS NEAR THE VICTORIA AT BUT-TERMERE" and "AT THE SEAT IN LANTHWAITE WOOD, SCALE HILL"—undulating horizon lines, printed horizontally across the page, with numbered peaks and promontories keyed to a list of names for reference and identification (Figure 2). The book then directs readers to the single "Yew-tree which Wordsworth has celebrated," quoting now the poem's first thirteen lines—

"There is a Yew-tree, pride of Lorton Vale,
Which to this day stands single in the midst
Of its own darkness, as it stood of yore,
Not loth to furnish weapons for the bands
Of Umfraville or Percy, ere they march'd
To Scotland's heaths"—

through to " 'Of form and aspect too magnificent / To be destroyed' " (87).

If "Yew-Trees" marks the height of Wordsworth's blank verse—one of his "best specimens," as he claimed[18]—*Black's Picturesque Guide* marks the height of the guidebook genre's conscription of verse as illustrative technology. Activating the poem's indexical gestures by their division and distribution across the chart and outline views—"But worthier still of note / Are those fraternal four"; "There is a Yew-tree, pride of Lorton Vale"—*Black's* transforms the passages into discrete views, such as tourist might see reflected in a Claude glass or in the steel-cut engravings leafed within the book. In line with new large-scale maps, which helped tourists "in tracing the rambles" described in prose, and the outline views which enabled them "to name most of the hills" in a particular range (73), the excerpts closely focused the yews, heightening their status as best "specimens" (87) within the national landscape for their age, girth, and connection to England's nation-building battles. Having furnished material for the "sounding bows at Agincour," "Cressy or Poictiers," the yews as rendered and arrayed among the printed inscriptions of the hills in the *Guide* now served also to draw sound out of that landscape. "The hill" near the yews, *Black's* notes, "bears the fine sounding British name of Glaramara"; "By

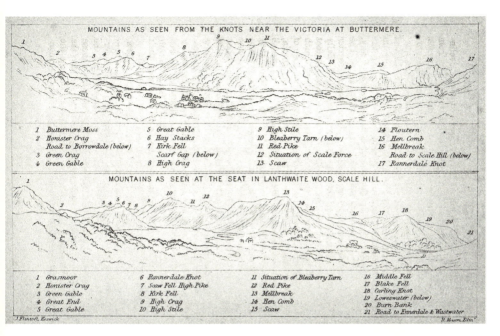

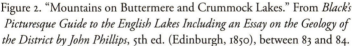

Figure 2. "Mountains on Buttermere and Crummock Lakes." From *Black's Picturesque Guide to the English Lakes Including an Essay on the Geology of the District by John Phillips*, 5th ed. (Edinburgh, 1850), between 83 and 84.

a little stretch of fancy," the compilers add, slightly misquoting the poem's last line, "the stranger may perhaps hear the streams 'murmuring in Glaramara's inmost caves'" (87).

Perhaps those etchings and engravings of the hills also helped also to draw sound out of the blank verse. For while the "literature of the district" (4) co-operated with the cartographic depictions to cultivate the stranger's knowledge of and feeling for place, those depictions also refocused the literature—and, in the case of "Yew-Trees," shaped the reading of a verse form recognized, and also criticized, for its difficult enjambments and unrestricted placement of pause and variety of feet. They did so not by notating cadences and patterns of stress—"tracing the rambles" of Wordsworth's long sentences as they extended across the lines—but by setting them amidst pictorial and diagrammatic renderings of the area's forms and features. These fields of reading cultivated the interpretation, and correlation, of miscellaneous "shapes," scales, and views, such as the mountains as depicted from above in the shaded charts and as etched in profile in "serpentine" outlines (82). Thus *Black's* conditioned the reading of a sometimes abstruse poetic form by cultivating *cartoliteracy*—visual and verbal attention to the printed marks and symbols of heterogeneous topographical fields. Whereas Thelwall sought to reform the minds and bodies of pupils by teaching them to reveal with a system of marks the "English rhythmus" hidden within print and, by reciting those rhythms, to retune their minds and bodies to the "feelings and principles of nature," *Black's Picturesque Guide* mixed graphic, metrical, and mensural grammars to give the traveler unparalleled access to the finest "combination of sublimity and beauty" in Britain (1) while "elevat[ing] the feelings and improving the heart" (4).[19]

In the Preface to *Lyrical Ballads*, Wordsworth famously cast off "poetic diction" for a conversational language derived from ordinary people's unmediated communication with the "best objects" of rural life (LB 747, 744). Although he aligned his poetry with speech and nature, in practice that poetry took shape in the context of print, within a culture actively engaged in measuring and marking the English language and landscape on paper. Wordsworth resisted writing poetry "by prescription" (LB 747) while participating in this dynamic culture of inscription.

Recent criticism has interrogated Wordsworth's self-presentation as a "man speaking to men" (LB 751) in light of his conflicted attitudes toward and complex processes of writing—the fact that composition involved intense and idiosyncratic scriptorial strategies for drafting and redrafting on paper.[20] His themes, forms, and figures, this criticism shows, emerged from insistent revision of past manuscripts.[21] Other critics have tied Wordsworth's oral investments to the cultural figure of the minstrel and traced his poems' revisions of the "oral-literate conjunctions" that characterize eighteenth-century ballad collections, revealing thereby a significant facet of Wordsworth's engagement with the realm of print and reflexive awareness, writes Maureen McLane, of the "trans- and inter-medial" workings of poetry "across oral, writerly, and print modalities."[22] In *Romantic Marks and Measures: Wordsworth's Poetry in Fields of Print*, I bring to light his poems' deep—and surface—marking of their engagement with two less examined domains of print, whose conjunctions in the poems both reveal and recast the "media situation of Romantic poetry."[23] Scriptorial, visual, metrical, and typographic, Wordsworth's poetry of "speech" and "nature" materialized, I show, within a matrix of inscriptional projects not traditionally considered part of the Romantic canon: the charting of terrain and the notating of language by cartographers, elocutionists, prosodists, and the writers of tours and guidebooks. Wordsworth's poems were written and read amidst new practices of measuring and marking, and of rendering measures and marks and in print, that reconfigured topographic and typographic fields and brought verse into heightened visibility and meter into national importance.

The inscriptional projects that affected Wordsworth's writing stemmed from Enlightenment initiatives to improve the reading aloud and speaking of English and the mapping of Britain. Interested in the effects and affects of sound, eighteenth-century grammarians, elocutionists, and prosodists forged new understandings of the English language in essays on versification, in books on the art of reading, in treatises on punctuation, in graphs of emphasis and inflection, and in new vernacular systems of scansion. Mapmakers and tour writers published reconfigurations of landscape on large-scale topographical maps, in guidebooks which increasingly featured charts, diagrams, tables, and pictures, and in essays on cartographic methods. These projects of making apparent the morphologies of land and language involved empirical scrutiny, new forms of quantitative and qualitative assessment, and searches for signs for "expressing on paper" newly recognized features of objects of national value.[24] Like the *Encyclopédie* of Diderot and D'Alembert, they effected a diagrammatic turn, altering representations on the two-dimensional page and charting new passages through space and speech.[25] They also turned the rendering of language and land into subjects of inquiry in their own right, as rival systems of measuring and marking became topics of debate. In the span of a century, the "arts" and "sciences" of mapping and speech modified fields of linguistic and graphic expression, modulated practices of seeing and reading, and offered new possibilities for inscription into the scene of print.

The historical scope of my study is broad, reaching from elocutionist John Mason's conversion of the printed page into ratios of cognitive and affective time, in 1748, to Matthew Arnold's assertion of the government's duty to restore shade lines on the Ordnance Survey maps of England, in 1862—a period in which the cultural work of expressive marks assumed national importance. Within this period, I locate points of intersection between Wordsworth's "natural delineation of human passions" (LB 739) and new delineations of speech and space. I explore the representational dilemmas pertaining to these inscriptional grammars and investigate debates surrounding them, particularly those concerning quantification and codification. I track their effects upon Wordsworth's composition and reception at the level of theme, form, trope, word, and mark, and consider the effects of Wordsworth's verse upon those grammars. How the poetry materialized within a shifting and contentious print milieu is the story each chapter differently tells. By exploring relations among Wordsworth's writing and the marks and measures of speech and space, I show how Wordsworth's topographically and orally invested poetry registered at a thematic and textual level, and also intervened in, a print culture in which Britain's linguistic and geographical self-conception as a modern nation was in vexed formation.

A central concern of *Romantic Marks and Measures* is the emergence of blank verse as a "national metre"[26] within a burgeoning print culture that highly valued oral delivery. Wordsworth did not inherit blank verse as a national meter—an uncontroversial medium commonly regarded, since George Saintsbury's *History of English Prosody*, as an embodiment of Englishness for its due mix of freedom and order and representative accommodation of the "inherent rhythms of English speech"—a medium that Anthony Easthope and Celeste Langan have viewed, following Marshall McLuhan, as in fact the product of a particular bourgeois class.[27] In Wordsworth's time, to write in unrhymed heroics was to choose a metrical form that was neither universally agreed to be poetry let alone an embodiment of Englishness. Blank verse could achieve aesthetic coherence and force when interpreted by bodies and voices on the stage, some conservative critics held, but on the page it seemed to lack vitality and form. By the later nineteenth century Wordsworth may have succeeded, with the aid of such followers as Keats, Shelley, Tennyson, and Browning, in naturalizing blank verse as the "metre of genius . . . a type and symbol of our national literary spirit," or, in more royalist terms, the "distinguishing crown of English poetry itself."[28] But in 1798, 1807, and 1814, it was treated by some arbiters of taste as inferior to rhyme, loose and long-winded, and, in Wordsworth's hands, a license for puerile and self-indulgent egotism. "This will never do," began Francis Jeffrey's review of *The Excursion*.[29]

By 1865, however, passages from that poem were being memorized and recited by teachers in the New National School, as part of a program to instill English "character." What had changed, and what role did print play in revaluations of the meter? What cultural projects conditioned its writing and reception? Here I take up McLuhan's understanding of blank verse not merely as a historically constituted institution, but as an effect, more fundamentally, of the technology that shaped the society that discovered it. For McLuhan, blank verse "answered the new need of the vernacular" in the Gutenberg era "to have recognition and implementation as a public address system"; whereas the "jigging" of rhyme confined, the "sweep and volume" of blank verse enabled English to "roar and resonate" (198). The "rising iambs" of Elizabethan drama "outered" and amplified personal views and public news. Although McLuhan here furthers the problematic identification of the vernacular with the iambic and, in Blakean spirit, exaggerates the metrical consistency of blank verse to fit his thesis about the typographic ordering of consciousness, his depiction of early-modernists' triumphant use of the form on the stage mirrors eighteenth-century laments about the fate of the vernacular on the page. According to the dramatist-turned-lecturer who galvanized the elocution movement (Thomas Sheridan), the deplorable conventions of writing, print, and speech pedagogy prevented Milton, Shakespeare, the Book of Common Prayer, and even the latest printed news from resonating. But not only lectures on the "art of reading" worked to make the sounds of English perceptible to and pronounceable by a broadening readership. In answer to charges, leveled by Dryden and Johnson among others, that blank verse was insufficiently acoustically delimited and merely *looked* like poetry by appearing in printed lines, essays on English "numbers" exploited the visual capacities of print to make apparent the accents and emphases that they too were heralding as the "genius" of the language. While both verse and prose were annotated, reformatted, and relineated in these typographic contexts, the blank verse that was attacked throughout the eighteenth century as a trick of print, or prose in disguise, was employed as a special illustration of English and heralded in the new century, by Thelwall, as a super-medium of the "English rhythmus." With the blank verse of Milton as a privileged example, the "nerves and energy"[30] of the language were visualized, spatialized, and temporalized: its syllables and pauses were displayed, arrayed, and staved across the page. English was revealed as an architecture of force and feeling in time, and the "national character" that was "sufficiently impressed" on its "tongue" (its "gravity and thoughtfulness," "strength and energy") was made visible in print.[31] Beyond these theoretical and practical contexts, the new vogue for elocutionary punctuation highlighted the language's dynamics of pace and sound, force and feeling.

New spatiotemporal visualizations of the English language coincided with new visualizations of Britain. Put to use also in picturesque guidebooks and on maps, blank verse directed readers' attention to newly appreciated features of the landscape—its complex forms and elevations—and was itself subject to new modes of visual attention and forms of feeling in these visual contexts. These cartographic contexts, which mixed profile views of mountain outlines with large-scale overviews and multipaneled itineraries, complemented the new spatiotemporal grammars of printed English—and Wordsworth, I show, was sensitive to both. A poet recognized for the subtlety of his exploitation "of the white space at the end of the line," Wordsworth took a broader interest, I argue here, in the medium's visual aspect.[32] His writing in blank verse, from the first fragments on the Discharged Soldier (1798) to *The Excursion* (1814) and the manuscript revisions of *The Prelude* (1850), reveals a joint fascination with the representation of speech and landscape in print; and the care he took with punctuation, layout, and diction suggests his sensitivity to the reception of blank verse, under these shifting conditions of publication and literacy, as a graphic medium. Thus I approach Wordsworth's "blanks" neither through literary history's genealogy of poets after Milton—a method inaugurated by the great nineteenth-century historians of English meter, Edwin Guest, T. S. Omond, and George Saintsbury[33]—nor by application of contemporary schemes of prosodic analysis,[34] but rather as material and ideological formations that were spatially and temporally refocused within indexically intensive fields of print that mixed numerical, verbal, phonetic, pictorial, and other symbolic codes. Under these complex conditions of writing and reception, blank verse became a medium in which Englishness was expressed in print.

The first half of *Romantic Marks and Measures* examines the shaping of Wordsworth's blank verse within a burgeoning cartographic culture; the second half, within a thriving print culture of English. Both parts also consider inscriptional responses to Wordsworth's poetry. The early chapters investigate the Romantic construction of the "Lake District" and discuss Wordsworthianism in Victorian debates about the mapping of Britain. The later chapters explore the Romantic-era elocutionary reception of Wordsworth's blank verse and also address the late twentieth-century Anglo-American editing of his poetry. One goal of the book is jointly to consider discourses that historians and literary scholars tend to approach independently. Cultural historian Benedict Anderson has taught us to see the nineteenth-century institution of "national print-languages" and the production of official state maps as joint instruments in the formation of national consciousness.[35] Despite this pioneering work across different print genres, literary scholars have tended to approach print encodings of land and language as discrete cultural phenomena with independent relations to literature.[36] My intention is to articulate them as related aspects of a diagrammatic and accentual turn in British culture that produced new forms of the spatial and temporal organization of print, new kinds of literacy, and new modes of feeling. By their conjunction, the nonnumeric mark of emphasis and indefinite "space of time" emerge as means of connecting English readers—and speakers—across ever more accurately quantified distances.[37]

The first chapter introduces this diagrammatic and accentual turn in British culture by reading the "Lakes in Cumberland, Westmorland and Lancashire" as a geographical and print domain of intensifying visual discrimination. In this context, how did the media, marks, and measures of picturesque tourism influence the materialization of poetry on the page? And how did Wordsworth play up the visual and verbal interactions of this inscriptional context in his prose and verse and further the development of the guidebook genre? Taking a long view of tourist publications, from Thomas West's *A Guide to the Lakes in Cumberland, Westmorland and Lancashire*, 1778–1851, through *Black's Picturesque Guide to the English Lakes*, 1841–1883, I track the practices of increasingly close reading and seeing engendered by the texts' combinations of prose description, verse quotation, picture, map, and diagram. In addition to consolidating what became known as the "Lake District," this mix of inscriptional modes changed the way people saw and interacted with topographical as well as typographical fields. While the representational strategies of tours and guidebooks brought the "images of nature" "forcibly" and "closely to the eye,"[38] they also heightened the graphical features of verse, which readers encountered inset within paragraphs of descriptive prose, on the face of large-scale maps, and in complex diagrams. Further, these representational innovations had formal and ideological effects on poetry: they affiliated its variable patterns of stress with Britain's native landforms and contours; they also familiarized blank verse as a short form of poetry. Wordsworth participated and influenced these developments I show in a reading of his *Guide to the Lakes*[39] (1810–42), the blank verse he quotes within it, and blank verse of his own that is reprinted in later guidebooks. This media context reveals the referential and graphic conditions of poems that twentieth-century criticism taught us to read as autonomous "lyric" as well as the collaboration of poetic and cartographic writing in the production of the "Lake District" and the formation of a national imaginary.

Chapters 2 and 3 consider Wordsworth's innovative project of poetic autobiography in the context of radical developments in European and British cartography. I first explore Wordsworth's reinscription of his 1790 Alpine tour in *The Prelude* in the context of the era's Alpine maps. Redressing scholars' neglect of historical maps as intertextual media, I examine the defining problem of eighteenth- and nineteenth-century cartography—the rendering of altitude and volume on the two-dimensional page—and show that the semiotic complexity of period maps informed Wordsworth's account of his loss of way at the Simplon Pass. As Wordsworth continued to hone Book VI, he employed terms derived from geometry and cartography, a vocabulary of *mark, trace, line, spot,* and *point,* to accent the growth of his imaginative vision. This notational lexicon signals the trans- and intermedial conditions of the autobiographical project, involving crossings between kinds of print, between print and writing, and between William and his sister Dorothy as writers and route-tracers.[40]

Chapter 3 explores the intersection of Wordsworth's notational diction with charged terms of contemporary cartographic debate in Britain. I divide my attention between the Ordnance Survey of Britain—the ambitious, scientifically modern survey of the nation begun in 1791 that aimed to represent the nation according to one standard scale and code[41]—and Wordsworth's attempts to trace the history of his mind in *The Prelude* during the same period. Wordsworth's near encounter with Ordnance Survey engineers on the western edge of Westmorland, in 1811, resulted in two short poems about cartography that have been read by historians and critics as demonstrations of Wordsworth's ideological ambivalence about the national cartographic project.[42] Looking more closely at the poems' marks and measures, I show how the period's cartographic projects were reflected not only in their formal shaping but also at the level of diction and punctuation, as Wordsworth self-consciously differentiates his dynamic poetic "lines," dashes, and parentheses from the "lines" of the Ordnance Survey triangulation that fixed the landscape in mathematical space. Examining Wordsworth's blank verse in relation to the nonliterary print media to which it refers thus reveals an unacknowledged "family of language" (LB 747) in the poems and uncovers significant trends in their revision over time. Wordsworth's inflection of *The Prelude* with a notational lexicon in extensions and revisions, for example, not only indexes the cultural conditions of his writing but also alters received understandings of his poetry's relation to the Ordnance Survey. In his emphasis of his imagination's growth—his "tracing" of visionary perception on the page with "line" terms—Wordsworth inscribed a mode of representing landscape that has unacknowledged affinities with the Survey's topographical maps, which employed artistic, nonquantitative techniques of shading to depict hills and mountains. Where critics have emphasized the Ordnance Survey's epistemological mastery of the landscape, I thus uncover arenas of resistance to this cartographic grand narrative so as to reveal unexpected ideological, formal, and representational affinities between the new cartographic "portraits" of the nation and Wordsworth's epic song of himself that emerges, as he claims, from intercourse with the "face of Nature" (1850, I: 587).

Behind the idea of an accurate and impressive map that affiliates readers with the nation and each other lies the eighteenth-century conception of language as a medium of social communication. In an essay that serves as an Interchapter midway through the book, I link naturalistic escapes from cartographic "flatland" to elocutionary escapes from the muteness of print.[43] From the mid-eighteenth century, elocutionists and prosodists reconceived English as an essentially "emphatic" language, one that required the phonetic marking of feeling and intent for full communication between minds and one whose harmonies were built upon the stresses of speech. Like guidebooks to the native landscape, guides to the speaking and reading aloud of English graphically encoded new understandings in printed texts using new signs and diagrammatic techniques in order to represent the nation to itself and to spread Englishness abroad. Focusing on scientific and popular accounts of intonation and inflection, I suggest that the graphic schematization of blank and topographical verse within manuals that sought to standardize the "accenting" of English across England, Wales, Ireland, and Scotland, implicated iambic pentameter, as a visual and vocal medium, in the national and imperial print project.

In Chapter 4 I explore the problems of marking and measuring that trouble the discourse of emphasis and I examine Wordsworth's engagements with these problems as he develops a blank verse for the printed page. While elocutionary manuals all extolled the semantic and affective effects of emphasis— understood as word, as distinguished from syllable, stress—they both regretted the lack of a system of signs for representing emphasis on the page and worried over its codification. How could Britain fix in print the oral mark of feeling and intent on which depended the "life" of the English tongue and the integrity of the national culture? Looking at graphical schemes developed by Thomas Sheridan, John Walker, and William Cockin, I link ambivalence about standardizing this ever-variable feature of speech to the proliferation of blank-verse illustration and to the meter's construction as the embodiment of British freedom of movement and force.

The concept of emphasis was also central, I suggest, to Wordsworth's affective poetics, articulated in prefaces and notes, and to his self-presentation as a poet in his earliest blank verse of 1797–98. In passages destined for *The Prelude* Wordsworth reworked elocutionary concepts into themes, and he gauged the animation of speakers and listeners in elocutionary terms—by their tones, looks, and gestures. I explore the Infant Babe passage as an embodiment of the emphatic ideal and read the Discharged Soldier as its antithesis. As

Wordsworth became a blank verse poet, I conclude, he adapted the contemporary discourse of emphasis for his own ends, assimilating the "spirit" that animates national culture to the "Poet" whose feeling rhythms, and resistance to "uniform control" (1799, II: 306–7), forges a greater universal community. In the process, he inscribed blank verse as a materially and spiritually energetic measure and medium.

But going into print as a blank-verse poet was another matter. After the anonymously issued *Lyrical Ballads* of 1798, cowritten with Coleridge, Wordsworth added, for the 1800 republication under his own name, a preface in which he appealed to a passionate form of speech derived from "hourly" communication with the "best objects" of rural life (LB 744). However, as I show in Chapter 5, the manuscripts of the 1800 edition reveal that the poetry of feeling was bound up with inscriptional technologies for rendering speech and place. One of these technologies was punctuation. Wordsworth's numerous revisions to the punctuation by which the rural subjects, speakers, and landscapes of the 1800 *Lyrical Ballads* were presented to the public—together with the new poems, notes, and Preface composed as he was preparing the volume for print—indicate his registration of contemporary controversies about the mediation of passion and his concerns about bringing local place before the public eye as a site of feeling. The effect of these graphic and thematic interactions is to query the power of print both to represent the "plainer and more emphatic language" (LB 743) that he aspired to imitate and to elicit sympathetic response from a distance. With its circa 1,300 lines of blank verse, the new volume of *Lyrical Ballads* materializes at the intersection of contemporary discourses concerned with codifying ways of moving readers—moving them affectively and spatially through a geographic locale—and Wordsworth's conflicted relation to both discourses. The "blank line," or double dash of emphatic pause, emerges as a sign of local—topographical and historical—knowledge and feeling; it is a mark of epitaphic deixis that Wordsworth teaches his distant readers not to measure but to "Touch,——" as it were, with the eyes ("Nutting," line 53; LB 220).

Chapter 6 makes interventions in two related debates: one is about the editing of Wordsworth's texts; the other about the figure of address, which deconstructionist critics have regarded as the defining trope of "lyric" if not "poetry in general."[44] Although influential readings of Romantic poetry reveal how apostrophe and address, by evoking voice, constitute the poet as poet, less attention has been paid to the historical circumstances in which Wordsworthian voice was produced and to the materiality of textual production, matters focused by Virginia Jackson in her groundbreaking reading of Emily Dickinson.[45] Against this neglect I read the compositional history of *The Prelude* in terms of the development of its principal vocal figure, showing how address to the "Friend!" was incorporated at key junctures in the writing of the poem and formative on several levels. Historically associated with the blank verse "conversation poems" of the late 1790s, the trope is also materially linked, I show, with poems and prose sent between the Wordsworths and Coleridge, during the winter of 1798–99, in Germany. Arising from physical correspondence sent over long distances by post, friendly address, as inscribed in *The Prelude*, remains inflected by this geography and history. Although the trope rhythmically and graphically figures a wished-for point of affective solidarity outside of space and time—a being together here and now—as Wordsworth incorporated the address among his accumulating lines, he shaped a history of his life as traversed distance and thematized feeling over time as a complex metrical subject.

I pay particular attention to Wordsworth's addition of the exclamation mark to the five books copied in 1804 for Coleridge to read in Malta and to his later inscription of the problem of emphasis in later books of the poem. Although Wordsworth activates the potential of the exclamation mark to emphasize sound and feeling, he also goes on to critique, in Book VII, the force of culturally instituted, as opposed to natural, signs of emphasis. This conflict between the poem's marks and its thematization of "conspicuous marks" (1805, VII: 567) registers Romantic-era disagreements about the exclamation mark's emotional and cognitive value and shows how the "business" of punctuation (EY 289) was influential beyond the production of the 1800 *Lyrical Ballads*. Yet this business is incompletely represented in one of the main twentieth-century editions of *The Prelude*—the parallel text Norton Critical Edition—which, while claiming to reproduce the thirteen-book poem "as it may be presumed to have stood after the immediate corrections of 1805–06," omitted the majority of the exclamation marks from the manuscripts on which the text is based, notably those in the repeated apostrophes to Coleridge: "Friend!," "My Friend!," and "O Friend!"[46] The Norton edition not only flattens the intonational and emotional contours of the thirteen-book poem, I conclude, but also obscures the 1805 text's visible symptoms of authorial anxiety and effaces its traces of personal, professional, and textual intimacy and estrangement—responses to the cultural, geographical, and social situations in which Wordsworth wrote.

Chapter 7 considers an earlier editorial intervention in Wordsworth's texts. Here my subject is the reformer, orator, physiologist, and poet John

Thelwall who visited Coleridge and Wordsworth in Somerset, in July 1797, at the height of Wordsworth's turn to blank verse and who took up the meter himself upon departure. My chapter examines Thelwall's scanned and marked copy of Wordsworth's epic poem *The Excursion* (1814) and explores the implications of Thelwall's prosodical act for the poem and in the context of his larger elocutionary project, which furthered his predecessors' critiques of grammatical punctuation and indicted the "false" prosodic notations and illustrations circulated in books. While in *Lyrical Ballads* Wordsworth offered a poetry of more nuanced feeling to counteract the blunting effects of sensational publications, and in the blank verse periods of *The Excursion* sought to re-tune readers to the spiritual energies that accented and organized the nation, Thelwall prescribed a practical and more broadly democratic program of scansion and recitation, and, for advanced students, further liberal education involving composition and oration. His therapeutic prosody, or what I call his *therapoetics,* entailed material interaction with texts in line with his physiological understanding of meter. On the pages of *The Excursion*, these notations mark out the conservative cultural politics that outraged many of the poem's earliest readers as a conservative politics of meter and print—one that mystified blank verse by subsuming its measures within the national landscape. Conversely, the marks of the "English rhythmus" still visible in workbooks across the United Kingdom, United States, and Canada map popular aspirations toward the freedom embodied by the language's most representative measure.

This book has many precursors in its development and practice of a newly historicized study of poetics. Marjorie Levinson's contextualized readings of Wordsworth's poems were germinal; historical accounts of meter and figures of address by Adela Pinch, Yopie Prins, and Virginia Jackson were exemplary. Susan Wolfson modeled criticism of Wordsworth's revisions. Where she shows how the poems "reflect on rather than conceal their constructedness (not only aesthetic, but social and ideological),"[47] I consider how they mark their constructedness in ways that are not immediately apparent to modern readers. I do so by incorporating a range of print genres in my analyses, prompted by reflexive scenes of poetic making in Wordsworth's verse that invoke contemporary marking and measuring systems and the modes of attention they inscribe. This cultural range also distinguishes my book from valuable studies by Andrew Bennett and Sally Bushell that have focused critical attention on the material technologies of writing, shed light on Wordsworth's compositional processes, and argued the significance of these processes to his poetic themes, figures, and subjects. Like Bennett, I build on influential readings of Wordsworth's inscription poems by such critics as Geoffrey Hartman, Paul de Man, and Cynthia Chase. Where we both foreground the material dimensions of Wordsworth's writing, Bennett reads Wordsworth's poetry as the effect of his "resistance to [a] conception of poetry as written" and simultaneous fascination with the "act and process of writing itself."[48] I contextualize and more broadly historicize Wordsworth's writing, approaching it as produced and received within a matrix of Romantic-era inscriptional systems and practices.

By attending to this matrix, I contribute to a current of critical interest in eighteenth- and nineteenth-century print culture represented by works by Paul Keen, William St. Clair, Adrian Johns, Leah Price, Tom Mole, Nicholas Mason, Heather Jackson, and Deidre Lynch among others.[49] Like Janine Barchas and Andrew Piper, I pay close attention to the kinds of linguistic and graphic interplay that new book formats, technologies, and conventions engendered.[50] Where Piper considers the subjective implications of what he calls the "intermedial" line—a form of line that blurs the boundaries between reading and seeing—and which he locates within the transnational, European context of the illustrated book, I explore books and other print media—as well as manuscripts and letters—in order to understand the complex conditions within which blank verse lines came into national focus and within which Wordsworth emerged as the national poet. Like many others, my materialist approach to the text is indebted to the pioneering work of Jerome J. McGann, who demonstrated in *Black Riders: The Visible Language of Modernism* how the graphic, retrotextual environments of William Morris' Kelmscott productions inspired modernists' "writerly exploitation of the spatial field of the printed page and codex forms."[51] Looking beyond the book and the productive literary community of writer, copyists, editors, publishers, printers, and readers that McGann describes in *A Critique of Modern Textual Criticism*, I examine epistemic and semiotic innovations and instabilities within the broader media and marking ecology that conditioned Wordsworth's experiments with the spatial field of print and made legible, and voiceable, his "visible language" of Romanticism.[52] Thus while I practice a method of historically informed formalist analysis throughout this book, I also practice a formally informed historical analysis that ranges across genres, media, and types of cultural practice.

Answering, in this way, calls for historical accounts of English prosody, I offer a new approach to the study of meter by prying open unexplored relations between English metrical and mensural systems.[53] How does the positioning of a scale bar between stanzas of poetry on a map affect the reading of poetic measure? What does the indeterminate temporality of the "blank line" matter to the meter of blank verse? Building on Brennan O'Donnell's impressive analyses of Wordsworth's blank verse in *The Passion of Meter: Wordsworth's Metrical Art*, I situate that art within the nation's inscriptional grammars, practices, and debates, offering an alternative to the primarily sonic readings that his formalism produces. Like Christopher Ricks, who argues that Wordsworth's "delicately aware" blank verse lessens the dominance of the reading eye and heightens the activity of the listening ear, O'Donnell deftly illuminates the tension between what Wordsworth called the "passion of metre" and "passion of the subject," or the interplay between the abstract theoretical pattern and "actual speech sounds and the passions that motivate them,"[54] in order to enable readers to "hear expressive subtleties—and to grasp with the mind's ear emblematic possibilities—that otherwise would be lost."[55] Like Prins, who develops John Hollander's attention to the "poem in the eye," I read sounds and stresses as effects of print.[56] Further, I approach "expressive subtleties" as the effect of historical interactions among acoustic and visual grammars and systems of emphasis—both public and personal ("My Friend!"), tropological and typographical, literary and nonliterary. It is not simply that line juncture and syntactic schemes such as chiasmus exert visual and rhythmical effects in Wordsworth's blank verse, as Hollander has shown.[57] I demonstrate, rather, that the poems produce their particular effects (lexical, rhythmical, vocal, visual) under heightened, intermedial conditions of marking and amidst conflicting aesthetic and ideological charges.

By approaching meter as a matter of national culture, as Prins and Catherine Robson have done for Victorian Britain and Meredith Martin for Victorian, Edwardian, and Georgian Britain,[58] I bring to an exciting new critical conversation a multifaceted analysis of a metrically crucial earlier period, before George Saintsbury had normalized "foot-based" descriptions of meter, and when "accent," "emphasis," and "quantity" were being urgently defined and disambiguated in a host of language texts.[59] If blank verse was a response to needs generated by print, as McLuhan has argued, I suggest that its nationalization and naturalization depended on a Romantic media context: on new forms of attending and feeling produced by reconfigurations of topographic and typographic space and time, and by new practices of interacting with texts.

Recent media-studies approaches to poetry have identified blank verse as a form that downplays its typographic presence in the age of print capitalism, when the "oral medium" of poetry grew increasingly outmoded. For Langan, "Tintern Abbey" is exemplary of the form that " 'affects not to be poetry' " by

"occult[ing] its technology for producing 'soul' "—or sound.[60] Andrew Elfenbein reads the same poem as an example of poetry's development of a "prosaic"
form of blank verse that engaged with new strictures of grammatical correct-
ness but rejected print's new "elocutionary interface," which novels, he argues,
excitedly absorbed.[61] In a short aside on the dash as a technology of "elocutionary voice" in "A Night Piece," however, Elfenbein acknowledges the continuing
significance in the production of voice of poetry's visual display on the printed
page. So, too, Pieter Simonsen's ekphrastic reading of typography in the late
sonnets opens the way for an historical criticism of Wordsworth that investi-
gates the materiality of the text.[62] I pursue this criticism here in a fuller account
of Wordsworth's engagement with elocutionary discourse in his poems, poetics, and post-"Tintern Abbey" print. Mediating between vocalic (Elfenbein)
and visual (Simonsen) readings of typography, I also address the visual effects
of vocalic signals. Wordsworth's pointing, lining, and spacing of the verbal
domain, I argue, relates and refers to new chartings and experiences of geographical space. Typographic consciousness, that is to say, implies topographic
consciousness—even when, as in *The Excursion*, Wordsworth strives to efface
the material condition of his national *"Song"* (Preface: 88) by subsuming
printed blank verse and topographical maps into nature.

Chapter 1

Lines on the Lake District

Poetry and the Print Culture of Tourism

What we now call the Lake District was, when Wordsworth first made it the subject of his nature poetry, neither a distinct region nor a blank page. By 1800 the lakes in Westmorland, Cumberland, and Lancashire were already described and promoted in tours and guidebooks: over the next fifty years such publications proliferated until what was now viewed as a "Lake District" was more intensely represented in print than any other place in Britain. My purpose in this chapter is to consider the implications for poetry of this visually intensive print culture by examining the implication of poetry within it: poetry's places on the pages of tour narratives, aesthetic manuals, guidebooks, and maps and the uses to which it was put. I will also consider the implications, for place, of poetry's interactions on those pages with prose, diagrams, maps, surveys, charts, and itineraries. By these interactions, what was known in the 1770s as the "lakes in Westmorland, Cumberland, and Lancashire," had by the 1840s become known, more concisely, as the "Lake-District." It was, however, neither simply the production of more guidebooks and maps, nor the ever-increasing scales at which these represented the Lakes region, but the incorporation of poetry into loco-inscriptive formats that gave those maps and guidebooks a purchase upon the region. The interactions of increasingly sophisticated representational technologies, and the perceptual practices they fostered, shaped the "Lake-District" and brought it into national consciousness as an emblematically English region. I suggest a similarly consolidating formal and ideological trajectory for nature verse. As publication sites for the poetic excerpt, the place-specific genres of picturesque tourism gave cultural impetus to a poetry of locality and affective brevity, shaping the production and reception of "nature lyric" and also shaping the perception of the meter that is most characteristic of that poetry: blank verse.[1]

One of the foremost critics to remind us of the affiliation of Wordsworth's versification of place to contemporary practices of topographical writing, including tours and guidebooks, was Geoffrey Hartman. In his seminal "Wordsworth, Inscriptions and Romantic Nature Poetry," Hartman derived Wordsworth's "nature poetry" from the merging, in the eighteenth century, of elegiac and locodescriptive modes of poetry and from a "species" of the inscription that he calls the nature-inscription. Where inscription designates "any poem conscious of the surface on which it is written," nature-inscription names a brief poem inscribed upon an object in the landscape that commands a beautiful prospect, such as a bench in a garden.[2] Wordsworth's achievement, Hartman claims, was to "liberate" the nature-inscription from "its dependent status of tourist guide and antiquarian signpost . . . into a free-standing poem able to commemorate any feeling for nature or the spot that had aroused this feeling" (208). While the nature-inscription "points to the landscape" (221), or directs "a cold, lapidary finger" to the external world, the Wordsworthian "nature lyric" evolved from it draws "the landscape evocatively into the poetry itself" (222); it is an "oracular apostrophe pointing to humble truth" (230). The "lapidary inscription" is "replaced by the meditative mind" (223), Hartman asserts, as "Romantic poetry transcends its formal origin in epigram and inscription and creates the modern lyric" (229).

Hartman's evolution of "Romantic and modern lyric" (221) from prior poetic modes and forms entails the shearing of poems from their contexts of composition and reception. His account of Wordsworth's perfection of blank verse as a "lyric" form—historically restricted to dramatic, epic, and didactic genres—would have us regard context and, with it, the referential or indexical function, as that which mature blank verse overcomes in the realization of "Romantic nature lyric" (221). Thus, by illuminating the subsumption of the inscription within Wordsworth's "nature poetry" ("the poet reads the landscape as if it were a monument or grave," 223), Hartman effectively reminds us of, only to turn away from, the actual inscriptional conditions of that poetry: the tours and guidebooks, maps and itineraries on and in which "nature poetry" was printed, and which were transforming both landscape and poetry when Wordsworth began writing poetry as a boy and began writing "nature lyric" toward the century's end. Hence the formal implications for "nature poetry" of intensifying representational attention to the English landscape—and the complex nature of that attention, involving not merely prose assessment but also mathematical surveying, diagramming, picturing, and cartographic plotting—have not been sufficiently explored.

In an important essay critiquing the telos of Hartman's argument and the formal closure he ascribes to lyric, Cynthia Chase opens lyric to the social and to history by considering Wordsworth's ongoing writing of poems that he designated "Inscriptions."[3] To Chase, Hartman's intentional model of lyric relies upon a cognitive and phenomenal model of language that elides its material and figural dimensions. In this model, words reflect ideas; they function unproblematically to represent feelings, thoughts, and things. Wordsworth's inscriptions, Chase counters, not only presuppose a material site of writing but also incorporate a reader who attempts to make meaning out of the "*indeterminably meaningful* mark" that is the inscription. Inscriptions are emblems, then, of the material conditions of all texts and of "the figural nature of language, or indeterminable performance" (73): the fact that such "nonsemantic" elements of language as "letters, punctuation, [and] grammar" get "confused with meaning" in the process of reading. Inscriptions are not monuments of (and to) the poet's intention, figures of the "meditative mind," but rather suggest the history to be written in the act of reading, should an instance of reading ever occur. Chase thus exposes the ideality of formalist conceptions of lyric that close off history and the social (Hartman's "free-standing poem"), but leaves unasked the question of the history of "the possibility of history": the history of the "inseparability of literary and nonliterary language," of the material dimension, and of the performance of reading.

On what surfaces, then, was the "nature poetry" of the era, including Wordsworth's, printed? How did the publications that pointed out the lakes in northern England involve poetry in their representational repertoires and visual agendas? What play of relations between the linguistic and extralinguistic did these complex print conditions make possible—and with what implications for place and poetry? I suggest that the print culture of lakes tourism, while evincing the "inseparability of literary and nonliterary language," enables us to rethink the history of poetic form, the Wordsworthian "nature lyric" in particular. Its insetting of poetic lines among prose and among a variety of lines, figures, notations, numbers, and codes from diverse representational grammars elevated the material dimension of "nature poetry" and activated its "nonsemantic" elements—print, punctuation, meter—so as to naturalize blank verse and focus its rhythmical patterns and variations in relation to the physical contours of the landscape.

I begin the chapter by discussing some of the publications that preceded Wordsworth's in representing the lakes of Westmorland, Cumberland, and Lancashire as a place of aesthetic and national interest. As Peter Crosthwaite's *Seven Maps of the Lakes* reveal, these publications shaped readers' perceptions of *"the native Isle"* and its poetry, directing attention both to the landscape and to its visual, verbal, and metrical encodings.[4] Implicitly patriotic, these tour narratives, picturesque manuals, and guidebooks invited readers to delight in specifically English landscapes that had previously been ignored in favor of the Grand Tour of Europe. They celebrated native scenes and quoted national poets to do so—frequently offering up blank-verse extracts from Milton's *Paradise Lost*, Edward Young's *Night Thoughts*, James Thomson's *Seasons*, and William Mason's *English Garden* as pictorial supplements to the landscapes rendered in prose. Increasingly featuring maps and other diagrammatic forms, these aesthetically and visually demanding books activated the indexical force of the quoted verse (its pointing, or deictic, function) while also foregrounding its metrical, graphical, and print materiality. They also prepared the way for Wordsworth to quote his own verse in his anonymous introduction to Joseph Wilkinson's *Select Views in Cumberland, Westmoreland and Lancashire,* which he composed in 1810, republished several times, and retitled as a *Guide Through the District of the Lakes* in 1835.[5] The interactions of prose and poetry in Wordsworth's introduction, and the ongoing development and republication of that text and its verse extracts, suggest the formalizing effect of this print culture on Wordsworth's poetry as well as his poetry's formalizing effects on the lakes in Westmorland, Cumberland, and Lancashire. These effects, I conclude, are evident in the most popular Lake guidebook of the Victorian era, *Black's Picturesque Guide to the Lakes* (first edition, 1841), a book that reveals the interrelated development of the "Lake-Guide," the large-scale map, and the short blank-verse poem and, in the process, the production, by the interactions of the mensural and the metrical, of a national subject of memory and imagination.

Focusing the Lakes: Blank Verse in Prose Tours

The Victorian "Lake-Guide" grew out of publications that marketed the lakes in Westmorland, Cumberland, and Lancashire to tourists in the 1750s using a single medium only. The region was represented in visual art and verbal text, but these media remained distinct. For example, in 1752, London topographical artist William Bellars printed and sold his *View of Derwent-Water toward Borrodale. A Lake near Keswick in Cumberland*, followed in the next two years by views of Windermere, Haweswater, and Ullswater. John Brown's epistolary *Description of the Lake at Keswick*, which included a "poetic rhapsody," circulated in manuscript after 1751 and was first published in the *London Chronicle* in April 1766. Meanwhile, in 1755, John Dalton published *A Descriptive Poem, addressed to two ladies, at their return from viewing the mines near Whitehaven*.[6] In 1768, when Brown's prose letter reappeared as a footnote to a reprint of Dalton's "Descriptive Poem" in a *Collection of Poems in several hands*, the culture's characteristic mixing of modes and artists began.[7]

In the 1770s, the representation of the Lakes became more complex, when verse began to appear regularly in tour narratives, guidebooks, and aesthetic manuals along with some pictorial engravings and simple diagrams. These publications celebrated native scenes and quoted both classical and national poets to do so—frequently offering non–site-specific extracts from blank-verse epics by Milton, William Mason, and James Thomson as pictorial supplements to the landscapes rendered in prose. As William Gilpin explained in his *Observations, Relative Chiefly to Picturesque Beauty*, which circulated in manuscript after 1774, verse comes to the aid of prose description in "bring[ing] the images of nature, as forcibly, and as closely to the eye, as it can."[8] To bring a sunset more "closely" to the eyes of readers, he quotes Miltonic blank verse that he calls "a grand picture from the pencil of a great master" and then supplements those lines with some from Thomson's *Seasons*: "the same picture," he claims, though more "suitably picturesque" (175–76). Throughout the *Observations*, Gilpin inscribed a diversity of verse pictures to convey images of the English landscape more "forcibly" to the eyes of the readers and instruct them in picturesque aesthetics.

What I call Gilpin's verse pictures work differently than his engraved sketches. While the *Observations'* pictorial engravings lead the eye across vast spaces—typically a foreground valley, middle-distance lake, and distant mountains—its verse pictures focus the landscape tightly.[9] Something similar occurs in later tours written under the influence of Gilpin, such as *An Excursion to the Lakes, in Westmoreland and Cumberland, August 1773*, by the antiquarian and historian William Hutchinson, who made numerous verse quotations, including these lines from William Mason's *English Garden*:

——"In this path
"How long soe'er the wanderer roves, each step
"Shall wake fresh beauties, each short point present
"A different picture . . ."[10]

In the context of Hutchinson's tour, these lines comment upon the function of the short verse excerpt to present a single picture and the function of successive verse pictures to present a sequence of illustrations. The lines also suggest the structural importance of verse citations to the genre of the prose tour: citations bring about the requisite pause of visual attention before "each short point" of interest along the path and permit, thereby, a moving on. The metrical excerpt measures a period of attention; enacts, when read, a temporal span of visual and affective intensity. This is vividly displayed in Hutchinson's treatment of the falls of Lodore, when after noting in prose its "stupendous rocks," dashing "spray" and rainbows, Hutchinson focuses attention on the rushing water by quoting verse. "One would conceive Thomson had this cataract in his eye, when he wrote his seasons," he says, delivering the falls to the reader's eye by way of Thomson's lines:

"Smooth to the shelving brink, a copious flood
"Rolls fair and placid; where collected all
"In one impetuous torrent down the steep
"It thundering shoots, and shakes the country round.
. . . .
"With wild infracted course and less'ned roar
"It gains a safer bed, and steals at last
"Along the mazes of the quiet vale." (141–42)[11]

Malcolm Andrews claims that the object of picturesque tourism, for the general journal writer, was "not so much to find something new to describe and then experiment with a new vocabulary, as to find scenery which resembled familiar paintings or poetic descriptions."[12] For the picturesque tourist, then, a point of interest is sufficiently apprehended if it summons landscape illustrations *in situ*. For the tourist at home with a copy of Gilpin, West, or Hutchinson, reading at a remove from the actual spot, interpellated, printed verse approximates aesthetic apprehension of that spot. The capacity of metrical composition to substitute for and simulate moments of visual and emotional intensity is suggested by Mason's punning "step": "each step / Shall wake

fresh beauties, each short point present / A different picture." Not unlike a
Claude mirror, the convex glass used by tourists and sketchers to focus a scene
and harmonize its tints, the metrical excerpt focuses a pictorial and affective
interest—but by refracting the landscape in question through an idealized
picturesque scene set elsewhere. Offset from the prose that dominates the book
page, the verse excerpt brings an unknown and extensive landscape into concentrated coherence. Thus by metrical (the temporal organization of words)
and typographic means of emphasis (the spatial foregrounding of the excerpt),
verse quotation brings "the images of nature" "forcibly" and "closely to the
eye," enabling the writer's progress, and that of his readers, to a new "point of
interest." By providing aesthetic and affective finish, the verse form notorious
for the fluidity of its ends fulfills the closural needs of the tour genre: its need
to complete a scene and proceed to the next.[13]

Lakes tour narratives and guidebooks conventionally unfold as a sequence
of pictorial citations; prose description with verse picture follows prose description with verse picture, shaping aesthetic judgment and modeling an emotional response to points of interest along the route.[14] But these extracts were
themselves subject to the visual dictates and formalizing tendencies of their
new print contexts. The effect, I suggest, was to recalibrate the measure and
the matter of the blank verse that hardly seemed to be poetry because its music
was lost on the ears of some influential eighteenth-century critics.

Samuel Johnson's remarks in his "Life of Milton" (1779) reveal the aesthetic value of the poetic line's auditory phenomenality. In this *locus classicus*
of formal critique, Johnson complained that the

> musick of the English heroick line strikes the ear so faintly that it is
> easily lost, unless all the syllables of every line co-operate together;
> this co-operation can be only obtained by the preservation of every
> verse unmingled with another as a distinct system of sounds, and
> this distinctness is obtained and preserved by the artifice of rhyme.
> The variety of pauses, so much boasted by the lovers of blank
> verse, changes the measures of an English poet to the periods of
> a declaimer; and there are only a few skilful and happy readers of
> Milton who enable their audience to perceive where the lines end
> or begin. "Blank verse," said an ingenious critick, "seems to be verse
> only to the eye."[15]

The acoustic indistinction Johnson ascribes to blank verse was the result, first,

of the heroic measure's "faintness," a charge that Paul Fussell has attributed to
a general eighteenth-century insensitivity to stress.[16] On top of this weak metrical substratum, a liberal dispersal of pauses (beyond the medial position) only
confounded the perception of a verse line already unmarked by rhyme. If the
"measures of an English poet" were heard by the ear as the periods of an orator,
those same verses, Johnson warned, could pass on the page for poetry. Really
prose mesurée, as Dryden had insinuated, syllabically regular and spatially organized writing appears to the eye as poetry—particularly in print. William
Coward gibed in heroic couplets that "Declamations ty'd to Measur'd Feet"
could yield "Harmony as truly sweet" if "the Printer please to set the Frame."
John Mason went so far as to refer to blank verse as the "Printer's measure." To
some critics, the verse of blank verse was predominantly a visual effect of the
printed page.[17]

But perhaps the print culture of tourism demarcated "English heroick"
lines on the page while also amplifying their "musick," or meter. Hutchinson
so frequently invokes poetic passages prompted by particular landscapes—and
through such curious devices—that he draws attention to the very act and
form of poetic quotation on the page. There is the Gilpinesque shift from prose
to poetry mid-sentence: "The Lake beneath was a perfect mirror—" Hutchinson states in ten syllables of measured prose, and then quotes,

> "O'er which the giant oak, himself a grove,
> "Flings his romantic branches, and beholds
> "His rev'rend image in th'expanse below." (134)[18]

Blank verse appears here as the more "rev'rend" aesthetic form, its "romantic
branches" framed by and differentiated from the expanses of prose above and
below. In another instance of citation, recounting the more sublime experience
of boating on Derwentwater, Hutchinson claims "almost" to hear emanating
from the landscape lines from Young's *Night Thoughts*, voiced jointly by the
poet and a long-dead hermit of St. Herberts' Island. He then quotes,

> "Blest be that hand divine, which gently laid
> "My heart at rest, beneathed this humble shed;
> "The world's a stately bark, on dang'rous seas,
> "With pleasure seen, but boarded at our peril:
> "Here on a single plank, thrown safe on shore,
> "I hear the tumult of the distant throng,

"As that of seas remote, or dying storms;
"And meditate on scenes more silent still,
"Pursue my theme, and fight the fear of death." (123–24)[19]

The aura of madness associated with the inspired poet-prophet is transferred to Hutchinson on the open lake, as the event of "almost" hearing the English landscape utter a blank-verse passage sinks him into a reverie and prompts an extemporaneous "soliloquy." This philosophical muttering on friendship and picturesque aesthetics itself serves as an occasion for voicing (and quoting on the page) yet another line from Young's *Night Thoughts*. Thus inspired by a resonant landscape, one steeped in the music of English poets, Hutchinson the quoter of blank verse becomes Hutchinson the vocalizing philosopher who continues to quote published blank verse. Through this sequence of citations, "Poor is the friendless master of a world" emerges on the page as a typographic crystallization of subjective isolation.[20]

Despite these claims to vocal, pictorial, and affective intensity, the insetting of blank verse within prose tours emphasizes its print materiality. Such reflexive puns as " 'unsandal'd feet, / Printless' " (from an excerpt of Mason's *English Garden*)[21] contribute to this effect, as does the notable tour and guidebook convention of quoting long passages of descriptive prose from already published tours. Tours and guidebooks follow in the footsteps of a rapidly reproducing print tradition (they are hardly "printless"), and they show it on the page—most saliently when the prose excerpted from published tours itself quotes verse. For example, while describing the mountain Skiddaw with Derwentwater at its feet in his 1800 tour *A Topographical Description of Cumberland, Westmoreland, Lancashire,* John Housman quotes a prose passage from Hutchinson's 1774 *Excursion,* a passage that itself contains a quotation of *Paradise Lost.* Housman quotes:

"The water was a plain of sable, studded over with gems reflected
from the starry firmament; the groves which hung upon the feet of
the mountains were wrapt in darkness; and all below was one grave
and majestic circle of Skiddaw,
              ——'till the moon,
          'Rising in cloudy majesty, at length,
          'A parent queen, unveil'd her peerless light,
          'And o'er the dark her silver mantle threw;'
when the long protracted shades the mountains cast on the bosom

of the lake shewed the vastness of those masses from whence they proceeded; and still as the moon arose higher in the horizon, the distant objects began to be more illumined; and the whole presented us with a noble moonlight piece, delicately touched by the hand of Nature." (290–91)[22]

Under the right (and repeatable) viewing conditions, the English lakes and fells offer up their *Paradise Lost* as lines that rise from the left margin of the page. Like the rising "peerless" moon that organizes "a noble moonlight piece," the verse dignifies the landscape and is, in turn, dignified by its distinction from the prose surround. Blank verse is elevated to national textual heritage that illuminates Britain's native forms and figures. Though visibly printed, blank verse is no mere "Printer's measure";[23] it brings into view the delicate touch of the "hand of Nature" and, in its rhythmical rise and fall, embodies it.

"A Body of Still Water Under the Influence of No Current": Verse in Wordsworth's *Guide*

The inscription of the Lakes in maps, poems, tour narratives, and guidebooks was significant to Wordsworth throughout his career. The library at Rydal Mount contained several topographical works, including the ninth edition of West's *A Guide to the Lakes in Cumberland, Westmorland and Lancashire* (1807) and Housman's *Descriptive Tour, and Guide to the Lakes, Caves, Mountains, and other Natural Curiosities, in Cumberland, Westmoreland, Lancashire, and a Part of the West Riding of Yorkshire* (1802). He read Hutchinson's *Excursion* (1774) and owned both Gilpin's *Observations, Relative Chiefly to Picturesque Beauty, Made in the Year 1772, on Several Parts of England; Particularly the Mountains, and Lakes of Cumberland, and Westmoreland* (1786) and James Clarke's *Survey of the Lakes of Cumberland, Westmorland, and Lancashire: Together with an Account, Historical, Topographical, and Descriptive, of the Adjacent Country* (1789), which was inscribed by Clarke to Wordsworth. When the latter came to articulate the Northern lakes as a region at the heart of Britain (both in his verse and the essay that described an "almost visionary mountain republic"), he did so in dialogue with the topographical texts that he had studied.[24] And just as Gilpin, Hutchinson, and Housman had set excerpts—often of blank verse—within their prose, where it acquired formal distinction and stature, so too did Wordsworth.

One of the most suggestive extracts of Wordsworth's essay on the lakes is a section of "There was a Boy," a poem that Wordsworth had previously published in thirty-two lines in the second edition of *Lyrical Ballads* (1800) and would republish in Book V of *The Prelude* (1850) within the current of recollections between the child prodigy and drowned man episodes. As one of the earliest written episodes of the epic autobiography (dating to 1798), and as a lyric that Wordsworth would classify in 1815 as a "Poem of the Imagination," "There was a Boy" suggests the Romantic-era versatility of the meter that was once reserved for epic, dramatic, and didactic genres. In Wordsworth's introduction to Wilkinson's *Select Views*, Wordsworth quotes the lines to illustrate an aesthetic principle: that "the form of the lake is most perfect when, like Derwent-water, and some of the smaller lakes, it least resembles that of a river."[25] His explanation hinges on the attitude this form induces in the spectator: "when being looked at from any given point where the whole may be seen at once, the width of [the lake] bears such proportion to the length, that, however the outline may be diversified by far-receding bays, it never assumes the shape of a river, and is contemplated with that placid and quiet feeling which belongs peculiarly to the lake—as a body of still water under the influence of no current" (*W Prose,* II: 179). The blank verse that follows is dramatically illustrative. Where the prose claims that a "small lake" is capable of "reflecting the clouds, the light, and all the imagery of the sky and the surrounding hills" and thus may be contemplated with a "placid and quiet feeling," the verse quotation translates the aesthetic claim into individual experience:

————The visible scene
Would enter unawares into his mind
With all its solemn imagery, its rocks,
Its woods, and that uncertain heaven received
Into the bosom of the *steady* lake!
(*W Prose,* II: 179)

The verse illustrates the prose by evolving quiet contemplation into unconscious internalization of imagery. In a like manner, the prose shapes our perception of the verse quotation. The aesthetic concerns of the prose—the valorization of smallness, wholeness, and proportionality—redound upon the blank-verse excerpt, tempting us to see the five lines of "There was a Boy" as typographical instantiation of formal proportion: five lines long by five feet wide, the verse floats on the page like a "body of still water under the influence of no current," a medium portraying the "all" of a "visible scene." Wordsworth's claim that "the form of the lake is most perfect when . . . it least resembles that of a river" thus indirectly glosses the lyric excerpt, anticipating the poet's conception of the sonnet as "an orbicular body,—a sphere,—or a dew drop," a productive tension between rhythmic license and regulations of rhyme.[26] The association of this blank-verse excerpt with a "body of still water" perceivable "at once" is far from Johnson's conception of blank-verse lines as "systems of sounds" that run on without perceptible distinction. In its context in the guidebook, the blank-verse extract surrounded by prose is defined visually, not aurally: distinct on the page, it attains a recognizable aesthetic wholeness, which is for Wordsworth analogous to, and in this case representative of, the lake, focusing and reflecting "its rocks" and "Its woods."

Wordsworth follows Gilpin in employing blank-verse quotation to explore the landscape's effect on mind. For Gilpin, "the power" that natural scenes "have over the imagination" demands a gradual approach to the Lakes and a part-by-part exposure to its grandest features, a point he underscores by way of William Mason's verse drama *Caractacus*: "Surely there is a hidden power, that reigns / 'Mid the lone majesty of untamed nature, / Controuling sober reason————."[27] He then quotes a passage from *Paradise Lost* to show Adam's sinking response to the panorama of human history revealed by the archangel Michael:

> So deep the power of those ingredients pierced,
> Ev'n to the inmost seat of mortal sight,
> That Adam now inforced to close his eyes,
> Sank down, and all his spirits became intranced.[28]

The guidebook context reveals Adam's all-too-knowing panoramic vision to be a suggestive intertext for the story of "mortal sight" told by the lyric and epic versions of "There was a Boy." If in those poems the entrance of "solemn imagery" into the mind signals the boy's premonition of death, in the context of the guidebooks, that event works to differentiate the "placid and quiet feeling" (*W Prose*, II: 179) of a "*steady* lake!" from the overwhelming power of the visually ranging panorama. The short blank-verse passage offers a moment of concentrated aesthetic reflection outside the "current" of history and its sublime representation.

The role of Wordsworth's prose in mediating between his epic and lyric blank verse is further suggested by his inclusion, in the 1823 edition of what later became known as *A Guide to the Lakes*—a set of lines that he had written toward *The Recluse*:[29]

> Mark how the feather'd tenants of the flood,
> With grace of motion that might scarcely seem
> Inferior to angelical, prolong
> Their curious pastime! shaping in mid air
> (And sometimes with ambitious wing that soars
> High as the level of the mountain tops,)
> A circuit ampler than the lake beneath,
> Their own domain;—but ever, while intent
> On tracing and retracing that large round,
> Their jubilant activity evolves
> Hundreds of curves and circlets, to and fro,
> Upward and downward, progress intricate
> Yet unperplex'd, as if one spirit swayed
> Their indefatigable flight.—'Tis done—
> Ten times, or more, I fancied it had ceased;
> But lo! the vanish'd company again
> Ascending;—they approach—I hear their wings
> Faint, faint at first, and then an eager sound
> Past in a moment—and as faint again!
> They tempt the sun to sport amid their plumes;
> They tempt the water or the gleaming ice,
> To shew them a fair image; —'tis themselves,
> Their own fair forms, upon the glimmering plain,
> Painted more soft and fair as they descend
> Almost to touch;—then up again aloft,
> Up with a sally and a flash of speed,
> As if they scorn'd both resting-place and rest! (*W Prose*, II: 183)

Building on the practices of Gilpin, Hutchinson, and Housman, Wordsworth embeds the verse extract in prose in which he explicitly teaches the tourist to read the landscape as a dynamic of shapes, forms, and lines—"by directing his attention at once to the distinctions in things which, without such previous aid, a length of time only could enable him to discover." Wordsworth hopes to inculcate "habits of more exact and considerate observation," allowing the tourist to register the landscape as a field that discloses marks. Thus he traces "the perpendicular sides" of mountains "seamed by ravines" that "entrench and scar the surface with numerous figures like the letters W. and Y." (*W Prose*, II: 171, 175), and he discriminates the straight edges of the larch plantations from the uneven borders of uncultivated forests. In patient prose he delineates the "gracefully or boldly indented" "*boundary-line*" of the lakes and magnifies the natural detritus of exposed "bays": "the curved rim of fine blue gravel, thrown up in course of time by the waves, half of it perhaps gleaming from under the water, and the corresponding half of a lighter hue" (*W Prose*, II: 181–82).

Having illustrated in prose the fine lines that are formed by strong wind and water currents, Wordsworth then turns to verse to show such lines in their making.[30] Foregrounding a natural geometry, "Mark how the feather'd tenants" directs the tourist to observe the "grace of motion" with which the birds trace and retrace a "circuit ampler than the lake beneath"; it then focuses our attention on more minute patterns of lines:

> Hundreds of curves and circlets, to and fro,
> Upward and downward, progress intricate
> Yet unperplex'd . . .

While the surrounding prose delineates landscapes—or land shapes—formed by water and wind, the verse delineates ampler "circuits" and the finer "Curves and circlets" shaped in midair above the lake. As such, it offers the visual figures traced by the birds as a figure for the interactions of meter and rhythm. Shaped into the metrical current, two first-foot inversions ("*Hun*dreds of *curves*"; "*Up*ward and *down*ward") and a final pyrrhic foot ("*progress in*tricate") make for a musical "progress intricate / Yet unperplex'd, as if one spirit swayed / [The] indefatigable flight" of these lines. The guidebook construes the blank verse as a coherent crosscurrent of natural forces traceable by the eye, and coming into the range of the ear.

For Johnson, it was a failing of blank verse that it was hard to detect by ear ("the musick" of the heroic line "is easily lost") and thus overly dependent upon its visual appearance on the page, without which it lacked metrical form. Inverting Johnson's aesthetic values and views, in "Mark how the feather'd tenants" Wordsworth exploits print not to manifest the "musick" of regular measures but rather to manifest a striving to track the variable and intermittent sounds of birds in flight:

—'Tis done—
Ten times, or more, I fancied it had ceased;
But lo! the vanish'd company again
Ascending;—they approach—I hear their wings
Faint, faint at first, and then an eager sound
Past in a moment—and as faint again!

Contra Johnson, Wordsworth's quotation not only employs but also graphically foregrounds its prosodic license, a playful freedom with pause and stress. The excerpt produces a feeling of sensory immediacy through high graphic mediation: dashing caesurae inscribe the flight of birds across the pentameter and thereby advance the formalizing effect of the *Guide to the Lakes* upon the landscape it evokes. The reader is invited not only to see and hear the birds circling over the circular lake in the turns and returns of the lines of type ("an eager sound / Past in a moment") but also to regard blank verse as a meter of such dynamic, sight- and sound-evoking lines. Set into the visual order of Wordsworth's guidebook, "Mark how the feather'd tenants" is indicative of Wordsworth's larger purpose of attuning readers to subtle "lines of demarcation" in the landscape (*W Prose,* II: 210). He follows Hutchinson and Housman in associating blank verse with nature's "careless and graceful hand" (*W Prose,* II: 209) but he does so by materializing the finer lines of nature's "hand" within the lines and line marks of the verse that inscribes them.

It is also significant that Wordsworth published the lines (marked "M. S.") in the 1823 *Guide to the Lakes* before republishing them in his 1827 *Poetical Works* as one of the "Poems of the Imagination."[31] The prose text marked out "Mark how the feather'd tenants" as a lyric entity in a way the lines are not so marked when just lines among many in the *Recluse* manuscripts. The *Guide* formalized the verse excerpt by involving its lines in lake-like circuits that dynamically demarcate the visual and sonic boundaries of "Water-Fowl."

Wordsworth's guidebook differed from those of Gilpin, Hutchinson, and Housman in that they were not themselves poets and did not therefore extract, and then publish separately, their own verse. Nevertheless, it is not untypical: what Wordsworth did with "Mark how the feather'd tenants" is but an extreme instance of the effect of the new print culture of extracts of which the guidebook is a salient example.[32] The print culture of tourism shifted the terms of poetic integrity; the new publications that aesthetically measured the landscape gave new form to nature poetry by excerpting passages from longer poems and by associating their measures with the figures and forms of the landscape.

Further, through Wordsworth's development of inscriptional convention and his modification of the picturesque visual agenda, tourist culture formalized blank verse by making prominent its graphic techniques of emphasis (the line of punctuation, the line of print) and by aligning these with nature's marks in land and sky. The production and reception of "nature poetry" was conditioned by the visual retraining (topographic and typographic) of tourists in tour narratives and guidebooks, and, as I will show in the next section, by the introduction of maps to this culture.

The Poem in the Map: Peter Crosthwaite's Innovations

In cultivating a form of visual attention that moves between the marks of the landscape and the printed poem, between "figures" in topographic and typographic fields, Wordsworth followed the earliest mapping projects of the Lakes region. Indeed, once introduced to the print culture of tourism, maps played an increasingly significant role in the representation of the region, and, as I suggest here, promoted a form of cartographic literacy that affected the writing and reading of poetry.

For the first decades in which tours and guidebooks started to appear, the forms and contours of the lakes were made visible to tourists by drawings, paintings, engravings, and verse but rarely by maps.[33] Arthur Young's *A Six Months Tour Through the North of England* included three engravings of Young's sketches from Keswick but appeared mapless in 1770. Hutchinson's *Excursion to the Lakes in Westmoreland and Cumberland* appeared mapless in 1774 but with engraved drawings of antiquities in 1776.[34] Gilpin's *Observations* offered a few spare outline sketches of the lakes. The region's first official guidebook for tourists, West's *Guide to the Lakes* (London, 1778), contained neither maps nor engravings though it famously directed tourists, in prose, to particular locations—stations—for viewing scenic prospects. The second edition of West's *Guide* contained a single picturesque frontispiece, a view of Grasmere; only in the third edition, in 1784, did a map of the region first appear. West's editor, the schoolmaster and elocutionist William Cockin, believed that the inclusion of a map "might tend to perfect the work" and "be very acceptable to the tourist."[35] At one-quarter inch to the mile, this was a small-scale map, described by Peter Bicknell as "little more than a diagram" with "emphasis on main roads, lakes and the principal towns and villages."[36] Relief—the depiction of the terrain's undulations—is almost nonexistent.

To see the region in greater detail than afforded by West's limited map, and to gain a sense of the fells, tourists of the 1770s and 80s could refer to county maps published independently of tour literature: Thomas Jefferys' map of Westmorland (1770) and Thomas Donald's map of Cumberland (1774). Based on the first mathematical surveys of these counties since the sixteenth century, these one-inch-to-one-mile maps register the importance Britain now attributed to detail and accuracy in terrain depiction—although their focus was the valleys and towns, not the peaks of the fells. Thus William Wilberforce carried the first edition of West's *Guide* and an unidentified map "that occasionally led him badly astray" when he toured the region in 1779, relying on the knowledge of human guides when venturing into the relatively unmapped, rugged terrain of the peaks.[37] In 1783, publisher Thomas Hodgkinson catered to tourists by reducing Donald's map to a more convenient size; and in 1800, Charles Smith produced the first pocket map of the region for tourists.[38] His *New and Accurate Map of the Lakes, in the Counties of Cumberland, Westmorland, and Lancaster,* which was constructed for active use by being "mounted on linen and folded in a neat slip-case," crossed county lines to depict a topographical area.[39] In sum, more detailed maps of a more firmly defined region were newly available in the last quarter of the century and, by its turn, had become something not merely to peruse but to carry close to the body and to consult on the spot.

As the map developed as a technology of picturesque tourism, it became more portable, more accurate, and more detailed; it also became a component of landscape experience and apprehension for travelers, who could scan a region of the earth as if from above, perusing indicated features. And in the hands of Peter Crosthwaite (1735–1808), the Lakes map, like the tour and guidebook, became a mixed-media publication that featured engraved drawings, prose descriptions, and lines of verse.[40] Recognized by historians as "the first man to try to turn the exploitation of Lake District tourism into a full-time occupation,"[41] Crosthwaite settled in Keswick a year after the 1778 publication of West's *Guide* and in 1780 established the Peter Crosthwaite Museum, which displayed natural curiosities and artifacts from home and abroad. At the sign of the "Quadrant, Telescope, and Weathercock," Crosthwaite sold his maps, Donald's map of Cumberland, and West's *Guide.* He sold the landscapes of Smith, Joseph Farington, and other artists; and tourist devices including tinted landscape glasses, Claude mirrors, and pocket compasses.[42] Crosthwaite also rigged devices that further opened the landscape to view. The journal of an unknown "Gentleman of Oxford" recalls "a

number of little reeds, fixed to the foot of a window sash, through each of
which by applying your eye, you are directed to the principal objects or stations on the Lake."[43]

An impresario of Lakes tourism, Crosthwaite brought the Lakes out to the
English public in order to lure tourists back to his museum at Keswick. He
commissioned sales agents for his maps throughout the country and led a
subscription campaign in the principal English towns, a campaign that promoted domestic travel as a patriotic activity. Crosthwaite's maps, which praise
the "*native Isle*" while quantifying its features, are recognized as the first accurate hydrographic maps of the Lakes; they thus mark a confluence of late
eighteenth-century impulses toward the natural world. With scientific, aesthetic, commercial, and ideological interests encoded, the maps focused the
Lakes and their shores at a remarkably large scale (all but one at three inches
to the mile) for a large number of the public, including "Country People" who
could visit the museum for half price.[44] Crosthwaite revised, updated, and
reissued the maps five times between 1783 and 1819. In 1789 alone he ordered
4,450 sheets for printing, and in a 1792 handbill claimed to have "sold many
Thousand Maps of the Lakes." They are considered to have "aided [scores of
tourists] in their quest" for picturesque scenery.[45] Wordsworth, Samuel Taylor
Coleridge, Robert Southey, John Dalton, and a handful of royals and aristo-
crats signed the museum's guestbook during Crosthwaite's lifetime, and the
museum remained a popular destination for visitors to Keswick until its close
in 1870.[46]

In 1783, Crosthwaite published the first of his seven large-scale portrayals
of the Lakes conjoining map, verse, prose, and picture to show "every Thing
which could be thought necessary or useful to the Tourist."[47] Navigational
tool, propaganda, and souvenir, the maps presented a complex field of sign
and image: lake depths, water currents, cardinal directions; villages, properties, parks, woods, roads, and hills are marked on the maps with different
kinds of sign (pictographic, abstract, conventional).[48] Following Jefferys, who
had included picturesque landscape vignettes in the borders of his countywide
maps, Crosthwaite inset captioned pictorial views of topographical features
and architectural curiosities, enhancing the maps' souvenir value. Profile views
of the "Bowdar Stone," "Lofty Skiddow," and "*The large* YEW TREE, *near
Coniston Waterhead, 9 feet Diameter*" intermingle with verse excerpts, prose
annotations, and directions to viewing stations. By consolidating these diverse
grammars on a simple surface, the maps fulfilled in a rich medium some of

the key elements of cartographic and picturesque touring publications, transforming the representation of place and shaping a multirepresentational topographical literacy.

Crosthwaite's maps offered a more accessible terrain than existing tour and guidebooks or even the single map introduced into West's *Guide* in 1784, the small scale of which precluded the marking of the viewing stations that West had made famous. To find the stations using West's guide, the tourist had to trace intricate paths of verbal description: "Mr. *Gray*'s most noble view of the vale of *Lonsdale*," for instance, is pointed out by the quotation of a footnote from Gray's text: " 'This scene opens just three miles from *Lancaster*, on what is called the *Queen's road*. To see the view in perfection you must go into a field on the left. †' " But the quotation, it turns out, is insufficient, prompting West to append a footnote of his own: "† As several mistakes have been made respecting this station, it is necessary to point it out more precisely. About a quarter of a mile beyond the third milestone, where the road makes a turn to the right, there is a gate on the left, which leads into a field, where the station meant is shown by a pole erected for that purpose, by Mr. *Jones*, the proprietor of the field, who gives travellers liberty to go into it with their horses, or carriages."[49] West's guide has no straightforward means of directing readers. Though Mr. Jones's pole promises to "point . . . out more precisely" the elusive view of Lonsdale, the fact of the pole is still conveyed by a footnote to a footnote.

Crosthwaite remedied the situation, turning West's convoluted prose directions into cartographic writing. In a representational paradigm shift, he denoted West's "picturesque points" directly on his maps: "*with West's 4 Stations pointed out thus* □ *and 3 of the* Author's *marked in the same manner,*" reads the map of the Lake of Coniston.[50] In an analogous manner he placed verse on his maps, using it to focus tourists' views as the tour narratives and guidebooks did. Crosthwaite, however, used the verse differently; whereas they quoted poetry that referred to scenes from elsewhere, he inscribed verse that was specific to the locality and worked with the devices of the map—such as the compass rose—to orient tourists within the scene. Thus on the map of Broadwater,

> *Adorn'd with Giant Skiddow on the East,*
> *The Towering Banks of Withope on the West;*
> *The North displays much Cultivated Land;*

The South the Vale of Keswick ever grand,
And winding Shoars with variegated Wood;
Compleat the Scene and Circumscribe the Flood. (Broadwater)

In these stanzas, verse annotates space. More radically, it acts as a cartographic sign, marking a physical area by occupying a corresponding place on the map:

Here Fletcher's Lofty Oaks from Nature's hand,
Bow down to every Blast and thus they stand;
A Living Ornament let them Remain,
(Until the present Age is past and gone:)
And Oaks Mature our Guardian Fleets Maintain. (Broadwater)

The map context intensifies adverbial deixis, heightening the force of *"Here"* above its force when quoted in a guidebook by transforming the lines of verse that follow into locational signs—material marks on the map for a stand of oaks on the ground, endowed here with martial might and national significance.

Thus by mapping the terrain without omitting pictorial representation—and by recruiting verse both to picture place and to mark spots on the map—Crosthwaite produced a new composite form, the significance of which his early "Ulls-water" map (first issued in 1783) makes explicit by celebrating the *"crystal Lakes"* and commending the tourist who *"leaves the Plains"* to visit them (Figure 3). If this was a means of flattering his customers, it also made claims about the purpose of tourism:

Henceforth let British Youths their native Isle explore,
Before they visit France, or from their Canaan Tour;
A Patriotic Plan, more so they scarce will find,
'Twill make them like the Sage of old, & bless their native Land.
                                                                (Ulls-water)

In rhyming hexameter and heptameter, Crosthwaite's *"Patriotic Plan"* enlists *"British Youths"* into veneration of the *"native Isle,"* offering itself and the map series as a national resource—regional representation with synechdochal force.[51] By focusing the *"enchanting Lakes"* and their surrounding features, the maps strive to promote a feeling for the nation as a whole.[52] The *"Lakes"* emerge as emblematic of Britain through the dynamic interaction of representational modes—verse stanza, prose annotation, pictorial vignette, and cartographic

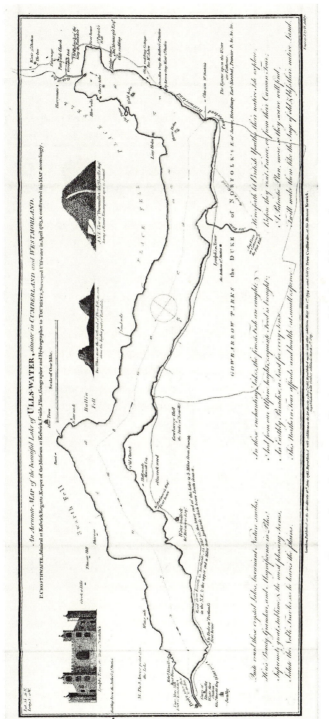

Figure 3. Peter Crosthwaite, "An Accurate Map of the Beautiful Lake of Ulls-water," 1783 (London: n.d.). Reproduced by permission of the William L. Clements Library, University of Michigan.

writing. And verse, as both linguistic and graphical signal, appears essential in that emergence.

While recalling the linguistic and graphic complexity of the traditional emblem,[53] Crosthwaite's were a new form of print text intended to facilitate a new form of experience: the map-mediated tour of a representatively British region. They encouraged physical exploration and demanded the interpretation of intersecting modes of measure, associating both with patriotism. In the "Accurate Map of Buttermere, Crummock & Lowes-water Lakes," first issued in 1794, the performance of national feeling gingerly encompasses the new activity of touring on foot, and in so doing it experiments with a logic of space new to tourist maps: "*The Company who go from* Keswick *to* Scale Hill (*10 Miles*) *in a Chaise, will be able to Visit the 1.st 2.d & 4.th Stations; and the Scale Force,* (*a Water Fall,*) *in one day, by the help of the Chaise, and a Boat; provided they can walk 2 Miles of the whole days Tour, at 3 intervals of time.*" Readers are asked to conceive of space in terms of durations of time as their bodies move through it, aided and unaided, at different rates. Crosthwaite's emblematic terrain is thus a multiply measured thing; landscape measured in numbers of yards, miles, and fathoms is measured also by intervals of time and modes of passage, and measured yet again by hexameters, pentameters, and the pauses of Crosthwaite's profuse punctuation—measured, that is to say, by the temporalizing patterns of language.[54] An array of spatial and temporal signs confronts and constructs the new "*British*" reader of the "*native Isle*," conditioning a hybrid form of national literacy in which measures of land and language interact.

Crosthwaite associated his name with the convergence of cartographic and poetic innovation, claiming to have invented not only a new method of surveying the land ("a machine 'for taking landscapes by rule'") but also an "improved Aeolian harp" which he sold alongside his maps at his museum shop.[55] On the map surface, the conjunction of cartographic and poetic codes intricate England with the English language. On the earliest maps, those of Ullswater and Windermere, three hexameter and pentameter quatrains appear beneath the lengths of the centrally positioned lakes, establishing a horizontal visual symmetry and neoclassical sense of balance.

Whereas the scale bar of one mile appears between the lake and the title of these maps, underscoring their scientific rigor (and the authority of the "Geographer and Hydrographer to Tourists"), maps issued later in the series construct a more dynamic conceptual relation between cartographic codes and verse. On the maps of Broadwater and Coniston a visually prominent "scale of one Mile" spans the distance between two stanzas of heroic verse (Figure 4),

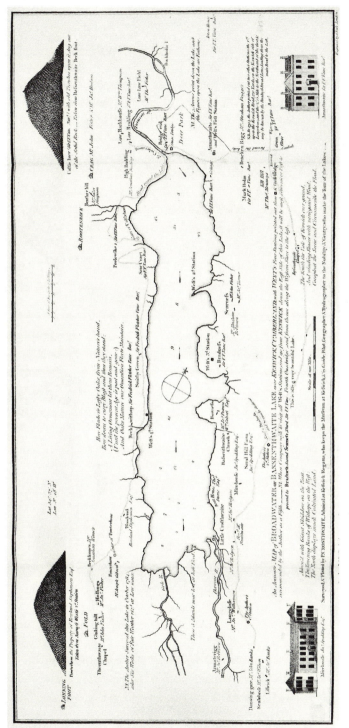

Figure 4. Peter Crosthwaite, "An Accurate Map of Broadwater or Bassenthwaite Lake," 1785 (London: n.d.). Reproduced by permission of the William L. Clements Library, University of Michigan.

demanding that the eye of the reader-viewer pass over the mark of topographical length as it moves between lines of patriotic verse. By this crossing of poetic and cartographic measures, I suggest, both lines accrue graphical salience and national significance. In conjunction with the English statute mile—modified from Roman precedent and instituted in 1593—the heroic line materializes as a standard unit of English verse length affiliated with the native terrain.

It is the Derwent map (Figure 5), however, that most suggestively exemplifies the inscriptional conditions of late eighteenth-century nature poems. Verse strikingly appears on the other maps in stanzas that enframe the central lake and balance the visual field; on this map, by contrast, between a segment of the Derwent River and the map edge (called the neat-line), Crosthwaite fits three and a half lines of blank verse that add to the map's visual density and asymmetry. On the right margin, beneath the place name "*ORMATHWAITE*" and a building pictograph is a property note:

> *Here Stands the Beautiful*
> *Villa of W. Brownrigg Esq.*
> *M.D. — F.R.S. It came to*
> *J.B. Walsh Esq.* in the Year 1800* (Derwent)

Above and to the left, a block of text similarly begins "*Here lie,*" activating the locational function of the lines as a lilting rhythm asserts the matter of verse:

> *Here lie the Splendid Spoils of Mountain Floods;*
> *Those Fertile Plains, brought Captive from their Sides,*
> *And yon Stupendous Chasms (Cloud high) have left;*
> *Bereft of Soil.* (Derwent)

For the tourist, the modulation of the landscape—the evocation of fluvial plains and mountain chasms—coincides with the modulations of meter; in reading of the contours of the land, the tourist is made aware of the stress contours of verse (and vice versa). Blank verse is not posing on Crosthwaite's map as poetry; the paragraph emerges as poetry as meter makes its mark in language—associated here with the forces and processes of climate and geology.[56] As both locational sign and topographical annotation, the verse interacts with neighboring signs that modulate the area's surfaces: the depth measures and flow arrows that figure the concavity and currents of the lake, and the hachuring and curvilinear writing that show its *"Alpine heights."*[57] Blank verse

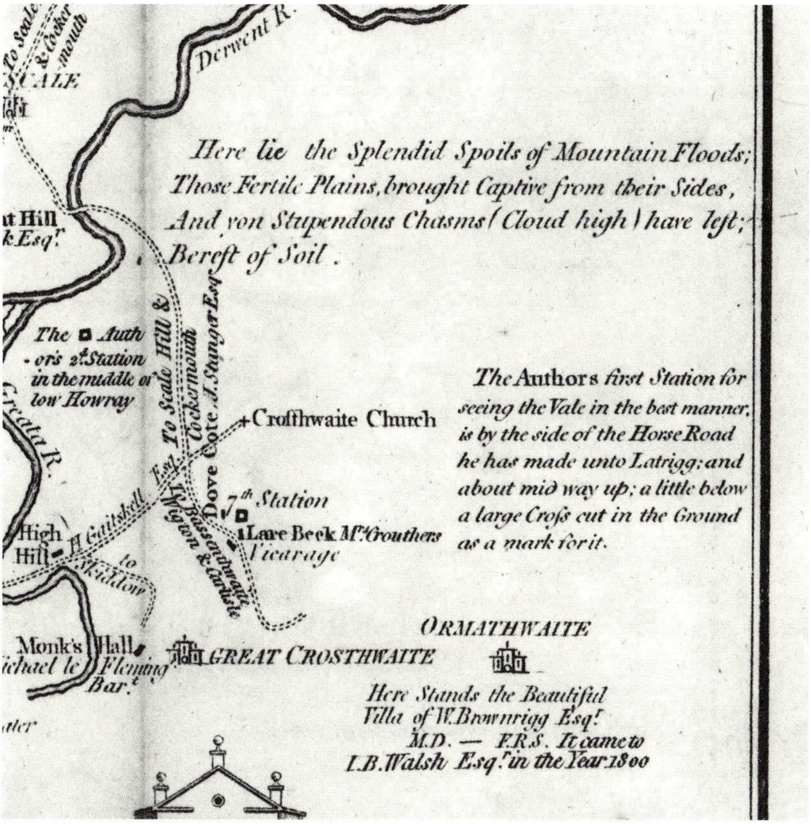

Figure 5. Peter Crosthwaite, "An Accurate Map of the Matchless Lake of Derwent," 1783 (London: n.d.), detail. Reproduced by permission of the William L. Clements Library, University of Michigan.

formally materializes as it serves its indexical function in the cartographic print context.

But the map attunes readers not only to its thick array of signs on the page—but also to the signs on the land to which the map refers. Below the verses, Crosthwaite informs the tourist of a "mark" that he cut in the ground to signal an additional viewing station:[58]

The Authors *first Station for*
seeing the Vale in the best manner,
is by the side of the Horse Road

he has made unto Latrigg; and
about mid way up; a little below
a large Cross cut in the Ground
as a mark for it. (Derwent)

Crosthwaite here inscribes a spot of real ground in the same way that he denotes
a spot on the map—such as Crosthwaite Church, marked by a small cross to
the right of this very note. He scores the terrain as if the ground itself were a
legible page on which he was placing an asterisk—the principal footnote mark,
along with the dagger or cross, in West's *Guide*: "† As several mistakes have been
made respecting this station, it is necessary to point it out more precisely." Improving on West's and his editor's attempts to point out viewing stations more
precisely—with footnotes to footnotes—Crosthwaite disperses notations beyond the printed sheet to the landscape it evokes, as if the landscape were now
a map of itself. Crosthwaite's prose legend thus reveals a historic moment in
British topographical representation: an intensification of the graphic sign now
inscribed within interreferring fields—both the printed field of the map sheet
and the literal field of the ground through which the tourist moves. His "large
Cross cut in the Ground" signals an inscriptional climate of heightened visual
discrimination, revealing a nature and a landscape that are now brought into
knowledge by visual codes that derive as much from cartography and guidebook conventions as they do from the spoken words of local people.

The blank-verse lines that limn Lake Derwent's shore, and whose stresses
complement the rises and falls of the neighboring Mt. Skiddaw, are telling. The
nature verse that took form and gained popularity during the publication and
reprinting of Crosthwaite's maps was conditioned by increasing print-pressure
on the terrain, when new ways of experiencing the British landscape—touring
on foot as well as by boat and carriage—were supported by new forms of engraving and publication, including large-scale mapping and mixed-media
guidebooks, that trained attention to landmarks and print marks simultaneously.[59] Poetry was an integral part of a complex visual culture that activated
the metrical and graphic dimensions of verse by recruiting it in projects of
locating and characterizing features of the landscape. Crosthwaite's own mixing of verse, prose, illustration, notation, and symbol was a commercial innovation that developed out of scientific and cultural practices (including
picturesque touring, sketching, and versifying) concerned with taking the measure of Britain. His maps reveal the confluence of impulses to measure and
mark—aesthetic, scientific, affective, ideological—at work in the consolidation

of the Lakes as an emblematically British region. They highlight the interactions of poetry and cartography in the articulation of national space and the dependence of national feeling on complex forms of carto-poetic literacy.

Interdependent Forms: *Black's Picturesque Guide to the English Lakes*

Lakes verse took place in a dynamic field of visual media; its production and reception was shaped by increasingly sophisticated conditions of diagrammatic and cartographic representation, as the century's many guidebooks reveal—including Wordsworth's own evolving *Guide to the Lakes* in which the poet, modifying convention, published his own poetic excerpts. Partly as a result of this poetic self-inscription, and also of the publication of the 1820 version of the *Guide* together with his River Duddon sonnets, Wordsworth's poetry was taken up and reprinted in other guidebooks, including *Black's Picturesque Guide to the English Lakes*, which became the standard. First published in 1841, and diversified in subsequent editions by increasingly complex forms of display, *Black's Guide* evinces the intensifying graphical and conceptual interplay between Lakes verse and other topographical media in the sixty years since the first edition of West's *Guide*. Further, its cutting and quoting of Wordsworth "Yew-Trees," which I explored in the Introduction, marks the treatment of the short blank-verse poem like the epic blank verse cited by eighteenth and early nineteenth-century tours and guidebooks. *Black's* "Yew-Trees" thus signals the completion of a cycle in Lake publications: the partitioning and recirculation of a form of poem that its guidebook predecessors had enabled.

Black's Guide also imaged the "District" in large-scale maps. Pasted into the front board is William Hughes' *Map [of the] Lake District of Cumberland, Westmorland and Lancashire*. This 3½-miles-to-the-inch foldout map afforded a more detailed view than the map Wordsworth added to his *Guide* in its 1822 incarnation as *Description of the Scenery of the Lakes in the North of England*. *Black's* map also outscaled Jonathan Otley's four-miles-to-the-inch *New Map of the District of the Lakes* (1818), the first of the Lakes' topographical publications to name the area a "District," and influential, no doubt, in Wordsworth's 1835 renaming of his "Book on the Lakes" a *Guide Through the District of the Lakes*.[60]

Interleaved throughout the book, *Black's* "Four Charts of the Lake District," at 1½ inches to the mile, afforded even closer views of the "District." We might liken these detailed cartographic renderings to the literary excerpts that also brought "the images of nature, as forcibly, and as closely to the eye" as possible. And insofar as *Black's* "availed [itself] to a considerable extent of the literature of the district," as it announces, it made the "Lake-Guide" a fully physical and literary compendium.[61] Whereas eighteenth-century tour narratives and guidebooks had increasingly quoted English over classical verse, *Black's* shows a concentration on local writers, trading, above all, on the name and poetry of Wordsworth. Indeed, *Black's* suggests the degree to which the culture's new categories—"Lake-District," "Lake-Guide," and "Lake Poets"— were mutually supportive and sustaining.[62]

Achieving twenty-two editions by the end of the nineteenth century, *Black's Guide* represents the mature, Victorian type of the Lake guidebook: graphically diverse and information rich, with map, charts, engravings of picturesque views, illustrated itineraries, and "Synoptical Tables of Mountains, Lakes, and Waterfalls." Even more thickly interleaved, the fifth edition of 1850 adds twelve "Outline Views of Mountain Groups" and sophisticated cross-sections of geological strata and of the district's aqueous deposits.[63] Prefaced by etymological dictionaries of place-names and regional terms (*barrow*, *tarn*, *thwaite*, and so on), and concluded with an essay on the "Geology of the Lake District," the guide presents the area as an achieved space: shaped not only by geological and sociolinguistic forces over time but also by the literary personalities of the era, including Wordsworth, Coleridge, Southey, Radcliffe, Keats, Hemans, Jewsbury, and De Quincey, through whose writing—and often because of it—tourists are directed to apprehend the landscape.[64]

The distribution of "Yew-Trees" amidst prose, chart, and "Outline Views," I showed in the Introduction, turns the tourist's attention between metrical and mensural grammars, topographical and typographical views. These turnings are perhaps nowhere more acute than in the novel feature of the "illustrated Itinerary," *Black's* elaboration of simple lists of stopping places and distances (such as those included in Wordsworth's 1835 *Guide*) (Figure 6).[65] The three-paneled scheme charts a course along a route (middle column) and plots features of interest to the traveler's right (left column) and left (right column) by means of prose annotations and verse excerpts. In the Keswick to Cockermouth itinerary, the Bowder Stone, five miles out of Keswick and 20½ miles before Cockermouth, is marked by lines from *The Excursion*:[66]

> A stranded ship with keel up-
>   turn'd that rests
> Careless of winds or wave. (166)

ON RIGHT FROM KESWICK.	From Cockerm.	KESWICK.	From Keswick	ON LEFT FROM KESWICK.
		Road to the Lake.		
Vicar's or Derwent Isle.	25¼ 25		¼	Castle Head, an eminence from which there is a beautiful view of the lake.
Lords Isle. Friar Crag projects into the lake a little beyond. Cat Bells are fine objects on the opposite shore, Grizedale, and Causey Pikes are to the left of them.				Wallow Crag. Falcon Crag.
Behind Barrow House is a cascade of 124 feet fall.	23½	Barrow House. Pocklington, Esq.	2	Road to the hamlet called Watendlath, placed near a tarn in a desolate and narrow vale.
The many topped Skiddaw, lifting its gigantic bulk beyond the foot of the lake, is a grand object. Crosthwaite Church will be observed lying at its base.	22½	Lowdore Inn.	3	Thrang Crag. The celebrated fall lies behind the inn, on the stream running from Watendlath Tarn. Its height is 100 feet. Gowder Crag on the left, Shepherd's Crag on the right of the fall.
Grange Bridge, and the village of Grange. The road returns to Keswick by the west margin of Derwent Water. Borrowdale, a valley 6 miles long, and containing 2000 acres, is now entered. It is watered, in its whole length, by the river Grange, which, after it issues from Derwent Water, takes the name of Derwent. At Castle Crag the road and the bed of the river occupy all the level portion, but beyond the vale widens considerably. Above Rosthwaite the valley divides into two branches; the eastern branch is called Stonethwaite. Borrowdale formerly belonged to Furness Abbey.	21¼ 20¼	Castle Crag on the right. " From the summit of this rock the views are so singularly great and pleasing, that they ought never to be omitted." WEST.	4 5	Grange Crag. There is a good view from this eminence. Shortly before reaching this point, a road deviates to, and passes, Bowder Stone, re-entering the main road a little beyond. This mass of rock has been likened to A stranded ship with keel upturn'd that rests Careless of winds or wave. It is 62 feet long, 36 feet high, and 89 feet in circumference. It has been estimated to weigh 1971 tons, and to contain 23,000 cubic feet. The view hence is exquisitely beautiful.
Here is a small inn. This is the widest part of the valley. The mountain Glaramara is seen in front. Scawfell Pikes, Scawfell and Great Gavel are seen over Seathwaite.	19½	Rosthwaite vill.	6	Half a mile beyond, near Borrowdale Chapel, a road diverges to the valley and village of Stonethwaite. Eagle Crag is a fine rock near the latter. A mountain path proceeds over the Stake, a lofty pass, into Langdale.
	18	cr. Seatollar Bridge.	7½	Near this bridge the road into Wastdale, by Sty Head, strikes off.
The ascent of Buttermere Haws, which rises to the height of 1100 feet above the sea, is now commenced. The retrospective views are fine. A portion of Helvellyn is seen over the Borrowdale and Armboth Fells.	17½	Seatollar. Abraham Fisher, Esq. Descend into Buttermere dale.	8	The well known black lead mine, and the immense Borrowdale Yews, are near Seatollar. The former is the only mine of the kind in England. The largest of the yews is 21 feet in girth.
Yew Crag. The upper part of this vale is exceedingly wild and uncultivated.	15½	Honister Crag.	10	Honister Crag, 1700 feet high. Here are some valuable slate quarries belonging to General Wyndham.

Figure 6. The first page of the two-page Keswick to Cockermouth "illustrated Itinerary." *Black's Picturesque Guide to the English Lakes*, 2nd ed. (Edinburgh, 1844), 166.

The itinerary constitutes an extreme disciplining of vision and movement, and thus an intriguing context for poetry; as *Black's* 1842 preface announces, "not only are the *distances* minutely stated, but the *objects of interest,* on either side of the road, are pointed out and briefly described" (v). The lines that figure the Bowder Stone as a stranded ship, indifferent to its proper medium and progress ("Careless of winds or wave"), seem particularly unsuited to the forward-moving itinerary but also illustrative of their own recontextualization. Their turning up within a mimetically structured typographic field—left, right, and center—heightens their referential function, making them point forcefully to the external world while also intensifying their tropological force: their troping or turning of the stone itself into another order of being.

Their force is topological as well as tropological. In a development of Crosthwaite's placing of verses within his maps (placing them "Here," as a mark of a spot), poetic lines play the role of locational sign along a fixed route. In their brevity and locational force—their approximation to the site itself— the lines come close to epigram. That is to say, the lines on the Bowder Stone evoke lines *on* the Bowder Stone—lines inscribed on stone, or epigram. "Romantic poetry" does not transcend but is recalled to "its formal origin in epigram and inscription"[67] within the hypermimetic field of the Victorian itinerary, where, paradoxically, it is called upon to point, trope, materially mark, and, like the other poetic quotations, cast a "spell," so as to permit, in future moments, a recollection of "the pleasures of the past" and a revisiting "in imagination of the scenery" (4). Metrical writing enlivens and extends the print tour; "*Care*less of winds or wave," subtle rests and rhythmic inversions disrupt the quantified field that brings them into focus. Like the excerpts from "Yew-Trees," they convert the reader into a subject of memory and "imagination"—a Wordsworthian form of consciousness that depends upon interpretive turns between mensural and metrical grammars, rhetorics of visibility and revisibility.

Black's Guide was the culmination not of an isolated genre (the tour narrative) or aesthetic fad (the picturesque) but of a rich, new print culture, serving tourism and patriotism, in which tour narratives, guidebooks, aesthetic treatises, maps, and poems were brought into new relationships and transformed in the process. *Black's* suggests the implicated maturation of the "Lake-Guide," the large-scale map, and the short blank-verse nature poem, as well as the cooperation of these grammars in the construction of both the "Lake-District" and a kind of touristic patriot: the new "*British*" reader of the "*native Isle*" who deciphers a literary and physical landscape. Participating in this print culture both as a guidebook writer and as a quoter and writer of landscape poems, Wordsworth attuned readers to the material forms and stress patterns of each. His poetry was written and read in a culture that associated poetry with intensely focused periods of perception and feeling in addition to encouraging readers to see lines, signs, and other figures within new kinds of inscriptional grammars and to visualize their relations to the world beyond the page. Not only does the Lake District come into focus as a site of national feeling as a result of these new forms of graphic and notational literacy: Wordsworth emerged as the national poet by means of these intersecting aesthetic, scientific, commercial, and ideological agendas. So, too, the short blank-verse nature lyric, a genre that scarcely existed at the publication of Dalton's *Descriptive Poem* in 1755, became a central—quotable—part of the new textual landscape within which Britain could be known and imaginatively recollected.

Chapter 2

"I Trace His Paths upon the Maps"

Cartographic Inscription in *The Prelude*

While his classmates remained at Cambridge during the summer of 1790 to prepare for final examinations, Wordsworth was not to be found within the precincts of his university. Instead, he was traveling by boat and foot through Europe and the Alps with his friend Robert Jones. "Nature," Wordsworth explains in *The Prelude*, was "sovereign in my heart, / And mighty forms seizing a youthful Fancy / Had given a charter to irregular hopes" (1805, VI: 346–48). After landing in Calais on the eve of the anniversary of the fall of the Bastille, the college friends journeyed over two thousand miles through France, Switzerland, Italy, and Germany.[1]

Much of what we know about Wordsworth and Jones's 1790 tour of the continent comes from a letter Wordsworth wrote to his sister during the trip and from the account he gives in *The Prelude*, Book VI, over seven hundred lines of blank verse composed in 1804 and revised periodically throughout his life.[2] From these and other sources, biographers and critics have substantially reconstructed the Alpine portion of the tour, motivated by the powerful yet enigmatic account of the crossing of the Simplon Pass.[3] Introduced as an event of "deep and genuine sadness" (1805, VI: 492), but interrupted by a rejoicing paean to the human imagination, the Simplon crossing has long captivated scholars, and criticism of the episode has come to define generations of Romantic scholarship.[4]

Despite the scholarly fascination with the crossing of the Pass, relatively little attention has been paid to one of the most fundamental and at the same time richest contexts informing both the event and its reinscription in *The Prelude*—cartography. And yet the letter to Dorothy composed over ten

September days of that 1790 tour provides a clue to cartography's significance for Wordsworth, from the very outset of his trip. Maps, the letter shows, were vital figures in Wordsworth's literary representation of his European tour. They were vital, I shall argue, not just in the 1790s when he wrote to Dorothy, but also, in a more complex and conflicted way, in 1804 when he again put the tour on paper. Maps, as figures in Wordsworth's verse—and as representational pages that themselves bear figures on their surfaces—shed light on Wordsworth's rendering of journeying on the two-dimensional pages of *The Prelude*.

Maps, both as artifacts produced by a cultural practice (cartography) with scientific, touristic, and military functions, and as figures in written discourse—letters, journals, and poems—had multiple effects on Wordsworth's representations of his journey. Few critics, however, have investigated their importance. In his *Prelude* annotations, Raymond Havens provides only the sparest of maps of France and Switzerland traced by a student from an undated *London Times Atlas* (first edition, 1895).[5] Similarly, in separate works Max Wildi and Donald Hayden reproduce modern-day sketch maps and photographs of the region in order to plot the tour and to situate the pivotal missed turn at the Pass: "One would like to know which were the three unforgettable hours [of Wordsworth's 'walk among the Alps']," Wildi muses. "Where did Wordsworth spend them? What was it that impressed him so deeply that he returned to this experience again and again as to one of those 'spots of time' in connection with which the deepest revelations were vouchsafed to him?"[6] Assuming the significance of geotemporal fact to the Simplon episode, these studies neglect to regard the map as a historical representational form in its own right—a form conditioned by particular representational imperatives and dilemmas—and as an object shaped by historically specific practices. Thus they leave unquestioned the relevance of the visual language of maps to Wordsworth's charting of his poetic and affective development in Book VI. Even Michael Wiley's cartographically informed reading of the Simplon episode omits local maps in its pursuit of an analogy between Wordsworth's "blanking" of the landscape in the apostrophe to the imagination and the lingering blank spaces on African and West English maps of the period (signifying the limits of cartographers' geographic knowledge).[7] I suggest, by contrast, that our understanding of "Cambridge and the Alps" may be illuminated not by an absence of marks on other maps but by the graphic particularities and thicknesses of period mappings of the Pass, as well as by the inscriptional engagements these mappings elicited from their users.

This chapter rectifies the omission of period cartography from the critical literature on Book VI while suggesting that some of the causes for that omission lie in the poem's narrative tactics. In the first section of my argument I consider the relations between writing and mapping that are implicit in Wordsworth's 1790 letter and in Dorothy's response to that letter. I then discuss the cartographical discourse of the period, including several maps that represent the Alps according to rival notational conventions for illustrating altitude and three-dimensional space, or relief. Turning to *The Prelude*, I then consider Wordsworth's use of the map as an emblem for his mind during his days as a Cambridge student before examining his rendering of the Simplon Pass in the light of the visual challenges presented by period maps: both the narrative of the crossing and its notational diction and emphatic gestures. The maps reveal that the "plainer and more emphatic language" (LB 743) to which Wordsworth aspired, and which he grounded in communion with the natural world, was inflected by a technical semiotics that he did not explicitly acknowledge but which, nevertheless, remains visible within the poem's ostensibly natural language. This persistence has implications for some of the critical discussions of Wordsworth, nature, and history that since the 1980s have dominated debate about Romanticism in general and *The Prelude* in particular.

The Letters of 1790

Between September 6 and 16, 1790, Wordsworth wrote to his sister "endeavouring to give [her] some Idea of [his] route."[8] Since last writing, he and Jones had "gone over a very considerable tract of country," but a short supply of writing paper would limit description of what he had seen and felt: "it will be utterly impossible for me to dwell upon particular scenes," he warns, "as my paper would be exhausted before I had done with the journey of two or three days" (32–33). This distinction between geographical and scriptorial space hangs over the letter. References to "scenes" and pictures multiply from page to page as the urge to description is repeatedly thwarted by insufficient "room": of the "celebrated s[c]enes" of the glaciers of Savoy, he writes, "any description which I have here room to give you must be altogether inadequate." Similarly, when he is "Among the more awful scenes of the Alps," he writes, "I had not a thought of man, or a single created being; my whole soul was turned to him who produced the terrible majesty before me. But I am too particular for the limits of my paper" (33–34).

Whether Wordsworth finds his exposition of nature, God, and the soul actually arrested by the material conditions of writing—the amount of paper available to the traveler—or whether he uses the idea that he lacks paper as an excuse not to get too metaphysical, the trope of material limits pervades the letter.[9] Wordsworth uses it here with reference to his memory: "ten thousand times in course of this tour have I regretted the inability of my memory to retain a more strong impression of the beautiful forms before me," he laments (35). While more paper might have relieved some of this pressure on the memory, Wordsworth wished instead for the instantaneous presence of his sister— wished, in effect, to circumvent the constraints of time and space that motivate communication by letter in the first place: "I have thought of you perpetually," he confesses, "and never have my eyes burst upon a scene of particular loveliness but I have almost instantly wished that you could for a moment be transported to the place where I stood to enjoy it" (35).

Wordsworth introduces the subject of maps in a manner that links them to his desire to overcome his distance from Dorothy. In a sudden break from the past tense of the narrative chronology, the letter takes on an exceptional immediacy:

> From Constance we proceeded along the banks of the Rhine to
> Shaffhouse to view the fall of the Rhine there. . . . We followed the
> Rhine downwards about eight leagues from Schaffhouse, where we
> crossed it and proceeded by Baden to Lucerne. I am at this present
> moment (14th of Septbr) writing at a small village in the road from
> Grindelwald to Lauterbrunnen. By consulting your maps, you will
> find these villages in the southeast part of the Canton of Berne not
> far from the lakes of Thun and Brientz. (35)

The fact of his "at this present moment (14th of Septbr) writing" supersedes the possibility of Dorothy's transport, "for a moment," to his side; and the maps, to which he then refers, graphically reveal the impossibility of such transport. Thus the maps function less as a solution to than an admission of the sibling's spatial remove and the letter's spatial restrictions. Only in the wishful conditional can Dorothy stand alongside William to enjoy a "scene of particular loveliness." "I" and "you" are separately positioned before the letter-in-progress and the map: William on location in Switzerland, Dorothy in England. The rhetorical form of the compositional present—"I am at this present moment (14th of Septbr) writing"—and the textual form of the map thus emerge in tandem, the map attesting to the locatedness of the writing "I" in time and space and signifying, by contrast, the limits of the writing paper. While the letter is insufficiently extensive to allow for Wordsworth "to dwell upon particular scenes" and record his turns of thought and feeling, the formal conditions of the map are such that he can project his position of writing ("at a small village in the road from Grindelwald to Lauterbrunnen") into both cardinal and topographical space ("in the southeast part of the Canton"; "not far from the lakes of Thun and Brientz"). The maps allow Dorothy to look over what William can only under-recall and under-describe, but without satisfying, the letter implies, the aesthetic and affective urgencies of the tour experience.

Although William directed his sister to note his current position on her maps, Dorothy did more than locate him in cartographic space. She used the names of places and the description of the routes taken between them ("along the Pays de Vaud side of the lake"; "up the Rhone to Martigny" [33]), to trace his way upon her maps. In a letter of October 6, 1790, to her friend Jane Pollard, Dorothy writes: "when I trace his paths upon the maps I wonder that his strength and courage have not sunk under the fatigues he must have undergone." She encourages Jane in this practice: "It may perhaps be of some amusement to you to trace his route upon your maps therefore I will give you a rough sketch of it mentioning only the principal places he stopped at."[10] Dorothy thus elaborates her brother's suggestion into a mode of affective experience (one evoking "wonder" and "amusement"), making what could have been merely an act of reference into a dynamic encounter between letter and map. In recommending the activity in writing to Jane and in reproducing for her friend the principal stops of the itinerary (a several-page, nearly verbatim transcription of parts of William's letter), Dorothy makes the cartographic encounter into a moving interpretive method for those, like herself, at a spatial and temporal remove. While William's letter is governed by the claim to have no "room" to dwell on the scenes he found so affecting, and while the map attests to these material constraints on writing, the map functions in Dorothy's letter as a textual surface for the production and transmission of knowledge and affect.

Criticism has neglected the cartographic renderings of *The Prelude*'s geographical locations despite, since the 1980s, much New Historicist scrutiny of Romantic "nature" and "imagination." Alan Liu, for instance, exposes the embeddedness of both in culture and history, reading the nature of Wordsworth's Alpine travels not as a sensuous power the imagination uncomfortably displaces in the recognition of its independence but as a convention of eighteenth-century tour literature that Wordsworth manipulates in a staging of the self. Identifying a three-fold structure of signification in what he calls Wordsworth's "tour painting," Liu reads nature as a necessary middle ground between the background plane of history and the foreground plane of the self. Nature, "really only an idea or mark of naturalness," crucially "deflects the arrow of signification" of the historical signifier such that it "points" not to the orbit of politics, civilization, and culture but "invisibly to the foreground self, which thus originates as if from nowhere, or from nature itself." A "denial of history," nature thus serves the goal of Wordsworth's tour "to carve the 'self' out of history."[11]

Liu helpfully situates Wordsworth's travel writing in relationship to the historical practice of the tour and to tour literature, noting, with others, Wordsworth's likely familiarity with William Coxe's 1789 *Travels in Switzerland in a Series of Letters to William Melmoth, Esq.* It is possible that Wordsworth "indeed had not just read but had actually studied Coxe before leaving Cambridge."[12] He certainly consulted a French translation of the work for the 1791–92 composition of *Descriptive Sketches*, and so would then if not before have come across the other "nature" of tour literature that goes unmentioned by Liu: the visual rendering of the physical environment in the form of the map.[13] Coxe's epistolary tour opens with a map of Switzerland and northern Italy that spans three pages and is "Marked with the Routes of Four Tours" made between 1776 and 1786 (Figure 7).[14] On Coxe's map, a set of red lines superimposed upon the engraved lines of the map proper pass across the terrain and through the conventional symbols denoting towns and villages, marking out the paths of traversal.

Hardly eccentric then, Dorothy's practice of tracing William's routes upon her maps reinscribes the conventions of tour literature wherein distance traveled is denoted in the form of lines marked out between points, a practice that superimposes a plane of personal history on a nondiachronic, impersonal form. Indeed for Dorothy, the act of tracing William's route foregrounds his physical and emotional state while also piquing her wonder: "when I trace his paths upon the maps I wonder that his strength and courage have not sunk under the fatigues he must have undergone." When viewed in the context of late eighteenth-century tour culture, William's epistolary "sketch of [his] route" (32) and Dorothy's scribal or gestural tracings on the map are of a bibliographical piece, and Dorothy's letter to Jane is a highly valuable document for exposing the way in which the itinerary and the map functioned as complementary

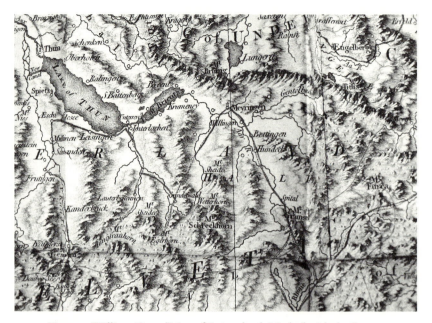

Figure 7. William Coxe, "Map of Switzerland, Marked with the Routes
of Four Tours made in the years 1776, 1779, 1785, 1786," from *Travels
in Switzerland*, 3 vols. (London, 1789); detail showing "the road from
Grindelwald to Lauterbrunnen" (EY 35). Reproduced by permission of the
John Hay Library, Brown University Library.

forms. For Dorothy, Jane, and any other reader-tracer of William's itinerary, a
sense of Wordsworth's psychic and physical state in addition to feelings of awe
and pleasure could be evoked by tracing lines through preexisting points on
the map surface.

According to Liu, Wordsworth's nature is "really only an idea or mark of
naturalness."[15] I suggest rather that "nature" recalls the marks of nature—and
of roads, towns, and boundaries—on maps that were significant to the textual
culture of the era in ways not immediately perceivable to us. What I explore,
then, is not how Wordsworth "carves" the self out of history, but how a historically adjacent visual grammar informs Wordsworth's narrative of poetic and
affective progression.

Alpine Mapping at the Turn of the Eighteenth Century

What would Dorothy, Jane, and William have seen in late eighteenth- and early nineteenth-century maps of the Alps—what configurations of pictures, words, and notation? What sorts of demands might have strained existing technologies of representation, impairing the signaling functioning of lines, points, and letters and making them salient features in their own right?[16] What effects might these configurations have had upon Wordsworth's representation of the journey and the self that journeyed?

The visual texture of maps of the Valais, the canton in which Wordsworth and his friend Robert Jones were walking when they unknowingly crossed the Alps, changed substantially between the second halves of the eighteenth and nineteenth centuries. The Homann family's 1768 map of the Valais and the celebrated Dufour map of Switzerland (1842–64) dramatically illustrate these changes. The most apparent differences include the switch from profile to plan view of mountains and a thickening of geographical detail on the map surface. In the Homann map (Figure 8), the Valais and neighboring Italy appear as flat space punctuated by streaks and pools of water, sudden uprisings of outlined mountains, and the lettering of place-names.[17] The visual effect is of prominent figures on negligible, inexpressive ground.[18] Relief and water iconography— mountains, lakes, rivers, and glaciers—are neighboring entities lacking geologic relation. The lake on *Simpleberg*, for instance, appears substantively foreign, an effect of the map's conflicting visual logics: while the map's peaks appear in profile view, from the side (also called elevation view), rivers, lakes, and glaciers appear in plan view, from above. Overall the surface features give an impression of incoherence and random contiguity. Through this compositional busyness, lines that formally echo one other—but bear no substantive relation—come into focus; the schematic outline of the sugarloaf peaks, the forks in rivers, and the inverted V-shape indentations of the prominent red-and-green boundary line are visual rhymes without reason.

By contrast, Dufour's 1854 map gives the same region an impression of deep coherence (Figure 9).[19] The region appears everywhere pinched, wrinkled, and creased, as if subject through and through to the operation of the same geological forces. Rivers hug the jagged bases of slopes, indicating valleys and ravines and showing descending altitude. Lakes, such as the Lago de Vino in the upper right portion of the map, are integrated into slope faces, the same aerial logic governing the depiction of relief and water features. Harmony of

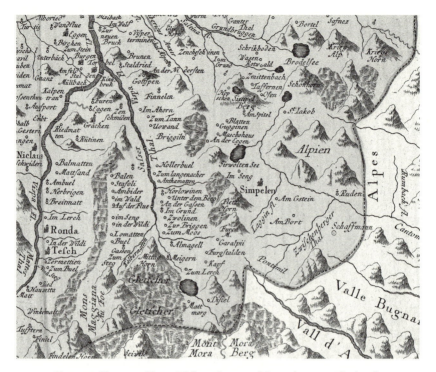

Figure 8. Homann Heirs, *Vallesia Superior* (Nuremberg, 1768), detail.
Lionel Pincus and Princess Firyal Map Division, New York Public Library,
Astor, Lenox and Tilden Foundations.

view and density of detail engage the eye continuously and encourage focus on
particular formations and their logics of relation. While the eye perusing the
Homann map is easily stopped by the disjunctions of the material surface or
seduced by formal echoes, the eye perusing the Dufour map can steadily travel
the Napoleonic road (constructed in 1805) over the Pass from *Caploch* on to
Ruden without disruption.

    To view Homann's nonnumerical relief lines of 1768 beside Dufour's
highly numerical relief lines of 1854 is to participate in two vastly different
orders of knowledge. I want to focus, however, on what happens in the in-
terim. Samuel Dunn's map of 1786 is an example of British cartographic endeavor during the rise of naturalism and the unsteady shift toward plan
representation of relief. The map shows some attempt at differentiation of
actual topographical form, which it renders with hachures, or lines tracing the
direction of slope; these are visibly rough relative to the fine lineation of the

Figure 9. Guillaume Henri Dufour, *Topographische Karte der Schweiz*
(1854), detail. From *Ingenieure unter der Aufsicht des Generals G. H. Dufour*
(Bern, 1833–63). Lionel Pincus and Princess Firyal Map Division, New York
Public Library, Astor, Lenox and Tilden Foundations.

Dufour map (Figure 10).[20] Impressionistic in their disposition, ungoverned by
any numerical framework, Dunn's hachures produce the illusion of three-
dimensional form in three competing views: profile for the highest peaks, high
oblique (or bird's eye) for the middle range, and plan for the lowest peaks. In
this late Enlightenment cartographic window after the embrace of naturalism
but before the systematization of relief, when methods for assessing form and
means of producing its illusion were not only unstable but contested, the
commitment to rendering actual physical form confronted the eye with unstable logics of line that demanded heterogeneous forms of viewing.[21]

It also produced new forms of visual incoherence and confusion. While
the mountain pictographs of the Homann map rely on outline in combination
with shade lines on the southeastern slopes (implying high oblique, northwest

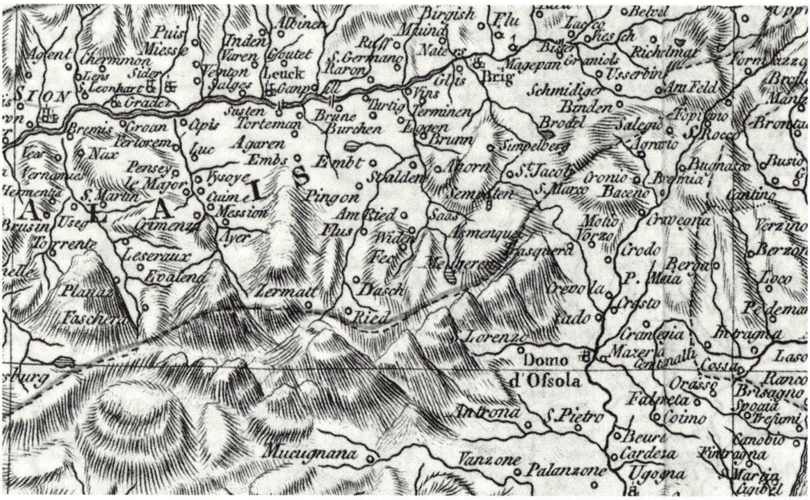

Figure 10. Samuel Dunn, *Switzerland Divided into Thirteen Cantons
with their Subjects and their Allies* (1786), detail. In Dunn's *A New Atlas
of the Mundane System . . . with a general introduction to Geography and
Cosmography* (London, 1788). Lionel Pincus and Princess Firyal Map
Division, New York Public Library, Astor, Lenox and Tilden Foundations.

illumination), the mountain forms of the Dunn map are rendered by hachures
(slope lines) on multiple sides. The reliance on slope lines rather than outline
to show form effects a higher saturation of lines on the map—and occasionally
an overlapping of different symbolic registers. In the northeastern quadrant of
the detail I reproduce here, a tributary leads the eye from *Brig* up the Pass to
Simpleberg, where the line of the river merges into the upper arc of the *p* in
Simpleberg. This fusion of the alphabetic and the pictorial leaves a mark that is
both alphabetical and pictorial at once—or is it neither? Another river begins,
after an interval, from the descender of the same *p*, leading the eye down the
other side of the Pass through *St. Jacob* and across the hand-colored, provincial
and Italian boundary. Codes cross—the transparency of signs falters—briefly
but not catastrophically.

Dufour's mid-century map, by contrast, more effectively layers and separates information.[22] Two developments were crucial: indirectly, the invention
of the contour line (curved lines of equivalent elevation first used to show the
overall form of landmasses on a French map of 1791) and, directly, Johann
Georg Lehmann's 1799 invention of shadow-hachures, an arrangement of

hachures that emphasized the "transition from level ground to steep gradients." Simply put, Lehmann subjected previously impressionistic slope hachures to a dual system of arrangement; in a section of slope, hachures seem to end on an implied line of consistent vertical height (like a contour line), and vary in thickness according to steepness of slope. The steeper the slope, the thicker the line; this way, "steep gradients appeared dark from the accumulation of heavy hachures, and gentle slopes with fine hachures appeared lighter."[23] On the Dufour map, these two logics tightly control hachuring such that the production of the illusion of geomorphic three-dimensionality, which is enhanced by consistent northwest illumination, interferes with no other cartographic information. Thicker, darker lettering seems to float at a distance above the finer thatch of the shadow-hachures beneath. Unobtrusive spot heights—meter measurements marked with point symbols—signal the government of the whole composition by numerical knowledge of altitude.

Two maps published in the very decade of the inception of *The Prelude* evince a commitment to the representational challenge of relief while eliciting a sensuous engagement with the marks on the surface of the map. Graphic surface is particularly thick in mountainous areas where crucial differences between up and down and between notation and alphabetic code are obscured. As cartographic historians have observed, before the era of legibility brought about by the introduction of contour lines to topographical maps, the difference between rivers and roads on slopes, as well as the differences among rivers, roads, and slopes, could be difficult to distinguish.[24] Chauchard's 1791 mapping of the Pass shows the road as a double line climbing the valley from *Glis* with the sinuous river to the left (Figure 11).[25] Interrupted by point symbols denoting places, the double lines fade suddenly into the dark shading and the barely legible italics spelling *St. Jacob*. At the base of what must be the letter *o*, the road appears again. A tangle of squiggles denoting either a river or a slope face of indeterminate orientation touches the arc of the road symbol before it disappears into the dark interlineations of letters and hachures on the way to Italy. Bacler D'Albe's *Carte générale du théâtre de la Guerre en Italie* (1802) similarly materializes an overlay of road and water in the Pass (Figure 12).[26] The road appears as a faintly dotted line. In the interval between the place names *Simplon* and *Gondo*, the dotted road line is dominated by arrows marking the route of Napoleon into Italy. In one spot, at the foot of the *R* in *Ruden*, the point of one arrow occludes not only the road but also the river iconography.

Wordsworth writes in Book VI that he and Jones lost their way in the Simplon Pass because they failed to distinguish "the road / Which in the stony

Figure 11. Captain C. A. Chauchard, *Carte de la Partie Septentrionale de l'Italie* (Paris, 1791), detail. Reproduced by permission of the Map Library, University of Michigan.

channel of the Stream / Lay a few steps" (1805, VI: 515-17). The Simplon maps reveal the lack, when Wordsworth was traveling and writing, of any one agreed code for the cartographic representation of space, a lack that called attention to the very artificiality of rendering a three-dimensional world into two-dimensional space. The maps also reveal historically particular forms of semiotic difficulty: how does one trace one's brother, friend, or prior self across the map when the map contains occasional pockets of illegibility that put on display not place but technologies of cartographic representation?

Thus if we trace Wordsworth's route on the map, as his sister once did, we see that the climactic event of Book VI narrates a problem of decipherment that is already inscribed on the maps of the period. Neither Dorothy nor any other reader could straightforwardly commune with him, beyond the limits of his paper, by tracing him on their maps. Cartography, it seems, could not be a

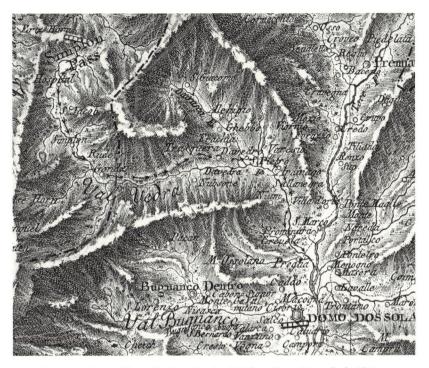

Figure 12. Louis Albert Guislain, Bacler D'Albe, *Carte Générale du Théâtre de la Guerre en Italie et dans les Alpes* (Paris, 1802), detail. Reproduced by permission of the Map Library, University of Michigan.

simple supplement to the inadequacies of literary representation, as it was invoked in the 1790 letter—but it could produce an ostensibly biographical event of landscape misreading. Significantly, the event of getting lost is not reported in the letter of 1790; however, when Wordsworth narrates the journey in 1804, he purports to recollect his eyes' failure to perceive the road in the stream and their attraction to the upward climbing path across it. He could just as easily be narrating the failure of period Alpine topographers to achieve a clear and consistent representation of three-dimensional forms and topographical features.

"We have several times performed a journey of thirteen leagues over the most mountainous parts of Swisserland," William wrote in his letter (37). Dorothy's conversion of the letter's dates, distances, and place names into a practice of route tracing implies a mode of cartographic viewing that anticipates William's retrospective narration in *The Prelude*:

Day after day, up early and down late,
From vale to vale, from hill to hill we went,
From Province on to Province did we pass . . .
(1805, VI:431–33)

With their unlocated vantage point and compression of both time and space, these measured lines suggest the acts of cartographic tracing we know Dorothy to have practiced—and they produce the image of the poet hovering over Alpine maps in the act of writing his *Prelude* account. We might even say that Wordsworth here engages in *cartospection* under the grammatical aegis of retrospection.[27] To read the quoted lines as performances of tour convention without considering the possible mediation of tour convention by cartographic form and practice is to overlook a key interaction between tour writing and map reading announced in Wordsworth's letter and disarticulated in Book VI.

"Behold a Map": Map as Figure

In Book VI, "Cambridge and the Alps," Wordsworth strategically revises the relations between writing and mapping inscribed in the 1790 tour letter. To trace the effects of cartography as a practice and as a figure in Book VI requires that we step back from the Simplon and begin where Wordsworth does—in Cambridge before he departed for the Lakes and then France, when the "Poet's soul" was newly "with [him]" (1805, VI: 55). Whereas in the tour letter Wordsworth invokes the map as a visual and affective supplement to prose description, at the beginning of Book VI he uses the map to complete his depiction of a shallow self that knows itself (and the world) only schematically and to figure a correspondingly shallow poetic that only schematically represents. Thus, recollecting his time as a student in Cambridge, Wordsworth likens his blank verse to a picture and then to a map, associating his immature poetics and Cambridge persona with simple mimesis:

And, not to leave the picture of that time
Imperfect, with these habits I must rank
A melancholy from humours of the blood
In part, and partly taken up, that lov'd
A pensive sky, sad days, and piping winds,
The twilight more than dawn, Autumn than Spring,

A treasured and luxurious gloom, of choice
And inclination mainly, and the mere
Redundancy of youth's contentedness.
Add unto this a multitude of hours
Pilfer'd away by what the Bard who sang
Of the Enchanter Indolence hath call'd
"Good-natured lounging" and behold a map
Of my Collegiate life, far less intense
Than Duty call'd for, or without regard
To Duty, might have sprung up of itself
By change of accident, or even, to speak
Without unkindness, in another place.
(1805, VI: 190–207)

Here Wordsworth suggests that the selfhood belonging to that period of his life requires representation not by poetry but merely by mapping. Cueing the self-referentiality of the passage is the word "behold" (202), an imperative identified by Quintilian as a signature verbal gesture of *hypotyposis*, the figure that "*sets things before the eyes*" and that is associated with "*topographia*," or the "luminous and vivid description of places."[28] However, asked to "behold a map" of Wordsworth's "Collegiate life" (203), readers note a passage that is bound by the word-axes of "time" (190) and "place" (207) and that lists clichés of poetic melancholy—a taste for pathetic landscapes and an internal weather mixing contentedness with chosen gloom. The largely undifferentiated feelings associated with that period are governed by a logic of repetition ("Redundancy of youth's contentedness" [198]) while the figuring of those feelings in writing employs a correlative logic of addition ("Add unto this a multitude of hours" [199]) and quotative iteration (" 'Good-natured lounging' " [202]).[29] Undistinguished by an event of psycho-visual interest, Wordsworth's final two years at Cambridge warrant no more complexity of rendering than is offered by the "map," which sufficiently communicates time and place lacking intensity or point. The map, as figured here, is an unproblematic survey, a syntactical sequence easily read but revealing little of difference, detail, or value.

At this point in Book VI, the map functions as an emblem—a sign of a limited self, lacking emotional maturity and depth. As such a figure, the map befits a poet who is as yet too little traveled to have had to represent more complex and meaningful experience: a decisive or critical juncture. But the map also reflects an environment that neither stirred the imagination nor disciplined the mind, and thus participates in Wordsworth's indictment of the social and intellectual world of the university.[30] We get a similar critique of social environment in the "Immortality Ode," which refers to the map as a rudimentary "fragment from [the] dream of human life": an uninspired rendering of a typically unitary emotional event, such as "a wedding or a festival / A mourning or a funeral."[31] The "plan or chart" which the six-year-old child draws, and to which he then "frames his song," is on the spectrum of conventional representational forms: he then "fit[s] his tongue / To dialogues of business, love, or strife," and then "cons another part" "As if his whole vocation / Were endless imitation" (90–107). The boy who leaves Cambridge for the continental tour has, like the boy of the Ode, a language and consciousness not yet liberated from an organizational scheme within which, however, he already feels a sense of restless confinement.

Against the "map" of Cambridge life, with its summary recounting of past habits and indolent contentedness, Wordsworth posits an inscriptional mode—and a possible poetics—that transforms the feelings of the inscriber. That mode is geometry, and I turn to it now so as to trace the way in which Wordsworth, by introducing a different kind of figure of writing—geometry's lineal representation of space and volume—seeks to show that his development as a poet involved a turn away from the kind of self that can be readily imaged by a map toward the kind of self of which geometry, with its claim to represent infinitude, is a better emblem. As an illustration of the salutary effects of "geometric science" (1805, VI: 137)—a marking practice that gave the emerging poet pleasure at Cambridge—Wordsworth offers the anecdote of the castaway John Newton, "beyond common wretchedness depress'd" (167), "draw[ing] his diagrams / With a long stick upon the sand" (171–72), a "Treatise of Geometry" (165) by his side. The diagramming of planes and volumes "Did oft beguile his sorrow, and almost" made Newton "Forget his feeling" (173–74). Though it does not transport Newton from his desert island, the practice of inscribing geometric abstractions temporarily undoes a depression that has been caused by fixity of place over time. Wordsworth claims as a student also to have found in geometry "Enough to exalt, to chear [him], and compose" (141); from it, he

                                        drew
      A pleasure calm and deeper, a still sense
      Of permanent and universal sway
      And paramount endowment in the mind,
      An image not unworthy of the one

Surpassing Life, which out of space and time,
Nor touch'd by welterings of passions, is
And hath the name of God. (150–57)

Whereas the "map" recounts Wordsworth's moods and dispositions, framing terrestrial, temporal feelings, the "clear Synthesis" (182) of geometric abstraction manifests "an independent world / Created out of pure Intelligence" (186–87). Geometric diagramming gives visual form to the infinite and thereby releases the moods belonging to time and place.[32]

Significantly, Wordsworth's meditation on the ameliorating effects of "geometric science" occurs within the overview of his Cambridge years, which records a new ability to think of "printed books and authorship" as graspable possibilities: "Such aspect now, / Though not familiarly, my mind put on" (71, 75–76). Geometry, then, offers a prospect of representing himself on paper that is quite distinct from the kinds of self-representation that are figured by cartography. No "fragment from [the] dream of human life," the "single Volume" of geometry that Newton "brought / To land" (163–64) suggests that it might be possible to inscribe, rather than typical passions tied to typical events and places, a transcendence of such temporal and spatial limitations—and to produce a corresponding transformation in feeling.

In the poem, Wordsworth locates at Cambridge both an emotionally shallow self that can be imaged by a chart and a writing self with limited representational capacity. As he describes Newton's geometrical consolations, and indeed his own, Wordsworth shows himself practicing a kind of "writing" that does not mimetically represent but productively transforms emotion. Let us cut to the crossing of the Simplon in the Alps portion of the Book, which measures the poet's distance from his collegiate artistic self still more and does so by revising the geographical and scriptorial conditions of the original tour letter—a process of revision in which both cartographic and geometric terminology take on new significances.

Book VI's description of the European tour seems at first notable for its lack of reference to cartography. Whereas Wordsworth conjoins writing and mapping in his 1790 letter to Dorothy, he narrates his crossing of the Alps without ostensibly linking cartography to literary representation. The contrast is quite evident at the level of verbal detail: after being lured by the "only track now visible" "up a lofty Mountain," the travelers are redirected by a "Peasant" who verbally plots their position and route (504, 506, 513). The 1850 text focuses visual attention on the vocal organs of "mouth" and "lips," marking this

as a time of seeing and hearing someone speak the lay of the land, and not a
time of beholding it on the map:

> By fortunate chance,
> While every moment added doubt to doubt,
> A Peasant met us, from whose mouth we learned
> That to the Spot which had perplexed us first
> We must descend, and there should find the road,
> Which in the stony channel of the Stream
> Lay a few steps, and then along its banks,
> And that our future course, all plain to sight,
> Was downwards, with the current of that Stream.
> Loth to believe what we so grieved to hear,
> For still we had hopes that pointed to the clouds,
> We questioned him again, and yet again;
> But every word that from the Peasant's lips
> Came in reply, translated by our feelings,
> Ended in this, *that we had crossed the Alps.*
> (1850, VI: 578–92)

Whereas the words "time" and "place" had framed the "map" of the Cambridge
passage, here facial features of "mouth" (580) and "lips" (590) frame topographical features of "road," "Stream," "banks," and "course": a difference of aspect
that submerges the topographical map. The right course emerges instead from
speech as the Peasant articulates landmarks and route. A speaking topographer,
the Peasant is a foil for the poet, who construes himself by contrast as nontopo-
graphically speaking. This foregrounding of the self in the act of composition
should ring familiar.

As we know, in the 1804/5 text the invocation of imagination and reference
to song ("Imagination! lifting up itself / Before the eye and progress of my Song"
[1805, VI: 525–26]) effect a sense of the poet's voice, which is reinforced by the
ensuing trope of self-address ("to my Soul I say / I recognize thy glory" [531–32]).
Thus, following the past-tense, narrative reprisal of their route and unnoticed
crossing, the poet reflexively figures himself in the act of composing—a structure that replicates the 1790 letter, but with a significant difference. In the letter,
past-tense narrative chronology unfolds and is then suddenly interrupted with
a reference to the present time and place of writing: "I am at this present moment (14th of Septbr) writing at a small village in the road from Grindelwald to

Lauterbrunnen" (EY 35). This reference to writing precedes a suggestion to Dorothy, who could not share the scenes that "burst upon" (35) William's eyes, to position him on her maps. Fourteen years later, past-tense narration of the tour again cuts to the compositional present—but with an emphasis on vocalizing, not on the act of writing time, place, and feeling under spatial constraints. Whereas the limits of the epistolary page everywhere check Wordsworth's 1790 geographical and theistic awe ("it will be utterly impossible for me to dwell upon particular scenes" [32–33]), in the poem Wordsworth sings that his "home / Is with infinitude, and only there" (538–39). The mature poet is off Dorothy's maps: his "Song" needs no cartographic supplementation. He does not locate himself in cardinal space but identifies with the transcendent realm plotted previously in Book VI by Newton. It is as if Wordsworth eschews maps not just because the Simplon, as we recognize, has revealed the constructedness of cartography, but because by doing so he can figure his growth both as a writer and as a being. If he needed the map in 1790 to supplement the writing of his feelings before God's work of "Nature," in 1804 he demonstrates the sufficiency of poetry both to produce and convey exaltation.

This signature passage of the poem has been read by Geoffrey Hartman as apocalyptic.[33] My goal is to resituate what Hartman sees as world-renouncing and mind-exalting within Wordsworth's real-world history of tour writing. Attention to limits is common to both letter and poem. Yet in the poem Wordsworth rewrites the relations between geographical and scriptorial space. If in 1790 thoughts spurred by "the terrible majesty" (34) before him are bound by the letter's margins, in Book VI Wordsworth reconceives the material nature of the limit so as to identify the poetic mind, in sublime fashion, with boundlessness. As Thomas Weiskel has shown, the power of imagination halts the "mental journey of retrospection":[34]

> Imagination! lifting up itself
> Before the eye and progress of my Song
> Like an unfather'd vapour; here that Power,
> In all the might of its endowments, came
> Athwart me; I was lost as in a cloud,
> Halted without a struggle to break through . . .
> (525–30)

Whereas an insufficiency of paper restricts the expansion of writing in 1790, in 1804 "Imagination" figured as threatening atmospheric excess halts the progress of "Song" (526). The tour letter is repeatedly checked by insufficiency of "room"; the 1804 tour "Song" is checked by a "Power" figured as rising "vapour" (527) and "cloud" (529), a semi-opaque spaciousness that blocks topographical retrospection. By recognizing that limiting power as an agent or emanation of his soul ("to my Soul I say / I recognize thy glory" [531–32]), Wordsworth identifies with that power, eroding its quality as limit to the "Song" while simultaneously resolving—in a trope of speech—the very problem of insufficient paper. The self-address has subtle figurative implications for the poet; doubly invoked as a speaking and listening presence,[35] he seems to resonate with sound before casting his "mind" ("soul" in MS D) as replete: "blest in thoughts / That are their own perfection and reward" (543, 545–46).[36] Checked in 1790 by his paper's limits and his memory's insufficient retention of forms, his mind now suffices for his thoughts, obviating the need for "room" on paper. A pressing consciousness of the finiteness of writing pages is relieved and released by identification of consciousness with "infinitude" (539).

Simplon's narrative sequence, as has long been understood, recounts a feeling of "deep and genuine sadness" (492) produced by the travelers' tough recognition of their failure to perceive Alpine form; Simplon's lyric sequence shows the poet feeling strength and "joy" (547). Wordsworth stages an unwilled confrontation with his imaginative soul and, Newton-like, confronts a sensible image of the "one / Surpassing Life" (154–55) that counteracts dejection by producing pleasure and wonder. Book VI thus uses the map to plot the growth of the poet's mind over time—to show an affective, cognitive, and artistic evolution. While Dorothy gives the present-tense "I" ("I am . . . writing") duration and emotional force by tracing her brother's day journeys into the map, William traces in Book VI an artistic evolution from visual map, through geometry, to "Song." Mapping the Cambridge unities of time, place, and feeling ("behold a map") and then displacing them in self-address at Simplon ("I recognize thy glory"), Wordsworth performs a journey from a print-conscious "Poet's soul" (55) to an imaginative "Soul" (531) revealed as his own. Thus to trace self-history, Wordsworth archly displays the limits of his maplike pages—scoring the verse-paragraph *topographia* with the words "time" and "place"—and then shows himself superseding those limits in the unmappable "Imagination" passage.

Marks of Emphasis

If the Simplon evaded the map as in *The Prelude* account, it did not do so for long, for although the 1805 text seems to most critics Wordsworth's best formulation of his soul's freedom from spatiotemporal limits, he nevertheless persisted in revising it. Over at least the next thirty-five years, he altered the words of Book VI several times, as if never satisfied that he had achieved a final expression of the journey.[37] I turn to these revisions now because they unexpectedly restore to the text a cartographic context that in 1804 Wordsworth had eschewed. *Spots, points,* and *lines*—terms suggestive of mapping's visual encoding of landscape—make a reappearance in Wordsworth's vocabulary of touring. For example, the initial "to the place which had perplex'd us first" (1805, VI: 514) becomes the notational "to the Spot which had perplexed us first" of MS D, a manuscript copied "by, and perhaps before, 1832."[38] The earlier text's "close upon the confluence of two streams" (576) becomes, in 1838–39, "at a point / Where tumbling from aloft a torrent swelled."[39] Aspects and features of the physical terrain are thus abstracted into marks. Wordsworth uses this notational lexicon to limn his cognitive and affective condition as well. Depicting the interview on the slope with the Peasant (who informs Wordsworth and Jones of their mistake and sets them in the right direction), the 1805 text has "Hard of belief we questioned him again" (520). But a phrase added during or after 1838–39 spatializes the affect and adds a cartographic inflection: "For still we had hopes that pointed to the clouds."[40]

Like the arrow's point on D'Albe's map that cannot be removed to reveal the stream and road beneath, the insistent hopes of the two travelers block the knowledge that the Peasant relays; still aiming to go higher, Jones and Wordsworth resist acknowledging that their way lies downward with the stream. Flecks of notation are thus constitutive of the poem's grammar of both nature and mind. The poet isolates himself and a cloud in Book I: "should the guide I chuse / Be nothing better than a wandering cloud / I cannot miss my way" (1805, I: 17–19).[41] However, with "we had hopes that pointed to the clouds," the point intervenes to emphasize a disjunction between desire and geographical experience. Print and engraving culture edge into the poem as affective inflections, signals of acuity and modulation of feeling.

The notational terms that Wordsworth deploys derive, of course, from geometry as well as cartography, in which discourse the symbols have a related but different use. The point and line feature prominently in the foundational principles of Euclid's *Elements*, a text which appears by name in Book V's Dream of the Arab episode and which editors identify as the "Volume" belonging to the castaway who draws diagrams of "an independent world" upon the sand (VI: 164, 186). Having largely been absent in 1805, notational terms entered the Simplon episode as a significant part of Wordsworth's language of nature and the self, and became more strongly significant as he struggled to formulate the Simplon passage to his liking. If Wordsworth, then, was one of the "Prophets of Nature" (XIII: 442), he was so because he was also a manipulator of contemporary cultural discourses in which our spatial and temporal relationships with the external world are encoded (cartography) and which permitted him to "meditate / Upon the alliance of those simple, pure / Proportions and relations with the frame / And laws of Nature" (geometry) (VI: 143–46).[42]

It would seem, then, that Wordsworth's use of notational terms to signal depth and progress of feeling has the effect of geometrizing his account of the topographical tour, and thus of elevating the physical places of his journey into symbolic locations in his larger spiritual and poetic journey. Revisions to the final lines of the tour account enhance the symbolic quality of the continental journey. Insisting that "the mind" he possessed during his tour was no "mean pensioner / On outward forms" (667–68), Wordsworth again invokes the emphatic "point" of geometry and cartography. The 1805 version of lines suggests unmediated retrospection:

> Finally whate'er
> I saw, or heard, or felt, was but a stream
> That flow'd into a kindred stream, a gale
> That help'd me forwards; did administer
> To grandeur and to tenderness, to the one
> Directly, but to tender thoughts by means
> Less often instantaneous in effect;
> Conducted me to these along a path
> Which in the main was more circuitous.
> (1805, VI: 672–80)

But an interlineal insertion in MS D hints of a divinely rendered, affective cartography. "Every sound or sight," he adds,

> Led me to [grandeur or to tenderness] by paths that in the main

Were more circuitous, but not less sure
Duly to reach the point marked out by heaven.[43]

The graphic mark is translated into the verbal medium as a "point marked," enforcing the idea of providential direction and ultimate arrival. Here, as in the 1790 letters, the map provides a structure and language for affective (psychological, spiritual) experience and progress. The mind thus seems not off the map, as the earlier manuscripts imply, but of the map. Wordsworth, that is to say, only seems to eschew cartography: in fact, his verse retains traces, in the form of the lexical-graphic accent, of cartography's importance as a supplement to his writing of the tour. Phrases that construe his life as a progressive, spiritual journey employ a geometric terminology, a terminology whose deployment is acutely problematic in period maps.

I turn now to consider another set of verbal instabilities in the poetic manuscripts, the historicity of which is illuminated by the shifting conventions of the Simplon maps. Some of the poem's terminology of lines was also added after 1805, and some of it was introduced into manuscripts but never incorporated. For example, in the middle of a page with interlineations and marginalia assumed to have been added between 1818 and 1820,[44] the narrative of the Simplon crossing begins with the words, "Upturning with a Band / Of Travellers." The page's last easily legible lines read "Right to a rivulet's edge, and there broke off. / The only track now visible was one." Mark Reed's transcriptions show the poet sampling phrasal descriptions of the look of the "track" that he and Jones mistakenly took. Reed just makes out, or misreads, the word "line" above the first deletion; uncertain of his decoding, he prints the word in brackets with a preliminary question mark:

> *The only track now visible was one*
> 　　　　　　　that showed its [?line]
> *Upon the further side, ~~right opposite,~~　　~~course~~*
> 　　~~Traced out, mockingly, in bold ascent~~
> *~~And up a lofty Mountain. This we took~~*
> 　　　　　　　~~chose~~
> 　　　　　　　(1805, vol. II, p. 669; lines 504–6)

The interlineations ("[?line] / Traced out, mockingly, in bold ascent") position the poet-viewer before a topographical map burdened by contemporary representational difficulties.[45] The characterization of the "track" as a "[?line] /

Traced out" uplifts the "track" from the order of the physical environment to the cartographic.[46] The Latin "trace" means "to mark, make marks upon" and "to mark or ornament with lines, figures, or characters"; and more crucially, "to mark out the course of (a road, etc.) on, or by means of, a plan or map."[47] A "[?line] / Traced out, mockingly, in bold ascent" thus brings to the fore the historical moment in cartographic production when roads were newly being inscribed on topographical maps and their lines could be alluringly uncertain in mountainous areas. In this period, a river line could blend into a letter; a slope line into a river; a trail into the point of an arrow. As this manuscript page and so many others illustrate, the "natural fact" and "visual detail" which Hartman[48] and others discover in the poetry is traversed by the cartographic detail. The Simplon Pass was already engraved when Wordsworth embarked upon his trip, and it was in the process of being reengraved according to different line systems for encoding relief when he wrote and rewrote the poem. For these reasons we should not dismiss the *cartospection* at work in retrospection, even if Wordsworth did not actively consult a map in the rewriting of the passage. The matter of the map coincides with the narrative of the tour at thematic and lexical-notational levels, particularly in the inscription of emphasis.[49]

The cartographic effect attending this manuscript passage is not merely lexico-visual, the combined effect of a notational lexicon on a page made more overtly (carto)graphic by crossed strokes of deletion. The "[?line] / Traced out" also locates the poem in a personal sociohistorical frame in so far as the image recalls the activity of route tracing that Dorothy advocates in her letter to Jane and claims to have practiced ("when I trace his paths upon the maps . . ."; "It may perhaps be of some amusement to you to trace his route upon your maps . . ."). The image thus invokes an engraved route as well as a route marked manually by a map user. Many Romantic-era maps preserved in collections contain evidence of such writing atop engraving. For instance, on the copy of Bacler D'Albe's map that I consulted, brown crayon skirts the Italian border and inscribes what are presumably altitude numerals in the area of the Pass. The image of the "[?line] / Traced out" is thus reflexively intertextual, mediating poem, letters, and period maps, the latter in their pure formality and as received objects used—and sometimes marked on—by people. It is unclear why Wordsworth rejected the image of the mountain track as a line ("track" is retained in C-stage revision).[50] If "Traced out, mockingly" too explicitly invoked the surfaces of maps, then Wordsworth's rejection of the bold image in the Simplon episode would comport with the larger strategy of Book

VI to represent poetic maturation by invoking and progressively rejecting the topographical map as a representational model. The rejection further suggests a considered reservation of geometrical terminology for the marking, in revision, of poetic and spiritual progress.

Apparently then, the structure of Wordsworth's Alpine progress into his imaginative self is paradoxical. On the one hand there is a gradual excision of cartographic reference—such reference is relied upon at the outset, in the Cambridge section; occluded in the Simplon Pass, it is after all structurally present since cartographic terms inform Wordsworth's very rendering of his apparent liberation from spatiotemporal relationships and the texts, including maps, that represent them. We see that the major event of Book VI—semiotic perplexity in the decoding of both the landscape and the Peasant's words—registers the notational context of the era's maps, a conflicted context in which the constructedness and historicity of all representational texts is made apparent precisely because maps are so explicitly conventional even as they strain to depict nature so exactly. It was, perhaps, because Wordsworth felt the continuing difficulty of overcoming his own poem's conventionality that he continued to add terms to it that derive from geometry and cartography. Maps—and volumes such as Euclid's *Elements*—gave Wordsworth a lexicon of figures in which his central subject—the struggle to make language "natural" (LB 762)—was encoded.

"'Tis not my present purpose to retrace / That variegated journey step by step" (1805, VI: 426–27), Wordsworth announces—but when we do so, by reading the letters, maps, and poem manuscripts in parallel, cartographic technologies emerge within the verbal texture of the poem. It becomes hard not to read Dorothy's "trace" in *The Prelude*'s signature verbs of autobiographical activity: "How shall I trace the history, where seek / The origin of what I then have felt?" (II: 365–66). And again,

> Thus far, O Friend! have we, though leaving much
> Unvisited, endeavour'd to retrace
> My life through its first years, and measur'd back
> The way I travell'd when I first began
> To love the woods and fields . . .
> (1805, II: 1–5)

The idea of life-writing as map-perusing—a tracing of past paths—impinges upon the figure of autobiography as a re-viewing or walking back over a "prospect in [the] mind" (II: 371). The map thus edges between the privileged Romantic categories of mind and nature as the poem inscribes its intermedial historical conditions at the level of the graphic and verbal mark. Map notation and practice thus coincide with the poem's trope of composition, renewing the energies of the 1790 letters in the central passages in which Wordsworth describes his writerly project.

Traces of cartographic language, structure, and practice are not reserved to Wordsworth's revisions of Book VI; with their addition to other books, Wordsworth overlays a poem already laced by notational diction with a providential cartography. Claiming that Wordsworth's "'poem on [his] own poetical education' converts the wayfaring Christian of the Augustinian spiritual journey into the self-formative traveler of the Romantic educational journey," M. H. Abrams observes that the poem's "literal journeys through actual places . . . modulate easily into symbolic landscapes traversed by a metaphorical wayfarer."[51] This modulation, I would qualify, functions by a notational symbolism that is a feature of poetic revision. When Abrams writes that "In the course of" the literal walk that opens Book I, "the aimless wanderer becomes 'as a Pilgrim resolute' who takes 'the road that pointed toward the chosen Vale,'" he quotes the 1850 text's alteration of 1805's more unequivocally literal "I resolved / To journey towards the Vale which I had chosen" (1805, I: 100–101). Thus if "at the end of the first book," as Abrams adds, "the road translates itself into the metaphorical way of his life's pilgrimage" ("'Forthwith shall be brought down, / Through later years the story of my life. / The road lies plain before me . . .'"),[52] it is because, in revision, an implicit cartographism mediates between the literal and metaphoric orders. The Pilgrim reads, and moves within, a landscape "marked out by heaven."[53]

Wordsworth developed *The Prelude*'s notational lexicon over the course of its production and through revisions of the fourteen-book poem in or after 1839. The geometric point effects the 1850 text's sense of *telos*, binding the self and poem in a joint "tending towards that point / Of sound humanity to which our Tale / Leads."[54] This assimilation of a cartographic lexicon demonstrates the increasing emphasis of a distinction between a willful narrative ordering of the mind's growth and a poetic tracking, or limning, of imagination's divine progress. This distinction is more deeply inscribed, or reflexively marked, within the poem after Wordsworth's formative encounter with the Ordnance Survey engineer Colonel Mudge and his composition of the Black Comb blank verse, which I consider in the next chapter.

Chapter 3

"Points Have We All of Us Within Our Souls, / Where All Stand Single"

Poetic Autobiography and National Cartography

In *The Prelude* of 1798–99, Wordsworth registers his sense of his subject's resistance to orderly and definitive exposition by making an implicit, and dismissive, analogy to cartography:

> I hasten on to tell
> How nature, intervenient till this time
> And secondary, now at length was sought
> For her own sake.— But who shall parcel out
> His intellect by geometric rules,
> Split like a province into round and square;
> Who knows the individual hour in which
> His habits were first sown, even as a seed;
> Who that shall point as with a wand and say,
> This portion of the river of my mind
> Came from yon fountain?
> (1799, II: 239–49)

In this complex critique of cartography, first, as a misguided analytic that imposes arbitrary order on the land and, second, as a specious fixing of spatial relations, mapping represents a mode of life writing motivated by the rational determination and systematic display of behavioral origins and mental causes. The analogy might seem to obviate comparisons between autobiography and cartography, and yet, having discredited the visual analytic, Wordsworth went on to develop the motif of spatial deixis when he extended, reorganized, and revised the poem. "And here, O Friend! have I retrac'd my life / Up to an eminence" (1805, III: 168–69), he comments in Book III, as if pointing to a spot on the map. Qualifying this, he then employs an array of semiotic terms to indicate what his subject is not and, then, to gesture toward the difficulties of representing human interiority:

> Of Genius, Power,
> Creation, and Divinity itself
> I have been speaking, for my theme has been
> What pass'd within me. Not of outward things
> Done visibly for other minds, words, signs,
> Symbols, or actions; but of my own heart
> Have I been speaking, and my youthful mind.
> O Heavens! how awful is the might of Souls
> And what they do within themselves, while yet
> The yoke of earth is new to them, the world
> Nothing but a wild field where they were sown.
> This is, in truth, heroic argument,
> And genuine prowess; which I wish'd to touch
> With hand however weak; but in the main
> It lies far hidden from the reach of words.
> Points have we all of us within our souls,
> Where all stand single; this I feel, and make
> Breathings for incommunicable powers. (1805, III: 171–88)

Speaking not of "things done visibly for other minds" but of that "genuine prowess" that "lies far hidden from the reach of words," Wordsworth constructs a semiotic opposition between a "field" of "outward things" ("words, signs, / Symbols, or actions") and the "Points" of an interior topography. The mathematical condition of the point indexes the limits of Wordsworth's medium: those places where, despite having "retrac'd his life / Up to an eminence," he cannot "stand" together with Coleridge. Thus Wordsworth figures the soul's "might" and emphasizes its resistance to communication by invoking the logic and codes of the survey, map, and plotted landscape. In an authenticating inversion of a life-writer's "point[ing] as with a wand"—or projection of experience upon a plane of visibility—Wordsworth claims that his "hand" cannot "touch" such "Points" of internal depth. His subject "beyond / The reach of common indications," to borrow a phrase from Book VII (1805, VII: 608–9), Wordsworth claims to make "Breathings for incommunicable powers" that do not materialize as words upon the page.

As with *trace*, *point* and its variants are part of the poem's self-reflexive repertoire: a cluster of terms with which Wordsworth evaluates the progress of his tale and probes the limits and possibilities of his subject's verbal communication—and the verbal communication of subjectivity. As with *trace*, again, *point* summons a print domain and field of practice of personal interest to Wordsworth and of more conceptual and historical relevance to his poetry than the caricature of cartography as organization by "geometric rules" would suggest. Even as he emphasizes the oral nature of his efforts in the opening of Book III—that he has "been speaking" of (1805, III: 173, 177) but merely "mak[ing] / Breathings for incommunicable powers" (187–88)—the first two books of the poem disclose a graphic line of argumentation, based on the figure of the line in the landscape, that sets the autobiographical project in complex relation to nineteenth-century British cartography: an endeavor far less seamless than Wordsworth's allusion suggests and resistant to the order of "round and square" with which it too easily gets identified by cultural historians.

In fact, the very question of how to assess and by what methods to inscribe the land occurred within British cartography and took on increasing cultural importance during Wordsworth's poetic career. This chapter considers the inscription of mental growth and power in the poem that spans that career in relation to the Ordnance Survey's reorganization of British space and to controversies over its modes of national representation. The signal event in modern British cartography, the Ordnance Survey involved both the making of a precise trigonometrical survey of the nation and the production of complete series of standardized topographical maps from that survey. Like the blank-verse autobiography, the survey and its first series of national maps were produced in stages, extensively revised, and involved the hands and eyes of multiple makers. Both projects were dynamically evolving, conceptually totalizing, and procedurally ambitious. Both tested the limits of knowledge and strained the established conventions of their media as they strove to show, on two dimensional sheets and pages and at enlarged scales, an extent of the earth's physical surface and of the mind's development over time.

The Prelude's representational self-reflexivity and experimentation is matched by experimentation and debate in the cartographic representation of the nation. In the case of the Ordnance Survey, controversy arose not over the triangulation survey of the horizontal plane—the mathematical plotting of the island and the redrawing of the nation's outline—but rather over the rendering of Britain's hills and mountains, where anxiety about national figuration and reception became most keenly focused. The marks on the national maps increasingly mattered to mapmakers and the public because they not only put forth an idea of but also legislated a mode of relating to the nation by inscribing a way of knowing what had become, by the middle of the nineteenth century, a deeply sentimentalized terrain. At the climax of the controversy, following the exhibition of a contour map of Lancashire at the Great Exhibition in 1851, a parliamentary Select Committee debated the matter, pitting mathematical against representational truth, mechanism against imagination, and precision against the characteristic expression of a personified nation.

That their searches for suitable grammars led both autobiographical poet and national mapmakers to look over their shoulders to the other domain—for Wordsworth, to the marking of the "province," for mapmakers, to the marking of "character"—suggests both the power of the cartographic turn at the time of Wordsworth's writing and the influence of ways of imagining landscape that Wordsworth promoted and popularized during the course of his career.[1] Reading the projects of poetic autobiography and national cartography side-by-side, over the course of their production, not only illuminates shared epistemological and representational concerns but also exposes cross-fertilization between them. In this chapter I examine the ways in which the geometrical features of the point and the line were pivotal to, and focused anxieties about, the depiction not only of nation but also of mind, revealing the historical conjuncture of semiotic instability, contention, and reference across the print domains.

To begin, I detail the new national grammar of lines and points that the Ordnance Survey put into cultural play: a graphic and conceptual context for and counterpoint to Wordsworth's delineations of landscape in *The Prelude*. In a reading of the two-part poem of 1798–99, I show how the figure of an unmeasured "line" functions in Wordsworth's telling of his childhood "intercourse" (1799, I: 149) with nature to accent his imaginative vision and signal his mind's growth over time. Across the extending poem, Wordsworth self-consciously aligns these decidedly noncartographic delineations of nature with his poetic lines, which materialize on the page as (typo)graphical and metrical registers of his "Poet's History" and of the history of his poem. A turning point in its composition, I argue, occurs with the Black Comb poems of 1811–14 (published 1815), whose own lexical and graphical play with the figure of the extending line patently contends with the Ordnance Survey's fixed and finite delineations of "British ground."[2]

In the final section, I consider *The Prelude*'s delineations of nature and imagination in the era of its print publication. Here I broaden received understandings of the Ordnance Survey as a "geographic panopticon"[3] by shifting critical attention from the abstract survey of the nation to the widely embraced pictorialism of the Board of Ordnance's topographical maps. During their production, the first series of topographical maps of England and Wales accrued increasing cultural importance and visibility, and, in response to threats to their pictorialism, were defended as a vernacular visual form: an expressive "portrait" of a living nation to be seen, felt, and imaginatively experienced by its citizens amidst the overarching mathematical drift of the period. This form of map, its defenders argued, depended on a mode of unmeasured line, the hachure, derived from unmediated perception of natural forms that engaged the imagination of cartographer and user alike. Merely four years after the publication of *The Prelude*, the "common face of Nature" that "spake . . . Rememberable things" (1850, I: 587–58) to Wordsworth as a boy was made to communicate strikingly to "ordinary" Britons through the medium of the national map. As industrialization was altering the landscape, British governors chose to preserve a familiar but outmoded system of representation that emphasized the undulations of the terrain over and against other cartographic information—names, numbers, and triangulation stations—memorializing a mode of feeling and interacting with the nation that Matthew Arnold, in his elegies and commentary on mapping, implicated with Wordsworth's poetry.

Toward the "Great Outlines of the Country": A Grammar of Lines and Points

A conceptual shift in the ordering of British space occurred at the end of the eighteenth century with the inauguration of the Trigonometrical Survey of Britain. Since the second half of the eighteenth century, private English mapmakers had worked to re-demarcate the counties according to scientific principles, spurred in part by the Society of Arts' 1759 announcement of a series of prizes for the best county maps. Their criteria for cartographic superiority included accurate coastal outlining, a one-inch-to-one-mile scale (a scale larger than then conventional), the determining of positions on land by means of visual, angular measurement (triangulation), and the employment of the most modern instruments.[4] Thus accurate, scientific surveys were experiencing a rise in cultural prestige, and private, regional surveying and mapping were being pursued with a new rigor when English engineers responded to a French challenge to recalculate the relative positions of the Greenwich and Paris observatories by triangulation in 1783.[5] César François Cassini de Thury (1714–84), who helped produce Europe's first nationwide triangulation-based topographical map, the internationally influential *Carte Géometrique de La France* (1744–93), urged the cross-channel triangulation as a means of resolving France and Britain's long-standing dispute about the Greenwich coordinates while underscoring the scientific merits of international trigonometrical alignment.[6] Although military engineer of the Board of Ordnance and Fellow of the Royal Society William Roy (1726–90) had campaigned during the 1760s "to make a general survey of the whole island at public cost" (after trigonometrically surveying part of Scotland to reestablish political dominance in the Highlands),[7] it was Cassini's direct challenge to England's scientific reputation that convinced the Royal Society and the quasi-military Board of Ordnance to launch a triangulation of the whole of the island of Great Britain in 1791, intending the positional data to abet military interests, commercial cartography, and other civilian and scientific efforts. In 1795, the Board began to produce topographical maps from these trigonometrical bases, recognizing the need for distinct coastal maps in the event of a French military invasion.[8] Once the threat passed, however, the Board continued the triangulation of England, Wales, and Scotland (commencing the survey of Ireland in 1825) and the production of official topographical maps at the enlarged scale of one inch to one mile. Historians interpret the decision as an embrace of Roy's earlier assertion that the " 'honour of the nation is concerned in having at least as good a map of this as there is of any other country.' "[9] Scientific and political conditions, as well as a sense that British "honour" depended upon the production of an accurate cartographic self-image, turned cartographical attention at the end of the eighteenth century to the nation as a whole.

Before the widespread introduction of triangulation, topographical features were positioned with respect to each other by dead reckoning (measurement by ground traversal or chains) and by a handful of astronomical determinations: a mode of surveying and data compilation that introduces significant error and incorporates no strategies of self-correction. When a map is drawn from a previously determined trigonometrical survey, topographical features are positioned with respect to a framework of ground positions arrived at by techniques of instrumental observation and trigonometrical calculation. As Matthew Edney explains,

The surveyor first imagines a series of straight lines joining the tops of hills or tall buildings. The hilltops are selected so that the lines form either a long chain of triangles or a network of interlocking triangles spread out across the landscape. The surveyor determines the geometry of the triangles by measuring their interior angles. The actual size of the triangles is determined by the very careful measurement on the ground of the length of one side of a triangle; the lengths of all other triangle sides are calculated from this one "baseline" by means of trigonometry.[10]

The theodolite (which measures the interior angles of triangles) in conjunction with a "minimum of actual measurement on the ground" and "the application of sound mathematical theory" resulted in "a highly accurate framework for map making."[11] Mapmakers working from the basis of a triangulation survey, it is said, "hang" topographical features from the dependable frame of the encompassing triangle,[12] a method that promises "the potential perfection of the map's relationship with the territory mapped."[13] In the words of General Roy, advocating for a general triangulation of England toward his larger goal of the whole of Britain, "the Situation of all the material points would be truely fixed with regard to one another, and thence the Great Outlines of the Country would be truely determined."[14] Roy's confidence that a network of points plotted across the island's interior would permit true delineation of the island registers the cultural prestige of visual technology, systematic method, and mathematical precision, an Enlightenment ethos referred to as the *esprit géometrique*.[15] Indeed, the production of those "Great Outlines" put into cultural play a form of non-naturalistic line abstracted from the land's physical structure that rearticulated the nation according to a new philosophical and material logic.

With the publication of the trigonometrical data as it became available over the next thirty years in the *Philosophical Transactions of the Royal Society*, the national survey became a circulating scientific and representational form in its own right. By sending into the public domain this geographic data for civilian mapmaking, the Board of Ordnance put forward a cartographic underface—a new image and logic of nation based on the pointed intersections of quantified lines. Further, after publishing its first topographical maps, of the counties of Kent (1801) and Essex (1805), the Board "started to map the country according to the straight lines of rectangular sheets" rather than the highly irregular, unquantified outlines of counties, Britain's traditional administrative, political, and geographic divisions.[16] Ordnance Survey mapmakers did not cease engraving a copperplate at the boundary of a county but engraved as much of the *country* as could fit within the rectangular borders of the sheets on which the maps were printed—a practice called "squaring the map."[17] And just as the dimensions of the sheet took organizational precedence over the traditional cartographic division, so too did the geometrical network of the triangles, which observed neither county borders nor the divisions between England, Scotland, and Wales. Great Britain's evolving scientific spatialism was thus signaled by the straight lines of rectangular sheets and triangulation, and was underscored by the use of the rigorously positioned Greenwich meridian as the basis for map projections.[18]

The initial data was published also in William Mudge and Isaac Dalby's *Account of the Trigonometrical Survey of England and Wales* (1799–1811). The quantified lines and fixed points of their *Plan of the Principal Triangles* covers the interior of England, Wales and southeastern Scotland with interlocking triangles. The 228 points on the primary survey (there were larger-scale secondary and tertiary surveys) corresponded in actual space to stones approximately two-feet square topped by a small stake.[19] There is stillness at these stations, the "material points" Roy had envisioned, and in the intersection of lines that do not represent courses, ways, or routes-lines that, when followed by the eye, allude to physical motion across the featured territory, such as the Thames that winds just north of the Greenwich Observatory on the *Plan of the Triangles Connecting the Meridians of the Royal Observatories of Greenwich and Paris* (Figure 13). Nor do the lines imply forces that have produced over time such features as coastlines. The triangles rather signal perfect proportions determined by the laws of geometry. As such they organize and interpret the landscape, but they do not mimic or represent it.

Of a different visual order are the hachures that function to produce the illusion of hills and upland on *Part of Kent and Sussex Laid Down from a Trigonometrical Survey in 1795–1796* (Figure 14). As discussed in Chapter 2, hachures are a line technique borrowed from French maps in the second half of the century when British mapmakers began to experiment with naturalistic representations of hills. They suggest shadow (the fall of light is as from above) and mark the orientation and steepness of slope; they trace out actual ridges and terrestrial form, asking us to see the landscape.[20] While the geometric notation of the survey orders the plane topologically by fixing horizontal locations and relations, a pictorial mode of indicating relief simultaneously uplifts and dimensionalizes that plane. And thus two concurrently valued but contrasting modes

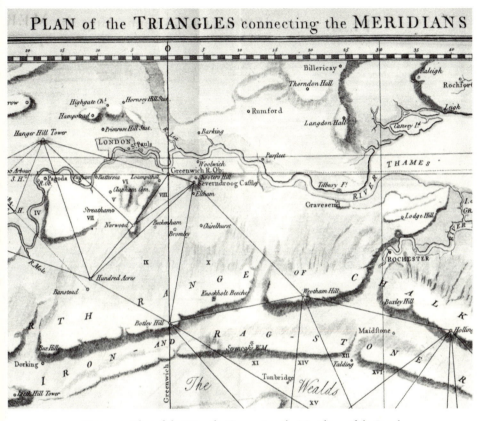

Figure 13. *Plan of the Triangles Connecting the Meridians of the Royal Observatories of Greenwich and Paris*, detail. William Mudge and Isaac Dalby, *An Account of the Operations Carried on for Accomplishing a Trigonometrical Survey of England and Wales; from the commencement, in the year 1784, to the end of the year 1796. Begun under the direction of the Royal Society, and continued by order of the honourable Board of Ordnance. First published in, and now revised from, the Philosophical Transactions, by Captain William Mudge, F.R.S., and Mr. Isaac Dalby*, vol. II (London, 1799–1811). Reproduced by permission of the Map Library, University of Michigan.

of articulating the nation—both new to cartographers in the second half of the eighteenth century—occupy the same geographical frame in the survey of part of Kent and Sussex, prefiguring a conflict between pictorial and abstract rendering that intensifies as the new century progresses.

The use of point symbols, "any non-linear sign which by its position on a map shows the location of some geographical phenomenon,"[21] exemplifies the

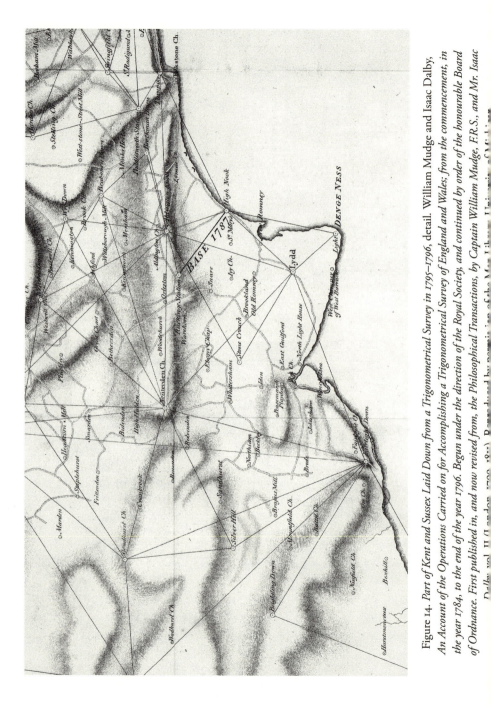

Figure 14. *Part of Kent and Sussex Laid Down from a Trigonometrical Survey in 1795–1796*, detail. William Mudge and Isaac Dalby, *An Account of the Operations Carried on for Accomplishing a Trigonometrical Survey of England and Wales; from the commencement, in the year 1784, to the end of the year 1796. Begun under the direction of the Royal Society, and continued by order of the honourable Board of Ordnance. First published in, and now revised from, the Philosophical Transactions, by Captain William Mudge, F.R.S., and Mr. Isaac Dalby.* vol. II (London, 1799, 1801). Reproduced by permission of the Map Library, University of Michigan.

abstracting tendencies of Ordnance maps and surveys. By the end of the fifteenth century, a small circle enclosing a dot or cross to symbolize town and city centers were conventional on European maps.[22] Sixteenth- through eighteenth-century county maps of England and Wales used the symbol for settlements, augmenting or substituting them with pictographs—conventional signs depicting recognizable objects, such as a church tower, building, or cluster of buildings in profile view—to mark larger towns and important cities.[23] On Mudge and Dalby's Ordnance Survey plans, however, the dotted circles mark not human settlements but particular points in space whose significance derives not from their social, cultural, or political function but from their function in supporting the mathematical national organization. As histories note, many triangulation stations were church steeples and hills, since elevation is good for sightings, but a scanning of the names beside the point symbols on the various plans shows that many other types of geographical phenomena were recruited to produce the framework; triangulation thus appears a great leveler. On the *Triangles for the Survey of Part of South Wales* (Figure 15), *Cilgerran Castle, Cardigan Steeple, Flat Barrow, Rock near Trecoon Farm, Mr. Jones's Summer House, Quarry Pile*, and *Direction Post* achieve parallel significance as all function equivalently to support the new mathematical, and predominantly Anglophone, frame. In effect, the triangulation of the island re-points the island: it subjects the territory to an alternative system of emphasis—or logic of showing—such that a rock and a castle and a post can be classed together as trigonometrical stations and marked by the same abstract sign.[24]

In its first topographical map, the Board of Ordnance dispensed with pictorial marking of human settlements. Towns and cities are indicated ichnographically as abstract grids of streets as seen from above.[25] The plan view of an actual horizontal arrangement, schematically rendered in straight lines, thus replaced the pictographic building profile so as to achieve a rational organization of human and physical geography consistent with the map's abstract, trigonometrical foundations.

Wordsworth's "Line of Motion"

Wordsworth's *Prelude* question "Who that shall point, as with a wand, and say, / 'This portion of the river of my mind / Came from yon fountain'?" (1805, II: 213–15) would seem to find an answer in the person of William Roy, who had conveyed his Enlightenment aspiration for accurate positioning and his

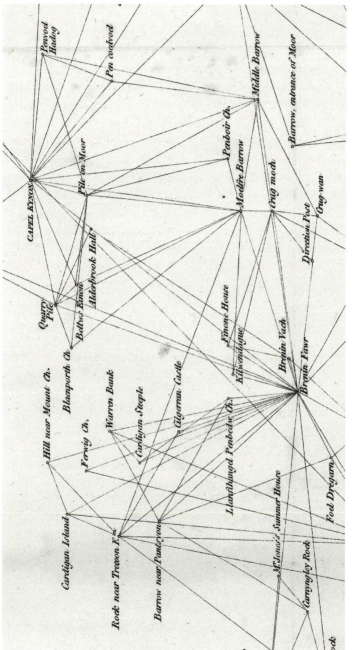

Figure 15. *Triangles for the Survey of Part of South Wales*, detail. William Mudge and Isaac Dalby, *An Account of the Operations Carried on for Accomplishing a Trigonometrical Survey of England and Wales; from the commencement, in the year 1784, to the end of the year 1796. Begun under the direction of the Royal Society, and continued by order of the honourable Board of Ordnance. First published in, and now revised from, the Philosophical Transactions, by Captain William Mudge, F.R.S., and Mr. Isaac Dalby*, vol. III (London, 1799–1811). Reproduced by permission of the Map Library, University of Michigan.

confidence in total visibility in no uncertain terms. While the Ordnance Survey engineers were taking sightings between trig points which they marked with stones and stakes across the nation, Wordsworth posited points of unrepresentability—"Points have we all of us within our souls, / Where all stand single; this I feel, and make / Breathings for incommunicable powers" (1805, III: 186–88)—employing the elementary Euclidean figure, and the sign of national triangulation, to organize a profound and potent human interior. The implication is that "What pass'd within" him (1805, III: 174) cannot be projected upon a plane surface or unfolded sequentially in verbal narrative, an idea that helps to interpret his characterization of "The face of every neighbour" from his childhood village as "a volume to [him]" (1805, IV: 58, 59). Nonetheless, as Wordsworth strives in the opening books on his boyhood education to "trace the history" and "seek / The origin of what [he] then [has] felt" (1805, II: 365–66), he invokes the figure of the line in the landscape as a signal of those "incommunicable powers"—"Genius, Power, / Creation, and Divinity itself" (1805, III: 188, 171–72)—that are fostered, according to his myth, by his "intercourse" with nature (1805, I: 450). With the figure of the unmeasured line Wordsworth neither surveys the landscape of his childhood nor chronicles his mental development, but traces a non-sequential history of the formation of his imagination in the landscape, and of the formation of a poetic line that carries the force and feeling of this primary experience.

As I showed in Chapter 2, despite his alignment of the map with simple mimesis in "Cambridge and the Alps," Wordsworth employs a cartographic terminology in his revisions, using terms such as *point, pointed*, and *marked* to accent his poetic and spiritual progress. In the opening books of *The Prelude*, he introduces the perception of the line in the landscape as a signal of his burgeoning imaginative vision—a signal by no means confined to *The Prelude* but given an origin story in that tale of mental growth and poetical education. One need only think of the "never-ending line" of daffodils added to "I wander'd lonely as a cloud" for its 1815 republication,[26] and of the Pedlar's "active power to fasten images / Upon his brain" and intense brooding upon "their pictur'd lines" until "they acquir'd / The liveliness of dreams" to recognize the importance of the trope in Wordsworth's corpus and its association with imaginative activity.[27] While critics such as Christopher Ricks and Susan Wolfson[28] have remarked the self-referring function of the terms *line* and *lines* in Wordsworth's poetry, none that I know of have registered their historical, intermedial resonance. As I suggest here, the figure of the line as it emerges in the two-part *Prelude* is suggestive of a visual epistemology, formal organization, and dynamic force that is noncartographic: it signals and prioritizes the loco-descriptive blank-verse line as it differentiates it from the totalizing Enlightenment grammars of the survey and history.

Wordsworth's penchant for the line relates to what Hartman has called a "spot syndrome." In his reading of Book III's "Points have we all of us within our souls, / Where all stand single," Hartman identifies "imagination" as the referent of "Points," interpreting it as a "force that isolates man, and from which he draws the consciousness of individual being."[29] Accordingly, he reads Wordsworth's attention to spots in nature, both in *The Prelude* and throughout the poetry, as a subliminal recognition of imaginative power, as the mind's tentative movement from consciousness of nature toward consciousness of self. It is the "*idea* of a spot that haunts Wordsworth: the idea of a point of powerful stasis, a concentration and fixation of power" (85). Hartman elucidates "the spot syndrome" with reference to the Simplon Pass and Snowdon episodes, explaining that "the imagination in its withdrawal from nature first withdraws to a single point. Its show-place is still nature but reduced to one center as dangerous as any holy site. This site is an *omphalos*: the navel-point at which powers meet, the 'one' place leading to a vision of the One. To describe it, the poet later resorts to the figure of an abyss which is a kind of verticalized point and a variant of the 'narrow chasm' and 'gloomy strait' he has actually crossed; while in another encounter he suddenly glimpses imagination in a 'breach' or 'dark deep thoroughfare'" (122). Hartman's reading of the point in nature as a meeting between the powers of nature and mind sheds light on the figure of the line and its tensions. In the two-part poem of 1798–99, before the Simplon, Gondo Gorge, and Snowdon episodes had been written and the figure of the abyss ("a kind of verticalized point") integrated into the poem, the line in the landscape emerges as the nexus of mind, nature, and the eternal or spiritual world, a signal, amidst the accounts of nature's impressive agency, of the boy's imaginative and visionary faculties and also of his inscriptional disposition.[30] Rather than a mark of man's isolation by imagination, or "a point of powerful stasis," the line in the landscape marks the boy's dynamic and poetically generative experience: his physical movements in space and imaginative transfigurations over time that "elevate the feelings" and anticipate an expressivist poetics. Emerging across the episodes of Part One as a mark of the edge between perception and vision, and culminating, in Part Two, with Wordsworth's offering of "these lines, this page" (1799, II: 384) to an adult reader, the figure of the line both encodes a history of nature-based imaginative process and accrues material associations with the blank-verse lines that it anticipates. In adding the reflexive accent to successive books of the extending poem, markedly in Book VIII, Wordsworth traces his own discontinuous history of seeing and models an active perception and moving reception of his own poetic lines.

Rather than employ a willful narrative analytic that would split the intellect into "round and square" and link "portion[s] of the river of [his] mind" to particular tributaries, in Part One of the two-part *Prelude*, Wordsworth relates episodes of his education by the "spirits" and "Powers" of nature (1799, I: 69, 73), both the "gentle visitation[s]" and "Severer interventions" that work to fashion the poet's mind from infancy and "form / A favored being" (1799, I: 73, 79, 69–70). Experiences of the "ministry / More palpable" leave the boy with "an undetermined sense / Of unknown modes of being" (1799, I: 79–80, 121–22)—with "Low breathings," "sounds of undistinguished motion," and "strange utterance" and with mental perceptions of "huge and mighty forms, that do not live / Like living men" (1799, I: 47–48, 64, 127–28): intimations of an order "beyond nature," to use Hartman's phrase, unfamiliar to the boy experiencing a nature of time and change.[31] In the boat-stealing episode (the third of the opening episodes), Wordsworth begins to signal the special effects of the boy's "intercourse" (1799, I: 149) with nature with the coalescence of circular impressions into a linear path, recalling that

>   not without the voice
> Of mountain-echoes did my boat move on,
> Leaving behind her still on either side
> Small circles glittering idly in the moon
> Until they melted all into one track
> Of sparkling light. (1799, I: 91–96)

The awakening of visionary power, as critics have noted, is strongly suggested in the multiple images of "liquid light";[32] but the resolution of "idly glittering" circles—produced by the boy's rowing—into "one track" is significant, too. The implications deepen in the next episode's depiction of ice-skating at twilight, where reflections on water (now frozen) appear to the boy whose motions again trace a line. The poet recalls "leaving the tumultuous throng / To cut across the shadow of a star / That gleamed upon the ice" (1799, I: 172–74), casting himself as incising, with deliberation, a natural medium and image. If the "Powers" of nature, "Impressed upon all forms the characters / Of danger or desire, and thus did make / The surface of the universal earth / With meanings of delight, of hope and fear, / Work like a sea" (1799, I: 194–98), the boy's movements across the earth's surfaces are reciprocally impressive.

Hartman has stated, in a reading of the "spots of time," that the boy has not yet recognized his imaginative power.[33] I suggest that Wordsworth's emphasis on the boy's proto-symbolic and proto-inscriptive interactions with nature foreground the material constituents of imaginative activity and suggest the foundation of Wordsworth's future poetic lines upon these experiences of marking natural forms: of making, perceiving, and inscribing them by his own motion. Thus when the boy, having given with his friends his body "to the wind," notes that "the shadowy banks on either side / Came sweeping through the darkness, spinning still / The rapid line of motion" (1799, I: 175–78), the perception of the "line of motion" marks a threshold in his experience of nature and in his poetic formation. Halting then his spinning, the boy gains a grander vision, as the "rapid line of motion" expands to an image of global revolution:

> yet still the solitary cliffs
> Wheeled by me, even as if the earth had rolled
> With visible motion her diurnal round;
> Behind me did they stretch in solemn train
> Feebler and feebler, and I stood and watched
> Till all was tranquil as a summer sea. (1799, I: 180–85)

The perception of the "line" marks the boy's cutting across the sensuous to a vision of nature's enduring forms, physics, and geometries, its grand circulations and extensions ("behind me did they stretch in solemn train / Feebler and feebler").[34] As both perception and narrative signal, the "line" highlights the intertwining of the boy's "passions . . . with high objects, with eternal things, / With life and nature" and his learning to recognize, with the coming of tranquility, "A grandeur in the beating of [his] heart" (1799, I: 134, 136–37,141). Without directly implying the future remediation of this visionary experience as poetry—lines organized by the beats of passion—the "track," "the cut," and "the line" intimate the fashioning of the mind for poetic inscription through unplotted, active "intercourse" with nature.

Unlike the national survey, with its systematic inscription of points and lines to build up the "Great Outlines of the country" (Roy), the two-part poem eschews compositional regulation. Like the boy who is "led" on by the "enchantment" of his "rod and line" (1799, I: 238, 236) to explore the pleasures of autumn woods and bowers, Wordsworth the writer proceeds unsystematically, enchanted by his own memories briefly to relate a series of autumnal impressions, "such effects as cannot here / Be regularly classed, yet tend[ing] no less / To the same point, the growth of mental power / And love of Nature's works" (1799, I: 255–58). Linking the boy in nature with the adult writer, the fishing "line" forecasts the poet to come,[35] motivated by fears and pleasures had and renewed in their telling, not by adherence to any abstract compositional order or compulsion to "class the cabinet / Of . . . sensations" and "Run through the history and birth of each" (1799, II: 258–60). While "point" signals the tendency of the boy's experiences and of the writer's inscription of those experiences (movement toward "the growth of mental power / And love of Nature's works" [1799, I: 257–58]), the fishing "line" flags their nonschematic nature and sequence as well as the poet's episodic dipping into the pool of memory, such as to those early childhood "spots of time / Which with distinct pre-eminence retain / A fructifying virtue" (1799, I: 288–90), working to nourish and repair the mind, "Especially the imaginative power" (1799, I: 293).

One of these "spots of time" associates the figure of the line with the imagination—with its emotional transfiguration of images "impressed" by powerful experience and with its spatial and temporal reorganization of those images into poetic lines (1799, I: 283). Introduced as leaving a power "Implanted" in Wordsworth's mind (1799, I: 330), the episode recounts the boy's impatient waiting on a "Stormy, and rough, and wild" (1799, I: 342) day for the arrival of horses to carry him and his brothers from school at the Christmas holiday. Rationally positioned, "half-sheltered by a naked wall; / Upon [his] right hand . . . a single sheep, / A whistling hawthorn on [his] left," (1799, I: 343–45), the boy had a purchase on the scene below. Not knowing which way the horsemen would come, he watched from

> a crag,
> An eminence which from the meeting point
> Of two highways ascending overlooked
> At least a long half-mile of those two roads . . . (1799, I: 335–38)

After his father's unexpected death during the holiday, and in the wake of feelings of guilt— "chastisement" for the "anxiety of hope" in which he had scanned those two highways (1799, I: 355, 357)—Wordsworth would "repair" to his imaginative revision of the scene and its feelings, to "drink / As at a fountain," deriving sustenance from seeing and hearing

the wind, and sleety rain,
And all the business of the elements,
The single sheep, and the one blasted tree,
And the bleak music of that old stone wall,
The noise of wood and water, and the mist
Which on the line of each of those two roads
Advanced in such indisputable shapes . . . (1799, I: 369–70, 361–67)

The abstraction of the "line" underscores the abstracting powers of imagination, the faculty which here removes the boy from the scene and distinguishes its features, articulating even the spread of mist, which had given intermittent views of the plane below, into "indisputable shapes." Rhythmical emphasis and coordinative syntax ("The *single sheep*, and the *one blasted tree*, / And the *bleak music* of that *old stone wall*") add eerie intensity to the images while also counterpointing the eventual emergence of the "line" in a steady pentameter sequence ("Which on the line of each of those two roads / Advanced"). This metrical and grammatical recuperation both evokes the advance of portentous shapes along the roads and anticipates the mind's unifying conversion of images and feelings into poetic lines.[36] The "line" is again associated with motion, linking the skater's vision of nature's grand turnings to the mind's transfiguration of images and feelings over time and to its reorganization of them into the spatiotemporal turnings of verse.

Significantly, the poetic rendering of the landscape, and of the past, is here distinguished from surveying. At first the boy casts himself as surveyor, or splitter, who scans from an eminence above their "meeting point . . . / At least a long half-mile of those two roads"; but in imagination he repairs to the unmeasured extension, the "line of each of those two roads," relinquishing the quantifying eye and control of the "meeting point"—a fatal crossroads, perhaps—for the indefinite stroke and its muted suggestion of eternity. In the 1805 and 1850 versions of the poem, which reposition the Waiting for the Horses episode to the end of Book XI, Wordsworth makes blatant the association of lines and the eternal, claiming to love, in the beginning of Book XII, a "public road," an "object" that "hath had power / O'er my imagination since the dawn / Of childhood, when its disappearing line, / . . . / Was like a guide into eternity" (1805, XII: 145–51, 148, 151).[37] "Waiting for the Horses" explores the circumstances and yields of these early visions and revisions—emotional, imaginative, and material; it offers the metrical line as a dynamic psychic structure linked to the relinquishing of visual command, the remission of powers of reasoning, and the unfixing of spatial and temporal limits.

Thus when Wordsworth first likens his history, in the next verse paragraph, to an act of tracing, the metaphor has literal resonance:

> [Nor sedulous to trace]
> How Nature by collateral interest
> And by extrinsic passion peopled first
> My mind with forms, or beautiful or grand,
> And made me love them, may I well forget
> How other pleasures have been mine, and joys
> Of subtler origin . . . (1799, I: 375–81)[38]

Rather than ordering the landscape of his mind "by geometric rules" (1799, II: 243), Wordsworth has been illuminating his mind's formation in the landscape, accenting the edges of perception and vision and signaling the processes of imaginative transfiguration with the figure of the line. If these episodes anticipate their own remediation as poetic lines, the sequence that follows these remarks on method suggests the process whereby nature's forms rematerialize in moving poetry. The passage traces the course of "lines / Of curling mist":

> Yes, I remember when the changeful earth
> And twice five seasons on my mind had stamped
> The faces of the moving year, even then,
> A Child, I held unconscious intercourse
> With the eternal Beauty, drinking in
> A pure organic pleasure from the lines
> Of curling mist or from the level plain
> Of waters coloured by the steady clouds. (1799, I: 391–98)

Wordsworth's "intercourse" with "the eternal Beauty" is appropriately signaled by the sinuous line, reminiscent of Hogarth's "line of beauty" and Burke's "varied line"—unmeasured, in motion, and insinuating itself into Wordsworth's affections via the "brain."[39] Such "scenes" of pleasure, he explains, "Remained, in their substantial lineaments / Depicted on the brain" (1799, I: 429–31); they "did at length / Become habitually dear" and "were by invisible links / Allied to the affections" (1799, I: 439–42), moving him to "love" nature and sense in it "a never-failing principle of joy / And purest passion" (1799, II: 495–96). *Lines, lineaments,*[40] *at length, links, Allied*: the associationist sequence of terms and sounds emphasizes the material and temporal process of impassioning. But the sequence does not stop here. After several episodes in which he "retrace[s]" his "round[s]" (1799, II: 1, 7) of childhood play, Wordsworth pauses to consider the emotional effect "these lines, this page" will have on a "passionately loved" but now distant childhood friend (1799, II: 384, 383). Lines materialize, in their "substantial lineaments," on the pages between poet and reader as the medium of their "intercourse." As Wordsworth traces his history, then, he traces a discontinuous genealogy of "lines" from domain to domain—from sky and sea to brain and ultimately to page, deriving his lines from passionate communion with nature and his own revisionary perceptions even as he queries their capacity to renew passions felt between friends in that landscape.

In an essay examining the "fluidity" and "suppleness" of line endings in *The Prelude*, Christopher Ricks observes the frequency of the words *line* and *lines* in Wordsworth's poems, including "the rapid line of motion" and "the lines / Of curling mist" from Book I, and asserts their occasional "covert metaphorical application to the verse-lines themselves."[41] Especially when poised in the final syntactic position, such terms as *line*, *hung*, and *end* evoke the line and the "white space at the end of the line," sensitizing readers both to the subtle plays of meaning effected by the visual boundary and to the individual line's easy accommodation within the aural structure of the blank-verse paragraph (7). "It is natural that the word *line* or *lines* should figure so often in Wordsworth's lines," Ricks argues, because the verse as an aesthetic form "is to epitomise" the poet's broader values of distinction without separation (5), transition without violence (9–10), and nontyrannical balance of the senses, particularly of sight and hearing. I have been suggesting that *line* and *lines* are not a "natural" self-reference in the blank verse of *The Prelude*. Inscribed from the earliest stages of the poem and incorporated in its latest phases of revision, they reflect shifting autobiographical concerns and representational strategies as well as a formal consciousness sharpened by contemporary projects of marking and measuring the landscape that had unprecedented cultural visibility and authority.

Ongoing invocations of the figure of the line reveal the historical nature of their reflexivity. In extensions and revisions of the "Poet's History" (1805, IV: 71), Wordsworth marked with the figure his growing awareness of the powers of the "Soul" and his spiritualizing visions of "Man" and nature, subtly differentiating his poetic lines from instrumental delineations of nature by drawing out, paradoxically, their typo-metrical materiality. Consider his account of "priz'd and lov'd" walks taken during his first summer vacation from Cambridge. Wordsworth singles out his first "Circuit of our little Lake" (1805, IV: 121, 128) for the feeling of "restoration" it brings, for "swellings of the spirits," and for

> glimmering views
> How Life pervades the undecaying mind,
> How the immortal Soul with God-like power
> Informs, creates, and thaws the deepest sleep
> That time can lay upon her . . . (1805, IV: 146, 153, 154–58)

This "musing" on immortality touches down in a corresponding image of the landscape: "meanwhile," Wordsworth recalls, "The mountain heights were slowly overspread / With darkness; and before a rippling breeze / The long Lake lengthen'd out its hoary line" (1805, IV: 167–71). The young man's "Circuit" of the "little Lake" opens into the lake's own lengthening of its "glimmering" line—a visual intimation of immortality that metrically materializes in the slowing sequence of stresses ("The *long Lake lengthe*n'd *out*"). Wordsworth again used the poetic line in this way—to formalize, or mark, his moving perception of the unbound—as he moved a passage from the two-part poem to Book VIII of the 1805 text and subsequently extended it. Telling of nature's guiding him to an early "unconscious love and reverence / Of human nature" (1805, VIII: 413–14), he added an image of a grove whose boughs overhang Coniston Water

> With length of shade so thick that whoso glides
> Along the line of low-roofed water moves
> As in a cloister. (1850, VIII: 460–62 cf. 1799, II: 140–45)

With the sinuous, material tracing of the "line" across three lines of /l/ sounds—*length, glides, Along, line, low, cloister*—Wordsworth inscribes an active perception of nature's spatial and spiritual volume. The pentameter comes momentarily into view as part of a longer rhythmical continuum, suggesting also the joint agency involved in imaginative and poetic progress: nature's guiding as he "glides / Along."

The poetic line materializes again in a revision of Book VIII when Wordsworth uses the figure of the "boundary line" to heighten his ennobling perception of the shepherd among the hills. In the 1805 text, their volumetric fullness stages a spiritual turn: "When round some shady promontory turning, / His Form hath flash'd upon me, glorified / By the deep radiance of the setting sun" (1805, VIII: 403–5). The 1850 text delineates this transformation more decisively—

> as he stepped
> Beyond the boundary line of some hill-shadow,
> His form hath flashed upon me, glorified . . . (1850, VIII: 267–69)

—by formalizing his surpassing of merely empirical perception in the striding *enjambement* and hypermetrical poetic line ("Beyond the boundary line of some hill-shadow") that doubly signals hill representation. Fully dimensional "Man" emerges, an "index of delight," "spiritual almost" (1850, VIII: 275, 280, 282), as if from the two-dimensional poem or relief map. If Wordsworth's "present Theme / Is to retrace the way that led [him] on / Through Nature to the love of human Kind" (1805, VIII: 586–88), the figure of the line in the landscape not only marks that "way" but also leaves typo-metrical traces of it on the page—blank verses that reflexively remark his "having track'd the main essential Power, / Imagination, up her way sublime" (1805, XIII: 289–90). In revision, the poem's spiritual cartographism is materially pronounced.

Each of these additions conjures a line that appears to Wordsworth's eye, and to the readers', by virtue of movement. Biographically, they indicate the boy's unwilled apprehension of dynamic power (Nature, Imagination, the eternal); compositionally, they mark the poet's inscription of a providential "way." And while the figure recalls Dorothy's tracing of Wordsworth's continental route upon her maps, Wordsworth's "line" elides point of origin and terminus ("the principal places he stopped at")[42] so as to inscribe an eternal fit or cooperation, only occasionally glimpsed, between mind and nature. Finally, as a foil for the never-ending line and for the retrospective poet of 1850 who tracks the "way" of Imagination toward the "point marked out by heaven" (1850, VI: 754), Wordsworth introduces a terminal line into a revision of the boyhood boat-stealing scene. In the 1805 text, the image of the "one track" comes in a passage rich with naturalistic detail:

> nor without the voice
> Of mountain echoes did my Boat move on,
> Leaving behind her still on either side

Small circles glittering idly in the moon
Until they melted all into one track
Of sparkling light. A rocky steep uprose
Above the Cavern of the Willow tree
And now, as suited one who proudly row'd
With his best skill, I fix'd a steady view
Upon the top of that same craggy ridge,
The bound of the horizon . . . (1805, I: 390–400; cf. 1799, I: 91–101)

The 1850 text distinctly opposes the "one track" to the determinate line:

Until they melted all into one track
Of sparkling light. But now, like one who rows
(Proud of his skill) to reach a chosen point
With an unswerving line, I fixed my view
Upon the summit of a craggy ridge,
The horizon's utmost boundary . . . (1850, I: 366–71)

With the inscription of "line" and "point," Wordsworth visibly figures the boy's willful ambition, his effort to master nature by pursuing a straight and finite course toward a "chosen" goal; yet the "summit" that the boy had rationally "fixed" in view, not unlike an Ordnance surveyor, is powerfully revealed to be false.[43] This graphic plotting of a deviation from nature's lead and from his own imagination, symbolized by the dynamic counter-image of "Small circles" melting into "one track / Of sparkling light," supports the 1850 poem's more explicit providentialism and its intensification of geometric accenting to trace the boy's developing perception of earth's heavenly, immeasurable volumes: "whoso glides / Along the line of low-roofed water moves / As in a cloister" (1850, VIII: 460–62).

The Map in the Poem: The Black Comb Poems

The Ordnance Survey and the poetic autobiography developed in parallel. The relevance of the Survey to the counter-cartographic imaginative accenting and formal fashioning of *The Prelude* is indicated by a pair of short blank-verse poems Wordsworth began on an 1811 visit to the western edge of Cumberland, a tour that brought him into contact with the surveyors who were currently working on the mountain of Black Comb. Cartographic historians and literary critics have discussed the poems' ideological ambivalence toward the Survey.[44] My goal here is to show how the blank-verse poems foreground the competing epistemologies of topographical media and how their particular graphical-lexical expressivity emerges in reflexive relation to national cartographic pressures on the terrain.

"Written with a Slate-pencil, on a Stone, on the side of the Mountain of Black Comb" shows Wordsworth's awareness not only of what he is writing on—the poetic page—but also, coyly, of what he is not: the map surface. Nominally an inscription "on a Stone" that in actuality takes the material form of a printed text in a book, the poem evokes a diversity of graphic surfaces and technologies of writing. In the mode of an eighteenth-century nature inscription—a brief poem inscribed upon an object in a garden—the poem invokes and halts a passerby. But instead of pointing out a sight to a gentleman or woman, the spirit of the place interrupts a pedestrian on his climb to a hoped-for "terraqueous spectacle":[45]

> Stay, bold Adventurer; rest awhile thy limbs
> On this commodious Seat! for much remains
> Of hard ascent before thou reach the top
> Of this huge Eminence,—from blackness named,
> And, to far-travelled storms of sea and land,
> A favourite spot of tournament and war![46]

Like one of Wordsworth's first published blank-verse poems, "Lines Left upon a Seat in a Yew-tree" (*Lyrical Ballads*, 1798), the poem admonishes the passing tourist to appreciate nature's essential flux—here by identifying the view-seeker with a topographical surveyor. The first half honors the peak's powerful storms; the second relates the account of a "geographic Labourer" who "Week after week pursued" his "lonely task" of measuring "height and distance" until a "glimpse" of "Nature's processes" intervened (14–19). The inscription relays the surveyor's report,

> That once, while there he plied his studious work
> Within that canvass Dwelling, suddenly
> The many-coloured map before his eyes
> Became invisible: for all around
> Had darkness fallen—unthreatened, unproclaimed—

As if the golden day itself had been
Extinguished in a moment; total gloom,
In which he sate alone with unclosed eyes
Upon the blinded mountain's silent top! (21–29)

If Wordsworth's nature poems offer an "enlarged understanding"[47] of a scene, this one dramatizes the dynamic strength of nature, capable of thwarting in an instant the measuring of heights and fixing of spatial relations—an event, Wordsworth explains in the Fenwick note, that occurred to "one of the engineers, who was employed in making trigonometrical surveys of that region."[48] The flux of weather exceeds the powers of perception, bringing the work of knowledge to an unexpected end. By obscuring the surface of the map, "Nature's processes" (18–19) stay the surveyor's labor but drive his telling of the tale and the inscribing of the lines on stone. The inscription thus structurally embodies its enlarged understanding: whereas maps depend on visual clarity and offer specious images of an earth without weather (from "centre to circumference, unveiled!" [11]), the inscription accommodates oral report of "total gloom." Further, in a final image of the surveyor seated with "unclosed eyes / Upon the blinded mountain's silent top!" it opens the possibility of deeper, spiritual insight for tourist and surveyor alike.

A fragmentary coda introduced in manuscript enforces the inscription's aesthetic-epistemological statement—"I am not a map"—by referencing the inscription's material features:

though the keen elements will soon destroy
All trace of these slight labours wearing out
The feeble lines perchance before they meet
A human eye yet shall the Stone [?record]
Long as it may that a[49]

While allying the inscription and the map by their labor of production ("geographic Labourer," "these slight labours") and by their susceptibility to time and weather, the unfinished coda suggests the power of effaced stone to remain a silent monument to nature's compromising of cultural projects. My interest, though, is in Wordsworth's use of the word "lines" to carry forward this critique. At publication in 1815, the self-reflexive coda with its "feeble lines" is rejected, a cancellation that dissociates the inscription from the mark of the line. This logic is repeated in the addition, also at publication, of the lengthy but nonetheless elliptical title, "Written with a Slate-pencil, on a Stone, on the Side of the Mountain of Black Comb," when "Lines," the volume tells us, are the stuff of poems. The index to the 1815 *Poems* lists "Lines Left upon a Seat," "Lines Written upon a Stone," "Lines Written on a Blank Leaf in a Copy of the Author's Poem 'The Excursion,'" "Lines Written in Early Spring," "Lines Written at a Small Distance from my House," and "Lines Addressed to a Noble Lord." A synecdoche that refers not merely to those poems Wordsworth classes in 1815 as "Inscriptions," "Lines" make up the poet's volumes.

The poem's sensitivity to graphic media is augmented over time. Canceled with the coda and elided in the title, the term "lines" returns to the poem in Edward Moxon's 1836 edition of *The Poetical Works*—but now in an elaborated description of the map and as a mark of cartography's aspiration to accuracy of distinction. In the 1815 clause, the map is a creature of colors: "The many-coloured map before his eyes / Became invisible."[50] In the 1836 clause, "colours, lines, / And the whole surface of the out-spread map / Became invisible."[51] The term "lines" migrates to the map, then, as the "eyes" of the surveyor vanish—two changes that emphasize the ideality of cartographic rendering and its fiction of objective, vantage-free perception. By presenting "the whole surface of the out-spread map" to the reader of "Written with a Slate-pencil, on a Stone, on the Side of the Mountain of Black Comb," Wordsworth elaborates the contrast between stone and map, pencil writing and cartographic delineation, and the attitudes toward nature that they imply. The very form of the title, a slow climb of prepositional phrases intimating the magnitude of that "huge Eminence," contrasts with the "whole surface," synchronic presentation of the survey's instrumentally measured space.

Even while elevating, philosophically, the nature inscription over the survey, the poem resists a simple valorization of one medium—and mode of inscribing space—over others. By appending a topographical note to the poem at publication in 1815, Wordsworth evokes yet another discursive context: that of tourist publications and county maps, which, as we saw in Chapter 1, commonly included informative topographical annotations.[52] The horizontal block of text at the foot of the verse reads: "Black Comb stands at the southern extremity of Cumberland: its base covers a much greater extent of ground than any other Mountain in these parts; and, from its situation, the summit commands a more extensive view than any other point in Britain. See page 305, Vol. I."[53] The impersonal objectivity assumed in the prose vies with the intimacy of the verse inscription to which it is a gloss, recalling the reader from the stony scene of inscription to the fact of the printed "page" and book.

Although part of the note paraphrases Colonel William Mudge, Superinten-
dent of the Ordnance Survey (1798–1820), and implies knowledge gained by
surveying from summits, the note refers us not to the sheets of the Ordnance
Survey but to an illustrative companion poem, "View from the Top of Black
Comb," which is classified in the same volume of 1815 as a "Poem of the Imagination."[54] The archaic wisdom of the *genius loci* is thus not compromised by
contemporary scientific authority but linked with the poet himself and his
imaginative apprehension and inscription of landscape.

"View from the Top of Black Comb" shows Wordsworth's developing sensitivity to the linguistic and graphic capacities of blank verse—to its capacities,
particularly, as a medium for articulating national and imperial space. While
"Written with a Slate-pencil" withholds the promise of expansive view, its
companion "View from the Top of Black Comb" traces, as if in real time, "the
amplest range / Of unobstructed prospect" that "British ground commands":

> —low dusky tracts,
> Where Trent is nursed, far southward! Cambrian Hills
> To the south-west, a multitudinous show;
> And, in a line of eye-sight linked with these,
> The hoary Peaks of Scotland that give birth
> To Tiviot's Stream, to Annan, Tweed, and Clyde;—
> Crowding the quarter whence the sun comes forth
> Gigantic Mountains rough with crags; beneath,
> Right at the imperial Station's western base,
> Main Ocean, breaking audibly, and stretched
> Far into silent regions blue and pale;—
> And visibly engirding Mona's Isle
> That, as we left the Plain, before our sight
> Stood like a lofty Mount, uplifting slowly,
> (Above the convex of the watery globe)
> Into clear view the cultured fields that streak
> Its habitable shores; but now appears
> A dwindled object, and submits to lie
> At the Spectator's feet.—Yon azure Ridge,
> Is it a perishable cloud? Or there
> Do we behold the frame of Erin's Coast?
> Land sometimes by the roving shepherd swain,
> Like the bright confines of another world

Not doubtfully perceived.—Look homeward now!
In depth, in height, in circuit, how serene
The spectacle, how pure!—Of Nature's works,
In earth, and air, and earth-embracing sea,
A Revelation infinite it seems;
Display august of man's inheritance,
Of Britain's calm felicity and power.[55]

While, as I showed in Chapter 1, Crosthwaite had encouraged "*British Youths*" to "*explore*" their "*native Isle*" with the aid of his patriotic plans, Wordsworth renders the scene from the perspective of viewers imagined already within it. From the summit of Black Comb, eyes of a viewer-speaker range over points to the south and the southwest, linking these in a diagonal "line of eye-sight" with Scottish peaks to the northwest. After a break-inscribing dash, enhancing the effect of vocal immediacy, the poem scans a westerly line of view from a point of "British ground" in the east ("whence the sun comes forth") to Black Comb's "western base," out across the ocean, and "Far into silent regions blue and pale" (11, 13, 15).

In *Romantic Geography*, Michael Wiley asserts that Wordsworth's "poetic survey of the land" simulates "the procedures" of trigonometrical "measurement."[56] He reads the Black Comb poems as Wordsworth's ideological reconciliation with institutional modes of delineating Britain, of which the Ordnance Survey was one official expression.[57] But this oversimplifies both the cartographic context in which the poems function and the way they take the measure of the landscape. Wiley overlooks the formal and material dimension of the poems as well as the print context of tourist publications, which trained Britons to encounter the landscape through a range of signs that flexibly interacted on the page. In fact, lexical and notational revisions made to the Black Comb poems heighten the interactions of graphic and verbal codes. These revisions intensify the critique of the Ordnance Survey's institutionalization of the landscape and, as I will show, endorse the fluidity of the blank-verse measure as a medium for formulating national space. The status of the "line" as a unit of spatial fixity, or of spatial and temporal play, is a crucial aspect of this critique.

While Wiley is right to say the poem "delineates Britain from [the surveyor's] vantage point,"[58] it is also true that the narrator's roving eye attributes dynamism to the land: the "line of eye-sight" extending to "The hoary Peaks of Scotland" senses movement in those peaks "that give birth to Tiviot's

Stream" and the rivers "Annan, Tweed, and Clyde."[59] The "Gigantic Mountains rough with crags" are where "the sun comes forth"; and the ocean at the "imperial Station's western base" is an acoustic field "breaking audibly" and "stretched / Far into silent regions"—beyond the reach of ear and then eye. Across the poems and their enactive enjambments, the word "line" draws attention to contrary epistemological and graphic modes: whereas the "geographic Labourer" of "Written with a Slate-pencil" "measures height and distance" and sets finite, quantified "lines" on the "out-spread map," "View from the Top" traces sight lines across interrelated fields of land, sea, and sky—producing the simultaneous effects of an animated nature and imaginative perceiver.

A late lexical revision underscores this epistemological and representational difference:

> —Yon azure Ridge,
> Is it a perishable cloud? Or there
> Do we behold the frame of Erin's Coast? (23–25)

Longman's 1832 text of the poem substitutes "the frame" with "the line of Erin's coast," a refining of the image that might seem to ally the poem with cartography.[60] But the change abstracts the coast while emphasizing the activity, and partiality, of vision. "Do we behold the line of Erin's coast?" echoes "a line of eye-sight," uniting wavering geographical aspect with mobile perception. The lexical change narrows the gap between object ("the line of . . . coast") and eye ("line of eye-sight") to a fine line—a gestural and expressive line that inscribes within the poem a viewer-speaker of searching uncertainty and feeling. By contrast, the "lines" of the Ordnance Survey map derive from "instruments" to "measure height and distance," implying the practical separation of object and eye.

If the term "line" suggests the tracing of the topography with the eye and into language, so too does the typographic mark of the line. Interestingly, the poem gradually develops a graphic logic of punctuation that supports its epistemic and ideological critique of the new national cartography. While punctuation across the lengthening manuscripts is unstable, placement of the dashes is particularly fitful.[61] Promoted during the era as a signal of long pause, break in speech, and sudden shift in thought, as I discuss further in Chapter 5, the many instances of the dash in the manuscripts clearly function rhetorically. In the text of the 1815 *Poems*, however, the spatial effects of the mark come into focus. Now the dashes iconically represent horizontal vision, from south to north (5–10) and from east to west, "far into silent regions blue and pale;—" (11–15). Dashes "visibly [engird] Mona's Isle" on the page (15–23), even as the "Spectator's" view of the shore's streaked uplands is foreclosed by the island's apparent flatness from the summit of Black Comb. Dashes also now foreground discontinuities and equivocal visions "—. . . Do we behold the line of Erin's coast? . . .—" (23–28) so as to intimate gaps in the poem's "circuit" (29) of the landscape, its interruptive but humanizing shifts between lines of visual and verbal attention. Thus while suggesting the speech patterns and pauses of a viewing subject, the dashes in the 1815 text also index the motions of a non-quantifying eye and mind as it focuses, and fails to focus, a United Kingdom (Scotland, England, Wales, and Ireland) that exceeds its reach. The dashes trace, that is, a qualitatively perceived space and a progressive mode of topographic cognizance that the Ordnance Survey would not record—one that engages and strains both eye and ear. The dashes thus signal the simultaneity of visual and vocal experience as well as their fundamental fragmentariness; the poem marks the "breaking audibly" of waves and voice as it gestures toward but does not fully delineate Britain's extension "Far into silent regions" of the "globe" (19).

The rhetorical and spatial work of punctuation marks in "View from the Top of Black Comb" becomes more complex over time. After 1820, a reader encounters several sets of parentheses (round brackets), segmenting marks that were only gradually introduced to the poem. The earliest draft of the poem employs only a single set of parentheses to mark an atmospheric, etymological reference: "Black Comb (dread name, / From clouds and Storms derived)."[62] Upon publication in 1815, an additional set of brackets marks a vision of Mona's Isle

> That, as we left the Plain, before our sight
> Stood like a lofty Mount, uplifting slowly,
> (Above the convex of the watery globe) . . . (17–19)

Here the parentheses aid in the reader's recognition of an inessential phrase—but they also make a point about cartography. Graphically set aside from two views of the island taken from separate vantage points at separate times ("as we left the Plain"; "but now appears / A dwindled object"), the parentheses offer a vision of global convexity. Thus Wordsworth marks both visually, in the convex shape of the brackets, and linguistically, by the words held within the brackets, the eye's mobility—its ability to shift between local and global perceptions of space. This blank-verse encoding of a quasi-empirical and imaginative perception exceeds the interests and scope of the "out-spread" surface of an Ordnance Survey map.

Introduced into the text of the 1820 *Poetical Works*, yet another set of parentheses mark a grammatical and geographical aside—an untethering of vision from this world, a flight of fancy:

> —Yon azure Ridge,
> Is it a perishable cloud? Or there
> Do we behold the frame of Erin's coast?
> Land sometimes by the roving shepherd swain,
> (Like the bright confines of another world)
> Not doubtfully perceived.—Look homeward now![63]

Over time, then, the poem adopts a visual and visionary logic of punctuation: the dashes come to manifest the poem's several lines of geographic vision as well as the gaps between them; the parentheses come to mark the awe-inspired, imaginative turns that round and enrich here-and-now perceptions. They are more *tropographic* than topographic or cartographic. The poem concludes,

> —Of Nature's works,
> In earth, and air, and earth-embracing sea,
> A Revelation infinite it seems;
> Display august of man's inheritance,
> Of Britain's calm felicity and power. (30–34)

Wordsworth lodges nationalist revelation not in the "lines" of the surveyor but in the speaker-viewer's shifting lines of sight that register the features, motions, and obscurities of the land, its local lore (the etymology of Black Comb), and subjective visual impressions.[64] It is not the Ordnance surveyor but the blank-verse nature poet, Wordsworth discovers, who takes the more nuanced measure of the British landscape by more flexibly deploying the lines of his medium (line terms, line marks, line units). By these formal, linguistic, and graphical interactions, the poems enlarge the visual and aural imagination of the nation and bring blank verse into view as a mode of national portraiture that hovers between speech and print.

Significantly, when Wordsworth coupled these poems in the volume of

1815, effectively differentiating both from the Ordnance Survey, he also organized the volume's poems into a new system of poetic classification. I want to suggest that the cartographic consciousness underlying "View from the Top of Black Comb" suffuses, as well, the class Wordsworth devises to contain that poem: the "Poems of the Imagination," designating the verse produced when the imaginative power of the "Author's" mind predominates.[65] It is in contrast to the surveyor's use of instruments to "measure height and distance" ("Written with a Slate-pencil") that Wordsworth introduces the "Poem of the Imagination"; defines the conferring, abstracting, modifying, creative, and shaping powers of the "Imagination"; and illustrates her "recoil from every thing but the plastic, the pliant, and the indefinite."[66] He writes: "Having to speak of stature, she does not tell you that her gigantic Angel was as tall as Pompey's Pillar; much less that he was twelve cubits, or twelve hundred cubits high; or that his dimensions equalled those of Teneriffe or Atlas; —because these, and if they were a million times as high it would be the same, are bounded: The expression is, 'His stature reached the sky!' the illimitable firmament!" An angel of imagination also appears in "View from the Top of Black Comb":

> This Height a ministering Angel might select:
> For from the summit of BLACK COMB (dread name
> Derived from clouds and storms!) the amplest range
> Of unobstructed prospect may be seen
> That British ground commands:— . . .

The angel is the exalted other of the "geographic Labourer" who was "employed in making trigonometrical surveys of that region."[67] And, as the manuscript and print revisions of the poems suggest, she is an effect, as well, of the poet's labor and the labor of copyists, editors, and compositors. It is by honing diction and punctuation that Wordsworth traces a verbal and visual view in blank-verse time and space, graphically evoking nation and empire, as well as a speaking subject in the process of feeling and imagining.

Pictorial Relief in the Age of Numerical Accuracy

When his poetic autobiography was published in April 1850, the Ordnance Survey had completed the trigonometrical survey of England and Wales and was in the midst of surveys of Ireland and Scotland. The network of triangles upon the island outlines graphically displayed what the presence of stakes and stones materialized in real space: the new mathematical formalization of the British landscape. In this cartographic culture, *The Prelude*'s indefinitely extensive lines of landscape and imagination and its joint pointing of the "Soul" and ground over which the poet traveled would have been charged by their difference from trigonometrical points and delineations: the product of instrument-aided vision, the angle-measuring theodolite, and the geometrical rules by which distances were derived from those angles. But they also would have been read in the context of a controversy about the topographical representation of the nation—and particularly of hill country—by the Ordnance Survey. This controversy was significant enough to generate a Parliamentary inquiry into the respective merits of different modes of rendering relief, numerical or pictorial, and for Matthew Arnold to advocate publicly, as the Lake District was being topographically mapped, the preservation of fine pictorial representation of hills. Arnold's elegies on Wordsworth, and his polemic on mapping, took Wordsworthian modes of feeling and perceiving nature to the heart of debates about delineating the nation.

When the Ordnance Survey undertook the task of producing topographical maps based upon the new trigonometrical data, it faced the problem of representing relief accurately and at large scale. Whereas small-scale eighteenth-century maps such as Emmanuel Bowen's of Cumberland and Westmorland (1777) had used conventional sugarloaf signs to indicate upland, at a larger scale (such as the one-inch OS maps) these schematic profiles would not only occlude information behind the hills but also be conspicuously out of character with the otherwise detailed depiction of the ground. To show hills from above, in plan view, would resolve the problem of occlusion, but British mapmakers had to adopt these techniques from continental cartographers and hone them.[68] Further, as I discussed in Chapter 2, they had little practice in visualizing geomorphology and inadequate technology for gauging slope.[69]

In confronting the challenge of producing standardized, accurate visual renderings of the landscape, the Board of Ordnance pursued and developed a French mode of assessing and representing relief that countered the mathematical principles of accuracy emblematized by triangulation (and which were used in some of the Alpine maps discussed in Chapter 2). While many foreign cartographers in the early decades of the nineteenth century had adopted measurement-based techniques, the Ordnance Survey fostered the pictorial, field-sketching mode used for the *Carte Géometrique de La France* (1756–1816).

While continental cartographers now privileged the determination, with instruments, of altitudes and angles of slope, British cartographers continued to privilege the unaided impression of slope to the eye. Each mode of rendering relief differently disposed lines across the two-dimensional surface of the published map, and each elicited different modes of interpretation.

As on the Cassini map, the Ordnance Survey maps employed hachures: short, parallel shade-lines that trace the direction water would take down a slope, the darkness or thickness of which can indicate either height or gradient. As historian Yolande Jones has shown, the Ordnance Survey championed the "natural history principle" of relief representation developed by English artist, surveyor, and draftsman Robert Dawson, a method founded upon the draftsman's thorough visual understanding of the "physical substance and geological structure and formation of the land."[70] From 1803, landscape artists employing Dawson's methods used statues of the human figure and natural objects, such as stones and the knots of trees, to train surveyors to recognize variations in form, undulation, and gradient. Using watercolor and charcoal, surveyors interspersed color washes with fields of hachures to suggest the fall of vertical or oblique light on slopes (Figure 16).[71] Hill engravers transferred finished drawings to copper plates, cutting hachures in the metal to image what the draftsmen could show with color, ink, texture, and brush stroke.

By contrast, the contour lines coming into favor on European maps bore no relation to naturalistic effects of light and shade, and their production obviated visual interpretation of the surface of the ground. In contouring, surveyors methodically canvass the terrain, determining heights with leveling instruments, marking the points they have leveled on the ground, and plotting those points on paper. Contours—concentrically linked points of equivalent altitude—imply the overall form of a given terrain. Whereas hachures communicate form by tracing slope for the eye, in contouring, slopes must be inferred from the relative widths of blank intervals: the closer the horizontal lines, the steeper the slope. In areas of subtle gradation where contour lines are by definition widely spaced, the lines themselves do not even imply incline: a user must reference and compare the numerical information appended to lines to determine or clarify the direction of slopes.[72] Numbers encoding altitude differentials permit the translation of lines into landforms. Its supporters hailed contouring as less subjective, less costly, more accurate, more able to show forms in their entirety, and more conducive to the total legibility of maps. Unlike closely inscribed hachures, rationally spaced and numerically encoded contours left room for the clear inscription of place-names and other signs. In

Figure 16. Robert Dawson, fair-drawing of northern Wales, depicting part
of Caernarvonshire (1816–21); detail showing Snowdon. © British Library
Board. Reproduced by permission of the British Library.

Britain, Major General Sir James Carmichael-Smyth fueled an interest in legibility in an 1828 treatise claiming that the nation needed a system of "expressing the features of ground, in a clear and decided manner, by rules, and upon principle, so as to leave little to the taste, the imagination, or the fancy of the draftsman."[73] Although Carmichael-Smyth criticized the system of contouring, he believed that hachures were so inconsistently applied as to prevent the "inspector" of a map from forming "a decided idea as to the nature of the country." Ordnance Survey maps, he complained, "are like the ancient Egyptian hieroglyphics, conveying vague and undefined notions, instead of that positive and distinct information we require."[74] Whereas Carmichael-Smyth construed hachures as indecipherable foreign language, or cryptic code, their supporters in the 1850s construed them as expressive marks that need not be *read* at all: as direct representation of the country's variegated face.

After Carmichael-Smyth's treatise, matters began to change. The Survey experimented with the instrumental technique of contouring in Ireland, beginning 1839 or 1840, in England, in 1841, and in Scotland at the start of the survey in 1843. In 1851, at the Great Exhibition, it displayed a contour map of Lancashire on which numbers and strings of dotted lines denoting equivalent altitudes appeared where the public expected hill shading (Figure 17). What visitors to the exhibition saw challenged the protocols of British map viewing. Rather than see the form of the ground in hachures impressionistically patterned after actual slopes, they encountered rationally proportioned degrees of altitude; and between these lines of concentrically fixed points, they saw blank intervals.[75] Where the public expected a continuous surface of hachures showing the undulations of the ground—as in this map of northern England (Figure 18)—they got metric framework, as in the same portion of northern England marked by contours (Figure 19).[76]

The exhibition of Map 91 SE galvanized debate. Although the Ordnance Survey had completed the triangulation survey of England and Wales, it had not issued all of its topographical maps. How the land would be rendered on the completed series of maps, and whether Great Britain more largely would appear in stylistic uniformity, was thrown into question. The contour map shown at the Crystal Palace aroused enough concern for a Parliamentary Select Committee to enquire into "the respective merits of contours and hachures," superseding the issue of scale that it had initially intended to address.[77] In 1853, the Committee considered evidence from advocates of each method. When its proceedings stimulated further debate in the press, what might have been a technical issue became the subject of considerable controversy, as surveyors,

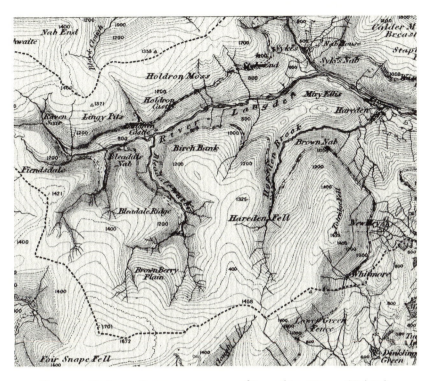

Figure 17. Ordnance Survey contour map of Lancashire, Map 91 SE (1851), detail.

journalists, and the public recognized that the way in which Britain represented itself to itself was at stake.

If, as General Roy of the Board of Ordnance believed, Britain's international standing depended upon a rigorous scientific triangulation resulting in the precise determination of longitude and latitude points and the accurate delineation of coasts, the portrayal of landscape and its undulations stirred other interests and brought competing criteria of value into the open. At the simplest level, the debate concerned the way in which public money would be spent; the defenders of hachuring, however, put liberal subjectivity and the coherence of Great Britain on the line. These, they asserted, could come only from "expressive" depiction of the country—from a mode of topographical "portraiture" that would bring British citizens into communion with the "face" of nature, as either the makers or viewers of unmeasured lines that were "faithful" to the particular forms of the country. Hachuring, its supporters reasoned, offered more "faithful

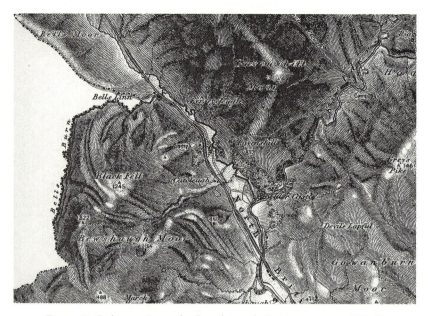

Figure 18. Ordnance Survey hachured map depicting area around Black
Fell. Sheet 108 SW, hill version (1868), detail.

representation" of the terrain than contouring. In a letter to Parliament, Lt.
Colonel Dawson (the son of surveyor and draftsman Robert Dawson) attacked
attributions of accuracy to contouring by contrasting its basis in mathematical
truth to hachuring's higher form of representational truth. Although the "principles" of the system of contouring are "theoretically and mathematically true,"
contouring only at widely spaced intervals of altitude, as it is practiced, misrep-
resents the land because its form between the lines is concealed.[78] Furthermore,
contour lines give only a weak impression of form: although mathematically
"accurate," they are not "expressive."[79] In an assemblage of contour lines on a
two-dimensional surface—and even in hachures sketched in the engraving office
from base grids of contour lines[80]—the map viewer will perceive merely "a flat
shade," not " 'literally and strikingly a correct representation of the physical relief,' " as its advocates claimed.[81]

Advocates of pictorialism pressed the claims of ordinary map users.
Against claims that contour lines " '[afford] the rigid accuracy the engineer
desires,' " Lt. Colonel Dawson asserted that "the forms" of the country "would
be better represented and more intelligibly to ordinary observers by the principles and practices of art."[82] Similarly, Robert Dawson asserted that

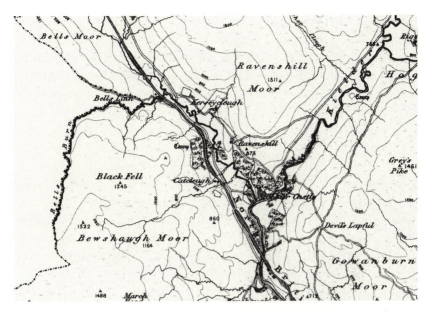

Figure 19. Ordnance Survey contour map depicting area around Black Fell.
Sheet 108 SW, outline version (1866), detail.

hill-shading gives "defined and accurate expression . . . expressively and immediately to the eye."[83] Hachures were construed as lines that communicate form
to the "'common eye'"—a value that Robert Dawson adopted from John
Ruskin, who had himself paid tribute to Wordsworth as "the keenest-eyed of
all modern poets for what is deep and essential in nature" while quoting lines
from *The Excursion*. The citation instances the revelation of nature's vital essence in the perception of a stem's shadow:

> "At the root
> Of that tall pine, the shadow of whose bare
> And slender stem, while here I sit at eve,
> Oft stretches tow'rds me, like a long straight path,
> Traced faintly in the greensward."[84]

The "eye demands natural drawing for natural subjects," Dawson asserted, and
for this reason, "neat and accurate delineation" should be combined with "pictural expression." By retracing nature's strikingly expressive lines, alive with
inner force, the topographer gratifies the eye and is able to "address the mind."[85]

To give cultural weight to their arguments against numerical modes of rendering relief, advocates of pictorialism aligned field sketching with the intertwined concepts of character and portraiture. Robert Dawson called the enterprise of hill delineation "full-face *pictural* representation" and "portraiture"; Lt. Colonel Dawson termed it "hill portraiture."[86] Essential to the rendering of topographical face was the scrutiny of surface particularities, which, Lt. Colonel Dawson insisted, "give distinctive character to different portions of the earth's surface."[87] If, in contrast, relief were depicted with contours, character-giving details would never appear. In a mountainous region contoured at 500-foot intervals, Lt. Colonel Dawson observes, "an abrupt slope of nearly 1,000 feet might pass altogether without notice in the map." The effect would rather be of a continuous, dull rise. To the hill sketcher, by contrast, "every separate feature, however small, is an object of special study, and the shading used to express it has reference to the inclination of its slopes, in comparison with those of other features in the limited field of the sketch sheet on which [the hill sketcher] works."[88] In stark contrast to the trigonometrical survey, what makes a map "faithful" is not its foundation in abstract truths but its commitment to the formal variations of particular locales.

Hachures based on hill sketching are thus expressive on two counts: insofar as they produce illusions of volume in the eyes of "ordinary observers" and insofar as they render the "characteristic expression" of terrain by fine attention to the details of the ground.[89] " 'Physiognomy,' " Robert Dawson claimed, " 'is no idle or doubtful science' " when it comes to terrain apprehension, and so he advocated close scrutiny of the bumps, ridges, and crevices of the land surface, the skillful representation of which requires practice and follows from "a power of figure-drawing (the human figure) with that truth and form of character which may mark, at least, the physical distinction of the natural races."[90] Where Dawson racialized the corporeality of the country in his defense of "*natural* figuration"[91] over and against numerical representation, one British officer gendered it in his vehement rejection of an early-century proposal to adopt continental methods of distributing hachures mathematically and varying their thickness according to a precise and rational schema (called the "scale of shade"): "It is a hopeless endeavour to restrict the graceful irregularities of nature to the absolute formalities of right lines and circles. . . . Even the colder scrutiny of the military draftsman will recognize the impossibility of cramping the variety of her swelling contours within the rigid scale of rectilinear features."[92] To the pictorialists, geometric and quantitative measure was not only misrepresentative but futile.

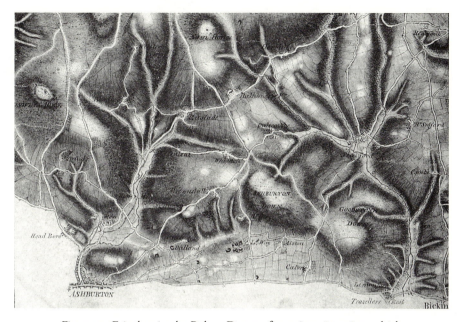

Figure 20. Fair-drawing by Robert Dawson from circa 1810–1820, which
shows the area around Ashburton, Devon, detail. © British Library Board.
Reproduced by permission of the British Library.

In the call for the reinstatement of hachuring on the public maps, pictorialists thus relied on tropes of body and face, implying that Britain could
distinguish itself from its European neighbors and vitalize itself as a nation
through topographical portraiture. Quoting Dr. Thomas Arnold's writings on
geography, Robert Dawson called for the depiction of the "'organic structure'"
of a "'country . . . the form of its skeleton, that is, its hills;—the magnitude
and course of its veins and arteries, that is its streams and rivers,' "[93] words that
aptly gloss a fair drawing of Dawson's from 1810–20, which shows the area
around Ashburton as translucent skin variably shaded and patterned by deeper
threads of organic tissue; rivers and roads that trace the edge of the downs are
like the veins of hands or leaves (Figure 20). The pictorial inscription of hills,
Robert Dawson insisted, gives "life and meaning, and harmony" to cartographic information that would appear "lifeless and confused" on a mere plan
outline of a country. To a "foundation" in trigonometrical technique, hachures
added a "finishing efficacy or grace," completing and fulfilling the meaning of
the national map.[94] Only pictorial treatment of the third dimension organized
an already mathematically plotted space into a nation; not the outline built up

from sets of trigonometrically fixed interior points but those base points over-
laid with pictorial accents made a national map throbbingly, distinctively
whole. Chiaroscuric effects, which alternately suggest on finished maps a fine
tissue of fingerprints and folds of skin (see also Figure 16), were necessary "ornament." Again quoting Ruskin, Robert Dawson claimed that "'no form
whatever can be known to the eye without its chiaroscuro,—that perfect and
harmonious unity of outline with light and shade by which the parts and projections of the body are explained to the eye.'"[95]

The rhetoric of pictorial relief insistently transferred attributes between
persons and land, subject and object, reflexively rooting "lively and intelligent"
representation of nation in the powers of the human mind to combine detailed
sketches of terrain into wholes.[96] Lt. Colonel Dawson stressed that hill drafting
was a two-stage process involving looking with the physical eye and then with
a disciplined imaginative eye. While a contoured topographic map involves
piecing together individual sheets of plotted elevations, a hachured map involves what the pictorialists claimed is a higher mental activity of imaginary
visual synthesis. In the two-stage process, first hill sketchers render the visible
details of local area ("characteristic expression"), then their collaborator the
draftsman "has to compass in his imagination the larger masses and assem-
blages of forms, assigning to individual features only their subordinate and
relative importance as parts of the general whole, and the tone only which
properly belongs to them in the scale of aerial perspective."[97] The hachured
map thus puts on display not only the "whole expression of forms," as Dawson
claimed, but also, by implication, "the mental apprehension" of the draftsman,
"his artistic judgment and skill," and his capacity for "the one whole imaginative view" that is required to produce the "*pictural effect* in maps."[98] By project-
ing himself above, he placed "'the whole character of a country before our
eyes.'"[99]

Thus the modern cartographic embrace of quantitative method was a
threat to portraiture and all it represented. Robert Dawson argued that impo-
sition of "rules and method" would restrict the "artistic judgment" of both
draftsman and engraver.[100] Further, Lt. Colonel Dawson asserted that an enlightened government would never adopt a purely mechanical process of topographic mapping. Only a textual look that is textural could faithfully represent
the country to its people, and a compelling textural look could come only from
human acts of looking at, not measuring, the ground. "'There is an expression
about all hill lines of nature, but it is not to be reduced to line and rule,'"
Robert Dawson stated, quoting Ruskin.[101]

Swayed by defenses of hachuring that invoked such cultural authorities—and Westmorland residents—as Ruskin and Thomas Arnold, in 1854 the Select Committee made the significant decision to give England and Wales a single textual look. They reinstated hachuring at the one-inch-to-one-mile scale—the scale at which south and central England and parts of Wales had been mapped since the 1790s, deciding that all of England and Wales would be represented pictorially, at the same scale, by hachures sketched in the field. What was called the Old Series (the one-inch maps of England and Wales) would be completed in stylistic uniformity, and the rest of Great Britain would likewise receive one-inch hachured maps. Thus the Committee empowered human imagination and judgment, for nonnumerical and noninstrumental hachuring had been made to support a form of unconstrained interpretive subjectivity, while also acknowledging the needs of "the more general and less instructed public."[102] To convey the variegated slopes of the countryside " 'literally and strikingly' " to the eye would enable "ordinary observers" to feel and know it. With their endorsement of hachures, Parliament construed the hills as a source of national significance and the topographical map as a popular medium of national feeling.

It was on behalf of the people that, in 1862, Matthew Arnold renewed the pressure on the Ordnance Survey to portray nature artistically for the " 'common eye.' "[103] Developing Dawson's Ruskinian aesthetic, Arnold wrote to the *London Review* complaining that although the Survey had in its new maps taken care to correct "obsolete nomenclature," "it had done nothing" "to amend their effaced shading." Scanning maps printed from worn-out copper-plates, Arnold asked: "where is the Cumnor hill country on the right bank of the Thames, as the original map gave it? Where is Bredon Hill, with all its beautiful staging from the plain to its summit? As they were in the Roman maps of Britain," he answers, "—absent."[104] Shading, Arnold continued, was the principal criterion of a good map: "A lover of maps would in general be only too happy if he could obtain the unworn sheet of thirty years ago, with all its imperfections of writing, in exchange for the indistinct catalogue of names which he now buys under the title of an Ordnance sheet. Names he can put in or correct for himself, but he cannot restore shading."[105] Shading not only gives definition to the nation but also measures cultural sophistication: "modern maps distinguish themselves from the ancient by the completeness and beauty of their shading."[106] Thus he concluded that the "Government's first and indispensable duty in the way of map-making is (we cannot repeat it too often), to provide a *good* map of its country, not to provide a cheap one.

The cheapness or dearness is a secondary consideration for it; the first consideration is excellence."[107] Whereas Roy and Cassini had based the goodness of a map on its trigonometrical frame, Arnold rested it on full, chiaroscuric representation of the surface of the ground—an expensive procedure but in his view both an essential aesthetic and informational element.[108]

If for the military-minded Carmichael-Smyth, hachures were "like the ancient Egyptian hieroglyphics, conveying vague and undefined notions,"[109] for Arnold they vitalized what would otherwise appear as an "indistinct catalogue of names." It was not orthography that made a map work but fields of lines that could be pursued by the eye: the "general public" of a "civilized European country" should be able to "trace in those finely graduated lines, mountain and valley, slope and plain, open ground and woodland, in all their endless variety."[110] Here Arnold was pressing for the picturing of slope in its subtlety and idiosyncrasy—exactly what contouring omits—and promoting a form of "civilized" visual experience that converted printed lines and names into the swells of a coherent country. (In Figures 18 and 19, notice the ridges circling the southwestern edge of Black Fell, visible on the left side of the hachured map and omitted on the contour map.)

Arnold's meditation on the viewer's engagement with the two-dimensional surface of the map suggests that in preserving shading he hoped to extend a sensory and imaginative mode of engagement with a country that exceeds the capacity of the mind to know it. The whole phrase, "trace in those finely graduated lines, mountain and valley, slope and plain . . . in all their endless variety," suggests not merely participatory creativity—as the viewer imagines printed lines into topographical fullness—but also unending discovery and wonder. No rational system of lines masters the variegated landscape or governs the movements of the eye,[111] which takes pleasure in freely pursuing the myriad of marks on the map and visualizing terrain organized, according to Dawson, by no rule other that the draftsman's "judgment." Hachures become the signs of an "enlightened Government" that not merely refrains from restricting but materially supports the interpretive and imaginative agency of its people.

Hachuring's association with empirical observation, imaginative apprehension, and an animate, organic country helps explain Arnold's anxiety about the "effaced shading" on Ordnance Survey maps. If hill shading fades, because of too-frequent impressing and poor preservation, so fades the "character" of the country and the traces of the visually acute and mentally agile landscape portraitists. Similarly, to replace lines that have "reference to the inclination of . . . slopes" with lines pictorialists consider "imaginary" for their nonreferentiality—that is, to replace hachures with contours—would alienate "ordinary observers" and preclude that felt sense of the nation as a vital whole. Hachures emerge as marks absolutely necessary to the cultural, not merely military and scientific, project of national cartography: they "convey" to the common eye what is "interesting and important in the knowledge of the ground" while also permitting what is "beautiful in a richly varied face of country [to] be beautifully portrayed."[112] The pictorialists thus allied the national map with portraiture and made topographical representation rhetorical by turning national cartography into a British vernacular: a visual language based in the abstract grammar of trigonometry but made fluently meaningful in its "natural" marks of inflection.

Arnold's obvious pleasure in tracing nature in the "finely graduated lines" on the map also speaks to the interests of personal and cultural memory—a desire for the map to revive and preserve past feelings. Wordsworth had linked the fine lines of nature's face with the revival of past joy in a scene of "unconscious intercourse / With the eternal Beauty." In the 1799 *Prelude*, by "Cumbria's rocky limits," the boy's

> eye has moved o'er three long leagues
> Of shining water, gathering, as it seemed,
> Through the wide surface of that field of light
> New pleasure, like a bee among the flowers.
>   (1799, I: 394–95, 400, 409–12)

The 1805 revision graduates that surface: the boy's "eye" now gathers pleasure as it moves "Through every hair-breadth of that field of light" (1805, I: 608), a refinement that works with the same passage's "lines / Of curling mist" to lineate the "common face of Nature" that "spake to [the boy] / Rememberable things" (1805, I: 592–93, 616–17). In "maturer seasons," Wordsworth would enjoy the fruit of that ranging gaze, when the "lineaments / Depicted on the brain" were called forth "To impregnate and to elevate the mind"—filling it with that original "joy" or with "obscure feelings representative / Of joys that were forgotten" (1805, I: 624, 629–30, 625, 635–36). Arnold's elegies on Wordsworth point to his memorial interest in the restoration of hill shading and his interest in generating a Wordsworthian feeling for nature on a national scale.

Hachure Nation

In endorsing hill portraiture, Arnold endorsed as a form of national experience
a visual and imaginative engagement with the printed face of nature. His intervention put Wordsworthian aesthetics into the public debate about Ordnance Survey mapping even more strongly than did Dawson's citation of
Ruskin. Arnold, of course, was not just an admirer of Wordsworth's verse but
from a young age had lived in the Lakes as the poet's neighbor. His position
on mapping reflects years of reading and hearing Wordsworth's poetry and
seeing the country through those texts, a double perspective manifest in his
elegies on Wordsworth.

In his "Memorial Verses" of April 1850, Arnold celebrated Wordsworth's
"healing power," his rejuvenation of benumbed Britons by returning them to
where they "lay at birth / On the cool flowery lap of earth":

> The hills were round us, and the breeze
> Went o'er the sun-lit fields again;
> Our foreheads felt the wind and rain.
> Our youth return'd; for there was shed
> On spirits that had long been dead,
> Spirits dried up and closely furl'd,
> The freshness of the early world. (51–57)[113]

Wordsworth's death marks a crisis in "Europe's latter hour": the elegy's echoes
of the Intimations Ode notwithstanding, "few or none" hear the voice of nature "right, now he is gone" or feel the maternal comfort of encircling "hills."
In a second elegy, "The Youth of Nature" (1852), Arnold deepens the association of Wordsworth with hill country as he lays him to rest "in the shadow" of
the very "mountains" that the poet had lived beside and animated in his verse.
Although the "spots which recall him survive, / For he lent a new life to these
hills" (13–14), Arnold doubts whether Britons are capable of feeling nature's
"joy" (61) without his mediation. In the voice of "Nature," Arnold calls for the
nation's attention:

> "Yourselves and your fellows ye know not; and me,
> The mateless, the one, will ye know?
> Will ye scan me, and read me, and tell

Of the thoughts that ferment in my breast,
My longing, my sadness, my joy?
Will ye claim for your great ones the gift
To have render'd the gleam of my skies,
To have echoed the moan of my seas,
Utter'd the voice of my hills?" (117–25)

With the "great" Wordsworth gone, Arnold's Nature challenges Britons to carry forward the work of truthful and vital representation. To know Nature requires that they "scan me, and read me, and tell"—that they rearticulate her forms, sounds, and surfaces in syntax, signs, and meters that embody her dynamic pulses and patterns. These rhythmic exhortations to "tell," or count, Nature's "thoughts" and feelings foreground Arnold's own triplets, his halving of elegiac hexameter into a dactylic trimeter that registers his sense of cultural decline but also prompts, in its forward swing, cultural revival. Not in the least rhetorical, his metrical questions spur the reader to aesthetic response: "Can thy pencil, O artist! restore / The figure, the bloom of thy love, / As she was in her morning of spring?" and "Can you make / With marble, with colour, with word, / What charm'd you in others re-live?" (110–12 and 107–9).

Arnold's public call for vital expression across media, after the loss of the poet who brought the "hills . . . round us," anticipates his call to the government to "restore [the] effaced shading" on the maps of England. If, in 1852, Arnold felt that Wordsworth gave "new life to these hills," and if the "spots which recall him survive," then by 1862 he fears that these hills and spots will be imperceptible on the national maps as their shading fades with official inertia—and if draftsmen and engravers fail to take care in their rendering of Cumberland's relief. Will the government give "new life to these hills," allowing its citizens to "scan" nature and trace themselves in the "finely graduated lines" of the most Wordsworthian parts of the country?

Arnold's elegies are steeped in Wordsworth's language; they echo him even as they debate his legacy. It is not surprising then that his discussion of the Ordnance Survey also derives from Wordsworth's engagement with the hills. Indeed, in arguing that national maps were vital precisely because, if beautifully delineated and shaded, they virtually connected the people who were not fortunate enough to live encircled by its hills, Arnold followed the agenda of *The Prelude*. Book VII shows how the impression of the northern hills and mountains upon the boy's mind had salutary effects after long intervals of time and in radical geographical circumstances (1805, I: 625), particularly amidst the disintegrating social, visual, and typographical mayhem of London. Against the many disorienting "marks" of London, its "meagre lines and colours, and the press / Of self-destroying, transitory things" (1805, VII: 739–40), the "mountain's outline and its steady form" (1805, VII: 723), impressed by habitual sight on Wordsworth's brain,

> Gives a pure grandeur; and its presence shapes
> The measure and the prospect of the soul
> To majesty; such virtue have the forms
> Perennial of the ancient hills; nor less,
> The changeful language of their countenances
> Gives movement to the thoughts, and multitude,
> With order and relation. (1805, VII: 724–30)

The mountain's "outline" and "steady form" function in the mind not as inert registers of past communion but as agents of cognitive and affective restoration. Sublime topographical impression fills Wordsworth with the feel of his own mental greatness, and by "shap[ing] / The measure and prospect of the soul / To majesty," stabilizes the poet. His reference to the patterning of light on the "ancient hills"—his seeing anew of the "changeful language of their countenances"—signals the reorganization of his feelings and reactivation of his personifying imagination: his capacity to perceive, with his mind's eye, a "face." Wordsworth thus offers an ideal of the national landscape that is perpetuated in arguments for a hachured map that gives "life and meaning, and harmony" by its imaginative faithfulness to characteristic expressions and total forms. If Wordsworth's urban memory of a mountainscape reestablishes dynamic order within the scene and self, Arnold, as it were, externalizes those internal impressions and literalizes them in printed maps. And, with the Dawsons, Arnold publicizes and politicizes their effects, extending to the British people a print-mediated communion with the nationalized "face" of nature. Nation would be consolidated not by the trigonometrical fixing of its form, the drawing of Roy's "Great Outlines," but by individual acts of scanning, reading, and telling, "Claim[ing] manifest kindred" (1805, II: 242) by the recognition of the country's "characteristic expressions."

INTERCHAPTER

Native Accents, British Ground

Changing Landscape in the Visual Display of Speech

In discussing the drive to make the countryside appear "literally and strikingly" to the ordinary eye, I compared hachured Ordnance Survey maps to a visual language. Since the 1980s, it has been common to think of the map as "a document presented in a visual language." "Like any ordinary verbal language," Martin J. S. Rudwick explains, the visual language of maps "embodies a complex set of tacit rules and conventions that have to be learned by practice" and that "imply the existence of a social community which tacitly accepts these rules and shares an understanding of these conventions."[1] Or, as J. B. Harley states, maps are "a class of rhetorical images . . . bound by rules which govern their codes and modes of social production, exchange, and use just as surely as any other discursive form."[2] Accordingly, in the last chapter I explored some of the historical, literary, and ideological determinants of Ordnance Survey topographical conventions and showed how Wordsworth's resistance to inscribing land and human life by "geometric rules" was memorialized in maps that aimed to portray an animate landscape to a social community of "ordinary observers." Like Wordsworth's "line," the hachure offers the possibility of imaginative engagement with the "face of Nature" and the feeling of social integration (Prelude, 1850, I: 587).

While scholars such as Rudwick and Harley introduced historicist methodology and ideological critique to the study of cartographic representation, they did not elaborate a parallel study of the "ordinary verbal language" that maps were said to resemble. Yet behind the idea of an accurate and expressive map that affiliates observers with the nation and each other lies the eighteenth-century conception of language as a medium of social communication involving visual and phonetic extralinguistic signals, including looks, gestures, tones, emphasis, and pause. From the 1750s, writers of the new dictionaries, practical grammars, prosodical essays, and books on the arts of reading and pronunciation stretched the capacities of the silent medium to display "intelligibly" their newfound understandings of the elements of written and oral communication.[3] Both prosodists and elocutionists established emphasis as the defining rhetorical feature of the English language, one that distinguished it from ancient and other modern European languages and, if well placed in the spoken sentence, promised to elevate British culture and affiliate its users around the globe. In addition to developing printed marks for this key oral mark of meaning and feeling, they created printed visualizations on the page— by means of diagrams, marks, staves, and other devices—to illustrate the relations among emphasis, quantity, pause, and other aspects of speech, and to identify patterns of tonal inflection that characterized the different forms of English spoken across the British Isles. Joshua Steele's and John Walker's graphical schemes show that before maps were ever conceived of as language, the English language was conceived of spatially and geographically—and configured in print in ways that reflected the increasingly large-scale mapping of Britain and the idealization of the English landscape. This spatialization of English had implications for poetry, too: in new scientific studies and guides to the speaking of the language—as in tour narratives and guidebooks, on maps and itineraries—lines of verse were conscripted to illustrate "natural," physical phenomena, shape perception, and direct performance.

In the next four chapters, I consider the implications for Wordsworth's poetry of the new accentual understandings and graphic displays of English. I begin, in Chapter 4, by historicizing "emphatic language" in the context of eighteenth- and nineteenth-century elocutionary and prosodic discourse and then consider Wordsworth's engagement of the matter during his turn to blank verse in the late 1790s. Of central concern are the rhetorical depictions of emphasis as animating force and key marker of Englishness and Wordsworth's developing conception of the "Poetic spirit" (Prelude, 1805, II: 276) within his autobiographical blank verse, which offers his poetic medium as an answer to the problem of spreading what Thomas Sheridan termed the "true natural mode of speech" around the globe in books.[4] In Chapter 5, I examine the production of the 1800 *Lyrical Ballads*, including the writing of new poems, the Preface, and notes, in light of Wordsworth's anxieties about publication and the larger cultural problem of encoding passion in print and communicating it to distant readers. I argue that Wordsworth exploited the spatio-temporal punctuation strategies of the elocutionists in his presentation of the poems and organization of the book, in an attempt to move readers not by "calling in the assistance of a lyrical and rapid Metre," as he wrote in the Note to "The Thorn" (LB 351), but by visually "mapping" local feeling in the book's slow measures and significant spaces.

The final chapters address the vexed issue of the inference of voice in Wordsworth's written and printed blank verse. Chapter 6 considers the role of punctuation in the development of *The Prelude*, in particular the role of the exclamation point as a mark of affectionate address. Manuscripts sent between the Wordsworth siblings and Coleridge from the start of their friendship reveal that punctuation was constitutive of the developing poem rather than a "superadded" (LB 750) afterthought or irregularly applied convention—despite some editorial claims to the contrary. Elision of the exclamation mark from contemporary editions of the thirteen-book poem produces a more meditative poet while also obscuring the history of troubled distance across which the poem was written and read, and which Coleridge's responding poem "To William Wordsworth" attempted to close. While the growth of *The Prelude* depended upon the absence of an intimate interlocutor, Coleridge's reply tries to overcome and compensate for the separation between the friends not so much by returning the remote reader to a present speaker but by renewing the gesture of exclamatory address.

Another interlocutor who had become a distant reader of Wordsworth's poetry was John Thelwall, who had discussed prosody and recited poetry with Wordsworth and Coleridge in the summer of 1797. As I discuss in Chapter 7, Thelwall responded to his reading of *The Excursion* by subjecting it to a strategy for returning voice to printed text through a system of prosodical marking. An extension of the pedagogical projects discussed here—schemes for visualizing the melodies and measures of speech—Thelwall's elocutionary analysis was also political critique: an act of physical annotation that made blank verse, and the "English rhythmus" it was supremely capable of mediating, available to a broader spectrum of readers and speakers, and thereby exposed the inherent social limitations of Wordsworth's nationalization and naturalization of the measure in the poem as well as its supporting religious ideologies.[5]

A few words about key contexts informing my arguments in the second half of the book. In the eighteenth century, the discourses of elocution and prosody were closely entwined; analyses and graphical displays of the stress-based nature of English—and the importance of emphasis in poetry and speech—served the instruction of eloquent and spiritually moving articulation as well as critique of neoclassical prosodic doctrine and ideologies of the poetic line. As I show in Chapter 7, Thelwall's project marks the radical physiologization, secularization, and democratization of these entwined discourses—and a radical extension of their interventions in print by a shifting of graphical agency to readers. Samuel Say, identified by Paul Fussell as one of the earliest "liberal" prosodists,[6] used simple diacritical marks to make apparent the accentual nature of English and the foundation of its "harmony" in its great "Variety in Numbers." Sound was integral to sense: it was by rhythmical variation that "all the Various Passions of the Human Soul, and all the Endless Variety of Ideas that pass thro' it" may be "sufficiently and strongly express'd."[7] This fundamental idea spurred Say's condemnation of the contractions and elisions favored by strict syllabists and practitioners of the rhyming couplet as well as his call for the printing of words in full and their pronunciation in a "Natural Voice"—one which gave "to every Sound it's [*sic*] proper Accent and Quantity of Time" (133). Say similarly called for the public representation of God's words in his "Remarks on the Scripture Sense of Preaching," which appeared in his 1745 *Poems on Several Occasions* with his essays "On the Harmony, Variety, and Power of Numbers, whether in Prose or Verse" and "On the Numbers of Paradise Lost." Here Say advised preachers to read aloud from the "*Holy Scriptures*" instead of merely sermonizing in order to enable parishioners to "hear God Himself speaking to [them] in his *own Words*"—just as the prophets of biblical history acted as public messengers of God by writing down "very plainly," posting up "where All might take Notice," or proclaiming aloud their visions.[8] Thus Say's own task of prosodic illustration, by which he made graphically apparent the "Secret Pow'r / Of Harmony" in *Paradise Lost*, conformed with his notion of preaching: "Where the Prophet seems to be commanded to hang up his Prophecy in some public Place, and to write it in such fair and legible Characters, that he that runs might yet be able to read it" (139, 172–73). Together the essays aligned accent and emphasis—"the very Sounds that give Life and Motion to the *English Iämbic*" (142)—with spiritual energy, and they charged printers, publishers, poets, and preachers with the responsibility of its representation.

What Fussell has characterized as a "gradually dawning perception" of the "accentual nature of the language"[9] across the eighteenth century was achieved by dramatic innovations in the figuration of speech, which the long career of Thomas Sheridan as a lecturer and writer on elocution aptly exemplifies. This Irish actor-manager, who was conscious of the need to erase provincialisms for success on the London stage, urged properly emphatic preaching, speaking, and reading—reading aloud from written text—in lectures across Britain between 1756 and 1761. Sheridan's treatment of "Pitch and Management of the Voice" demonstrates his early reliance on the verbal imagery to which his oral medium confined him, as he advised aspiring public speakers to estimate, before the event if possible, the "degree of loudness [pitch] . . . necessary to fill the room" and to "deliver all the more forcible, spirited, and impassioned parts of his discourse" with "this degree, or quantity of voice."[10] In a vivid visual analogy, he then compared "the undulation of sound" that issues from a well-pitched utterance in a well-constructed room "to the circles made in a smooth water by the gentle dropping in of a pebble, where all gradually increase in their circumference, and are regular in the figures." In a poorly constructed chamber, by contrast, the "sound is suddenly reverberated by an echo" and "rebounds like a tennis ball," a discord that Sheridan likened to the "motion of water when a stone is dashed violently into it, where all is irregular and confused." The speaker then must diminish the quantity of voice, and "energy"—or "emphasis"—he must "wholly give up."[11] In the packed lecture halls of Oxford, Cambridge, London, Edinburgh, Bath, and Belfast, Sheridan's visual metaphors would have demanded that listeners trace in their imaginations those regular "figures" of sound that they were simultaneously taking in with their ears, and then to picture the violent disruption of those circular undulations by redundant vocal energy.

In the first edition of his *Course of Lectures on Elocution* (1762), Sheridan had encouraged the modeling of speech on the most polite speakers in society—on living figures of eloquence—because he promoted a naturalness of style that he believed could best be achieved from observation and experience. Yet as phonological analyses and techniques of visual display became more sophisticated, print increasingly became the path to eloquence. In his two-volume *Lectures on the Art of Reading* (1775), Sheridan now "pointed out" the "verse-pauses, and some of the more remarkable emphases" in his graphic annotations of hundreds of lines of Milton's blank verse, devoting separate sections of his book to "Lessons of Practice in reciting Poetry"[12] and to "the Art of Reading" prose. When John Walker published his two-volume *Elements of Elocution* in 1781, he diagramed the "wave-like rising and falling of the voice, which constitutes the variety and harmony of speech," stating that it was unnecessary to enter the auditory range of polished speakers to achieve effective tonal modulation.[13] Walker's practical guides offered a communicative and pleasing voice, properly emphasized and tuned, without any living, oral instruction. In this, they owed much to the advances in the understanding and encoding of speech made by Joshua Steele, whose scientific approach to elocution and prosody resulted in the radical visual display of English speech: cross-sectional views of sentences that enabled the imagination of English as pervaded by upward and downward "slides"—and enabled the imagination of the countries of the British Isles as patterned by their prevailing tonal axis, or characteristic inflection.

In 1775 Steele illustrated the melodies and measures that pervade all English utterance—and verse and prose—by graphing parts of the church service, Shakespeare's and Milton's blank verse, and his own prosaic exposition on an expanded musical scale (Figure 21). Historians consider Steele's *Essay Towards Establishing the Melody and Measure of Speech To Be Expressed and Perpetuated by Peculiar Symbols* the "first attempt at a scientific account of English

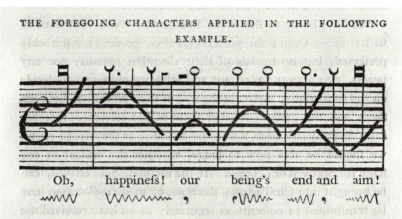

THE FOREGOING CHARACTERS APPLIED IN THE FOLLOWING EXAMPLE.

Oh,   happinefs!   our   being's   end and   aim!

In an attempt fo new in our age, as the reducing common fpeech to regular notes, it will not be expected that this firft

* I mean, by adopting thefe marks, to infinuate a conjecture; and, if I am right, will not the neceffity of *two spirits*, as well as two *accents*, be apparent?—Though very learned men have thought otherwife. In the ancient guttural languages, the forte was probably afpirated; that is, the found of the letter H was frequently thrown in: for a frequent energic afpiration is a principal caufe of the Irifh vicious tone in pronouncing Englifh; and that afpirated tone is derived from the original Irifh language, which, like all the other antient languages, is extremely guttural.

effay

Figure 21. Joshua Steele, *An Essay Towards Establishing the Melody and Measure of Speech* (London, 1775), 13.

intonation."[14] By "expressing on paper" (8) the inherent musicality of English utterance—its *"melody of modulation"* and *"rhythmus of quantity"* (2)—Steele hoped to improve both speech and writing and to persuade theater professionals to follow ancient Greek and Roman tradition by adding bass accompaniment to dramatic declamation. The elevation of the language arts would require the clarification of phonological analyses, however, which Steele believed were muddied because of "a want of terms and characters, sufficient to distinguish clearly the several properties or accidents belonging to language" (viii). Although he recruited and invented signs to mark five aspects of speech—accent, emphasis, quantity, pause, and force—the symbols that most excited Steele were those that marked his more accurate sense of "accent": the "imperceptible slides" (2) of ordinary speech. Attempting to differentiate and clarify the phonological aspects of speech, Steele gave to printed symbols the power of encoding sounds and demanded new, complex forms of interpretive engagement with the printed page.

Descriptively ambitious and radically experimental in its exploitation of print, Steele's essay principally worked to counter the widespread misunderstanding, reinforced most recently in Lord Monboddo's essay *On the Origin and Progress of Language*, that the English speaking voice is *"monotonous*, or confined like the *sound of a drum*, to exhibit no other changes than those of *loud* or *soft"*:[15] "Whilst almost every one perceives and admits singing to be performed by the ascent and descent of the voice through a variety of notes, as palpably and formally different from each other as the steps of a ladder; it seems, at first sight, somewhat extraordinary, that even men of science should not perceive the rapid slides of the voice, upwards and downwards, in common speech."[16] To Steele, speech, like song, is melodious. But where the singing voice *steps* perceptibly from note to note, the speaking voice *slides* imperceptibly, and rapidly, through them. To help his readers recognize this elusive melody, Steele appealed to the imperceptibility of topographical difference, remarking that in "travelling through a country, apparently level, how few people perceive the ascents and descents that would astonish them, if the man of art were to demonstrate them by his instrument, and to bring the sluggish stream to form a cascade! In like manner, when the modulation of the melody of speech shall be ripened into method by art, even the vulgar may be taught to know what the learned can now scarce comprehend" (5). On the verge of presenting his newly conceived method for notating the "ascents and descents" of speech on a musical staff, Steele thus invoked another "man of art": the surveyor or canal engineer who demonstrates gradient with his leveling "instrument" and exposes the landscape's undulations by modulating the flow of water through a lock or ladder of locks. A like feat can be accomplished, he asserts, by a skillful modulation of the vocal tones.

Michael Maittaire's English grammar of 1712 made no appeal to topography in its description of general discourse as being "uttered" in an "even and levelled voice."[17] Only at moments of interrogation and exclamation, admiration, or wonder—marked by the "Point of Interrogation" (?) and the "Wondering Point" (!)—did the voice rise and fall: "Here the Passion comes [into the discourse], sharper in the first, graver in the last, but vehement in both. The [interrogative] begins with an Acute accent, and then falls, with a quickness of the words, as being in haste to receive an answer to its Question: The [admirative] begins with a Grave, and raises itself gradually and slowly, as requiring more time to consider; since we are in no haste to be resolved about that, which is so wonderful to be past all answer and solution" (193). By 1775, however, when Steele challenged assumptions of the flatness of English utterance, he conceived of discourse as a "country, apparently level" but shot through with undulation.[18] The intervening years had seen developments in both topographical and phonological analyses. Sheridan's lectures had promoted the idea that tones mark the "infinite variety of emotions" attending operations of the mind, that they pervade discourse, and that they have a semantic function: "our very ideas can not be communicated, nor consequently our meaning understood, without the right use of tones; as many of our ideas are marked and distinguished from each other by tones, and not words."[19] William Cockin affirmed, "modulations of the voice, which indicate our passions and affections . . . more particularly point out the meaning of what we say."[20]

Also during this period, of course, natural historians and topographical artists had taken increasing interest in the forms of the countryside. More immediately germane to Steele's topographical analogy was the new rigor with which topographical mapping was being pursued and the rise in cultural prestige accorded accurate, scientific surveys. In 1759, sixteen years before Steele's essay, the Society of Arts had announced its series of prizes for the "best county maps," built upon original triangulations, and further awards for accurate determinations of the levels of navigable rivers, an initiative that fostered the work of canal building in Britain.[21] Several prize-winning county maps used the new French method of hachuring to illustrate orientation of slopes and steepness of the hills—a method, as discussed in the previous chapters, that did not quantify the heights of hills but traced their forms and faces. To the

Society of Arts and to the Royal Society Instituted for the Improvement of
Natural Knowledge, Steele co-dedicated his *Essay on the Melody and Measure
of Speech*, demonstrating a like concern with measuring and delineating "Natural" phenomena native to Britain—plotting the formal modulations of the
land.[22]

Although his analytic treats five properties of English utterance, Steele
designed his graphic illustrations to accommodate the subtle workings of "accent," which he defined as the slide within a syllable from a low note to a high
note (as in the acute "Oh") or from a high note to a low note (as in the grave
"and") (Figure 21). Tonal modulations do not merely occur at moments of
heightened passion ("Oh!" or "O!"), but throughout speech. They are "rapid"
and occur within single syllables—sometimes in two directions to form a cir-
cumflex, as in the turn from acute to grave in "our." Because modulations of
speech proceed not "by pointed degrees coinciding with the division of the
traditional musical scale, but by gradations that seem infinitely smaller," Steele
added quarter-tone interlineations to the five-lined scale.[23] By this significant
enhancement, Steele plainly demonstrated that "accent" (inflection) is an inherent element of utterance and that it is keyed to sense and feeling.

Steele's recognition of slide's ubiquity and significance prompted enlargement of scale. Enhancing the scale turned, as it were, a "sluggish stream" into
a "cascade," allowing "men of science" to see on the page what was aurally
elusive.[24] While the rigor of Steele's graphs and their intermixture of quantitative and qualitative codes reflect the *esprit géometrique* and aesthetic interests
of British topographical maps in the era of national cartography, it is the fact
that scale focused the matter of slope in both projects that highlights their
corresponding drives to demonstrate what was not fully apprehensible by the
senses. As cartographers were striving to make visible, in plan view, those formal relations and variations of ground unattainable by the eye, so too was
Steele striving to make visible—and virtually audible—the interacting dimensions of voice and the pivotal feature of slope that can "scarce" (5) be apprehended by the ear. In a further correspondence, Steele sought to illustrate not
absolute tones on the chromatico-diatonic scale but the relative steepness and
tilt of the slides in utterance—just as British cartographers, until the 1830s,
were more interested in determining slope and orientation of the uplands than
absolute heights.[25]

Steele's graphical displays, then, did not *level* English speech, prose, and
verse but rather show them to be equally pervaded by "*accent*," or "diversity of
tone" (11). Their likeness also hinged upon their organization in "emphatical

divisions," or cadences of equal time (11): "Every sentence in the language has a rhythmus peculiar to itself, whether prose or verse. That is, in the language of modern musicians, it is either in common time or triple time, videlicet, minuet time, or jigg time, or mixed" (28). Steele's graphical display of the "*rhythmus of quantity*"—the isochronous units of stress and unstress, or *thesis* and *arsis,* that course through speech, prose, poetry, and song—thus further democratized the language arts, and brought them closer to physiological process: "Our breathing, the beating of our pulse, and our movement in walking, make the division of time by pointed and regular *cadences*, familiar and natural to us" (20). Steele's graphical displays of the "emphatical" movements of English thus enabled such striking sociolinguistic claims as Wordsworth's that he writes a poetry in the *speech* of the common man, and that there is "no essential difference" between poetry and prose: the "same human blood circulates through the veins of them both" (LB 750).

Steele's diagrams made for particularly demanding reading. His plotting of the "To be or not to be" soliloquy expands the phonological dimensions of blank verse, marking *thesis* and *arsis* and tracing the upward and downward slides of syllables, in time, along the five-lined staff above (Figure 22). His iterations of a couplet from John Denham's "Cooper's Hill" likewise thicken poetic reading as they demonstrate, by showing emphasis, quantity, and rests, the "proper" measure of heroic lines into at least six temporally equivalent cadences rather than units of five feet: "Tho' | *deep,* | yet | *clear;* | tho' | *gen*tle, | *yet* not | *dull;* || *Strong,* | without | *rage;* | with | *out* o'er | *flow*ing | *full*"—and, in the voice of the revered actor David Garrick—who makes cameo appearances throughout elocutionary texts—"*Strong* with | *out* | *ra*ge; | with | *out* o'er | *flow*ing | *full* |" (31). First in a long tradition of the topographical genre, "Cooper's Hill" celebrates temperance in the English monarchy and poetic measures, a value the poem locates in the windings of the River Thames and in the rolling landscape. While it is tempting to read Steele's newly discovered "ascents and descents" (5) of voice in the poem's moralistic ranging across English "swells" and "wanton Vallies" and its positing of Windsor Castle on "an easie and unforc'd Ascent" to which "no stupendious Precipice denies / Access," it is John Walker's reprinting of the same couplet from "Cooper's Hill" in his 1781 *Elements of Elocution* that more closely aligns the ideas of an easily rising and falling English landscape and speech.[26]

Walker, an actor-turned-elocutionist and lexicographer, was more prescriptive regarding intonation. In his *Elements of Elocution*, which offered full, print instruction in standard English pronunciation without the aid of a

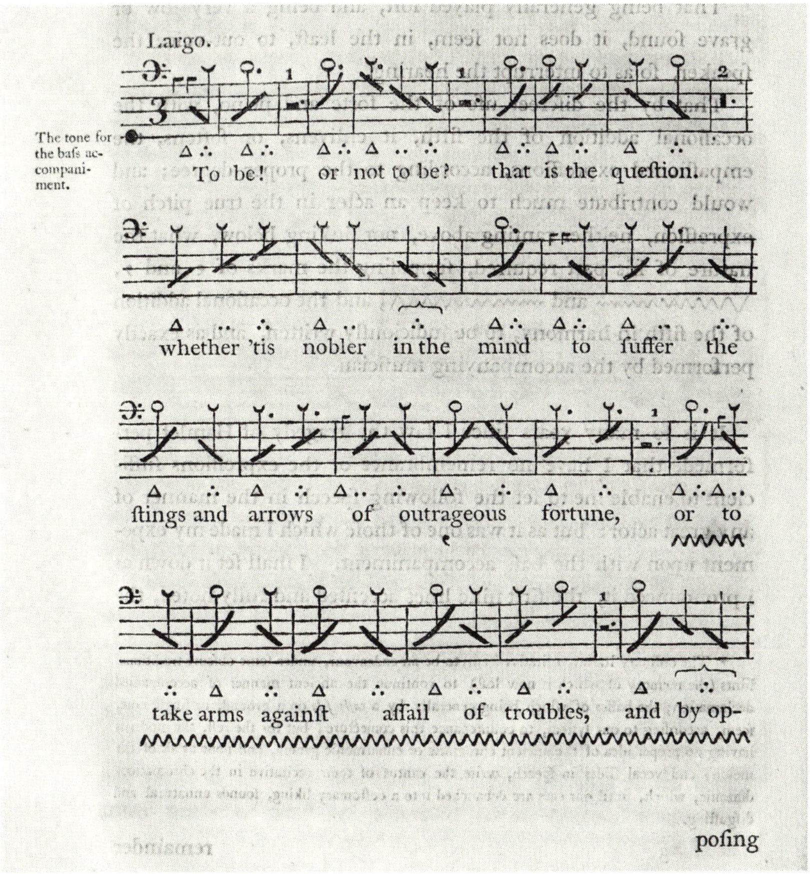

Figure 22. Joshua Steele, *An Essay Towards Establishing the Melody and Measure of Speech*, 40.

lecture, he seized upon Denham's moral lines to reinforce the alternating slides characteristic of what he considered the proper English voice. To standardize, Walker simplified: "Whatever other diversity of time, tone, or force, is added to speaking, it must necessarily be conveyed by these two slides" (I: 117), he asserted, or else "the true meaning of a sentence" will not be conveyed (I: 112). As I discuss in Chapter 4, Walker followed Sheridan in spreading the doctrine of emphasis and devised signs for marking in print the force that experts recognized as necessary to comprehension; but inflection, he insisted, was essential. A right "turn of voice"—a qualitative turn upward or downward—"finishes this emphatical word, or that member of a sentence where we pause" (I: 121).

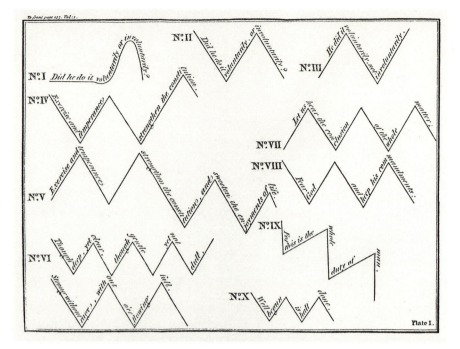

Figure 23. John Walker, *Elements of Elocution,* vol. I (London, 1781), Plate I.

Inflection becomes the master phonetic signal without which others fall short of their functions.

Walker's resolution of speech into essential "inflexions" takes the graphic form of a continuous line. Dispensing with Steele's scale, which functioned by degrees, and its detailing of tone, time, and emphasis, Walker figured utterance as sheer contour: upward and downward "turns" running through almost every word of a sentence but most perceptible at emphatic words and long pauses (Figure 23). A set of foldout plates offered aphorisms engraved to show their axial turns—the "great outlines of pronunciation" which "every ear, however unpractised, will naturally adopt in pronouncing them" (117)—including, on Plate I, "Well begun is half done" (No. X) and "Exercise and temperance strengthen the constitution, and sweeten the enjoyments of life" (No. V). No. VI graphed the perfectly alternating inflections of Denham's "Cooper's Hill" and thus aligned the court voice that rising professionals were to adopt with the vicissitudes of the Thames and the gentle "swells" and "Vallies" of the countryside. Thus Walker's graphs of rising and falling inflection strikingly belie the idea

of "*monotonous*" (Monboddo) and "even and level utterance" (Maittaire) as well
as the restriction of tonal modulation to moments of interrogation and admiration. As Walker stated, "by the elevation of voice [grammarians] impute" to
the notes of interrogation and admiration, "it is not unlikely that they mean the
pathos or energy by which we usually express passion or emotion, but which is,
by no means, inseparably connected with elevation of voice" (II: 324–35). His
"great outlines of pronunciation" (I: 117) represent English as a more broadly
prosodic system, in which accentual "slides" enable the semantic and affective
function of the emphases and pauses that structure sentences and that serve as
a ground for the qualitative, emotional tones that pervade utterance.

But these slides that Steele and Walker regarded as fundamental to communication were also indicative of nationality. Walker used the two "axes"—
the "most marking differences in reading and speaking"—to mark the outsiders
from the insiders, the rustics from the polite: "the Scotch pronounce the far
greater part of their words with the acute accent, or rising inflexion, and the
Irish as constantly make use of the grave accent, or falling inflexion, while
English observe pretty nearly a due mixture of each." Thus, he concluded, "the
Irish ought to habituate themselves to a more frequent use of the rising inflexion, and the Scotch to the falling, in order to acquire . . . the English accent"
(II: 14). Where Steele's differentiation of Irish, Scots, English, and Welsh patterns of "accent" attended descriptively to the larger British context, Walker's
diagrams of voice explicitly prescribed an English ideal of eloquence. More
readily consumable than Steele's complex illustrations, Walker's plates of plotted phrases could be referred to as "a kind of *data*" or set of "principles" on
which to mold all utterance (I: 118). They represent an ideological encoding,
and geographical standardization, of sound.[27]

Wordsworth's understanding of national and native accents developed in the
context of the graphic characterizations of accent and emphasis that elocutionists and prosodists made central to English speech, verse, and prose. But
whereas Steele and Walker, charting "Cooper's Hill," had implicitly linked
"emphatical divisions" and "inflexion" to the English landscape, nationalizing
its patterns of sound, Wordsworth explicitly naturalized these patterns.[28] This
naturalization is evident in an 1818–20 addition to Book X of *The Prelude* that
depicts his 1792 return from revolutionary France to the land of his birth. The
addition revises the 1805 text in the direction of a pointed patriotism defined
by the grounding of speech in native soil. In the process, it also naturalizes
blank verse, in print, as an English melody and measure.

In the 1805 text, Wordsworth returns to his "native Land, / (After a whole year's absence)" to find the discursive "air yet busy with the stir / Of a contention which had been rais'd up / Against the Traffickers in Negro Blood" (1805, X: 201–2, 203–5). In the later, revised text, the discursive air is neither political nor fractious but rather unified by feeling tones, the signature inflections of "native speech" (1850, X: 240).[29] Likewise, the land is represented as a rhythmical unity. The new passage begins by naturalizing the rhythms that inform cadence (from *cadere*, to fall) as it takes the measure of time spent away from England's shores, which are marked by the "Beat" of the waves upon them:

> Twice had the trees let fall
> Their leaves, as often Winter had put on
> His hoary crown, since I had seen the surge
> Beat against Albion's shore, since ear of mine
> Had caught the accents of my native speech
> Upon our native Country's sacred ground.
> A Patriot of the World, how could I glide
> Into communion with her sylvan shades,
> Erewhile my tuneful haunt? (1850, X: 236–44)

Recalling the temporally and topographically condensing, bird's-eye *cartospection* of his Alpine walk (Chapter 2),[30] Wordsworth here imagines a linguistic return flight, over the wild anapestic surges of the coast ("surge / Beat against Albion's shore"), to an aural pattern bodily recognized—the tones of "native speech" "caught" by the ear as if from the air but derived from, and grounded by, "our native Country's sacred ground." The regular iambic march of the pentameter (beginning at "Upon") signals Wordsworth's return to a stable literary tradition, to the measures of Shakespeare, Milton, and Cowper, which he not only domesticates but naturalizes—grounding their "accents" in a landscape of swells and valleys that unfolds across the rhythm of the line.

However, it is not just by the conceptual conjoining of meter and "ground" that Wordsworth naturalizes "accent"; he also does so by the way he displays the sentence across the lines. The different spatial locations in the circulation of accent between air and ground are allotted to different verse lines, creating a visual cross-section:

> Had caught the accents of my native speech
> Upon our native Country's sacred ground.

Whereas Steele graphs "accent"—the upward and downward "slides"—on a scale bar above a line plotting "emphatical divisions" (see Figure 20), Wordsworth uses the visual organization of blank verse on the page to figure the oral/aural relationship of "native speech" and "Country": tones float above but emerge from, and are heard as one stands upon, or walks across, the ground. He thus takes advantage of blank verse's horizontal and vertical array as lines upon the page to nationalize and naturalize it. The passage visually emphasizes the patterns of accent that are said to be native and patriotic; these patterns, in turn, naturalize and nationalize the visuality of the medium. Insofar as oral, aural, and visual are mutually reinforcing, Wordsworth's blank verse is aligned with the native accents and emphases it describes—and contrary to eighteenth-century critical orthodoxy, still represented as "tuneful," or poetic.

This prosodic and topographic configuration also implies an incarnation: "native," transferred from "speech" to "Country," invokes, via allusion to Milton, the nativity of Christ.[31] At least, such an implication accounts for the next adjective Wordsworth chooses, "sacred," which makes English "ground" the material form of the moving spirits that are English "accents." The young Wordsworth is shown to have been up in the air—ungrounded—in espousing a more universal language of feeling, marked by the strong divergence from the iambic in the next lines: "A Patriot of the World, how could I glide / Into communion with her sylvan shades?" Glide suggests a facile mobility—an all-too-easy way of entering a state that in the Anglican Church must be prefaced by an effortful act of repentance and entreaty. Gliding in, the young Wordsworth is figured as too migratory a bird; moreover, "sylvan shades" is an unspecific cliché, an example of the eighteenth-century poetic diction that Wordsworth denounced in the Preface to *Lyrical Ballads*. The lines thus criticize the internationalist idealism of the republican Wordsworth of 1792: to be a "Patriot of the World" appears an empty paradox, lacking affiliation to a speech that returns the speaker to a common birthplace. One's "native" country is a fatherland (from *patria/pater*); the "World" is not.

The 1818–20 addition crucially channels the narrative of developing poetic identity away from revolutionary engagement and international republicanism into the renewal of "native speech." Though not on the tip of his tongue, the "accents" of "native speech," or tones of native feeling, that unify the country are deeply interfused within his being (his English "ear" catches them) and will reassert themselves as he stands upon England's "ground" (as his strong iambic cadence suggests). "Tuneful haunt" also hints at the means of renewal, for it suggests that "native" "accents" are natural: birdsong, a kind of natural communication in melodic tones, em-placed in local woods, will retune his tongue and resonate in Wordsworth's future's verse (the "tuneful haunt" of the poem on the page).

The 1818–20 passage exhibits the reflexivity of a poet comfortable in his art. It offers a fairly seamless relationship between poetry, speech, feeling, nation, and nature—and uses that relationship to revise his youthful political self-portrait. When Wordsworth first began to articulate their relations in the blank verse of 1798, however, the project of self-portraiture had not yet begun—but would emerge, in part, from his explorations of the emphasis said, by Say, Sheridan, Steele, Walker, and also Hugh Blair and Thelwall, to animate English speech, prose, and poetry. It was in the context of their graphical displays and verbal elaborations of the significance of emphasis that Wordsworth negotiated the turn from a blank verse for the stage to a blank verse for the page.

Chapter 4

Eighteenth-Century Emphasis and Wordsworthian Ontopoetics

In 1800, Wordsworth authorized his emergence into print as the sole named author of *Lyrical Ballads* by means of a Preface in which he sought to justify the experimental poetry that had delighted some reviewers but baffled many others when it had been published anonymously in 1798. Whereas the first edition had proposed to test the adaptability of "the language of conversation in the middle and lower classes of society" to the "purposes of poetic pleasure" by means of poems that offered a "natural delineation of human passions, human characters, and human incidents" (LB 738–39), the second declared its bold purpose "to make the incidents of common life interesting by tracing in them . . . the primary laws of our nature: chiefly as far as regards the manner in which we associate ideas in a state of excitement" (LB 743). To achieve this object of universal, human import required that Wordsworth swap "poetic diction" for rural speech, a language that directly reflected the feelings. "Low and rustic life was generally chosen," Wordsworth explained, "because in that situation the essential passions of the heart find a better soil in which they can attain their maturity, are less under restraint, and speak a plainer and more emphatic language; because in that situation our elementary feelings exist in a state of greater simplicity and consequently may be more accurately contemplated and more forcibly communicated" (747, 743). Although Wordsworth derived this "plainer and more emphatic language" from "passions" rooted in the "soil" (743), in placing it at the center of his poetic project, he was adapting a contemporary discourse concerned with the forcible and feeling delivery of English printed on the page. Reflecting new philosophic and prosodic understandings of the language, and featuring blank verse prominently in its illustrations, the British elocutionary movement aimed to restore the "true natural mode of speech, . . . that of the emphatic kind," in order to give life to the dead letter of foundational English texts and to unify the disparate speakers of the language. Across Ireland, Scotland, Wales, and England's rural counties, far from the eloquence of London's "court-end," disagreeable dialects reigned, but with the dissemination of the emphatic creed, "no changes of note in the voice will be used, but what results from meaning and sentiment."[1] Wordsworth's "more emphatic language" spoken by the "passions" thus reflected British elocutionary ideals while inverting the movement's metropolitan bias.

While Wordsworth's poetics of speech has received much critical attention, the contemporary resonances of "emphatic language" have received less scrutiny. In his detailed commentary on the Preface, W. J. B. Owen treated the figure of the man "who gives vent" to "the basic, and permanently surviving passions of mankind" as implicitly consonant with Wordsworth's attempt to align his poetry with nature.[2] After Hans Aarsleff based Wordsworth's expressivist embrace of meter and figurative language on Condillac's theory of a primitive language of the passions, scholars more closely examined Wordsworth's engagement of continental natural-language theories and speculative histories of the origins of language.[3] For Alan Richardson, a "real language of men" that "forcibly" expresses "elementary feelings" and "passions" evokes Rousseau's and Herder's founding of human language in physical gestures and instinctual accents, cries, and tones, as well as their belief that contemporary languages maintain some these emotive features in their repertoires of articulation.[4] Noting the apparent contradiction of Wordsworth's call for a "more emphatic" and at the same time "plainer" language, given the Royal Society's sense of "plain" as free from the veils of metaphor, Richardson draws on Horne Tooke's notion of " 'plainer' language" as one that is simultaneously "more sensuously concrete and more metaphorical and emotive than the overly abstract and specialized sociolects of urban culture."[5] He concludes that Wordsworth's "plainer and more emphatic language" would be both rich with figures and punctuated by sounds, calls, and passionate interjections.

Of the significance of "emphatic language" within popular British print discourses and debates relatively little has been said, and yet the notebooks in which Wordsworth wrote after failing to bring *The Borderers* to the stage suggests the importance of the concept to his development as the writer of a blank verse for the page.[6] Between late January and early March 1798, Wordsworth drafted 1,300 lines toward *The Recluse or Views of Nature, Man, and Society*, the philosophical project consigned to him by Coleridge, who admired his friend's brief, nondramatic endeavor in the measure (EY 214).[7] As Wordsworth elaborated "The Ruined Cottage" in the notebooks by composing a brief history of the Pedlar, he made geographical and linguistic claims that strikingly anticipate those of the 1800 Preface. Having "wandered far" from his "native hills," he wrote, much had the Pedlar

> seen of men,
> Their manners, their enjoyments and pursuits,
> Their passions and their feelings, chiefly those
> Essential and eternal in the heart,
> Which 'mid the simpler forms of rural life
> Exist more simple in their elements
> And speak a plainer language. (MS B, 58–65)[8]

Notably absent from this sketch of rural speech is any reference to force; but within the same notebook, that same winter, Wordsworth also began drafting the passage on the Discharged Soldier—his first exploration of "emphatic language."[9] Though intended for his philosophical poem on nature, man, and society, the passage would be incorporated into his account of his own poetic development in *The Prelude*.[10] This is fitting, for the passage reflexively regards its status as metrical composition, as Celeste Langan has observed in a reading of the scene as part of Wordsworth's attempt to naturalize blank verse in *The Prelude* and to identify himself with the voice of nature.[11] But in 1798, I suggest, the passage shows no fully fledged identification with nature but rather an engagement with contemporary debates concerning the fitness of blank verse as a mode of turning English speech into poetic measures to be read on the page. Instead of writing blank verse for the stage, as he had in *The Borderers*, in the Discharged Soldier passage Wordsworth dramatized the production of blank verse along a "public way" (line 2, LB 277). Invoking measures of speech and space—elocution but also cartography and surveying—in his account of an encounter with a nearly lifeless body, he shaped his meter in self-conscious relation to contemporary systems of inscription, or ways of marking and measuring nature, man, and society. In doing so, he interrogated the passion and vitality of the nation and of his new medium.

A scene of encounter and quiet assessment that modulates into active walking and talking, the passage concerns the registration of bodily and mental energy and the power of poetry—or moving "discourse" (90)—to provide "restoration" (23). Coming upon "an uncouth shape," Wordsworth presents himself as one who marks and measures, translating the immobile presence into feet:

> I could mark him well,
> Myself unseen. [He was in stature tall,]
> A foot above man's common measure tall,
> And lank, and upright. (38, 40–43)

The phrase "common measure" alerts us to the line's uncommon measure. Not the alternating four- and three-beat lines of hymn meter (known as "common meter") but the five-beat blank verse ("A foot above") traditionally reserved for lofty themes is provocatively employed to measure out a physically lofty subject. Wordsworth notes the great length of the man's arms and legs, but the measure that most matters is his spiritual and emotional alienation from the human community, which is suggested by the "mile-stone" along the road:

> from behind
> A mile-stone propp'd him, and his figure seem'd
> Half-sitting, and half-standing. I could mark
> That he was clad in military garb,
> Though faded yet entire. His face was turn'd
> Towards the road, yet not as if he sought
> For any living object,—he appeared
> Forlorn and desolate a man cut off
> From all his kind, and more than half detached
> From his own nature. (51–59)

Traumatized by military service in the "tropic isles" (99), the soldier is a war victim whom Wordsworth signals by his physical alignment with the "mile-stone," a surveyor's marker on which a standard unit of distance was inscribed. An instrument of the Roman empire, turnpike roads, and also of the Ordnance Survey—the stone raises the specter of England's military subjugation of first Scotland and then India.[12] The soldier's dehumanized petrifaction—his shocking approximation to the stone counter—suggests that the imperial wars that consume the bodies and minds of soldiers begin and end on home turf—with a culture that wields science and technology to measure, control, and exploit terrain.

The taking of a man's vital signs is the central problem of the passage. As an arbitrary tool for national and imperial mensuration and inscription, the milestone is insufficiently subtle to gauge the soldier's enervated yet residual human vitality—as the repetition of "Half" suggests ("Half-sitting," "half-standing," "more than half detached"). What come to distinguish his "nature" (59) from the stone against which he is "propp'd" (52) are the vestigial traces of animation discoverable by an eighteenth-century grammar of signs different from cartography and surveying. Rather than organize human space by the quantitative signs and mathematical plottings of surveyors, elocutionary discourse rooted the communication of ideas and feelings, and thus the organization of human community, in the "natural" signs of the passions: looks, gestures, and tones. Attending to just these signals, the poet as he is figured in the scene notes the features of the soldier's face—

> [His visage, wasted though it seem'd, was large
> In feature, his cheeks sunken, and his mouth]
> Shewed ghastly in the moonlight . . . (49–51)

And he reads "gesture," noting that the soldier, after being hailed,

> with his lean and wasted arm
> In measured gesture lifted to his head,
> Returned [the poet's] salutation. (87–89)

He reads, as well, the phonetic sign of tone. As he walks the soldier to shelter, "measur[ing] back / The way" which they had separately come (109–10), he weighs the feeling in his voice, noting "a strange half-absence, and a tone / Of weakness and indifference" (141–42) that modulates, gradually, into "a reviving interest, / Till then unfelt" (167–68). The means of revival—a motivating motion or measured tread rather than a "propp'd" station—suggests Wordsworth's self-conscious interest in the animating effect of his own poetic measures and his acknowledgment of their dependence on speech intonations. Whereas the "Poet" of the Preface will be wary of the figures of speech typical of eighteenth-century verse, the personification of abstractions most particularly (LB 747), the "I" as figured in this passage activates the energies of actual speech, recalling a person from the brink of abstraction. The passage implies that by drawing out the soldier's vestigial emphases and by setting them to a blank verse that becomes, by this incorporation, a more "common measure," the poet may more broadly restore the ability to feel and to speak feelingly.

In presenting his meter in this way, here and in related writing toward *The Prelude*, Wordsworth was not only adapting an elocutionary discourse that he encountered at school, at university, and in conversation with his sister Dorothy, Coleridge, and John Thelwall, but was also bringing to that discourse a subject it failed to figure: the enervated speaker alienated from his own feelings. He was also offering a solution to one of the principal problems that discourse confronted: how to communicate "emphatic language" on the page. Constructed by writers on the language as critical to the communication of ideas and feelings, the moral animation of listeners, and the force and meaning of English literature—critical, that is, to Britain's national and cultural self-articulation—emphasis was nonetheless slippery. Variable in speech, unfixed in sentences, and without signs for its indication in writing, emphasis generated attempts to create typographic systems—diagrams, accents, and punctuations marks—that might overcome the incapacity of the printed word to represent emphatic speech and to spread the Englishness that it represented to the far reaches of a broadening empire. For Wordsworth, this variability became a virtue that he increasingly identified with the creative power of the poet as he shaped blank verse into a written medium of "emphatic language" and material structure for vital force or energy.

Classical Rhetoric and Elocutionary Discourse

A seventeenth-century English adjective, *emphatic* is defined in the first edition of Samuel Johnson's *Dictionary* (1755) as "forcible; strong; striking" ("In proper and *emphatick* terms thou didst paint the blazing comet's fiery tail"; "Where he endeavors to dissuade from carnivorous appetites, how *emphatical* is his reasoning!") and "striking the sight" ("It is commonly granted, that *emphatical* colours are light itself, modified by refractions"). But Johnson also defines *emphatic* as "appearing; seeming not real," providing no examples of its use. He drops this sense from the fourth edition of the work, in 1773, to make the term more determinately denote strikingly expressive language or representation.[13]

A parallel shift occurs in the sense of the noun *emphasis*. The *Oxford English Dictionary* notes the obsolescence after 1653 of "optical illusion, mere appearance" for *emphasis* ("Some think Comets . . . a meere Emphasis or apparency") while recording the formal "prominency, sharpness of contour" for *emphasis* beginning in the 1870s: "You never saw a Ben rising bolt upright with a more distinct emphasis"; "The bones which mark the features . . . lose their emphasis"; "An . . . oriel-window, the base of which is formed by a gradual emphasis of the brick wall."[14] The use of *emphasis* to denote physical prominency in things—landscape, anatomy, or architecture—follows from its use with respect to the English language, which in the eighteenth century was widely approached as a medium registering the processes of thought, rather than a logical system reflecting a divine or natural order, and requiring that the most significant words be made conspicuous.[15] Joseph Priestley recorded the following lesson in his 1761 *Rudiments of English Grammar*: "Q. Wherein consists the art of *Pronunciation?*" "A. In laying the *accent* upon the proper syllable of a word, and the *emphasis* upon the proper word of a sentence."[16] According to commentators, public speakers and readers had to mark for their listeners the signs, or as they were interchangeably called, the "marks" of their ideas.[17] As John Herries wrote in his 1773 *Elements of Speech*, "the species of utterance which conveys our sentiments in the most lively and forcible manner is the most perfect. Here comes in the use of emphasis. When a man is deeply engaged in any subject, he pronounces some words with a greater exertion, others, with lesser. His chief aim is to be clearly understood."[18]

Classical rhetoric had treated emphasis as a matter of diction. In the *Institutes of Oratory*, Quintilian describes emphasis as a trope (of the same class as metaphor, hyperbole, irony, and so on) that "intimates a deeper meaning than the words used actually express." He offers the Homeric example, "where Menelaus says, that the Greeks *descended* into the horse; for by that one word, he shows the vastness of the horse." "Virgil, too, when he says that the Cyclops *lay stretched through the cave*, measures the prodigious bulk of his body by the space of the ground that is occupied."[19] Heinrich Lausberg explains that the "word-trope" *emphasis* "is the use of a word of lesser semantic content in customary use (with a broader semantic range) to designate a greater (more precise) semantic content." He also helpfully characterizes *emphasis* as a "cryptic verbal imprecision whose more precise representational *voluntas* [purpose] is revealed by the (linguistic or situational) context and by means of *pronuntiatio* and thus has the effect of surprise."[20] In Quintilian's examples, the immensities of horse and Cyclops are indirectly, and thus powerfully, disclosed rather than directly stated or delineated.

Classical rhetoricians also understood emphasis as a figure of thought, one of the "general tactical processes" in oratory classed with digression, rhetorical question, and anticipation of objection.[21] According to Quintilian, in such devices of pleading "consists the life and energy of oratory; and, if they be taken from it, it is spiritless, and wants as it were a soul to animate its body."

The figure of emphasis is used "when some latent sense is to be elicited from some word or phrase,"[22] and thus, as Lausberg explains, the "phenomenon of emphasis" is precisely "the relation of the scant utterance to the presentient representation of a great content."[23] In this framework, it is appropriate, stylistically striking, or argumentatively expedient under certain conditions to intimate a greater, more precise, but unstated meaning.

These senses were carried into English tradition by early modern commentators, such as George Puttenham, who categorized emphasis (or "the Renforcer") as one of those verbal ornaments that had the quality of "*Energia* of *ergon*, because it wrought with a strong and vertuous operation." "One notable meane to affect the minde," he wrote, "is to inforce the sence of any thing by a word of more than ordinary efficacie, and nevertheless is not apparent, but as it were, secretly implyed."[24] Whereas Johnson's 1755 examples of "*emphatick* terms" and "reasoning" reflect the classical notion of extraordinarily efficacious words and thought, elocutionists transferred virtuous energy to the sounds of speech. The predominant sense of emphasis shifted from the classical verbal device of implication and suggestion; it now denoted that reinforcing vocal stress attached to a word to bring an idea into prominence and to impress it upon the minds of listeners. Writers on the English tongue now insisted that the basic comprehension of English sentences under ordinary conditions of communication required the forceful or energetic utterance of particular words.[25] As the prestige of classical rhetoric waned,[26] writers referred to the *laying of emphasis on* a word, and by the nineteenth century, in a continuing trend, it became possible to *emphasize*, even with the feet: "This philanthropic wish Miss Slowboy emphasized with various new raps and kicks at the door."[27]

The quirky, technical, and proto-psychological discourse of emphasis is fascinating for the glimpse it affords of early studies of the vernacular—especially for the understandings it conveys of social communication in an oratorical but increasingly print-centered age. In such an age, the prospect of reading aloud to friends "a copy of verses, a passage of a book, or news-paper" gives as much reason to polish the tongue, Sheridan claimed, as "sitting in parliament, . . . pleading at the bar, . . . appearing upon the stage, or in the pulpit."[28] Heeding John Locke's 1690 call to study "propriety of speech,"[29] commentators analyzed words and their arrangement, producing grammars, spellers, dictionaries, and pronouncing dictionaries for the instruction of children and adults in their native tongue, rather than the Latin that dominated education in the public schools. In 1712, Michael Maittaire turned the spotlight on the concept of vocal emphasis by identifying it as a spoken mark of punctuation. Credited with being the first commentator on English to recognize that "intonation was con-nected with emphasis," Maittaire advocated leaving "it to the judgment of the Reader to distinguish, what word carries the most sense in [a sentence], and ought therefore to be pronounced above the rest."[30] Accordingly, he advised against printing the "Emphatick and more Significant words" in italics and re-fused on philosophical grounds to capitalize the first-person singular.[31] From the beginning, then, the oral mark was construed as a problematic of print: essential to its vocal realization but resistant to encoding.

In lectures and guides to the art of reading, the device of emphasis (word stress) was closely paired with accent (syllable stress), but because accent was appropriate to a syllable notwithstanding the context—diverging only under rare and codifiable conditions—the correct location of that "smart percussion" could be tabulated in spellers and dictionaries.[32] Such was not the case with emphasis, which depended upon the "Design" of the maker of the individual sentence. Emphasis did not inhere in words. In some sentences a word should have it; in others, not. To complicate matters, a sentence could have any num-ber of emphatical words, all of which should be pronounced with "Stress or Force of Voice"—"for 'tis for the sake of that Word, or Words," Isaac Watts explained, that "the whole Sentence seems to be made."[33]

Emphasis mattered because of its newly realized semantic power. Whereas Locke had observed that the attachment of different ideas to the same words could hinder communication, Watts demonstrated in 1721 that the same ar-rangement of words had several potential senses—and thus that communica-tion could be hindered even if people attached the very same ideas to words. While insufficient stressing or an entire mis-stressing of a sentence could "con-ceal the Meaning of it from the Hearer," a proper placement of stress allowed "*the Force and Meaning*" of a sentence to "*best appear.*" "To make it appear of how great Importance it is to place the *Emphasis* aright," Watts wrote, "let us consider that the very Sense and Meaning of a Sentence is oftentimes very different according as the *Accent* or *Emphasis* is laid upon different Words."[34] Commentators never tired of demonstrating this new observation by cycling emphasis through the principal words in a sentence. Sheridan repeated it in his 1762 *Course of Lectures on Elocution* and Lindley Murray adopted Sheridan's example sentence in his 1795 *English Grammar*.[35] In its numerous reprintings throughout the next century, Murray's grammar sent forth the idea that "on whichever word we lay the emphasis . . . it strikes out a different sense, and opens a new subject of moving expostulation."[36]

Commentators' "habit" of demonstrating this "strikingly new idea,"

Murray Cohen remarks, reflects their "conception of language in terms of speakers and listeners and a commitment to the priority of the oral over the visual."[37] Yet, I suggest, they conceived of oral emphasis in highly visual ways. Where Locke claimed that with words, or the "*sensible signs of his* ideas *who uses them*," users "bring out their *ideas*, and lay them before the view of others,"[38] Sheridan claimed that the "true Meaning" of a sentence was believed to lie latent unless made to "appear" by vocal effect, recalling Johnson's second definition of *emphatic* as "striking the sight," a legacy of the ancient Greek *emphanés* (manifest, visible).[39] Emphasis, Sheridan says, brings forward "the true meaning,"[40] indicating not just a pictorial but also perspectival conception of communicative language. Watts warns that the omission of oral emphasis would not only "make a Sentence lose all its Force" but also cause the sentence to dissipate into a "meer catalogue of words"—just as a map without hill-shading, Arnold would warn, presents an "indistinct catalogue of names" rather than a country.[41] Emphasis was both integrative and activating, as Sheridan's personification made clear: "in speech, words are the body, pauses and stops give it shape and form, and distinguish the several parts of the body; but accent and emphasis, are the life, blood and soul, which put it in motion, and give it power to act."[42] Stress enlivens the body of speech, vividly manifesting meaning to and affecting a listener.

Emphasis became an increasingly popular concept in the new genre of practical and concise vernacular grammars. It also featured in the elocutionary lectures and manuals that sought to improve the fluency of speakers, from London to the provinces, and to prove that the "*English tongue* is as capable of all the Art and Elegancies of *Grammar* and *Rhetorick*, as *Greek* or *Latin*, or any other Language in the World."[43] This was not merely a matter of standardizing the pronunciation of words. Taking issue with Locke's neglect of "the signs of internal emotions," Sheridan and the elocutionists he inspired surveyed gesture, facial expression, and tone—those "other parts" of language "*absolutely necessary to the communication of what passes in our minds*, which can not possibly be done by mere words."[44] To Sheridan, tones were the "speech of nature" while facial expressions and gesture constituted nature's "hand-writing."[45] Unlike socially fashioned words—and the print in which they were packaged—these signs "cannot be mistaken" and do not mislead. But while gesture, facial expression, and tone conveyed the feelings that the sentence maker attaches to ideas, emphasis worked at the level both of the understanding and the passions. According to Sheridan, the complex form of emphasis superadded to force a change of tone. By the superaddition of a tonal mark of the "energies and affections of the mind" to force, not only is the "plain meaning" clearly pointed out but the "affections and passions are excited, the fancy agitated, and the attention of the hearer engaged."[46] An antecedent of Wordsworth's "plainer and more emphatic language," emphasis of this kind mediated both meaning and feeling.

To the liberal prosodist Samuel Say, the "ancient Poets" and Milton represented the most impressive of communicators.[47] But public readers of printed texts had to deploy energy consciously. As John Rice observed, conveying an author's intention to an audience involved determining in advance which words are to be emphasized and then "giv[ing] the Energy of the living Voice to the Precision of the dead Letter."[48] Thus in practice emphasis was often mismanaged, and the consequences were not merely technical. The disintegration of a sentence threatened political disaster in Parliament and cultural debilitation on the stage, where the genius of Shakespeare could be entirely obscured. In church—of particular concern to Sheridan—false emphasis was spiritually and morally dangerous, for it could lead the mind astray, while an "un-animated" "manner" could "lull the whole parish to sleep"—a combination that would pervert foundational English discourses and preclude the spiritual and social energies that emphatic discourse could summon and organize.[49]

Because a cold, unanimated tongue threatened the fabric of the sentence and the nation, Sheridan advised speakers preparing to recite or read aloud a text in public first to reflect where to lay the emphasis by supposing the sentiments their own. The speaker should then commit those words to memory, or better yet, "give a particular mark to those words . . . that whenever he reads he may be put in mind of laying a due stress on them."[50] This particular mark, inscribed by the reader on the printed page, would go some way to compensate for the lack of a typographical system for indicating emphasis in print. Regarding the mis-stressing of an Anglican verse about the acknowledgement of our "sins," he claims, "Had there been proper marks invented for emphasis, such gross errours could not have been committed."[51] The deficiency of print made for a moral error and, moreover, prevented the desired dissemination, within Britain and abroad, of the all-important concept on which the "Life" and merit of the English tongue were seen to depend.[52]

Marking the Oral Mark

Although Sheridan and fellow elocutionists are mostly remembered for help-ing the "newly affluent English middle class" to "acquire court speech in a se-ries of lessons," they should also be recognized for promoting what we might call a *cosmopolitongue*—a standard language divested of its regional affiliations that could be instructed across the British Isles and exported to continental Europe and "through all parts of the globe."[53] In their pan-Britain and global aspirations for a standard English tongue, the elocutionists questioned both how to mark the oral mark and the implications of doing so. Popularizing the English tongue first on the Continent, where it would face automatic contest with French and the more amorous Italian tongue, demanded making explicit its force to readers—something elocutionists believed could not be achieved by typographical manipulation alone, the usually prescribed italics or capitals. Further, italics and capitals are not "marks" by which readers could annotate their own texts; they are a change in the face of a character. "As there is no pointing out the very meaning of the words by reading, without a proper emphasis, it surely has been a great defect in the art of writing, that there have been no marks invented for so necessary a purpose" (78), Sheridan complained.

Elocutionists never fail to register their skepticism about systems of nota-tion; like the existing marks of punctuation, any new marks would be inferior to the "natural" signs and would be subject to the false assignment of tones by language instructors (about which more will be said in Chapter 5). Nonethe-less, both Sheridan and the equally prolific John Walker acknowledged the usefulness of the printed page to their purposes.[54] But to spread emphatic language, from "the court end" of London to the counties and abroad would require a restructuring of English pedagogy and an expansion of "the visible marks offered to the eye."[55]

The highly visual way the elocutionists figure the work of emphatic force focuses their concerns about the necessity of the printed page to their objective of spreading the emphatical language. Explaining that the more important the idea to the speaking mind, the more forcefully the idea will be uttered, Walker asserts that a speaker who varies the "degree of force" in a sentence supplies "that light and shade, which is necessary to form a strong picture of the thought."[56] "Loose cursory" speakers, he similarly claims, who "want a firmness of pronunciation are like those painters who draw the muscular exertions of the human body without any knowledge of anatomy."[57] This sister-arts analogy derives from the classical rhetoricians' figuration of the figures as bodily postures and of tonal distinctions as a means of their promotion: "just as painters who use but one colour nevertheless make some parts of their pictures appear more prominent, and others more retiring, without which difference they could not even have given due forms to the limbs of their figures."[58] Modern elocutionist John Herries figures the formalizing and animating power of emphasis as face making. It

> is to speech what colours are to a portrait. When the painter would imitate nature with the most success, he properly disposes the light and shade. The lustre darts from the eye, the cheeks receive their bloom, and every feature is so strongly marked, that the whole piece seems almost to start to life. But if he should daub the whole countenance over with one dull undistinguishing colour, the just proportion would be entirely lost, and every trace of nature erased. In like manner, if every word in a sentence is uttered with an uniform energy of voice, the meaning and spirit of the whole must be destroyed.[59]

Variations in energy make sentences meaningful and compelling; features coalesce into face. References to color and chiaroscuro imply that conventional signs, and black-on-white typography, can only fall short of the task of displaying and disseminating an emphatic English that functions by degrees. Sheridan's personification of speech suggests as much ("in speech, words are the body"), emerging at the moment he complains that "the very life and soul of speech"—accent and emphasis—"consists in what is utterly unnoticed in writing."[60] Elocutionists most vividly figure emphasis as an animating force when they register the lack of "visible marks" to designate it.[61] To circulate the globe, "the true natural mode of speech" requires a living human speaker, but typographical marks will have to do.

Marking systems grew more complex as the century progressed. In his 1775 *Lectures on the Art of Reading*, Sheridan employed an instructional scheme that pointed out the "emphatic words" with "the grave accent of the Greek [`]" and indicated lengthening pauses with single, double, and triple acute accents. Two horizontal lines (=) signaled "a pause longer than any belonging to the usual stops."[62] Hundreds of pages of the church service, annotated for the use of clergymen, and of Sheridan's own "DISCOURSES, *Properly marked, to serve as Lessons to practice on in the Art of Reading,*" enforced the cooperation of emphasis and pause in presenting ideas clearly and forcefully to the mind:

> Now there are twò sorts of language in use" . . . The òne´ mani-
> fested by the li`ving vòice" the other´ by the dea`d letter´" The one´
> Divìne´ given by God himse`lf" the other´ hùman´ the invention of
> m`an ´"[63]

Where these annotations attempted to disseminate in a printed book the "li`ving vòice" of the lecturer himself, his "Lessons of Practice in reciting Poetry" illustrated the speeches of *Paradise Lost* and the sounds of its narratorial blank verse, limning the "verse-pauses" and "some of the more remarkable emphases" to aid in the expressive realization of English heroic poetry:

>   IS thi`s the region" thi`s the soil´ the clime"
> (Said then the lost Arch-angel)" thi`s the seat
> That we must change for Heaven?"[64]

Sheridan's 1775 *Lectures* thus shows a late-career confidence in print: as if subtle graphical analysis, tailored to his theoretical and practical purposes, could meet his populist vision of diffusing "the emphatic language" through "all ranks of people, in whatever part of the globe English shall be taught" (I: 146, 148).

Walker took a different tack. In his 1785 *Rhetorical Grammar* he countered the imprecision of italics with a "notation" to clarify the "several forces of speaking sounds" (111). This involved reformatting English sentences to display their essential architecture of three principal degrees of force: unaccented, accented, and emphatic. He thus re-presented a passage of rhyming couplets from Pope:

> Britons, attend ! beworth likethis approv'd,
> Andshow youhavethevirtue tobemov'd.
> . . . .
> Suchplays alone shouldplease a*British*ear,
> AsCato's*self*hadnot disdain'd tohear.

In imitation of the logic of word formation, a clustering of unaccented syllables around the accented syllable in a word, Walker visibly joined the unaccented words in a phrase to the "accented," more significant, word that integrated the phrase—such as "virtue" in "youhavethevirtue." He reserved italics for the "emphatic" words in a sentence that were to be uttered with the highest degree of stress, as in, "a*British*ear" and "AsCato's*self*"[65]—demonstrating, in the process, that "emphatic" words need not be rhyming.

While "intended to heighten communication," as Andrew Elfenbein has observed, the visual techniques of Walker and Sheridan "defamiliarize English into strange new forms." But if their schemes manifest print's "control over elocutionary voice," as Elfenbein suggests,[66] Sheridan and Walker were the first to acknowledge the resistance of emphasis to codification, typographic display, and vocal reproduction. While maintaining confidence in the heuristic function of his typographic scheme, Walker admitted that his complex "notation" could never encode the precise distribution of force across a sentence; the degree of force with which words should be uttered depended upon "the degree of passion," which in itself could not be quantified. Further, this "mode of printing" was entirely unsuited to elocutionary use: it would only "perplex and retard" students.[67] Walker instead proposed the practical strategy of marking the inflection of all significant ("accented") words in a passage or, better yet, simply the most significant ("emphatic")—the method he uses to illustrate blank-verse passages by Young and Milton. The rare mark of the upward or downward "slide" would illuminate the whole, but the communication of this principle required pages upon pages of exposition.[68]

According to theorists of the so-called "natural school," the proper use of emphasis could never be achieved by the application of abstract rules; expressive variations of stress, tone, and quantity depended upon sense and feeling and so required a "due degree of attention and practice" and the cultivation of the ear.[69] Sheridan's hundreds of pages of typographical and discursive analysis attest to the irreducibility of English pronunciation to rule and demonstrate his hopes for print as a technology of both illustration and liberation—a liberation of the body and soul of the English language from the tyrannical application of Roman (quantitative) prosodic strictures, the "false ornaments" of French rhyme, and the "squeezing stays" of its numerically minded syllabic measure (II: 383). Sheridan's analysis of *Paradise Lost* in *Lectures on the Art of Reading* reveals, and patriotically revels in, English heroic poetry's expressive variety of feet ("eight species" [II: 68]) and unrestricted placement of emphasis and caesura:

Let us leave to the sallow French their rouge and ceruse, but let
the British red and white appear in their genuine lustre, as laid on

by Nature's own pencil. Let them torture the body into a fantastic shape, or conceal crookedness under an armour of steel; let them cover puny limbs, and a mincing gait, under the wide circumference of a hoop; but let the easy mien, the comely stature, the fine proportioned limbs decently revealed, and the unrestrained majesty of motion in the British muse, be displayed to sight in their native charms. (II: 384)

Sheridan's print is both self-remarking and self-effacing, aligning itself with "Nature's own pencil" in the remediation and remobilization of the "British muse."

William Enfield addressed the underlying paradox of the elocutionary project's reliance upon "artificial helps": "particular characters or marks," he professed, "will always be found" to "mislead instead of [assist] the reader, by not leaving him at full liberty to follow his own understanding and feelings."[70] In *The Art of Delivering Language* (1775), Cockin directly criticized the encoding of emphasis and the instruction of readers in pronunciation, arguing that *emphasis of sense*, as the "work of *nature*," falls "spontaneously upon its proper place" and that the finer distinctions pertaining to the ornamental *emphasis of force* (which gave grace to speech) were the effect solely of social refinement.[71] Nonetheless, just as he had used graphic means to represent landscape—as editor he introduced a map to West's *Guide to the Lakes* (see Chapter 1)—Cockin chose to italicize instances of ornamental emphasis throughout his handbook. His graphic interface thus offered glimpses of a soundscape that it could not reproduce. The subtleties of ornamental emphasis could be learned only by living in the city—a "more favourable soil for the cultivation of the arts" than the "depths of rural rusticity"—and by a polishing of the "taste . . . with a more extensive intercourse with the world."[72] Wordsworth, who would ultimately derive emphatic language from real, not figurative, soil, first construed blank verse as a technology for its dissemination in print while also challenging the patriotism of elocution's personification of speech.

"Feeling It No Longer": The Discharged Soldier

In 1798, Wordsworth was living in rural rusticity, close to Coleridge in Nether Stowey. It was here that Dorothy began the Alfoxden journal and here, responding to that journal, that William explored a "plainer and more emphatic" blank verse. "Perhaps the earliest surviving draft" for the Discharged Soldier passage appears on the last page of the Alfoxden Notebook (DC MS 14)—the first page when used in reverse, as the Wordsworths did. At the top are eight lines in Wordsworth's hand that he may have copied from the first entry of Dorothy's journal (dated January 20, 1798), may have composed himself, or may have co-written with his sister:[73]

> the green paths down the hill sides
> are channels for streams—the young
> wheat is streaked by silver lines of
> water running between the ridges—
> the sheep are are gathered together
>   wet
> on the slopes—after the ~~long~~ dark days
> the country seems more populous it
> peoples itself in the sunbeams. —
>   (DC MS 14, 50v, LB 503)

The lines for the Discharged Soldier passage below certainly drew from Dorothy's entries for January 24 and 27. These describe a "sea of a sober grey, streaked by the deeper grey clouds"; the "half dead sound of the near sheep-bell"; and the "strange, uncouth howl" of a local dog, which "howls at the murmur of the village stream."[74] William's verses take up not only her words but also her patterns of stress—his "Howls to the murmur of the village stream" reveals a haunting pentameter within her prose that veers psychologically away from his openly iambic opening line ("Without a touch of melancholy thought"). Similarly, her "half dead sound" of the "near sheep-bell" is echoed in his "dead grey light," "sober dead grey light," and "dead shade" (LB 503). These monosyllabic recombinations link monotonous sound to monochromatic light, drawing out the eeriness of nothing being "strongly marked." "The sky is flat," she continues, "unmarked by distances."[75] By contrast, the lines at the top of the notebook page offer images of marked contrast and vitality: the "green paths down the hill sides" and the "silver lines of / water" streaking the wheat make the country seem "populous"; the country "peoples itself in the sunbeams" (LB 503). Against those unmarked expanses and flatlining rhythms ("dead grey light"), the energetic shimmer of pastoral "paths" and agricultural "lines" gives the slopes living form.

That William and Dorothy were thinking about the animation effects of visual and verbal emphasis is also suggested on the notebook's next page, on which Dorothy copied a footnote from Richard Payne Knight's *The Progress of Civil Society*:

> [Dr.] Johnson observed, that in blank verse, the language suffered more distortion to keep it out of prose than any inconvenience or limitation to be apprehended from the shackles & circumspection of rhyme. Boswell's life Vol. 1st. p. 584
>
> This kind of distortion is the worst fault that poetry can have; for if once the natural order and connection of the words is broken, & the idiom of the language violated, the lines appear manufactured, & lose all that character of enthusiasm & inspiration, without which they become cold & vapid, how sublime soever the ideas & images may be which they express.[76]

Payne Knight's remarks concern the integrity of the idiom: the effort to make audible the faint "musick of the English heroick line" distorts the patterns of stress used by living speakers and erodes the syntax of genuine feeling.[77] The citation reflects the new cultural importance of emphasis and the contrary pressures on blank verse it effected. Blank verse was, at once, supposed to sound like "poetry" and like idiomatic language: it was to seem aesthetically patterned—with marked iambs and medial caesuras—so that listeners could easily detect where lines began and ended; it was also to sound "natural," coursing with feeling inflections—like "green paths down the hill sides" channeling the "streams," like "silver lines of water running between the ridges." Resetting "sublime . . . ideas & images" into regular iambic order deprived them of force and feeling—thus, on the first page of the Discharged Soldier drafts, Wordsworth's markedly *un*-iambic "sober dead grey light" and the anapestic tilt of "Howls to the murmur of the village stream."

Perhaps the Wordsworths copied Payne Knight into their notebook because they took it as a challenge and a spur. How to write blank verse without producing "measured prose," turning sublimity into mechanism and violating the natural idioms and cadences of common speech? The couplets from *The Progress of Civil Society* that Payne Knight glossed with his footnote lay out the challenge more pointedly by focusing the crucial issue of blank verse on the page:

> Oft, too, the rhyme, with neat and pointed grace,
> Fixes attention to its proper place;

Directs with truer aim the shafts of wit,
And marks, with emphasis, the spot to hit;
And guides the gleams of fancy to the heart.
        But cold, in blank and unmark'd metre, flows
The turbid current of our measured prose;
Unless when Shakespeare's genius breathes it fires,
And the brisk bustle of the stage inspires;—
When glowing passions melt it into ease,
And strong expression gives it power to please.
        (III: 525–35)[78]

Unmarked by rhyme, the "cold," barely perceptible "metre" poses a problem of meaning and feeling, but "measured prose" is given definitive form and motion when inflamed by the breath of "genius" and embodied by dynamic performers on the stage. If it is their "glowing passions" and "strong expression" that animate the meter, how to write a nondramatic blank verse about speakers who have no energy to give? The question for Wordsworth, the drafts suggest, was not only aesthetic but political. For where Payne Knight warns of the distorting and deadening effects on the language by nondramatic forms of the meter, Wordsworth dramatizes the distorting and deadening effects on a *speaker* by an imperial system of order. He addresses the depletion of force in a human body and soul and explores the restorative possibilities of his written medium.

A reflexively critical response to Payne Knight's aesthetic injunctions, the Discharged Soldier passage realizes the tropes of body and soul that pervade eighteenth-century prosodic and elocutionary discourse. Take Hugh Blair's *Lectures on Rhetoric and Belles Lettres*, which Wordsworth read while he was drafting the passage. Blair's chapter on "Pronunciation, or Delivery" recapitulated the emphatic creed: "On the right management of the Emphasis depend the whole life and spirit of every Discourse. If no Emphasis be placed on any words, not only is Discourse rendered heavy and lifeless, but the meaning left often ambiguous."[79]

The idea—and phrasing—would have been familiar. An admirer of Quintilian, Wordsworth knew emphasis as a stylistic effect of economical utterance and as a figure of thought in which the passion in the words forces us to understand some latent idea.[80] He knew, too, of Quintilian's attribution of the "life and energy," "spirit," and "soul" of oratory to the tropes and figures.[81] Wordsworth was also likely familiar with elocutionary conceptions of emphasis from William Enfield's *The Speaker* (1761), in which he and Dorothy read, and from James Burgh's *The Art of Speaking* (1762), a set book at Hawkshead grammar school that set Sheridan's analogy as its epigraph: "in Speech, Words are the Body . . . but Accent and Emphasis are the Life, Blood, and Soul, which put it in Motion, and give it Power to act."[82]

Eighteenth-century elocution's investment in the life of the language— not the speaker—would soon be challenged by the radical orator and poet John Thelwall, who met Wordsworth in the summer of 1797 at Alfoxden and continued there a discussion about metrical emphasis that he had conducted in correspondence with Coleridge. Where the arts of reading construed the reader generically, as a body and mouthpiece of the text, and were concerned, above all, with the "life" of English, Thelwall's science of elocution would address the psychological and physiological conditions of individual speakers. Wordsworth's drafts of the Discharged Soldier passage register and contribute to this disciplinary turn. Here Wordsworth explored discourse *in extremis*, at the limits of its "life," in the body of a contemporary human type and dramatized the putting of this body "into Motion" and returning to him of the "Power to act"—not by instructing him in the art of emphasis but by resetting his speech cadences to physiological motion and by incorporating his speech into his own poetic measures.

The passage is organized around a contrast between the vital, self-enjoying subject and the wasted body. As Wordsworth proceeds "step by step" (36, LB 277) along the "silent road" (21), his "body from the stillness drinking in / A restoration," "beauteous pictures" rise from his "soul" "in harmonious imagery" (22– 23, 28–29). His "consciousness of animal delight" and sense of "self-possession felt in every pause / And every gentle movement of [his] frame" (33–35) suggest his embodiment of organic poetic form.[83] More precisely, the portrait recalls Sheridan's articulation of the "body" of English numbers (II: 269) into pauses and feet—"They are called feet," he explained, "because it is by their aid that the voice as it were steps along through the verse in a measured pace" (II: 35)— as well as Sheridan's identification of "emphasis" as the "principle, which, like a soul, actuates and regulates all the parts," producing vivid pictures from sequences of words (II: 269). Wordsworth's manifest "freedom to slacken his pace"[84] also recalls Sheridan's analysis of *Paradise Lost*, where his personification of unrestricted poetic motion achieves patriotic heights ("let the easy mien, the comely stature, the fine proportioned limbs decently revealed, and the unrestrained majesty of motion in the British muse, be displayed to sight in their native charms" [II: 384]). Wordsworth writes no essay on "English Numbers," no *Lectures on the Art of Reading*, and he employs no special diacritical marks. But his formally self-referential heroics, I suggest, enact a historically particular form of self-annotation and critique. Incorporating an account of their own pedestrian production, they keep readers in the company of flesh and blood, discovering and accommodating a "British muse" with a "mien" far from "easy," a "stature" far from "comely," and "limbs" less than proportioned.

Wordsworth measures and "mark[s] him well" (40), attempting to assim-ilate the man to the known and to poetry:

> His legs were long,
> So long and shapeless that I looked at them
> Forgetful of the body they sustained.
> His arms were long and lean; his hands were bare;
> [His visage, wasted though it seem'd, was large
> In feature, his cheeks sunken, and his mouth]
> Shewed ghastly in the moonlight . . . (45–51)

While the allusion to Milton's allegory of Death ("uncouth shape" [38]) or to Dante's shade of Virgil give the soldier a tinge of the uncanny and sublime,[85] the parts fail to coalesce into any physical or poetic whole. Limbs, hands, and features, with no apparent body, he is a figure of disintegration—like a sen-tence without emphasis, drained of "its Force," as Isaac Watts warned, and resolved into a "catalogue of words."[86] Long arms and legs, "long, / So long and shapeless," show extension without organization, as do the "murmuring sounds, as if of pain / Or of uneasy thought" that "issued" "From his lips" (69–70, 68). In the absence of organizing accent, words have dissolved into indistinguishable sounds, leaking from the "mouth" (50)—a stark contrast to Wordsworth's holistic "self-possession" and mental theater of "harmonious im-agery." His mode of interpreting the indistinguishable sounds, of discovering a life force, resembles a poet's or a prosodist's: "Long time I scann'd him (67–68). But this interpretation is frustrated because the soldier's "murmuring voice" is one of "dead complaint" (77–78). The soldier's voice, and person, is unenlivened by passionate accent; any vehemence he once had has been spent.

The "wasted" face of the soldier suggests the implosion of the emphatic, oral ideal, and its promise of sympathetic communication and community. Instead of lustre darting from the eye, a "shadow / Lay at his feet and moved not" (71–72)—like an audience unmoved by a speaker. "To move, therefore, should be the first great object of every public Speaker," Sheridan stated, and "for this purpose, he must use the language of emotions, not that of ideas alone, which of itself has no power of moving."[87] The murmuring figure realizes discourse without "natural, forcible, and varied EMPHASIS."[88] He represents the ghastly underside of eloquence, and thus moves the narrator to question his history.

Burgh's complaint about a "total want of *energy* in expressing *pathetic* language"[89] is relevant to the soldier's response; it also illuminates Wordsworth's psychological and political deepening of the discourse of delivery. Though the soldier tells of "what he had endured / From war, and battle, and the pestilence,"

> in all he said
> There was a strange half-absence, and a tone
> Of weakness and indifference, as of one
> Remembering the importance of his theme
> But feeling it no longer. (136–37, 140–44)

Channeling Sheridan, Burgh wrote of the good clergyman who read "so *striking* a piece of scripture-history in a manner so *unanimated*, that it was fit to lull the whole parish to *sleep*." Burgh would

> never forget his manner of expressing the twenty-second verse,
> which is the Jewish general's order to bring out the captive kings to
> *slaughter*. "Open the mouth of the cave, and bring out those five
> kings to me out of the cave;" which he uttered in the very manner,
> he would have expressed himself, if he had said to his boy, "Open
> my chamber door, and bring me my slippers from under the bed."[90]

For Burgh, emphatic speech is something that can and should be cultivated. But while the dissociation of feeling from language he observes is striking, it is merely situational, emerging from the clergyman's failure to emphasize the text's "emphatical" words (those for whose sake the sentences were written), which itself reflects his failure to internalize the sentiments of the text.[91] It is as if, Sheridan explains, "we said it with our lips but did not think so."[92] What is troubling about the soldier, however, is that he relates his own "theme" (143), his own history, indifferently: with no differentiation of emphasis, or as Burgh says, "*natural* inflections."[93] "Natural Discourse," in which the voice carries "genuine expressions of sentiment," is disturbed not as a result of the speaker's alienation from the text but of his alienation from his own sentiments—as if his "theme" had become a text authored by another (compare the blind beggar of *The Prelude*, with the paper affixed to his chest, explaining his story).[94]

Self-alienation is a condition not accounted for in elocutionary theory. One spoke a naturally emphatic language in intimate conversation and also when reading aloud by identifying one's feelings with those of the author or narrator. Furthermore, this strategy of internalization and identification assumed the immediacy of one's own feelings. Burgh writes: "*reading* is nothing but *speaking* what one sees in a book, as if he were expressing his *own* sentiments, as they rise to his mind."[95] According to Peter de Bolla, elocution's insistence on an absolute identity between the "inner private voice" and the "outer public text" produces the autonomous subject as its excess.[96] The possibility emerges of a "split within the subject" arising "about the dividing line, or bar, of consciousness . . . which enables the speaker to distinguish between his 'intentions' in his emphatic vocalization and his 'unconscious' slavish following of the text's own intent" (167).

Wordsworth, I argue, raises a further problem within elocutionary theory as he brings a new subject—a dismissed soldier—to blank verse: how can the reader voice the text as though its sentiments and intentions were his own if he is already distanced from his own sentiments and intentions because he is the object of power?[97] "More than half detached / From his own nature" (59–60), the soldier has been severed from country, family, and self by participation in, and summary discharge from, his nation's foreign wars. He is neither the elocutionary subject who can speak the intentions of the text with "propriety" (as he would were the sentiments his own) nor the "proper" subject whose thoughts and feeling are legible as "surplus,"[98] but a man disintegrated by social and political forces that operate within him and without him. He does not possess the "energy" to infuse his own theme with feeling.

Wordsworth's passage sketches out a personal and implicitly political solution for the repair of the subject and the restoration of feeling to voice that involves the "natural" emphases that, he shows, organize his own poetry. It is clear that by hailing the "Stranger" (86), holding "discourse on things indifferent" (90), and then interestedly eliciting "his history" (94), Wordsworth begins a process of reinspiriting him. The "murmuring" man then speaks "unmoved, / And with a quiet, uncomplaining voice, / A stately air of mild indifference" (95–97)—that is, he shapes his sounds into words, and although no discernible feeling animates them, they carry a dignified "air" of detachment, as if to hint of the possibility of tune or melodic inflection. It is, however, by maintaining their "Discourse" (146) as he guides the soldier to the cottage of a rural "labourer" (111) that Wordsworth sets the man's self and social reintegration into motion. How does this reintegration occur? By a physiologization of speech in the process of a rhythmical pacing that is analogous to the pacing of verse. The discharged soldier and the poet who had "wandered, step by step" (36) "disposed to sympathy" (17) but enrapt in his own creations, together "measure back / The way which [they] have come" (109–10). Side by side, they calibrate their uncommon strides, "[advancing] / Slowly" (144–45). Although the exchange of words over a measured distance of road is suggestive of metrical lines and the turns and returns of verse, such overtly literal phrasing as "Back we turned and shaped / Our course toward the cottage" (120) signals the mutual accommodation of poetry and the soldier's speech, as well as their mutual shaping. By their "moving" (124) together toward a destination, the airy "imagery" that "rose / As from some distant region of my soul / And came along like dreams" (29–31) is grounded while the soldier's indifferent "voice" is inspirited. Indeed the poet's compassionate interest in the man (his decidedly not "indifferent" questions [90, 94, 125, 136]) is registered in a speech that is now differentiated by feeling and in a poetry that literally reports that differentiation: "in a voice that seem'd / To speak with a reviving interest, / Till then unfelt, he thanked me" (166–68).

The variegation of the landscape also plays a role in the portrait of the man and in his revival. Even as it recalls the classical device of the passage through the Underworld,[99] their passage "In silence, through the shades gloomy and dark" (147) and their "turning, up along an open field" (148), lit by "moon" (8) and "stars" (20), suggest a conversation shaped by nature—modulated, that is, by rural emphases or patterns of "light and shade."[100] Wordsworth realizes the elocutionary concepts of the "speech . . . of nature" and "natural . . . Discourse" in a physical nature that supplies its own chiaroscuro.[101] By their pedestrian movements and rural turns of speech and silence—the signaled materials of the poet's new measures—the discharged soldier "seems almost to start to life."[102]

As critics have observed, the encounter recalls the self-involved figure of the poet to his fellow humans and stages a movement from the Miltonic and Dantean sublime, and the Gothic of ballad and romance, to the natural world and human subjects.[103] Wordsworth also discovers in the encounter his social poetic register: the " 'man' that speaks in Wordsworth's poetry" emerges here as a " 'man speaking to men' " (LB 751).[104] Wordsworth's portrait of the man who comes to speak back to him, I have been arguing, drew on current ideas about "heavy and lifeless" discourse and the means of its enlivening, by dramatizing an encounter between a motionless body and a vital soul in "nature." As he identifies a political subject unimagined by that discourse, Wordsworth identifies his own poetic "soul" and medium with a type of the moving energy celebrated by the elocutionists. Not the emphatic haranguing that spurs the declaration of war and leads some "captive kings," and many ordinary men, "to *slaughter*,"[105] but the responsive though still purposeful—intentional and interested—turnings of discourse along a measured route to lead a man to "succour" (158). The poet shapes his measures to accommodate living speech—speech that has the power to provoke thought if not also the "Power to act."[106] At the door of the laborer, and the first time in the passage, the soldier replies not to one of the narrator's questions but to the reproving instruction "that he not linger in the public ways" but "at the door of cottage or of inn" to ask for "relief or alms" (156, 157, 160). "'My trust is in the God of Heaven / And in the eye of him that passes me,'" the man counters. The comment betrays the vagrant's lack of social and economic power, as Langan has observed, by falsely endowing him with choice.[107] However, if we pursue the suggestion of equivocal agency, the man's voicing of his intent to occupy "public ways" as an (en)countering force, we can observe Wordsworth's reflexive development of a blank verse for the page that does not suppress the emphases of conversational speech but rather trusts to the "eye" of the reader "that passes" over them.

In her discussion of *The Prelude* text of the passage and that poem's "glad preamble," Langan reads Wordsworth's "insistent materialization of the formal dimensions of the poem"—its references to walking and breathing, stepping, pausing, and measuring—as part of a broader strategy to present the poet as "an autonomous voice" in *The Prelude*: a poet of nature, free of social obligations.[108] Building upon Anthony Easthope's arguments, Langan sees blank verse as a form that "operates . . . to naturalize its formal determinations" and argues that its "antithetical structure," or constitutive "tension between the two orders (meter and speech intonation, or stress)," works to produce "the effect of a 'common' or 'natural' language" (168, 169). Wordsworth's highly self-reflexive writing in the measure thus supports his presentation as liberal subject and poet of imagination, enjoying a freedom of speech and motion that depends paradoxically, on successive encounters with the vagabond "figure of empirical deficit" (21).

Read in the context of the draft notebooks of early 1798, however, a less

exploitative, more critical and questioning Wordsworth emerges, one developing as a blank-verse poet by politically dramatizing contemporary warnings
about the form's distortions of idiomatic speech. The tension between meter
and speech intonation attributed to blank verse is not inherent but historically,
discursively, and typographically produced. By realizing Sheridan and company's personification of speech and spiritualization of emphasis, Wordsworth
critiques its characteristic patriotism so as to inscribe the absent figure of elocutionary discourse: the speaker/reader whose own feelings have been alienated. Wordsworth raises real questions about imperial power, human
enervation, and the dissolution of personhood—informed, perhaps, by Thelwall's radical physiological speculations on animal vitality (of which more will
be said in Chapter 7). That is, he does not subordinate politics to aesthetics.
Samuel Say had stated that accent and emphasis give "Life and Motion to the
English Iämbic," an otherwise torpid measure.[109] Rather than personify the
iamb, Wordsworth draws out the politics of personhood than underlie English
verbal and geographic marks and measures. Reflexively marking its constitutive features, he makes and displays a meter that is neither "cold" nor "unmark'd."[110] His exploration of the circulation of energy between speaking and
silent walkers in nature and the "restoration" of "animal delight" (lines 23, 33;
LB 278) on road and path recall the inscription of the hill scene in the notebook, which does not violate "the idiom of the Language" but seems to channel its "enthusiasm & inspiration" in the "lines" of ink on the page.[111] The
poet's early immersion in these circuits would be the subject of the autobiographical verses that followed. With the Discharged Soldier passage, the project of metrical self-fashioning begins.

Ontopoetics: "Emphatically Such a Being Lives"

Having explored the loss of emphasis from and its restoration to the soldier's
speech, Wordsworth turned to its earliest origins in the blank verse that he
began in Goslar in October 1798. This verse, the first sustained writing toward
what would become *The Prelude*, explores the acquisition, in infancy, of vital
energies and the development of measures for articulating these energies—
measures that channel their force without suppressing it. In MS JJ, Wordsworth posits the existence of a "creative" "power" (1799, p. 123) which infuses
the mind from its earliest stages and which closely resembles the "force" and
"energy" that was said to animate discourse:

> a mild creative breeze
> a vital breeze that passes gently on
> Oer things which it has made . . .

Like Sheridan who warned that an oversupply of vocal "energy" in a small room would cause sound to rebound "violently" against its own smooth undulation,[112] Wordsworth warned that this "breeze" could surge and cross itself. It

> soon becomes
> A tempest a redundant energy
> Creating not but as it may
> disturbing things created.—
>
> a storm not terrible but strong
> with lights and shades and with a rushing power
>
> trances of thought
> And mountings of the mind compared to which
> The wind that drives along th'autumnal [?leaf]
> Is meekness. (1799, p. 123, lines 3–12)

Thus it is that Wordsworth invokes the "steady cadence" of the River Derwent as a tempering counterforce to thought. "Was it for this," he asks,

> O Derwent—travelling over the green plains
> Near my sweet birth-place didst thou beauteous stream
> Give ceaseless music to the night & day
> Which with its steady cadence tempering
> Our human waywardness compose[d] my thought
> To more than infant softness . . .
> (1799, pp. 123–24, lines 24, 22, 28–33)

Here the mind of the infant poet is presented as potentially overcharged, in need of the river's metrical discipline and softening "voice" (26). But the strength of his inner energies, although it renders them difficult to regulate, is also their virtue—and thus like the emphasis theorized as vital to English discourse, vital to his poetry.

In a passage that Wordsworth wrote in winter 1798–99, which would become the Infant Babe passage of Book II of *The Prelude*, he developed blank verse as a medium of this stress principle that animates being and that he now called the "Poetic spirit" (1799, II: 306). His purpose, he announces at the outset, is "to trace / The progress of our being" from "torpid life" into active animation (1799, II: 268–69, 274), which occurs not in isolation but in a passionate communion between infant and mother that gradually broadens into communion between infant and universe. Arousal from torpor is initiated when the "soul / Claims manifest kindred with an earthly soul" by an intake of passion: the "Babe, who sleeps / Upon his Mother's breast . . . Doth gather passion from his Mother's eye!" (1799, II: 271–72, 270–71, 273). This "awakening" (275) absorption of passion registers elocutionists' understandings of looks, gestures, and tones as the true signs of the passions, as well their insistence that emphatic delivery will prevent the lulling of the mind to sleep: "the power animating and affecting the hearers depends much upon it," Sheridan had advised.[113] Indeed, the intake of passion from the eye makes the "mind" "prompt and watchful": "day by day / Subjected to the discipline of love / His organs and recipient faculties / Are quickened, are more vigorous, his mind spreads / Tenacious of the forms which it receives" (1799, II: 280–84).

In his Preface to *Lyrical Ballads*, Wordsworth would claim that the "essential passions" nurtured in rural soil "speak" not only "a plainer" but also a "more emphatic language" (LB 743). The Infant Babe passage renders at high resolution a pre-verbal phase of nurturing in which the essential "passion" gathered from the mother's eye issues into a condition of broader affective responsiveness to and engagement with the world—what Wordsworth seems to designate an emphatic ontological mode. The growth from private to worldly communion originates in the primary visual, tactile, and (in a later revision) rhythmic interaction between mother and infant (the 1850 text has "who sinks to sleep / Rocked on his Mother's breast" [1850, II: 235–36]). Growth is also stimulated by a supplementary "virtue" associated with their engagement: a "virtue which irradiates and exalts / All objects through all intercourse of sense" (1799, II: 289–90). Like emphasis, which "ennobles the word to which it belongs, and presents it in a stronger light to the understanding," this power lifts into prominence and consciousness what would otherwise lie latent, affectively and intellectually obscure.[114] By this virtue, the babe is attached—forcefully attracted—to the world:

No outcast he, bewildered and depressed:
Along his infant veins are interfused

> The gravitation and the filial bond
> Of nature, that connect him with the world.
> Emphatically such a being lives
> An inmate of this *active* universe;
> From nature largely he receives, nor so
> Is satisfied but largely gives again,
> For feeling has to him imparted strength . . . (1799, II: 291–99)

Wordsworth does not posit a static condition of bondedness between babe and world but a condition of always-bonding in a somatic pulsing of natural forces— as if the babe were the inmate of a uterine cosmos. He marks this pulsating connectivity metrically, the uncertain beats of "The *gravitation* and the *filial bond*" (my emphasis) evoking along the line the pulses of force along the "infant veins" of the babe.[115] He also places it under the cultural sign of emphasis— "Emphatically such a being lives / An inmate of this *active* universe"—prominently positioning "Emphatically" at the head of the line and clause so as to suggest the unusual idea that the being *lives* emphatically, as an inmate of, and because an inmate of, the "*active* universe." What might it mean to live emphatically? A reading that honors the line break observes Wordsworth's deepening and redirecting of elocutionary thought. Whereas the elocutionists had construed impassioned forcefulness of voice as capable of connecting speakers in private and public conversation, and in "whatever part of the globe English shall be taught,"[116] Wordsworth depicts a more fundamental condition of integration within a more extensive, implicitly energetic universal community—a belonging premised on an ongoing, pulsing interchange between human "being" and nature.[117]

Wordsworth's assertion of a forceful, pre-verbal ontological mode serves his construction of the poet, in whom this affective, stress-principle of being continues:

> ——Such, verily, is the first
> Poetic spirit of our human life;
> By uniform controul of after years
> In most abated and suppress'd, in some,
> Through every change of growth or of decay,
> Preeminent till death. (1799, II: 305–10)

Wordsworth hangs much upon the emphatic mode. "Such, verily, is the first / Poetic spirit of our human life," he asserts, as the signal of strongly felt intention—"Such, verily"—points back to "Emphatically such" at the center of the paragraph to warrant a rereading of "Emphatically such" along intentional lines: as in, "Emphatically, I say, such a being lives, / An inmate of this *active* universe." When read as modifying the poet's mode of statement (rather than the babe's mode of living), "Emphatically" inscribes the poet as a forceful speaker within the silent field of writing. By this slipperiness of modification, which is thoroughly apt given the eighteenth-century fixation on the unfixability of emphasis, the force and feeling that organizes the "*active* universe" is suggested still to course through the poet and his lines.

Indeed, at "Emphatically," the force of the "living tongue" disrupts the abstract metrical template.[118] We might scan *Em-pha-ti-call-y-such* as regular iambs but pronounce *Em-pha-ti-clly* as an iamb followed by a trochee or pyrrhic. The uncertain beating of "Emphatically" thus indexes the conception of the sentence as a dynamic architecture of force, while the strong stresses in the italicized "*active*" further evoke the idea of emphasis as the activating principle of speech: "accent and emphasis, are the life, blood and soul, which put [speech] in motion, and give it power to act."[119] The central lines thus strikingly display the intersection of Wordsworthian poetics and popular elocutionary discourse: the irruption of speech rhythms within the blank-verse line giving "life, blood and soul" to poetry.[120] As Wordsworth will go on to claim in the Preface, the "same human blood circulates through the veins of [prose and poetry] both" (LB 750); similarly, emphasis is suggested here to vitalize the "infant veins," or unspeaking lines, of blank verse. It is difference of energy that activates: as Herries stated, "if every word in a sentence is uttered with an uniform energy of voice, the meaning and spirit of the whole must be destroyed."[121] Compare Wordsworth on the "Poetic spirit": "By uniform controul of after years / In most abated and suppress'd" (1799, II: 306–8).

If the discharged soldier figures the inversion of the emphatic ideal in his disarticulated body and speech, the blessed infant babe personifies that ideal as a "being" of "veins" and "mind," a vital nexus of feeling and idea.[122] A medium of forces, the "inmate" then acts within and on "this *active* universe":

For feeling has to him imparted strength,
And powerful in all sentiments of grief,
Of exultation, fear and joy, his mind,
Even as an agent of the one great mind,
Creates, creator and receiver both,

Working but in alliance with the works
Which it beholds. (1799, II: 299–305)

The conception of "mind" as "creator and receiver both" recalls "the mighty world / Of eye and ear, both what they half-create, / And what perceive" of "Tintern Abbey" (lines 106–8, LB 119). Here, however, this imaginative work is decidedly founded upon that "virtue" associated with the passionate presence of the mother, "which irradiates and exalts / All objects" (1799, II: 289) and with a gravitational connection to nature, revealing how notions of affective force shape Wordsworth's early conceptions of creative perception. For the elocutionists, speech emphasis is integrative, emboldening, and luster giving: its energy makes the dead letter of print three-dimensionally vivid. For Wordsworth, a feeling, energetic mind acts on "the works / Which it beholds," to bring forward their life and meaning. A fragment from 1800 similarly registers the discourse of vocal force that informs Wordsworth's theory of imaginative perception:

There is a creation in the eye,
Nor less in all the other senses; powers
They are that colour, model and combine
The things perceived with such an absolute
Essential energy . . . (lines 1–5, LB 323–24)

These "powers," he continues, interact with the "impulses" of "Nature," and are felt as "A vivid pulse of sentiment and thought" that "Beat[s] palpably within us" (lines 20–23, LB 324). Animated by the stress principle, the creative perceiver beholds more vividly, and more essentially or truthfully, the things of this world—and communicates that more vital vision by the activating pulses of his patterned, but rhythmically flexible, medium. As Sheridan wrote of Milton's unusual emphases, "What an amazing force does this position give to the word *worse!* and in what strong colours does it paint to us the desperate state of reprobation in which Satan had fallen!"[123]

In an 1802 addition to the Preface to *Lyrical Ballads*, Wordsworth further developed his version of the emphatic ideal by endowing the Poet with a worldly and metaphysical importance that both evokes and surpasses the global reach of elocutionary discourse:

the poet, singing a song in which all human beings join him,
rejoices in the presence of truth as our visible friend and hourly

companion. Poetry is the breath and finer spirit of all knowledge;
it is the impassioned expression which is in the countenance of all
Science. *Emphatically may it be said of the Poet,* as Shakespeare hath
said of man, "that he looks before and after." He is the rock of de-
fence for human nature; an upholder and preserver, carrying everywhere with him relationship and love. In spite of difference of soil
and climate, of language and manners, of laws and customs: in spite
of things silently gone out of mind, and things violently destroyed;
the Poet binds together by passion and knowledge the vast empire
of human society, as it is spread over the whole earth, and over all
time. (LB 752–53, italics added)

Whereas elocutionists celebrated emphasis for its capacity to bind English
sentences and speakers "through all parts of the globe"[124] by its marking of
meaning and passion, Wordsworth celebrated the Poet for his capacity to bind
"the vast empire of human society . . . over the whole earth, and over all time"
by his access to truth and power of feeling. Thus in *The Prelude* manuscripts
and the prose, Wordsworth worked the single word "Emphatically" to make
his poetry that integrative force—"impassioned expression" in the "countenance of all Science," "breath and finer spirit of all knowledge"—that, surpassing dialects and languages, gives meaning and feeling to human discourses and
endeavors. Thus, when first written, the discharged soldier is not yet a "type of
the Romantic ventriloquist," whose speech "approximates the language of poetry precisely to the extent that it is distanced from the 'impassioned utterance'
Wordsworth identifies as the source of poetry in Preface,"[125] but a crucial figure
in Wordsworth's development of that ideal.

Revising for "Emphasis and Grace"

Wordsworth later returned to the concept of the force of poetry as elaborated in
the passage on the Infant Babe. The revisions highlight the abiding influence of
rhetorical and elocutionary discussions on his poetry and sense of the poet, and
also suggest the importance that typographical presentation would come to assume. In his discussion of the figures of interrogation and exclamation, Blair had
discouraged reliance upon "Typographical Figure[s] of speech," such as italic
characters, exclamation points without exclamations, and dashes, advising writers to arrange words on the page to give "most emphasis and grace."[126] Syntactic

figures can effect "strength or liveliness of impression" and give "every word, and every member [of the Period], its due weight and force" without doing "violence" to the language or "hurt[ing] the eye" (!) of the reader.[127] In arguing thus, Blair echoed classical rhetoricians' warning against obtruding figurality. Longinus had advised that the figurality of the figure should be kept in the shade to maintain its sublime force; Quintilian had warned, when writing on emphasis, "If a figure betrays itself, it ceases to be a figure."[128] "Emphatically such a Being lives / An inmate of this *active* universe"; "Emphatically may it be said of the Poet . . . 'that he looks before and after'" (Prelude, 1799, II: 294–95; LB 753). Wordsworth's emphatically flagged statements run the risk not of demonstrating the fundamental forcefulness of the poet's language but of exposing the infancy, or muteness, of the poet in the age of print—a poet forced explicitly to highlight and typographically to manipulate in order to inscribe himself as impassioned, animate, and vocal. Wordsworth's major revisions of the passage between 1824 and 1832, particularly of the lines framing "Emphatically such a Being lives," register his ongoing concerns about the inscription of forceful utterance in blank verse—about forcefulness that appears forced and thus falls short in "liveliness and truth" (LB 751).

The revised passage reduces the appearance of force in both the poet and the infant by eliminating the emphatic italics ("*active*") and by making illustrative additions. These changes present the poet and the infant as nonviolent users of signs and "marks." Following from the lines "Along his infant veins are interfused / The gravitation and the filial bond / Of nature that connect him with the world," an added section reads,

Is there a flower to which he points with hand
Too weak to gather it, already love
Drawn from love's purest earthly fount for him
Hath beautified that flower; already shades
Of pity cast from inward tenderness
Do fall around him upon aught that bears
Unsightly marks of violence or harm.
Emphatically such a Being lives,
Frail Creature as he is, helpless as frail,
An inmate of this active universe. (1850, II: 246–55)

The addition is indexical and affective, imaging the early language of a poet of feeling: the infant "points" and marks—noticing what "bears / Unsightly marks of violence or harm"—as his pure "love" and "pity" leave delicate traces, "shades" or emphases, on the objects of his interest. The sensitive babe gently signs himself into a natural world responsive to his feelings and intent, "Working but in alliance with the works / Which it beholds" (260–61). Separating "The gravitation and the filial bond / Of nature that connect him with this world" (244–45) from "Emphatically such a Being lives" (253), the lines subdue the sense of interpulsing connectivity, or force-based alliance with the universe, in illustration of affective communion and immediacy.

Wordsworth's verbal additions and cancelling of emphatic italics suggest concerns about the typographic marking of feeling and meaning. To signal typographically the activity of the universe forces the idea, or points too strongly; thus in revision, the italicization of "*active*" is replaced by a thematization of emphasis in added phrases about the infant babe who "points with hand / Too weak to gather" the flower, signaling his incipient communion with nature.[129] In line with the stylistic recommendations of Blair, Wordsworth replaces a "Typographical Figure" with a rhetorical figure:[130]

> Emphatically such a Being lives,
> Frail Creature as he is, helpless as frail,
> An inmate of this active universe.

The repetition of the first word of the line as the last, "Frail . . . frail," is an instance of epanalepsis. The figure reinforces the physical delicacy of the infant and schematizes the principal idea of his integration within a universe in harmony with which he acts.[131] Impassioned but nonviolent, the feelings and intentions of the babe are met and anticipated by the natural world ("already love / Drawn from love's purest earthly fount for him / Hath beautified that flower"). In stark contrast, the French military officers of Book IX are depicted as acting contrary to universal feeling by uttering forceful words which fly like "dart[s]" (1850, IX: 257) back into their speakers' faces ("their discourse" is thus "Maimed, spiritless" [260–61]). One local Royalist leader during the Terror reads aloud the daily reports at a "punctual" hour while punctuating his words with uncomfortable taps of his "sword" (1850, IX: 156, 159). The nervous gesture violates rather than works in alliance with the universal impulse ("His temper was quite mastered by the times" [143]). On the other hand, the infant inmate of the universe does not overtly stress—in speech, gesture, or looks—but subtly "points," in such a way as to recall "the relation of the scant utterance to the presentient representation of a great content" that is the phenomenon of classical emphasis.[132] The virtue of emphatic speech, as articulated in eighteenth-century elocutionary and rhetorical discourse, is thus modulated into creative, unspeaking (*infans*) perception and communication.

The revision, as late as 1832, of the Infant Babe passage demonstrates that Wordsworth continued to concern himself with ways of inscribing emphasis in blank verse. If he began this process in January 1798, it came to a head in 1800. The emphatical marking of communion with nature, visualized and re-visualized in the *Prelude* manuscripts, became a still more pointed issue when he prepared to publish, for the first time under his own name, his new blank-verse compositions.

Chapter 5

"—You Are Mov'd!"

Lyrical Ballads and the Printing of Local Feeling

Wordsworth explained his definition & ideas of harmonious Verse,
that it consisted in the arrangement of pauses & cadences, & not in
the even flow of single Lines—

CL, I: 442

In Book VI of *The Prelude*, Wordsworth recalls that moment at Cambridge
during his growth into a poet when

> the instinctive humbleness,
> Upheld even by the very name and thought
> Of printed books and authorship, began
> To melt away . . . (1805, VI: 69–72)

Yet the second edition of *Lyrical Ballads*, prepared for publication during the
summer and fall of 1800, marks an acute moment of self-consciousness with
regard to "printed books and authorship." After mixed reviews of the first
edition, and at the prodding of Coleridge, Wordsworth drafted a preface in
which he explained his aims and procedures and defended his choice of subject
matter and style. Picking up concerns from the Discharged Soldier and the
Blessed Babe passages of 1798–99, Wordsworth gave emphatic language prominence in his statements on poetry, discussing its acquisition by speakers and
its reproduction in verse. The new poems added for this edition and the old
ones of 1798, he claimed, explored incidents from common life and used the

language of rural speakers, because in that situation, "the essential passions of the heart find a better soil in which they can attain their maturity, are less under restraint, and speak a plainer and more emphatic language" (LB 743). Thus in contrast to some contemporary views about emphatic language—that it flourishes in polite society or that it can be learned from printed books— Wordsworth here posited a rural mechanics of forceful expression, deriving it from "hourly" communication with "the best objects" of nature (LB 744).

The Preface thus aligned the new edition with an oral and rural communicative ideal in stark contrast to the urban sphere of print and the newspapers' "hourly" gratification of "craving for extraordinary incident." The "rapid communication of intelligence" about "great national events daily taking place" has corrupted literary production and taste such that the "invaluable works of our elder writers . . . are driven into neglect by frantic novels, sickly and stupid German Tragedies, and deluges of idle and extravagant stories in verse" (LB 746–47). If the sphere of print is held up here as creating and supplying a demand for sensational event, reducing the minds of readers to "savage torpor," it is also presented as a repository of "phrases and figures of speech which from father to son have long been regarded as the common inheritance of Poets": language not generated by looking "steadily at [the] subject" but culled from books and repeated—and therefore not dictated by "real passion," Wordsworth would add in 1802 (LB 751). Between the literature of "extraordinary incident" and the unfelt phrases and figures of poetic tradition, between the too current and the recurrent, Wordsworth cleared a space in the Preface for "Poems" of "worthy *purpose*" (LB 744) arising from the fresh "impulses" of a mind that has "nourished" "feelings connected with important subjects." If "blindly and mechanically" obeyed, these impulses led the poet to "describe objects" and "utter sentiments" that enlighten the understanding, exalt the taste, and ameliorate the affections (LB 744–45). In this model of literary production, impulses issue into utterance.

But the affective and moral force of the poet's words emerges as a problem. The exalted figure of "good poetry" "as the spontaneous overflow of powerful feeling" produced by a "man . . . of more than usual organic sensibility [who] had also thought long and deeply" (LB 744–45) is followed by the admission that the poet's words may frequently "be incommensurate with the passion" (LB 756) he hopes to communicate, necessitating the addition of impassioning meters. Even the proposal "to imitate, and, as far as is possible, to adopt the very language of men" (LB 747) is hedged from the outset. Wordsworth thereafter explains that while he has "endeavored to bring [his] language near to the real language of men" (LB 757), it "may frequently have suffered from those arbitrary connections of feelings and ideas with particular words, from which no man can altogether protect himself" (LB 757). In 1802 he further problematized the mimetic aspect of his project, adding that because the poet only imitated a language "uttered by men in real life, under the actual pressure of those passions," his language "must often, in liveliness and truth, fall short" (LB 751). The Preface thus cast philosophical limitation as an effect of the general human susceptibility to "faulty expressions" derived from "arbitrary connections" (LB 757) and of the poet's ventriloquial relation to rural speakers—his imitation of the "forcibly communicated" language of "the essential passions" (LB 743). Grand claims introduced in the 1802 extension of the Preface—"Poetry is the breath and finer spirit of all knowledge; it is the impassioned expression which is in the countenance of all Science. Emphatically may it be said of the Poet . . . 'that he looks before and after'" (LB 752–53)— reinforce that "emphatic language" could not be taken for granted: it arose under the "actual pressure" of passion that the poet aimed to simulate but could not be assumed to reproduce—nor to represent on paper (LB 743).

That Wordsworth invoked "emphatic language" and indeed wrote the Preface in the midst of preparing the second edition of *Lyrical Ballads* for the press illuminates a related conflict: his relationship to the medium to which his vocation committed him—print. We might say that one of the chief problems Wordsworth faced in representing "the plainer and more emphatic language" spoken by "the essential passions" lay in the remove of written and printed media from speech. Or, conversely, that Wordsworth's perception of an unsympathetic distance between the poet and his readers prompted the figure of the speaking passions in the first place, a prosopopoeia that transfers the power of speech from rural "men" to the "essential passions" in order to lend sound to the pages of the book. The remove of print from speech had already exercised the elocutionists: in their effort to spread the "true natural mode of speech"[1] that had been corrupted by various influences, including the written and printed language, the elocutionists were, paradoxically, committed to print. This commitment, as I discussed in the previous chapter, led them to devise new symbols and schemes for representing emphasis on paper and for graphing its relation to pause and inflection. They also reconceived punctuation to encode speech in print, recasting the stops not as signals of syntactic relations—marks for clarifying grammatical structure—but of pauses for breath and emphasis in the delivery of written texts. The ideal of an "emphatic language" thus coincided with a critique of the written medium and was disseminated by a flourishing sector of the book trade: elocutionary lectures, rhetorical grammars and dictionaries, and handbooks on speaking and reading that drew their examples from poetry, prose, and the Bible.

Wordsworth's valorization in 1800 not merely of the "plainer language"[2] that he had linked with rural speakers in "The Ruined Cottage" but of a "plainer and more emphatic language" coincided with an intense period of book production and consciousness about the medium of print. If the "more emphatic language" by which Wordsworth hoped to improve the sympathies of his readers arose under the "actual pressure" of passions, it was articulated and theorized under the pressure to get a full volume's worth of poems into print for judgmental reviewers and readers who had had been deterred, Wordsworth believed, by "the old words and strangeness" of the opening poem of the 1798 edition, "The Rime of the Ancyent Marinere" (EY 264). The emphatic ideal gave the new edition currency while also signaling Wordsworth's recognition that his language would "fall short" in "liveliness and truth" if he did not find means of evoking sound, silence, and feeling in the medium of print. Wordsworth's valorization of rustic speech as a "more emphatic language" both is a product of and betrays anxieties about print publication and reception.

Wordsworth's anxieties about publication have been well documented. "There is little need to advise me against publishing; it is a thing which I dread as much as death itself," he wrote to James Tobin in March 1798 (EY 211). Lucy Newlyn, who diagnoses in Wordsworth a lifelong "paranoid fear that poets were at the mercy of a hostile public," argues that Wordsworth aimed with his critical prose and poems from *Lyrical Ballads* forward "to transform an anonymous public into a sympathetic readership." Acknowledging, with Stephen Gill, Wordsworth's preoccupation in the preparation of *Lyrical Ballads* with the "minutiae of presentation," including typeface, punctuation, and the shape of the volumes, Newlyn reads his close scrutiny of the manuscripts as a "defensive measure"—a way to secure his self-image before a hostile readership.[3] But we could also link Wordsworth's anxieties about publication to cultural concerns about the written and printed medium—particularly to historic perceptions of the muteness of pages and to indeterminacies in the value of printed signs; and we could read Wordsworth's close scrutiny of the manuscripts, as I do here, not as a "defensive measure" but as the reflection of material debates that, as Wordsworth grappled with them, informed his conceptions of the public and the poet and his ongoing writing of the poems and prose for the edition as he and his domestic circle prepared it for the press.

We can trace the generative effects of the problematic of presentation in the printer's copy of *Lyrical Ballads*, a set of sixteen letters sent from Grasmere to Humphry Davy and the Bristol printers Biggs and Cottle between June and December 1800. Written by Dorothy, William, and Coleridge, mixing verse and prose, directions to the printers and notes to the readers, the letters reveal an acute consciousness about the typographical presentation of the verse while directly expressing, in Wordsworth's words, uncertainties regarding the "business" of punctuation (EY 289). One context for these concerns, I suggest, is the elocutionists' reform of the written medium—their conversion of punctuation from a grammatical technology to a technology of voice and emotion—which I explore by highlighting their critique of the exclamation mark and their promotion of long pauses, including the "blank line," the dash, and the white space between paragraphs. Turning to the printer's copy, I consider the poems of volume two that bear the signs of revision and experimentation while also thematizing the language of feeling and the printed book. "There was a Boy" and "The Brothers" are newly marked by the "pauses of deep silence" (LB 140) that the elocutionists had made a key affective element of oral communication and had sought to indicate spatially on the page. Wordsworth's graphic repunctuation of these dramas of communication on the verge of their publication not only suggests an anxiety about being identified as the author of a collection of poems under his own name but also reflexively underscores the poems' thematic concerns about the capacity of printed books to represent local affections and communicate them to public readers.

Another context for Wordsworth's typographical concerns and experimentation is the topographical discourse that already delineated the place and its people—the tourist publications that I explored in Chapters 1 and 3. As Wordsworth prepared the poems of volume two for print, inserting "pauses of deep silence" that interrupt speech and slow the pace of reading, he also contrasted tour- and map-generated attitudes with local feelings. The long dashes added to "The Brothers" align his poems with the latter by inscribing the passions of local people not only as it marks their speech but also their experience of place—local rivers, hills, and valleys. Punctuation emerges, within this blank verse, as a topographic device. As the preparation of the copy proceeded, Wordsworth's consciousness of the print medium and of his authorship shaped the book more largely. In the late composition of "To Joanna" and the preface to "If Nature, for a favourite Child," Wordsworth experimented with ways to impassion the spatial field of verse, to prevent it seeming, as guidebooks and tour narratives often seemed, too facile an inscription in print of the passions generated in place. While these print inscriptions strive to heighten expressivity by investing the typographical surface with material and historical depth, Wordsworth's completion and clustering of the five "Poems on the Naming of Places" mark a joint impassioning of geographical place and book space—a topographical treatment of the book. Throughout this chapter I argue that Wordsworth's self-articulation as a rural and oral poet, as well as a theorist of poetry, does not precede but depends upon the edition's preparation for print. The final stages of this, the composition and copying of "Michael, A Pastoral Poem," culminate in Wordsworth's boldest experiment hitherto in deriving his self-figuration as a poet "among the hills" from the layout of his blank verse across the pages of the book (line 363; LB 264).

The Spacing of Passion in Eighteenth-Century Punctuation Debates

I shall turn to *Lyrical Ballads* in detail later in the chapter; first, however, it is necessary to explore the elocutionists' critiques of punctuation and the pedagogy of vocal delivery, which corrupted the "living Voice,"[4] they claimed, and sapped it of its passion. A flashpoint in their critique of the syntactical mode of punctuation favored by grammarians was the exclamation point, which was associated with an elevation of voice and the pause value of a period. In the course of their critique, elocutionists illuminated the semantic and affective value of the sounds and silences that pervade English speech. In doing so, they brought the broader typographic field, including the spaces between words and paragraphs, into focus.

A fourteenth-century Italian symbol whose name and function was as yet unstabilized in eighteenth-century Britain, the exclamation point entered the general repertory of Western punctuation in the fifteenth and sixteenth centuries along with the semicolon and the parenthesis—marks to guide comprehension during silent reading.[5] By the sixteenth, scholars had come to associate the mark with " 'passions of the soul' " and " 'affections of the mind.' "[6] Late seventeenth- and early eighteenth-century grammarians concurred in linking the stroke with "passion" and with "Words of Wonder," calling it the note of admiration, note of exclamation, and the sublimely resonant "wondering point."[7] As indicated in the Interchapter, they also showed an interest in the intonation of the point. Christopher Cooper's 1687 *English Teacher* advocated "a suitable raising of the voice" so as to effect in delivery a mimesis of the "affections of the author." In an exuberant description of the tonal modulation of passion, Michael Maittaire isolated the "Wondering Point" and the "Point of Interrogation" insofar as both require different tones and pronunciation from the rest of discourse. "Passion" does not suffuse but enters into speech with the quick falling accent of the interrogative and slow rising accent of admiration. It belongs squarely to the author or character in the text, who is questioning or wondering, curious or beyond curiosity. The role of the reader is to mimic vehemence by modulating the voice solely at those moments of minimally differentiated "Passion."[8]

Credited with stimulating the revival of elocution in Britain, John Mason's 1748 *Essay on Elocution and Pronunciation* shows how post-Lockean attempts to bridge the gap between minds incorporated the space of the page into the mechanism of punctuation. Concerned not merely with the reader's performance of the author's passion, Mason urged a "proper and just Pronunciation" that functions sympathetically to "raise" in the audience the "same Ideas [the author] intended to convey" and the "same Passions he really felt."[9] He advocated punctuating texts with the common long pauses, or "periods"—the "Period," and the points of "Interrogation" (?) and "Admiration" (!). But he also promoted what he calls the "Double-Period, or Blank Line, (——)" which he made equivalent in quantity to the time of two periods. Converting the page into regular ratios of time, Mason gave the paragraph break a pause equivalent to two "Blank Lines," and he allotted the "Double Paragraph," which he describes as an inserted "vacant" line between two paragraphs, the time equivalent of two paragraphs, or four "Blank Lines."[10] Long pauses have a communicative function, he claimed. Not only do they allow the voice to rest and permit the intake of breath, they also work on and within the reader or listener; they "at once compose and affect the Mind," he says, "and give it Time to think." "And therefore," he continued, "in printing the most *affecting parts of a Discourse*, there should be (as we sometimes see there is) a frequent use of long Pauses, *viz.* the periods, blank Lines, and Paragraphs."[11]

In a radical move, Mason thus invoked the space of the page to do the work of signaling affecting and thought-permitting pauses. This bringing of paragraph breaks and vacant lines into the sphere of punctuation—a semiosis of the page itself—highlights the mid-century's heightened concerns with affectivity and sympathetic response. Only then did intersubjective issues enter the discourse of points: the location of ideas and feelings in minds, the marks that transmit them, and the time sympathy requires. Only then was the exclamation point theorized as allowing time for ideas and feelings to sink into the minds of readers and listeners. In the process, however, the mark associated with "passions of the soul" and "affections of the mind" lost its status as the principal mark of affect. Lines, the blankness of the page, and other full stops were also theorized as devices of sympathy, and as I will suggest, could be manipulated to mark the temporal and spatial interval between minds that they simultaneously strived to cross.[12]

The elocutionists who followed Mason argued for a new way of thinking about punctuation. The marks should be used to indicate not grammatical relationships but the pauses of the speaking voice, declared Sheridan, lamenting that the "modern art of punctuation was not taken from the art of speaking, which certainly ought to have been its archetype."[13] Accordingly, Sheridan advised public readers to ignore the extant punctuation in printed texts, which had been assigned false tones and times by "grammarians" and bore no relation to the natural modulations of the voice. The uniform "elevation" of voice grammarians had assigned to words preceding the comma, semicolon, and colon, and the uniform "depression" of voice assigned to the period effected a monotonous, "unnatural manner" of reading. These "reading tones," grammatical signals of the incompletion and completion of sense, bore no correspondence to the "exceedingly numerous, and various" tones that occur naturally in speech, and that depend not upon syntactical structure but "the sense of the words, the emotions of the mind, or the exertions of the fancy." Readers should rather pause and intone according to sense and feeling. This necessitated recopying the passage without punctuation and repointing it according to one's own manner of delivery—using not the common "stops of writing, the sight of which would revive the use of their associated tones," but inclined lines marking increasing lengths of pause (see Chapter 4).[14] Expressive intonation, Sheridan argued, pervades whole periods and parts of discourse; it should be suitably varied and could not be prescribed.

Sheridan's explanation of the failure of "modern punctuation" to meet the needs of an orally invested print culture highlighted the cooperation of emphasis and pause. The "proportion of time in the pause should be regulated," he contended, not by the abstract formula of the grammarians but "by the importance of each idea."[15] It was not simply that pauses permitted the inhalations necessary for distinct and forcible delivery but that a "sufficient pause at the end of each member" gave "time for each idea to make its due impression on the mind."[16] The speaker was "at liberty to prolong" any pause "at pleasure" and, by taking "power over the pauses," could "strongly [inculcate] his meaning."[17] Inserting a "longer pause than usual" before a key "proposition or sentiment" would "excite uncommon attention" and "raise expectation" in the listener. Inserting a pause afterward would "allow time for the mind to ruminate upon it" and let it "sink deeper into [the mind] by reflection."[18] The voiced stress of oral emphasis and the silence of an extending pause thus worked in conjunction to express and impress ideas and feelings.

To wrest the punctuation marks from grammarians' tonal and temporal assignments, elocutionists elaborated the communicative work and cognitive effects of pauses in pictorial terms. The "pauses in discourse answer the same end that shades do in pictures," Sheridan claimed; "by the proper use of which, the objects stand out distinctly to the eye; and without which, were the colours to run into one another, it would be difficult to discriminate the several figures of the composition."[19] William Cockin compared pauses to the "blank spaces in pictures," which "set off and render more conspicuous whatsoever they disjoin or terminate."[20] As with emphasis, the highly painterly tropes of pausing register anxieties about the efficacy and anonymity of public discourse. Walker urged his students when speaking or reading in public to pause "much oftener [than when] reading and conversing in private; as the parts of a picture which is to be viewed at a distance, must be more distinctly and strongly marked, than those of an object which are nearer to the eye, and understood at the first inspection."[21] It was not an intensification of vocal stress (a wildly passionate mode of communication that Sheridan associated with Methodist preaching) that would bridge social distance but the more frequent insertion of blank spaces. While evoking an empiricist and implicitly typographical model of communication as the impressing of ideas upon the "white paper" of the mind, the spatial figuration of temporal pauses had material implications for punctuation and the spacing of words on the pages of books.[22]

Although critical of the system of grammatical punctuation, the elocutionists did not reject the existing marks but redefined them, while promoting one that was itself mimetic of the "'Space of Time'" of discourse.[23] Walker strongly advocated the use of the relatively new and controversial dash, a mark not included in Robert Lowth's 1762 grammar but exploited by mid-century novelists, including Samuel Richardson and Laurence Sterne, to mark omission, interruption, and pause.[24] Taking up Sheridan's discussion of the pause of suspension—a suspension of the voice before a continuation in the sense, for the "sake of breathing" or "where precision or energy require it" (I: 47)— Walker described the dash as "the point wanting to render our punctuation much more definite and complete" (I: 33). Influenced by the elocutionists, Joseph Robertson admitted the "dash" into his 1785 *Essay on Punctuation*, declaring that it was used properly "where the sentence breaks off abruptly . . .

where a significant pause is required; or where there is an unexpected turn in the sentiment."[25] His example of its use to mark a "significant pause" shows the dash cooperating, effectively and affectively, with the exclamation point:

> LORD Cardinal! if thou think'st on heaven's bliss,
> Hold up thy hand, make signal of that hope.——
> He dies, and makes no sign! (131)

Robertson's "dash" of "significant pause" has the semantic and affective force of Mason's "blank line," its length without its strict temporal designation. It visually marks, without precisely measuring, an "interval of silence" or "solemn pause," just as the short form of the dash signals, but refuses to precisely measure, a "short interruption."[26] As Walker stated, while critiquing grammarians' investment in the arbitrary "geometric" proportioning of temporal quantity, "every one feels a difference between a greater and a smaller pause, but few can conceive degrees of these."[27] Sanctioned by Robertson, and by Lindley Murray after him, dashes represented silences to be seen and felt, not precisely counted. As with other spatial figurations of pause on the page—such as the vacant line between paragraphs—they made the page an implicit register of the distance between minds in the public sphere that pauses sought to overcome.[28]

"Across the Watr'y Vale": The Printer's Copy and the Letter to Davy

"Pauses of deep silence" became crucial to Wordsworth's understanding of communication—both between a "man [and] men" (LB 757) and between men and nature. When he prepared *Lyrical Ballads* for the press in 1800, the representation of those pauses in print, so that they might be seen and felt by readers, preoccupied him at both practical and theoretical levels. Indeed, it was the demands of putting his verse into the material form of a published book that led him to sharpen his ideas about poetry's communication of feeling: as he repunctuated old poems and pointed new ones, as he deliberated on their layout in the volumes, he also composed the Preface explaining how they represented speech and articulated feeling. Thus the Preface's now-famous statements linking poetry to rustic orality, to "emphatic language" (LB 743), and to spontaneous emotion were elaborated in the context of grappling with the typographical and visual decisions required of an author going into print.

These decisions, too, were inflected by the reform of punctuation led by the elocutionists: like Sheridan and Walker, Wordsworth was concerned not just to make printed text reflect the emphases and pauses of speech, but also to utilize visual means—including significantly placed spaces and elongated dashes—to do so. He attempted, that is, in the elocutionists' wake, to make his book reveal spatially the vocal inflections by which feeling was temporally articulated. Thus print, while simulating the speech of Cumbrian locals and circulating it beyond that locale, might represent that rustic speech community without trivializing or commodifying it, as so many tourists and tourist publications did.

The process of preparing his old and new poems for print took place in the letters composed between July and December 1800 and sent to Davy, Biggs and Cottle at the press in Bristol. Written in Grasmere, where Wordsworth was living with his sister and more-than-copyist Dorothy, and during the long visit of Coleridge and his family, the first letter, addressed to Davy on 29 July, contained fair copies of "The Brothers," "There was a Boy," "Ellen Irwin," and "Hart-leap Well." Here Wordsworth asks Davy "to look [over?] the proof sheets of the 2nd Vol[ume] before they are finally struck off" and makes a special request with regard to the manuscript: "You would greatly oblige me by looking over the enclosed poems and correcting any thing you find amiss in the punctuation, a business at which I am ashamed to say I am no adept" (EY 289). There follow, at intervals, twelve letters to printers Biggs and Cottle with the poems for volume two, instructions about formatting and arrangement, title requests, corrections and addition, prose notes, and the Preface. Wordsworth composed the Preface, and the note to "The Thorn," relatively late in the process of moving the poems into print, mailing them in late September and early October when he began to compose "Michael" and also worked on completing the "Poems on the Naming of Places."

As Wordsworth's letter to Davy (and much of the manuscript material of the period) shows, marking practices could be idiosyncratic. Wordsworth uses at most one comma within the entire letter and no other marks of punctuation save for periods followed by dashes to mark the ends of sentences—as we can see in "I am no adept.__" and "pleased with their situation.__" but cannot see in de Selincourt and Shaver's repunctuated edition of the letters (EY 289).[29] That edition also elides the points and dashes that Wordsworth uses to bring the ends of paragraphs flush with the right margin of the page and that show his penchant for the horizontal stroke. Wordsworth does not use the line to conserve page space—to indicate and substitute for a paragraph break, as writers sometimes did—but to mark and traverse it. Though probably a technique to preserve neatness of lineation, the paragraph-ending points and strokes perform a casual disregard for the "business" of punctuation as well as the need for its regularization.

The poems sharing the page, however, indicate Wordsworth's scrutiny of the matter. "Hart-leap Well," "There was a Boy," "Ellen Irwin," and the first thirty-six lines of "The Brothers," all in Dorothy's hand, make visible the well-known social nature of Wordsworth's writing (Figure 24).[30] The darker, sometimes thicker marks—the commas, semicolons, periods, dashes, and question and exclamation marks—suggest additions to or alterations of the original text. They signal Wordsworth's recognition, with publication looming, that punctuation was an issue that mattered but at which he was "no adept."[31] They also respond to the poems' thematic emphasis on speech, writing, and the communication of feeling. Copied to the left of the letter to Davy, "There was a Boy" and the lines of "The Brothers" explore both the affective force and intersubjective dynamics of silent pauses while exemplifying, at the material level, the refining of poetic pacing. "There was a Boy," for instance, gains twenty-two extra commas,[32] showing a tendency toward finer temporal and rhythmic modulation at this late stage of copy; ten of these, as well as four periods, a hyphen, and a colon, appear to be corrections to the copy. The concentration of new commas in lines 15–19 is particularly suggestive; mini-interruptions in the metrical flow, they mimic the interruptions in the boy's vocal interplay with the owls that the poem describes:

There was a Boy, ye knew him well, ye Cliffs
And Islands of Winander! many a time,
At evening, when the stars had just begun
To move along the edges of the hills,
Rising or setting, would he stand alone,
Beneath the trees, or by the glimmering lake,
And there, with fingers interwoven, both hands
Press'd closely palm to palm and to his mouth
Uplifted, he, as through an instrument,
Blew mimic hootings to the silent owls
That they might answer him. And they would shout
Across the wat'ry vale and shout again
Responsive to his call, with quivering peals,
And long halloos, and screams, and echoes loud

Redoubled and redoubled, a wild scene
Of mirth and jocund din. And, when it chanced
That pauses of deep silence mock'd his skill,
Then, sometimes, in that silence, while he hung
Listening, a gentle shock of mild surprize
Has carried far into his heart the voice
Of mountain torrents . . .   (lines 1–21, LB 140–41)

The new pauses and the steady increase in syllables between them ("Then,
sometimes, in that silence, while he hung / Listening,")[33] effects the sense of
an extending silence. With the spondaic slowing across the line break and the
quiet unstresses that follow ("while *he hung* / *List*ening, a"), they heighten the
boy's—and our—attention to the gaping absence of sound. Pause, stress, and
line take the poem to a point of metrical suspension or stillness, mimicking
the experience of auricular hiatus that leaves such a deep impression on the
boy.

Wordsworth intensifies the sense of silent temporal extension in MS 1800
also with the notable horizontal stroke after "Mute" in the final line of the
poem—a striking rule, double the length of an em dash and dramatically
reflexive:

And there along that bank when I have pass'd
At evening, I believe, that near his grave
A full half-hour together I have stood
Mute____for he died when he was ten years old. (MS 1800)

The double em dash makes the first-foot caesura more boldly convention-
breaking than in previous copies; stepping beyond "Mute," in MS 16 and
"Mute,__" in MS 16(2), "Mute___" offers a scriptographic figure of speechlessness. Dorothy's fair copy had already added the poem's first exclamation
point—"ye Cliffs / And Islands of Winander!"—emphasizing the vocal nature
of the apostrophe that constitutes the poem.[34] By contrast, and like an inversion of the pointed apostrophe, "Mute___" marks a bold recruitment of pag-
inal space as expressive resource: a "full half-hour" stretch of wordless
consciousness that defers the subsequent verse by rendering time as space. The
poetic exploitation of the horizontal line that appears repeatedly in the letter
to Davy, and only twice in the 1798 *Lyrical Ballads*, belies Wordsworth's punc-
tuational modesty.[35] As the drafts of "There was a Boy" show, Wordsworth was

quite consciously experimenting with the rhythmical force and affective weight of forms of pause. The bold break both intensifies the stress on "Mute" and enforces the idea of muteness by extending the word's voiceless final consonant along the beating silence of the line. The line of wordlessness graphically registers the larger poetic structure of ramifying silence: one boy's occasional experience of "pauses of deep silence" becomes another's occasional speechless standing near his grave. Wordsworth affectively finished this poem about a boy, identified in first drafts with himself, by formally exploiting a mark used to less understated effect in the novels of Laurence Sterne, Charlotte Smith's *Elegiac Sonnets*, and Coleridge's effusions.[36]

By thematically, rhythmically, and visually focusing "pauses of deep silence," and by elaborating their affective and contextual dynamics, "There was a Boy" engages the fascination of the elocutionists with the "emphatical" pauses through which profound aural and visual impressions are made. As if illustrating Sheridan's claim "if there be any proposition or sentiment which he would enforce more strongly than the rest, he may . . . precede it by a longer pause than usual, which will rouse attention, and give it more weight when it is delivered," Wordsworth makes of nature a speaker in whose communion with the boy fall emphatic pauses—not by mechanism but in the natural course of things, as in an intimate and thus "naturally" emphatic, conversation with a friend.[37] "Sometimes," however, nature's pauses are especially profound. Sheridan writes,

> He may go still farther, and make a pause before some very emphatical word, where neither the sense nor common usage would admit of any; but this liberty is to be used with great caution. For as such pauses excite uncommon attention, and of course raise expectation, if the importance of the matter be not fully answerable to such expectation, it will occasion disappointment and disgust. This liberty therefore is to be seldom taken, and never but where something extraordinary and new is offered to the mind, which is likely to be attended with an agreeable surprise. For pauses of this sort put the mind into a state of suspense, which is ever attended with an uneasy sensation, and for which it will always expect to have compensation made, by a greater degree of pleasure, than it otherwise could have had.[38]

In Wordsworth's lines, something "extraordinary and new" is offered to the aroused mind, not in the form of a proposition but as sensation and sentiment:

the "voice of mountain torrents" heard in the distance but "carried far into his heart," and attended by a "gentle shock of mild surprize"—a feeling more equivocal than the "agreeable surprise," which, in Sheridan's model of reception, relieves a preceding "uneasy sensation." Wordsworth's emphasis, however, is not on emotional compensation but on the penetrating force, and affective depth, of the pause—its ability to enhance the power of sound; or, in the alternative scenario, to stream a range of visible objects into one impressive image:

> or the visible scene
> Would enter unawares into his mind
> With all its solemn imagery, its rocks,
> Its woods, and that uncertain heaven, receiv'd
> Into the bosom of the steady lake. (lines 21–25, LB 140)

Wordsworth's paragraph dramatizes the weight induced by Sheridan's pauses of suspense. Here, "pauses of deep silence" turn the lake's *reflection* of the sky into the impression of their *reception*—an image that closes the verse paragraph not with any statement of knowledge gained by mental reflection (for the scene "Would enter unawares" into the boy's mind) but by the sensual imaging of deep impression.[39] As a concluding figure of the boy's sensitivity to, and penetration by, the sounds and silences of the vale, the lake image aligns Wordsworth's language of nature with Sheridan's "vivifying energetic language, stamped by God himself upon our natures . . . which can penetrate the inmost recesses of the soul" but has been bartered for a language "which dies in the ear, or fades upon the sight."[40] It is as if that "energetic language" has bypassed the understanding to work at the level of the "inmost . . . soul."

Sheridan's assertion of a historical corruption of language—a fall from a natural (oral and gestural) language of emotion into writing and print—offers a way of reading the death of the boy and the subsequent transfer of attention to the language of the narrator. Read by Frances Ferguson as an "echo" of the boy, a repeater of his silence, and thus as a figure of autobiography's relation to epitaph, the narrator can also be recognized as a repeater and inscriber of the emphatic pause:[41]

> Fair are the woods, and beauteous is the spot,
> The vale where he was born: the Church-yard hangs

Upon a slope above the village school,
And there along that bank when I have pass'd
At evening, I believe, that near his grave
A full half-hour together I have stood
Mute——for he died when he was ten years old. (lines 26–32, LB
    141)

If, in the first verse paragraph, pauses acted upon the boy, enforcing nature's wild solemnity, now a visibly marked, "longer pause than usual" enforces for the reader the "extraordinary and new" idea of human vitality cut short.[42] The gravity of the boy's experience of nature is fully revealed by the affected and reflecting consciousness of the Wordsworthian "I," who recalls the boy's colloquies with the owls "Across the wat'ry vale" and repeats their suspenseful "pauses of deep silence" in his pauses upon the "slope" where the "Church-yard hangs." The "wat'ry vale" that was the medium of the boy's oral conversation is thus re-delimited as an arena of circulation, for from the narrator's absorption of nature's pauses emerges his sounding, and solemnly breached, apostrophe: "ye Cliffs / And Islands of Winander!" And, as with its only appearance in the 1798 *Lyrical Ballads*, the long, two-em dash is topographically evocative: here it suggestively traces the "grave" upon the "Slope"; there, it traces the woman's endless wandering "across this moor" ("——for no earthly friend / Have I——") and the "perpetual weight which on her spirit lay," dampening words.[43] The "blank line" that takes visible space, and time, in the first letter of MS 1800 inscribes "W. Wordsworth" as the poet of rural emphases—who with that spatial delineation of time extends the force of local circuits of communication, and their silences, into the medium of print. "A gap temporarily seems to open," Ferguson states, "in which articulation is impossible, and in which the reader's greatest responsiveness is to hear silence"—and also, I suggest, to see and trace its places.[44]

Two Books on a Dry Stone

"There was a Boy" is concerned with communication between nature and the local inhabitant within the "wat'ry vale"; how this communication may be circulated beyond the locale is at issue in the revision of its punctuation. In "The Brothers" (LB 142–59) the mediation of place to the outside is also thematically addressed as Wordsworth explicitly invokes the tourist publications—picturesque guidebooks and tours—that prescribe modes of moving through, seeing, and feeling regional landscapes. Opposing his own poem to such publications, he subjected it to an intense process of preparation for print that involved superintending its layout and punctuation so that it might visually render the force of local attachments—of people to each other and to place—and the strains upon those attachments. It is not merely that "silence" emerges as a potent feature of Wordsworth's poetry in "There was a Boy," as Ferguson observes; between that poem and "The Brothers," as the printer's copy shows, the graphic mark of a solemn pause emerges as a potent feature of the book.[45] The "blank line" or double dash functions as a mechanism for sympathetic extension in print and initiates a pattern of epitaphic deixis in the book.

Wordsworth's interest in crafting the look of the poem is clear. In a note at the head of the copy text, Dorothy asked Biggs to print the poem "with a whole page title as the Idiot Boy in the former volume" and not to print "the names of the Speakers as they are here written, by the side, but at full length in the middle of the page as in the Foster-mother's tale" (EY 289). This is not merely the styling of a commodity but also the shaping of reading. Floating the names of speakers in the midst of white space rather than printing them to the side of the first line of each speech increases the distance between verse paragraphs, slowing the turns between speakers and emphasizing the gaps in understanding that are the poem's themes. It also visually clarifies the splitting of the pentameter line across two blocks of speech—distinctly formalizing Leonard's separation from his boyhood village of Ennerdale, to which he has returned after twenty years of seafaring. Leonard hopes to resume his former life as a shepherd among the hills with his younger brother and fellow orphan, whom Leonard, in a type of re-orphaning, had left behind. Unwilling to ask directly for news of James at their "paternal home" (65) and fearing that an unfamiliar grave in the churchyard may belong to his brother, Leonard elicits the "history / Of half these Graves" (184–85) from the local vicar, who fails to recognize the grown man. Pursuing his own course of answers to Leonard's leading questions, the Vicar is slow to reveal the event of James' fatal fall from a cliff; and only after Leonard has left the village never to return does he divulge his identity to the Vicar in a letter. Early on, the poem offers a figure of its interlocking, dialogic form in the image of the "twin cards tooth'd with glittering wire" with which the Priest feeds "the spindle of his youngest child"; he lays them "with gentle care, / Each in the other lock'd" (22–23; 32–33) as he goes to engage in dialogue the man he mistakes for a tourist.

Leonard captures the attention of the Priest because he lingers in the churchyard a curiously long time—with nothing to read. Sitting beside his wife on a "long stone seat," doing "winter's work" of carding wool, he exclaims,

> "These Tourists, Heaven preserve us! needs must live
> A profitable life: some glance along,
> Rapid and gay, as if the earth were air,
> And they were butterflies to wheel about
> Long as their summer lasted . . ." (18, 20, 1–5)

While the Priest's daughter spins the carded wool, turning "her large round wheel in the open air / With back and forward steps" (24–25), tourists "wheel about" (4) effortlessly, aimlessly. "Rapid and gay" (3), they move without being affectively moved. And when they

> "Upon the forehead of a jutting crag
> Sit perch'd with book and pencil on their knee,
> And look and scribble, scribble on and look,
> Until a man might travel twelve stout miles,
> Or reap an acre of his neighbour's corn" (5–9)

they no more productively use their time, making marks with no apparent meaning or value. They are separated from the earth by the picturesque ways of seeing, reading, and marking the landscape that the new tourist publications were formulating and codifying.

Leonard, however, does not fit the tourist stereotype; he loiters—without a book in which to sketch or write and without a carved stone to see or read:

> "that moping son of Idleness
> Why can he tarry *yonder*?—In our church-yard
> Is neither epitaph nor monument,
> Tomb-stone nor name, only the turf we tread,
> And a few natural graves." (11–14)

Reversing the gaze of tourism, the Priest watches and ponders, unsettling cultural hierarchies by setting epitaphic reading against natural treading: knowledge of place and people gained by perusing commemorative inscriptions against knowledge accumulated by living close to the earth and in community.

The Priest later explains, investing the absence of written marks with feeling
and meaning:

> We have no need of names and epitaphs,
> We talk about the dead by our fire-sides.
> And then for our immortal part, *we* want
> No symbols, Sir, to tell us that plain tale . . . (176–79)

The time which the presumed stranger spends in a space that can only be a
blank to him piques the Priest's wonder: tourists do not tread the turf but
move about "'as if the earth were air'" (3). In the rendering of this half an
hour's "lingering" and puzzled looking, Wordsworth poetically validates the
turns and returns of local forms of movement. Like a local "man" traveling
"twelve stout miles" (9) or the girl working her treadle, step by step, in twelve
unfolding lines of verse, he invests the ordinary round with significance:

>   Towards the field
> In which the parish chapel stood alone,
> Girt round with a bare ring of mossy wall,
> While half an hour went by, the Priest had sent
> Many a long look of wonder, and at last,
> Risen from his seat, beside the snowy ridge
> Of carded wool which the old Man had piled
> He laid his implements with gentle care,
> Each in the other lock'd; and, down the path
> Which from his cottage to the church-yard led,
> He took his way, impatient to accost
> The Stranger, whom he saw still lingering there. (25–36)

By taking so long to narrate the Vicar's slow-growing impatience, the poet
aligns his measures with the spatiotemporal patterns of local production rather
than with those of tourism. It is through this opposition between the local and
the touristic that Wordsworth raises questions about the generation and communication of meaning and feeling—the value of "scribble" and swiftly perused epitaphs against the slow, careful, and repeated motions—the spinning
of wool or a tale, the ongoing talking of the dead by the fireside—that center
locals within the "bare ring of mossy wall" (27) which itself signifies the enfold-
edness of the human community within the larger enclosure of the valley.

Elsewhere, too, the poem addresses the problem of how to move the public who are no more local to the vale than the tourists whom the Priest derides— the public who know it through reading books—and in the process tacitly questions the role of the book called *Lyrical Ballads*. In relating the history of Leonard's childhood, the Priest describes how when the streams were "swoln into a noisy rivulet," blocking the boys' passage to school, Leonard would

> go staggering through the fords,
> Bearing his Brother on his back—I've seen him,
> On windy days, in one of those stray brooks,
> Ay, more than once I've seen him, mid-leg deep,
> Their two books lying both on a dry stone
> Upon the hither side: —and once I said,
> As I remember, looking round these rocks
> And hills on which we all of us were born,
> That God who made the great book of the world
> Would bless such piety— (252, 254–63)

The boys' books are not like tourist guidebooks: they do not move visitors through the air like " 'butterflies' " (4) or write nature to stereotype. Instead, they touch nature, itself "the great book of the world." Moved locally across "stray brooks" to safety on dry stones, they mark out a geographical sphere of affection and materialize the bond between the brothers. Leonard's bearing of those precious books and his brother "mid-leg deep" across the swollen streams raises the issue of larger streams of circulation and the capacity of books to carry affection beyond the local. The Bible that the priest put into Leonard's hand the "very night before he went away" did not succeed in bringing Leonard back to his brother when he was still living (277). Can printed books move distant readers—strangers and those estranged from the locale? Would readers, like the tourists of "The Brothers," " 'glance along / Rapid and gay' " (2–3) but unmoved by local affections?

While Leonard's books appear to be an emblem of the kind of book Wordsworth wants to produce (in contact with nature, local, and securing brotherly affections), he still has to acknowledge that *Lyrical Ballads*—a book published by a commercial press in London—will be consumed in the context of other contemporary publications that evoke place—including tours and guidebooks. Thus in preparing the poem for broader circulation among anonymous readers, Wordsworth supplemented his text with topographical explanation:

The great Gavel, so called I imagine, from its resemblance to the
Gable end of a house, is one of the highest of the Cumberland
mountains. It stands at the head of the several vales of Ennerdale,
Wastdale, and Borrowdale.

The Leeza is a River which flows into the Lake of Ennerdale: on
issuing from the Lake, it changes its name, and is called the End,
Eyne, or Enna. It falls into the sea a little below Egremont. (LB 153)

The note appears neither in Mary Hutchinson's fair copy of the poem nor in
earlier drafts.[46] Only in the printer's copy does Wordsworth offer the cartographic overview, situating the mountain and valleys and tracing the flow of
the Leeza through the vale. Here he also enhances the ground-level view of the
place—the emotional texture of the encounter between Leonard and the
Vicar—by graphically refining the rendering of their speech.[47] To Dorothy's
copy of the first verse paragraph alone he adds several commas, semicolons,
and periods, as well as an exclamation point ("These Tourists, Heaven preserve
us! needs must live / A profitable life" [1–2]), modulating the temporal movement of the poem and sharpening its emotional gradations (Figure 24). Inserting a dash after "yonder" ("Why can he tarry yonder?__In our church-yard /
Is neither epitaph nor monument" (12–13) draws out the Priest's wondering in
time and Leonard's lingering in place, emphasizing the deictic gestures, both
intonational and physical, that betoken local knowledge and feeling.

Throughout the poem, emendations to the punctuation of speech sharpen
the emotional contours of place. In the Priest's depiction of the landscape of the
brothers' childhood, the addition of colons gives weight and movement to the
lines.[48] "Like roe-bucks they went bounding o'er the hills," becomes "Like roe
bucks they went bounding o'er the hills:" (273); and "They play'd like two young
ravens on the crags" becomes "They play'd like two young ravens on the crags:"
(274). Parentheses are added to enclose a grammatical aside: "It is the loneliest
place of all these hills," becomes "(It is the loneliest place of all these hills)" (137),
lowering the Priest's intonation and enhancing the austerity of "that tall pike"
where two springs once "bubbled" (136, 138). The Vicar's history brings the place
into view for Leonard and readers as a site of feeling; in augmenting its punctuation, Wordsworth emphasizes the emotional contours of the landscape. What
the poem dramatizes, however, is the suspenseful determination of Leonard's
feelings about the place *now*. These hinge upon Leonard's identification of the
unfamiliar grave in the family plot. Here, too, corrections and additions to the

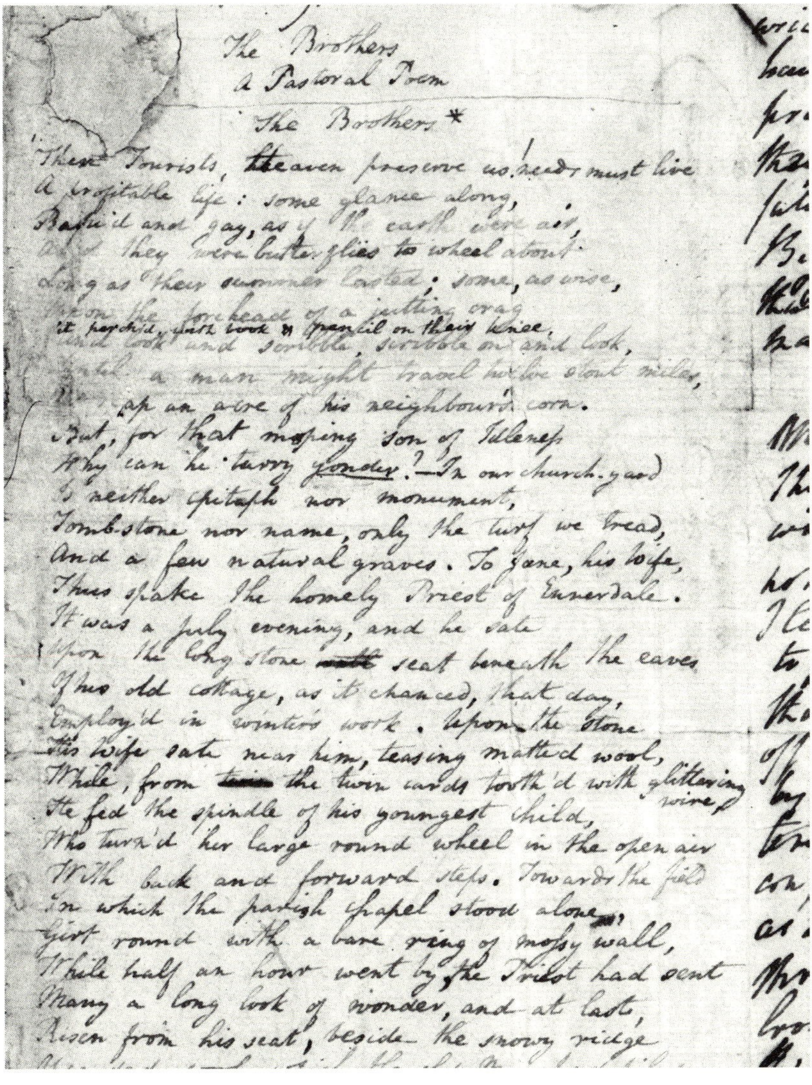

The Brothers
A Pastoral Poem

The Brothers *

These Tourists, Heaven preserve us! needs must live
A profitable life: some glance along,
Rapid and gay, as if the earth were air,
And they were butterflies to wheel about
Long as their summer lasted; some, as wise,
Upon the forehead of a jutting crag
Sit perch'd, with book & pencil on their knee,
And look and scribble, scribble on and look,
Until a man might travel twelve stout miles,
Or reap an acre of his neighbour's corn.
But, for that moping son of Idleness
Why can he tarry yonder?—In our church-yard
Is neither epitaph nor monument,
Tombstone nor name, only the turf we tread,
And a few natural graves. To Jane, his wife,
Thus spake the homely Priest of Ennerdale.
It was a July evening, and he sate
Upon the long stone seat beneath the eaves
Of his old cottage, as it chanced, that day,
Employ'd in winter's work. Upon the stone
His wife sate near him, teasing matted wool,
While, from the twin cards tooth'd with glittering wire,
He fed the spindle of his youngest child,
Who turn'd her large round wheel in the open air
With back and forward steps. Towards the field
In which the parish chapel stood alone,
Girt round with a bare ring of mossy wall,
While half an hour went by, the Priest had sent
Many a long look of wonder, and at last,
Risen from his seat, beside the snowy ridge

Figure 24. The beginning of "The Brothers." Letter of 29 July 1800 (*Lyrical Ballads* MS 1800), detail. Reproduced by permission of the Beinecke Rare Book and Manuscript Library, Yale University.

manuscript punctuation enhance the intensity of Leonard's feeling while more evocatively rendering place. Suspecting that "to the file / Another grave was added" (80–81) since his departure twenty years before, Leonard searches his mind and the landscape for evidence of his memory's failing, gaining hope, when he recalls his loss of the path "that afternoon, / Through fields which once had been well known to him" (89–90), that he had merely forgotten the existence of the grave. "And oh! what joy the recollection now / Sent to his heart:" is corrected in manuscript to "heart!" (91–92), intensifying Leonard's jubilant relief, in free indirect style, at the association of the grave with a forgotten landscape. Leonard's positive identification of James' grave, after the Priest's account of his fall, is similarly heightened. The understated, full stopped "And that then is his grave" is corrected to, "And that then is his grave!__" (cf. 380), evoking the emphatic intonation of a recognition contrary to hope and letting the force of Leonard's dismay "sink" more deeply into the minds of readers.[49]

The poem thus materializes in print between the impulses to make known and make felt to anonymous readers an unknown, unfelt landscape. These impulses converge in the rhetorical accenting of deictic speech (" 'Why can he tarry *yonder?*—' "; "that then *is* his grave!—" [12, 380]), as the man whose "soul was knit to this his native soil" (294) reencounters it as an estranged reader of its marks and ridges. Describing the "rhetorical force of what is left unsaid" between the speakers, Susan Wolfson observes that the questions Leonard asks of the Priest, "whether punctuated as such or conveyed by the protracted uncertainty of a dash, gravitate to a core of answers that scarcely requires articulation." Unlike the voices of "The Thorn" (1798), which are "engaged with deflections of scandal and sensation," the voices of the "The Brothers" are engaged with "inflections of pathos and silent grief."[50] These inflections, many of which were added to the printer's copy, also suggest that as Wordsworth was struggling with the "business" of punctuation, he found ways to renegotiate the conventions of rendering place in print. There is the addition of single dashes that limn Leonard's focus on the file of graves ("who is he that lies / Beneath yon ridge, the last of those three graves;— / It touches on that piece of native rock / Left in the church-yard wall—" (195–98).[51] There is also the long or double dash, which is used to further contour the locale. In the narrator's introduction, it traces the end of a patrilineal order: "they two / Were brother Shepherds on their native hills./——They were the last of all their race" (71–73). And then, in Leonard's invitation to the Priest to disclose mortal "changes" in the physical environment, a double dash inscribes Leonard's rhetorical indirection as well as his undisclosed hope for his brother's survival: "And you, who dwell here, even among these rocks / Can trace the finger of mortality, / And see, that with our threescore years and ten / We are not all that perish.——" (125–28). The long mark traces on the page the men's scanning of the landscape with their eyes "all along the fields / By the brook-side" where Leonard claims a "foot-way" once existed ("—tis gone—"), culminating in Leonard's pointing upward toward "that dark cleft!" which "does not seem to wear the face / Which then it had" (130–33). As a spatial sign of temporal passage, the two-em dash traces in the visual medium the "finger of mortality" (126) that has scored the landscape—a pattern of epitaphic deixis that Wordsworth develops in the preparation of the printer's copy. The Priest's suggestive narrative of the companion "Springs which bubbled side by side" (138) is also made more ominously symbolic by the addition here of the emerging mark of death:

> ten years back,
> Close to those brother fountains, the huge crag
> Was rent with lightning—one is dead and gone,
> The other, left behind, is flowing still.——
> For accidents and changes such as these,
> Why we have store of them! (140–45)

While the scoring of the page indexes the scarring of the landscape, its emphatic silence only barely conceals the human implications of the "brother" fountain tale.

The knowledge that looms in the Vicar's long pauses finally emerges when he narrates James' fall. MS 1800 reads,

> we all conjectur'd
> That, as the day was warm, he had lain down
> Upon the grass, and, waiting for his comrades
> He there had fallen asleep, that in his sleep
> He to the margin of the precipice
> Had walk'd, and from the summit had fallen head
>   =long
> And so no doubt he perish'd: at the time,
> We guess, that in his hands he must have had
> His Shepherd's staff; for midway in the cliff
> It had been caught, and there for many years
> It hung____and moulder'd there.[52]

A copy made by Mary Hutchinson by April 5 has "hung, and moulder'd there."[53] More dramatically, the long dash entered by Dorothy in MS 1800 links the rending of the crag and scorching of a "brother" fountain to the rending of the local family and loss of a brother, fulfilling but not subsuming the narrative portent (Figure 25). The sign of temporal passage that functioned as a device of gentle suspense and a figure of Leonard's knowing suspicion now visually indexes the literal suspension of James' staff, hanging "midway in the cliff." The long dash reinscribes on the page a local sign made by accident and attributed by the community to James' unconscious actions.[54] "Midway in the cliff" and amid the line of verse, the blank line carries the pathos of James' deep sense of loss and ongoing desire for his brother that the Priest had attached to his somnambulism (in sleepwalking "He sought his Brother Leonard" [349]). It also carries the "piety" and love that the Priest had attached to Leonard's carrying of his brother "mid-leg deep" across the streams. Thus the hanging staff is a material epitaph: a physical symbol of the boy's commitment to the pastoral life of his forefathers and of the invasion of that life by suspense—the

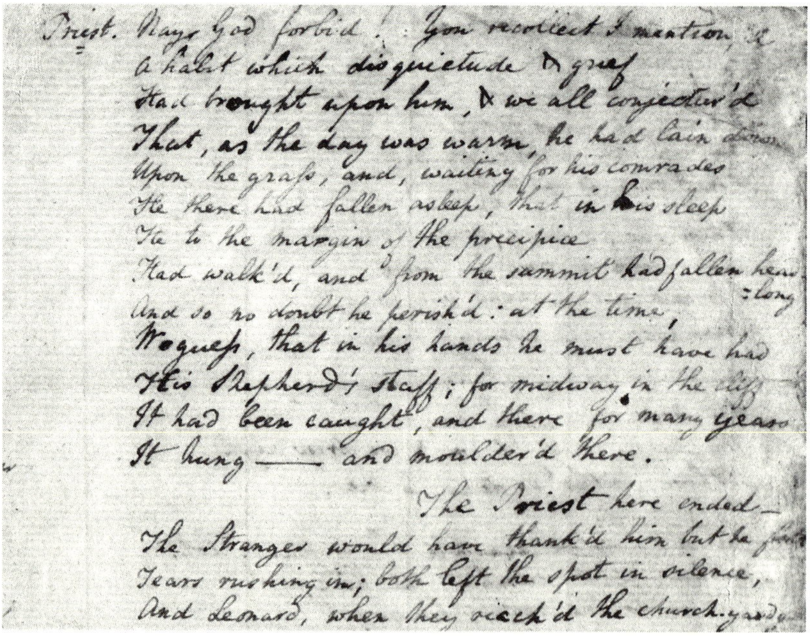

Figure 25. "It hung ___ and mouldr'd there." Letter of 1 August 1800 (*Lyrical Ballads* MS 1800), detail. Reproduced by permission of the Beinecke Rare Book and Manuscript Library, Yale University.

hope, never fulfilled, for his loving brother's return. As an icon of the sus-
pended staff, the double dash inscribes the brothers' strong attachment and
separation, and with that breach, the end of a pastoral line and patrilineage.
The community has "no need of names and epitaphs" because its most telling
and forceful signs are local and organic rather than public and conventional.
Wordsworth's preprint repunctuation of the poem contrives to give the anonymous readers of *Lyrical Ballads* something that consumers of tours and guidebooks do not gain—access to those local, potent signs. It generates a meaningful
sign for readers over the slow course of the poem, in a way analogous to the
ways that signs are gradually produced within the community.

Wordsworth questions the affective capacity of books in "The Brothers"
and, in its final preprint stages of copying and correction, graphically sharpens
the poem's critique of those books that bring people to the Lakes of Cumberland and Westmorland, move them rapidly through the area, but fail to move
them in emotionally significant ways. While the slow raveling of the tale embodies the time of local knowledge, feeling, and production—recalling the
Priest's carding and his daughter's spinning of the wool (now imbued with fatal
significance)—the many single and double dashes added to the poem for publication slow reading while foregrounding a landscape experienced in and over
time. They mark the suspension of conversation about communal place when
seeing eyes and remembering minds hover over a shattered crag and trace the
margin of a river where a path once lay. The dashes mediate a slowly changing
landscape, and rather than engage readers of the book *Lyrical Ballads* in the
"gay and rapid" iterations of a scene, they linger over scars and impress upon
us the image of a shepherd's staff which "hung _____ and mouldr'd there."
Wordsworth's book gets closer to God's "great book of the world" (262) by
mediating a nature in which the course of human life and death becomes
openly or plainly legible.[55] The value of the blank line, from its first telling emphasis of "the last of all their race" among the hills, is confirmed gradually, just
as "All that the Priest had said" gradually weighs more heavily upon Leonard:
"All press'd on him with such a weight, that now, / This vale, where he had been
so happy, seem'd / A place in which he could not bear to live" (417, 420–22).

Despite Wordsworth's typographic and topographic crafting of the Priest's
final speech, the two-em dash in "It hung _____ and mouldr'd there" was replaced in the printed text by a single em dash—most probably to conserve
space.[56] Elsewhere in the printed poem the visual accenting of feeling was reinforced—in one instance so as to stake a claim, inadvertently or not, for
punctuation's role in the sympathetic reception of printed texts. " 'Tis my

belief / His absent Brother still was at his heart" (343–44), the Priest tells Leonard, surprised then to detect a welling of emotion in his audience of one. MS
1800 reads,

> often, rising from his bed at night,
> He in his sleep would walk about, & sleeping
> He sought his Brother Leonard—You are mov'd
> Forgive me, Sir: before I spoke to you,
> ~~I wrong'd you in my thoughts~~
> I judg'd you most unkindly.[57]

The addition, by either Davy or the compositor, of an exclamation mark ("You
are mov'd!") more strongly evokes the sounds of surprise and even Leonard's
look of pained response to a story all too personal. If in the poems "feeling
gives importance to the action and situation and not the action and situation
to the feeling" (LB 746), as Wordsworth went on to claim in the Preface, the
added exclamation mark emphasizes the irony of the poem's affective warp and
weft: the Priest's happy reversal of expectation and Leonard's disappointing
confirmation of suspicion that slowly play out, in interlocking "back and forward steps" (25), across the pages of the poem. Moreover, "You are mov'd!"
highlights the poem's staging of concerns about the public reception of local
poems while revealing Wordsworth's lack of control over that reception. Neither approved by the poet, who did not read the proofs, nor canceled by him
in subsequent printings and editions, the mark is socially inscribed and the tale
variously received, no matter how determining the Priest's exclamation appears.[58] The effect of interactions among poet, amanuenses, proofer, and printers, the mark dramatizes the elusiveness of a distant readership, whose tones,
looks, and gestures, like the Vicar's when receiving Leonard's letter of self-
disclosure, exceed the scope of the poem and perception of the writer.[59]

The Space Words Occupy on Paper

If "There was a Boy" and "The Brothers" query the capacity of printed books
to transmit local feelings beyond the "wat'ry vale" of Winander and the "books"
and "brooks" of Ennerdale, the poems Wordsworth copied next attempt an
answer by representing the pages of the book *Lyrical Ballads* as surfaces for the
reinscription of local affections. In the former poems Wordsworth

experimented with punctuation, graphically slowing the flow of words to carry feeling to distant readers. In August, Wordsworth began to close the distance between book and place by experimenting with poetic form. The effect was to make place more explicitly the material foundation for affections—and the scene of their first expression—and to make the poetic page a material effect of place. In what follows, I term these poems of August 1800, *print inscriptions*—self-consciously typographical objects that nevertheless also disclose their material and historical relations to writing made on objects in the external world. These poems do not produce the paradoxical effect of what Andrew Bennett has called "impossible writing"—writing that supposedly exists *not* on the page in the book that one is reading but elsewhere.[60] They present themselves as the latest, typographical effect of a succession of inscriptions, which they carry forward and arrange. Far from denying or ignoring their condition as printed texts, they foreground that condition as a product of a stable relationship with other kinds of script that have determinate places in the material world.

Between August 8 and 13, in a small gap left by Dorothy in the printer's copy, William added a prefatory note to "If Nature, for a favorite Child" stating that the "*Author*" wrote the "*following lines*" opposite one of the names of the "*Schoolmasters*," inscribed "*in gilt letters*," on a "*tablet*" in the "*School of* ————" (LB 211). The headnote makes significant adjustments to a poem composed over a year earlier, at Goslar between October and December 1798, insofar as it explicitly presents the poem as a poem in a book and as a copy of lines appearing elsewhere. Though the poem points to itself—"Read o'er these lines; and then review / This tablet" (5-6)—it nowhere positions itself spatially; the title, "Lines written on a Tablet in a School," which Wordsworth does not seem to have written, appeared only in the table of contents of the printed book, not on the poem page.[61] The paratext, then, not only secures the poem's status as an inscription but also dispels any fiction of its being read in situ. Unlike "Lines left upon a Seat in a Yew-tree which stands near the Lake of Esthwaite" (vol. 1) or "Lines written with a Slate-Pencil upon a Stone" (vol. 2), the poem announces, through its new preface, its double status as inscription and print object.[62] How does this affect our reading?

Shaping reading is the acknowledged aim of the stanzas. Like other inscriptions in the poet's corpus (and the tradition more broadly), the poem addresses its own readers, but instead of urging a special sensitivity to a spot in nature, it instructs in textual reception.[63] "Read o'er these lines," it commands, singling out those readers who never let their feelings go "astray,"

and then review
This tablet, that thus humbly rears
In such diversity of hue
Its history of two hundred years.

—When through this little wreck of fame,
Cypher and syllable, thine eye
Has travell'd down to Matthew's name,
Pause with no common sympathy. (4–12)

Here Wordsworth is being verbally explicit about the pause that he made so graphically apparent in "The Brothers," and whereas that poem focuses on acts of speaking, this one foregrounds acts of reading. The "lines" do not merely instruct in the reading of the inscribed tablet but introduce an emotional and biographical supplement to it, which is inscribed in the three-stanza sketch of Matthew's intensity of feeling that follows (17–28). These stanzas strive to un-check a reader's "tear" by offering Matthew as an emotional model, quick to sympathize but now stagnant: "Poor Matthew, all his frolics o'er, / Is silent as a standing pool" (17–18).[64] With print publication on the horizon, moreover, Wordsworth supplemented this act of supplementation paratextually—not by adding long pauses but by attaching personal history to the plea for a feeling "Pause," as if, by identifying the Matthew mourned in the poem as a teacher in the "*School of*————" and attributing the lines to the "*Author*," he might stimulate imaginative identification with the beloved teacher scenario—an effect encouraged by the particularizing and privatizing elision of the name. Further, by contextualizing the "*lines*" as an inscription beside an inscription, Wordsworth implies an intimate act of writing at a scene of reading, modeling a reception so sympathetic that it culminated in expressive and commemorative writing. Positioning the lines in place thus also situates the texts in time.

The prefatory note also redoubles the lines' attention to the written medium but without issuing pointed directives about the pace of reading. Rather, the note revisualizes the inscribed tablet, taking time to describe the "*gilt letters*" of the Schoolmasters' names, with "*the time at which they entered upon and quitted their office*" and the "*lines*" written "*Opposite.*" To reinforce the "Pause with no common sympathy" (12) at "Matthew's name" (11), then, Wordsworth elaborates the material format and symbols, adding dates and thus the *idea* of distinct historical stages—not only within the "two hundred years" (8) of schoolmasters but also, implicitly, between that making of the "wreck of fame"

(9) and the writing of the lines, and between the writing of the lines and the printing of the poem. The note thus makes apparent a third inscriptional level—that of the page, with its own bipartite format and historical logic: the italicized prose printed above but written after the tetrameter stanzas. The printed poem emerges, on the page, as an effect of the "*Author*['s]" rereading of his own inscribed "*lines*" and as an effect of the series of historical inscriptions that the page organizes and represents. Going to press, then, Wordsworth fashioned a material and personal prehistory for the poem, activating the visual imagination and feelings of his readers by stratifying the printed plane with inscriptional and expressive dimensions.

Another print inscription is "To Joanna," which Wordsworth completed in the last week of August, reading it aloud on both 23 August and 1 September, the months in which he drafted the Preface (LB 244). In presenting itself as a personal letter to a friend distanced geographically from the region, "To Joanna" raises the question of writing's power to restimulate feeling associated with local place. Moreover, by distancing Joanna constitutionally from the Lakes (raised "Amid the smoke of cities" [1], her "heart / Is slow towards the sympathies of them / Who look upon the hills with tenderness" [5–7]), the poem positions Joanna as a figure for the public reader, who by this proxy may "gladly listen to discourse / However trivial" (14–15) concerning local people and experience. If the letter's purpose is to teach Joanna that those friends "with whom you once were happy" still "talk / Familiarly of you and of old times" (16–17), it does so by offering a genealogy of ongoing affection in a nested series of visual, aural, and inscriptional events that measure out the passage of time since her last visit, implicating the written and printed passages to Joanna with feeling.

As if through a telescope, the writer looks back in time from the present moment of the letter, first to "some ten days past" (18) to recount his response to the Vicar upon being asked why,

> Reviving obsolete Idolatry,
> I like a Runic Priest, in characters
> Of formidable size, had chisel'd out
> Some uncouth name upon the native rock,
> Above the Rotha, by the forest side. (27–31)

His explanation itself looks back to " 'One summer morning' " when he and Joanna " 'had walk'd abroad' " (36) and he had " 'gaz'd perhaps two minutes space' " (51) upon " 'that tall rock' " (42) above the Rotha—the point of greatest historical and visual magnification from the time of the letter. He then zooms forward, " 'when eighteen moons / Were wasted' " (77–78), to the moment of chiseling " 'Joanna's name upon the living stone' " (83). Distinctions of time then fade into the continuing present of affectionate and familiar reference— " 'And I, and all who dwell by my fire-side / Have call'd the lovely rock, Joanna's Rock' " (84–85)—and the continuing present of address, as represented by the letter and the poem "To Joanna."

The occasion behind the inscription in stone, the first cause, is the narrator's " 'two minutes' space' " of silent visual rapture that Joanna witnessed but did not share. At " 'that tall rock / Which looks toward the East,' " he tells the Vicar,

> "I there stopp'd short,
> And trac'd the lofty barrier with my eye
> From base to summit; such delight I found
> To note in shrub and tree, in stone and flower,
> That intermixture of delicious hues,
> Along so vast a surface, all at once,
> In one impression, by connecting force
> Of their own beauty, imag'd in the heart.
> —When I had gaz'd perhaps two minutes' space,
> Joanna, looking in my eyes, beheld
> That ravishment of mine, and laugh'd aloud." (42–53)

Joanna's laugh is reactive and deflective. The narrator maps its reverberations among the surrounding mountains (from Helm-crag to Hammar-Scar, Silver-How, Loughrigg, Fairfield, Helvellyn, Skiddaw, Glaramara, and Kirkstone [56–65]), which he obtrusively personifies as if to demonstrate the outsider's responsiveness only to a nature whose life force is writ large: " 'while we both were listening, to my side / The fair Joanna drew, as if she wish'd / To shelter from some object of her fear' " (74–76). He represents himself, by contrast, as an organizer of this energy—not recoiling in awe but moved, over time, to inscription. As he explains to the Priest, eighteen months later " 'as [he] chanc'd to walk alone / Beneath this rock,' " he " 'sate down, and there, / In memory of affections old and true, / . . . chissel'd out in those rude characters / Joanna's name upon the living stone' " (78–79, 80–83). The inscriptional act memorializes and stabilizes Joanna's endearing flux of passions, just as that " 'intermixture of delicious hues' " on the rock face, " 'all at once, / In one impression, by connecting force / Of their own beauty' " was " 'imag'd in the heart' " (47–50). By this analogy, the materialization of " 'affections old and true' " in the name accrues a residual graphic force.

Although the historical sequence of mediations—the original impression, the look of ravishment, the laugh, its report among the mountains, the inscription on the rock, the oral report to the Vicar, and the letter to Joanna—implies a symbolic evolution, " 'Joanna's name upon the living stone' " (83) is not superseded. The inscription has an ongoing existence that coincides with the letter to Joanna and, we are to believe, with the poem "To Joanna"—a column of print headed by the same name. That tall rock on which the name is chiseled is even made to appear typographically in the center of the poem, in thirteen lines that render the narrator's tracing of " 'the lofty barrier with [his] eye.' " His " 'two minutes' space' " of silent gazing from " 'base to summit' " is remeasured in *our* reading of the vertical column of blank verse, a set of lines framed by a pair of dashes (38–51). To read the printed passage, I suggest, is to retrace, that lofty barrier; it is to " 'to note . . . shrub and tree . . . stone and flower' " in the typographical array of words and lines on the page—and thus perhaps, by " 'connecting force of their own beauty,' " to have impressed upon us an image of the " 'living stone.' "[65] Whereas Wordsworth slows reading in "If Nature, for a favorite Child" by galvanizing the inscriptional imagination—the visual imagination of "Cypher and syllable" (line 10; LB 211), numbers and lines— "To Joanna" dramatizes the slow reading of rock face and printed space. The poem is cast as material effect and further cause: subject to, and partaking of, those local feelings and forces—an impression on paper with a traceable ancestry and material foundation.

The complex frame structure, by which the original incident is narrated once but made meaningful at multiple levels of mediation, is new to the volume, and it shows Wordsworth experimenting with the force of words and poetic form. How can a nondramatic poem "speak" to a reader? What was a blank to Joanna, simply a " 'tall rock' " facing " 'the East,' " (42–43) no longer is. Perceived as one of a chorus of personified crags and mountains, and inscribed with "characters / Of formidable size" (28–29) that tall rock becomes a " 'living stone' " (83)—as a blank page becomes a letter and a printed poem, an address eliciting a response ("—You are mov'd!" ["The Brothers," line 349; LB 155]). It is not simply the rhetorical device of the personal epistle that is functioning here: the facing and refacing of the rock as " 'Joanna's Rock' " (not the defacement that the Vicar perceives) bring the spatial field of the poem to the surface and activate the reader's material and sympathetic imagination.

Wordsworth's self-historicizing print inscriptions were written in the practical context of preparing *Lyrical Ballads* for print, which involved the drafting of the Preface. As Wordsworth was crafting poems that disclose their slow histories and material foundations, he was beginning to formulate his critique of the newspapers' "rapid communication of intelligence" about "great national events . . . daily taking place" and of their "hourly" gratification of readers' "craving for extraordinary incident."[66] In contrast to the ephemerality and relentless periodicity of "frantic novels, sickly and stupid German Tragedies, and deluges of idle and extravagant stories in verse" (LB 746–47), the poems of August 1800 enfold inscriptional prehistories that record the gradual and localized (not extravagant) growth of the feelings they express. Thus, for example, the printed characters of "To Joanna" evoke the rock carvings that embody "'affections old and true'" (81). So, too, the lunar measuring of the time to inscription, "'when eighteen moons / Were wasted'" (77–78), exemplifies the claim made soon after in the Preface that in rustic life "the essential passions of the heart find a better soil in which they can attain their maturity" (LB 743).

In the Note to "The Thorn," which Dorothy transcribed with the last part of the Preface in an undated letter probably of September 30 and October 1, Wordsworth explicitly addressed issues about the communication of passion that he had been grappling with in the poems of the previous month. His aim in composing the "The Thorn" (for the 1798 edition) was, he said, while adhering to the style in which "such [superstitious and talkative] men describe, to take care that words, which in their minds are impregnated with passion, should likewise convey passion to Readers who are not accustomed to sympathize with men feeling in that manner, or using such language" (LB 351). Significantly, he construed the impasse as a problem of reading—a mistaking of repetition for tautology—stating that "a Poet's words . . . ought to be weighed in the balance of feeling, and not measured by the space which they occupy upon paper" (351). Judging words' worth solely by spatial measurement, it turns out, is to devalue them, just as they are devalued in the crowded columns of newspapers, "frantic novels," and "deluges" of "extravagant stories in verse." Wordsworth, in effect, imagines the reception of popular print as a verbal relationship of inverse proportions: the greater frequency of a word, the more space it occupies on the two-dimensional plane of print, the less its affective value and efficacy. To weigh words "in the balance of feeling," by contrast, is to assess the "interest which the mind attaches to words," to sense a speaker's dissatisfaction with "the inadequateness of [his] own powers, or the deficiencies of language" or to sense the pleasure the mind takes in the material efficacy of the words ("<u>things</u>, active and efficient, which are themselves part of the passion"). In this model, thoughts are formulated into words in time. During "efforts" to "communicate impassioned feelings," Wordsworth continues, "there will be a craving in the mind, and as long as it is unsatisfied the Speaker will cling to the same words, or words of the same character" (LB 351). Ideally, the repetition of a word on paper should indicate the cognitive interest of its user, the stamp of its impregnation "with passion."

With their historical layering of inscriptional surfaces, a demonstration of interest over time, Wordsworth's print inscriptions affectively charge "the space [words] occupy upon paper" (LB 351). It is not the narrator's oral repetition of his words (as in the expansive ballad "The Thorn") but his nested reporting of inscription and expression that impassions "To Joanna," infusing both typographical space and geographical place with feeling. Thus we can read the Note to "The Thorn" as a self-conscious differentiation of that poem's narrator from the poet as figured by the letter writer of "To Joanna" and of that poem's pages from the pages of "To Joanna." Wordsworth worked to configure these pages not as an apparently arbitrary surface for the recording of a verbal sequence— from a mind, he feels compelled to remind readers, which thinks, feels, and articulates in time—but as a material register of historical feelings and mediations. Wordsworth, that is, brings the history of words and feelings, subjective and communal, to the surface. As he wrote in the Note, "the Reader cannot be too often reminded that poetry is passion: it is the history or science of feelings" (LB 351). The Note thus obliquely theorized Wordsworth's more recent experimentation with poetic form and passionate reception as he prepared to make *Lyrical Ballads* a printed publication by "W. Wordsworth."

This increasingly developed attention to the poems' disposition on the pages of the book and to the poems' affective configuration of those pages was reflected in mid-October when Wordsworth requested a "separate Title page" for the poems to be "classed under the title of 'Poems on the Naming of Places'" (EY 305; cf. LB 732). In this letter, Wordsworth sent the last of these to the press along with an "Advertisement" which identified them as a distinct affective cluster:

> By Persons resident in the country and attached to rural objects, many places will be found unnamed or of unknown names, where little Incidents will have occurred, or feelings been experienced, which will have given to such places a private and peculiar Interest. From a wish to give some sort of record to such Incidents or renew

the gratification of such Feelings, Names have been given to Places
by the Author and some of his Friends—and the following Poems
written in consequence.——— (LB 241)

In presenting the five poems under their own title and advertisement pages,
Wordsworth widened his attention from the typographical field of the single
poem to the sequence, and from the one spot to the several. This bibliographical decision, of course, had topographical implications—insofar as the "space"
words "occupy" in this distinctly bordered unit of the book evokes a geographical region and contemporary modes of geographical representation. Like certain words in a speaker's mind that are "impregnated with passion," certain
places are infused with "private and peculiar Interest"—their value determined
not by size, location, or status as marked or unmarked on a topographical map
or triangulation survey, but by the feelings and occurrences associated with
them by local residents. The name given to such places emerges as a special
type of "impregnated" word, a referent current within an intimate group of
friends and family, for whom it carries particular weight. While two of the
poems written "in consequence" of such private acts of naming strongly reference public place-names and locally designated landscape features (Grasmere,
the fells in the vicinity) and, like others in the volume, footnote those references, as a group the poems diverge from the rest by emphasizing authorial
incidents and feelings. The effect is to personalize the very real region that the
poems evoke—as if they were a foldout map of intimacies within the larger
book.[67] Interestingly, the poems that pin the private spots to the area of Grasmere vale were two that Wordsworth composed during the copying of the
volume—"A narrow girdle of rough stones and crags" and "To Joanna" (II and
IV in the sequence: see LB 24, 242–51). With them, then, Wordsworth made
real the very personal geography that the earlier poems evoke. And in opening
the group of poems to cross-reference within the broader ecology of print—to
the maps, tour narratives, guidebooks, engravings, and aquatints that depict
Grasmere and its surrounds—he succeeded in enhancing their typographical
and topographical charge: the exact location, within the region, of the "still
nook" named for "Mary" in "To M.H." (as with "Emma's dell" in "It was an
April morning") was, and would remain, "Unknown to [travellers]," a "calm
recess" away from "road" and "path" (lines 23, 17, 13, 2, LB 250–51). The point
is not to move tourists through the region—so that they "glance along / Rapid
and gay" ("The Brothers," 3)—but to create spaces of feeling, accesses to intimacy, within the printed book.

"More Than an Ordinary Interspace"

Wordsworth's attention to the book culminated, between October and December, in the composition of the long blank-verse narrative "Michael, A Pastoral," which, he insisted in a letter to the printers, must "conclude the work." Now Wordsworth closed the distance between book and place by focusing, and historically charging, the very blankness and form of the page. In a letter probably written between December 10 and 14, Coleridge copied the first 216 lines of the poem, and in addition to requesting "a separate title-page," asked for a "very large Capital Letter where there is one in the M.S., with more than an ordinary interspace between the Paragraphs" (EY 308).[68] Like the longer than ordinary dashes added to the poems throughout the volume, "more than an ordinary interspace" slows the pace of reading, but its more significant effect in "Michael" derives from its visual articulation of historical changes disclosed within the poetic narrative—a function also performed by the long dashes in "The Brothers," which "trace" the movements of "the finger of mortality" (126) across the human and physical environment. Here, however, Wordsworth recruited the blankness of the page to reveal that what seems to be blankness, on the hillside, has material and emotional significance.

The use of "interspace" as a means of signification intensified a relationship that had been developing throughout the late summer and autumn—the relationship between the material form of *Lyrical Ballads* and the thematic attention paid within it to printed books and authorship. In the first introductory verse paragraph of "Michael," the narrator prefaces his "Story" appertaining to the "straggling Heap of unhewn stones" beside the "tumultuous brook of Green-head Gill" (lines 17, 2, LB 252) with personal history; heard when he "was yet a boy / Careless of books," but led on by the "gentle agency" of "natural objects" to "feel / For passions that were not [his] own" (27–29, 30–31), it was the "earliest of those Tales that spake to [him] / Of Shepherds, dwellers in the Vallies" (22–23). Thus to read the tale is to enter into an ontological anteriority, to return to a period of sympathetic extension toward "man, the heart of man, and human life," mediated not by "books" but by "natural objects," including stones and brooks (33, 30).

The first paragraph also addresses the capacity of books to expand human sympathies by countering the guidebooks' leading of tourists through the landscape. The narrator, by contrast, gently leads readers to his boyhood locale and state of feeling, toward a topography of unexpected nondifficulty and clarity:

If from the public way you turn your steps
Up the tumultuous brook of Green-head Gill,
You will suppose that with an upright path
Your feet must struggle; in such bold ascent
The pastoral Mountains front you, face to face.
But, courage! for beside that boisterous Brook
The Mountains have all open'd out themselves,
And made a hidden valley of their own.
No habitation there is seen; but such
As journey thither find themselves alone
With a few sheep, with rocks and stones, and kites
That overhead are sailing in the Sky.
It is in truth an utter solitude . . . (1–13)

Encouraging, the narrator-guide claims that the fronting "Mountains" soon open out, from the seam of the "Brook" into a valley of visibility—on the model, it seems, of an opening book. And thus if we "turn [our] steps / Up" toward the pastoral nook, we cross imaginatively into a place of idealized interchange between solitary mind and nature, where the role of writing—marks bringing a surface into meaning—is performed by "a few sheep" and "rocks and stones" on the valley floor and by "kites" against the expanse of sky. The very distinctness of "natural objects" implies no gap between signifier and signified, nor even a symbolic order: an unfallen, unwritten pastoral.

The first paragraph is introductory and idealizing. To enter that place, and follow the story that made it mean in this way, the reader crosses, as she scans the page of the book, the "more than . . . ordinary interspace" that divides the first and second paragraphs. In effect, Wordsworth lays out the poem so as to mark the reader's passage into a world—and time of life—supposedly innocent of books. Here shepherds and hills, not books, are the bearers of memory. Because Michael had daily climbed the hills with "vigorous steps," the hills "had impress'd / So many incidents upon his mind / Of hardship, skill or courage, joy or fear" and "like a book preserv'd the memory / Of the dumb animals, whom he had sav'd, / Had fed or shelter'd" (67–69, 70–72). Meaning is actively produced, unmediated by language. It is made and preserved as Michael cares for the "dumb animals" and listens to the wind (48–60)—not by his reading and writing of books but what the narrative presents as a primitive alternative: watchful attention to the shifting weather and the purposeful climbing of the fells. Greenhead Gill is a locale of bookless memorialization, a place of topographical not typographical signification—which, from his adult perspective, the narrator can only construe in bibliographic terms.

The pastoral world into which Wordsworth's "more than . . . ordinary interspace" conducts the reader is also an economic order, in which the value of things is determined by the labor involved in shaping them—labor memorialized by the names given to these things. That "The CLIPPING TREE" (179) so baldly refers in the "rustic dialect" (178) to the shearing performed in its shade suggests its basic referential logic and the community's valorization of industry over imagination. In a letter to Charles James Fox mailed with a copy of the book, Wordsworth protested the parliamentary "measures" undermining the traditional existence of the "Northern statesman"—the small landowners represented by Michael and his forefathers—and bemoaned the erosion of the "domestic affections" that he associated with that existence by industrialization, urbanization, inflation, taxation, and inadequate relief for the poor (EY 312–15). And yet, as Marjorie Levinson has shown, [69] while the poem manifests the "forgotten material dimension of that highly literary and idealizing form, the pastoral," it does not organize its elements into stringent political critique but "affectionately" presents a "*modus vivendi*" in which the pleasure of life is derived from "material and productive relationships to specific fields, hills, and animals" (63, 62). The narrator sketches Michael and Sarah's engagement in a nonspecialized, unalienated form of labor which is "compensated by the realization of service or pleasure, not by their symbolic expression, money." This compensation, Levinson observes, extends to the inhabitants of the vale, whose appreciation of the light emanating from the oil lamp in Michael and Sarah's house, as the couple card and spin wool at night, is suggested by their naming of the house "The Evening Star" and their interpretation of it as a "public Symbol of the life, / The thrifty Pair had liv'd" (137–38). Michael also invests his energy, Levinson observes, in shaping his son Luke, who, like his material property (sheep, lamp, land, and dogs), increases in real value over time: "Thus in his Father's sight the Boy grew up, / And now when he had reach'd his eighteenth year, / He was his comfort and his daily hope" (214–16). The narrator's temporal and affective focusing ("now," "daily hope") prepares the dramatic turn of the next verse paragraph: Michael is called upon to pay the forfeiture of a contractual claim, entered into long before on behalf of his nephew (217–36). Wordsworth marks this economic crisis by a second manipulation of the layout of the poem that more radically engages the matter of the book.

In the second of three letters sent to the printer on December 18, Dorothy noted above line 217 (the first of the remaining 275 lines), "This must begin on a new page with no words between such as Part second or any thing of that sort." The intentional use of the page, in place of words, numerals, or other typographic marks, is to make the reader turn a "new page" just as the narrative takes a tragic turn; the reader is forced to break off reading as a breach opens in the "domestic affections" and the organic community is wrenched by the procedures of intensive capitalism. In a failed bid to raise money without having to sell "a portion of his patrimonial fields" (234), Michael, as Levinson has shown (69), converts Luke's use value into exchange value, a privileging of the land over the son he sends to the city as a wage laborer that results in the loss of both (456). The "new page" materializes in the poem's layout—and engages readers in—the passing of the pastoral order of Greenhead Gill and its incorporation within a mercantile economy: "The Cottage which was nam'd The Evening Star / Is gone, the ploughshare has been through the ground / On which it stood" (485–87). Whereas the hills had "like a book preserv'd the memory / Of the dumb animals" (70–71) that Michael had saved, the plow, in turning over the earth, has effaced those particular marks of productive relation and opened the hills to aesthetic representation in books. The capitalist economy threatens local knowledge and forms of feeling: "The Evening Star" that was a "public Symbol" is not just effaced but replaced by homogenous rows suggestive of print. The new symbolic (typographical) order of information and valuation—represented in the poem by the tourist books that prescribe the less strenuous "public way" (1)—disregards local meanings and marks of rural experience that fall outside the category of the aesthetic.

Levinson explains how the narrator-poet translates the significance of the "straggling Heap of unhewn stones" (17) to a broader, urban public of readers, and also how, in the frame narrative, he recuperates Michael's material and affective loss in the form of poetry. Although Luke never returns to complete the sheepfold at which his father "wrought" the "length of full seven years from time to time" (479, 480), and although the land is sold, the narrator-poet presents himself as "finish[ing] the sheepfold in finer tone, with language instead of stones" (Levinson, 74). Property inheritance is restored as poetic inheritance. As the narrator states at the outset, he relates the "history / Homely and rude" for the

> delight of a few natural hearts,
> And with yet fonder feeling, for the sake

Of youthful Poets, who among these Hills
Will be my second Self when I am gone. (34–39)

The narrator-poet realizes, then, not the primary material value of the sheep-fold as refuge from the weather, but its symbolic, "Christian" value as sign of the dangers of material possessiveness. This attempted "imaginative transcendence" or "aesthetic sublimation" of history, Levinson suggests (77, 75), pries the poet from the program of representational immediacy to which the Preface had committed him. Wordsworth, she argues, presents and celebrates the poet and poetic labor in the place of "external objects," betraying the poem's "historic materials" (77).

Yet it is not merely the figure of the poet who emerges in the framing narrative, alongside the mythical figure of the suffering shepherd whose loss he redeems, but also the historical material of the book. The book is heard and glimpsed in the slippery iterations of "tumultuous brook" (2) and "boisterous Brook" (6) and "tumultuous brook" (332) and "boisterous brook" (491)—a pronounced framing device; and it is implied in the unfolding, from several references to the "Sheep-fold" (417), of the "Fold of which / His flock had need" (470–71, cf. 430, 451, 476, 490). With the tale of Michael's leaving his "work unfinished when he died" (481), Wordsworth finishes the work of filling his octavo—not folio—"of which / His flock had need," a self-reflexive finale that raises readers' awareness of the new economic-symbolic order by engaging them, and keeping them in touch with, a book that he construes in close material relation to the fundamental "external objects" of the poem: its hills, brook, and fold.[70]

By the end of "Michael," even more than in "The Brothers," there is no place so local that it can remain innocent of the symbolic order (including contracts of guarantee and money) and therefore of the sign systems that represent it to a distant world and of which books are the embodiment. Working within this predicament, Wordsworth strives to represent the local for those who are far away without commodifying it—without uprooting its particularity and transforming it into an easily transferable sign ("the beautiful," "the picturesque," etc.). Michael sends his son Luke to the city—as Wordsworth, of course, sends his poems to the Bristol printers for the publishers of Paternoster Row, London (T. N. Longman and O. Rees). Indeed, this post-Preface poem invokes the urban world of commercial print and newspapers in Luke's writing of "loving letters full of wondrous news" (442) from the "dissolute city," where "at length," he "gave himself / To evil courses" (452–54).

Wordsworth's printed book, "Michael" suggests, quenches no "degrading thirst after outrageous stimulation" (LB 747); but by guiding readers "Up the tumultuous brook" (2) and into another realm of apprehension, where substances, not signs, expand the sympathies, it ameliorates the "affections" (LB 745).

Wordsworth, of course, had made a problem in the Note to "The Thorn" of sympathizing with a garrulous narrator of "slow faculties and deep feelings," and had employed a "lyrical and rapid Metre"—passionate by virtue of its pacing and association with exciting subjects—to facilitate the extension of sympathy (LB 351). As he had written in the Preface, meter is "something which will greatly contribute to impart passion to the words" (LB 756). In "Michael," however, Wordsworth went in a different direction. Having first drafted "semi-jocular" stanzas about the sheepfold and Michael's disappointment in a rapid, anapestic meter (in DC MS 15), when he returned to the subject in October—after dropping Coleridge's "Christabel" and needing more poems to fill the volume—he took up the steady, but versatile, measure that was dominating the new volume.[71] He also devised a frame narrative that explicitly dramatized the role of "Poet," as assigned by the Preface and Note to "The Thorn," in leading readers to feel for "passions that [are] not [their] own" ("Michael," 31). By no means "Careless of books" (28), Wordsworth here took the sympathetic spacing promoted by the elocutionists to a new level by employing "more than an ordinary interspace" to distinguish that place where "The Mountains have all open'd out themselves" (7) and to stimulate responsiveness to a more primitive and passionate order of language. Having recruited the space of the page to lead readers back in time, through the memory of the narrator, to a topographical (not typographical) economy—an economy both material and affective, he used the page break to emphasize its disruption. Thematically, formally, and materially, then, the poem works to elicit a sympathetic reading of plowed ground, showing that an apparently blank space actually retains traces of tragic history and feeling.

In "Michael" Wordsworth clearly developed the Preface's valorization of rustic life and language, but he also drew upon the material practices that informed the claims of the Preface (the copying, punctuating, and laying out of the poems for print) to bring into focus the historic actualities of that rustic life. The minute attention that Wordsworth and his domestic circle gave to the typographical presentation of his rural poems and to the impassioning of print is reflected in his well-known inscriptional metaphor for property in his letter to Charles James Fox, which he mailed with a copy of the book. Explaining the strength of the "domestic affections" among the small independent landowners of Northern England, while directing Fox's attention to "The Brothers" and "Michael," Wordsworth wrote: "Their little tract of land serves as a kind of permanent rallying point for their domestic feelings, as a tablet upon which they are written which makes them objects of memory in a thousand instances when they would otherwise be forgotten. It is a fountain fitted to the nature of social man from which supplies of affection, as pure as his heart was intended for, are daily drawn. This class of men is rapidly disappearing" (14 January 1801, to Charles James Fox, EY 314–15). The metaphor of the "tablet" explicitly relates an area of land and surface for the writing and reading of feeling. Implicitly it relates Wordsworth's book to a "tract of land" and to other delimited spaces for writing within the larger physical field—such objects as the "tablet" in the "*School of* ————," " 'Joanna's rock,' " and the "*Stone, the largest of a heap lying near a deserted Quarry upon one of the Islands at Rydale*" upon which "*LINES*" are "*Written with a Slate pencil*" (LB 209). With the departure of Leonard at the end of "The Brothers" and the sale and conversion of Michael's "tract of land," Wordsworth's metaphor transfers emotional power to the printed book and assigns particular political potential to the image of plowed ground—a new kind of "rallying point." But as Wordsworth seemed to know, despite his crafting of the narrative and dramatic blank verse toward sympathetic ends, the poems alone could not catalyze reform. As he wrote to Fox, it was his hope that the two poems "may excite profitable sympathies in many kind and good hearts" and "might co-operate, however feebly, with the illustrious efforts which [Fox had] made to stem [the sapping of feeling] and other evils with which the country [was] labouring" (EY 315).

In addition to the spatial and formal strategies discussed above, Wordsworth also worked to excite the sympathy of readers by exploiting marks of hesitation and suspension in the speeches of his "rustic" characters. In the climax of "Michael," a series of dashes accents the shepherd's emotional conflict: his reluctance to part with his son, and thus, by implication, the greater strength of his possessiveness of, or love for, the land ("——It looks as if it never could endure / Another master" [389–90][72]). After asking Luke to "lay one stone" for the sheepfold, "with thine own hands" (396–97), Michael's speech fractures:

> "—Heaven bless thee, Boy,
> Thy heart these two weeks has been beating fast
> With many hopes—it should be so—yes—yes—

I knew that thou could'st never have a wish
To leave me, Luke,—thou has been bound to me
Only by links of love, when thou art gone
What will be left to us!—But I forget
My purposes. Lay now the corner stone . . ." (407–14)

The lines exemplify how for the Wordsworth of late 1800, as he wrote in the Preface, "fitting to metrical arrangement a selection of the real language of men in a state of vivid sensation" (LB 741) was not a matter of assimilating this language to the abstract metrical template but of experimenting with expressive dislocations of time and stress—a strategy affirmed by his claim that the pleasure of meter derived from the "perception of similitude in dissimilitude," or regularity amidst irregularity (LB 756). The strong pauses are not merely temporally and rhythmically modulating, however, but also visually significant, and their midline predominance, despite the multiple fracturing of line 409, suggests more than that Wordsworth, in 1800, was moving toward the traditional blank-verse line of his maturity.[73] Concluding his speech, Michael straightens his syntax and organizes his emotions into singular purpose:

"Now fare thee well:
When thou return'st thou in this place wilt see
A work which is not here, a covenant
'Twill be between us——but whatever fate
Befall thee, I shall love thee to the last,
And bear thy memory with me to the grave." (422–27)

The long dash in the middle of the period—the pivot at the center of "When thou return'st" and "me to the grave"—traces out the fatal turn of Michael's silent thoughts in time, and, with his recovery into speech, marks the strength of repression that his determination requires. Poetry, here, is very palpably "the history or science of feeling" and also a "delineation of human passions" (LB 351, 739). In its prolonged interruption of the poetic line, the dash also suggests Michael's stretching of those "links of love," by which Luke had been "bound" to him, toward their breaking point. The pentameter, split dead center, is nearly parted in two. Although Michael's words are different, their patterning of the domestic affections across the period and the line recalls Sarah's words to Luke and expresses their truth: " 'We have no other Child but thee to lose, / None to remember—do not go away, / For if thou leave thy Father he will die' "

(306–7). Michael, indeed, dies in spirit and then in body, and Luke never returns to see "in this place" a "work which is not here"; but readers, "in this place" (424, 423) on the page, do. Whether a graphic indictment of Michael's material possessiveness or an illustration of his best efforts under strain, the long dash indexes this topographical and typographical place. It confirms the visual bond between poet and reader—the only that obtains—which Wordsworth has worked to shape throughout the making of this book.

Despite Wordsworth's elevation of his subject (his humanization, idealization, or apotheosis of Michael), Fox professed himself, in a brief response to Wordsworth, "no great friend to blank verse for subjects which are to be treated of with simplicity."[74] Wordsworth, undoubtedly, used the elite measure to dignify his rustic story and to abet the revaluation of a genre—pastoral—that the eighteenth century had held in low esteem.[75] It was also a measure that he had been seriously practicing. Between probably mid-1796 and early 1800, Wordsworth had composed over five thousand lines of blank verse and had published only two hundred and forty, all in the first edition of *Lyrical Ballads* ("Lines left upon a Seat in a Yew-tree," "Old Man travelling," and "Lines written a few miles above Tintern Abbey").[76] Running to fifteen hundred and forty lines, the thirteen blank-verse poems published in 1800, written predominantly in Grasmere, filled more than half of the new volume.[77] And though Wordsworth seemed to be judging his words' value "by the space which they occupy upon paper" when he expressed his hope to the printer that "Michael" and the "Poems on the Naming of Places" would "fill up so much space as to make the volume 205 pages" (EY 307), his practice of the meter shows his intent to distinguish his poetry from the "deluges of idle and extravagant stories in verse" flooding the marketplace (LB 747). Not only does he vary diction, cadence, and grammatical structure to lower the social register of his speakers, taking readers from the educated, meditative poet of volume I's "Tintern Abbey" into the vocal range of the local Vicar, Leonard, and the shepherd Michael in volume II,[78] he also uses varieties of pause visually to traverse the distance between book and locale, as when, in the pivotal moment of "Michael," he makes the two-em dash mark both "this place" on the page and "this place" on the ground; or when, in "To Joanna," single dashes etch into the black and white column of verse " 'that tall rock / Which looks towards the East' " (42–43), a shaped surface for readers' visual imagination of the rock's colorful complexities.[79]

Fox's reply reveals his inability, or unwillingness, to read the blank verse of *Lyrical Ballads* according to the terms Wordsworth was establishing, which asked that we not only listen to "pauses of deep silence" but also see them and

see *in* them the emotional contours of the landscape and people. Like the elocutionists who worked to free the marks of punctuation from their conventional associations (tonal and temporal), Wordsworth took a flexible approach
to the written medium. He did not simply adopt the marks of time, feeling,
and emphasis they promoted but contextually established their significance,
encouraging readers to feel the gravity of the blank line in "There was a Boy"
and to glimpse in that line "the grave in which he lies" (an 1805 variant of line
32; LB 141). In "The Brothers" Wordsworth deepened that visual association
with a grave by hanging upon the stafflike dash the pathos of forlorn hope. The
Vicar not only establishes the staff's local significance but also, by pointing to
the cliff where it once hung, foregrounds the mark on the page. "Michael"
culminates this pattern of epitaphic deixis, such that when Michael points to
"this place" where Luke had laid "one stone," and then pauses, the blank line
shadows forth Michael's "grave" (423, 427)—a graphic emphasis of the poem's
tragic irony, making plain the futility of Michael's plan. Volume II not only
teaches readers to interrogate objects in the landscape that "you might pass by,
/ Might see and notice not" (15–16), a heap of stones by a brook, lifted absently
perhaps but never shaped; it also attunes readers to the material gestures of
print—suggestive of a writing hand's movement across paper—and the gestures they represent: a speaker's pointing to the rocky landscape or a writer's
manual inscription of stone, wood, or paper. After shaping the "Poems on the
Naming of Places" into a "calm recess" within the book, enclosing spots that
cannot be reached with any certainty on foot, Wordsworth engages the reader's
hand in the moving forward of Michael's tale. Extrapolating from the narrator's address to the "dearest Maiden" in "Nutting,"—"move along these shades
/ In gentleness of heart; with gentle hand / Touch,——for there is a Spirit in
the woods" (lines 52–54, LB 220)[80]—Wordsworth leads readers to weigh words,
the silent gaps between them, and the pages on which they appear "in the
balance of feeling" (Note to "The Thorn," LB 351).

By the copying of "Michael," Wordsworth was consciously constructing
his printed book as a "place of refuge" from commercial weather ("When to
the attractions of the busy world," lines 11–12). "N.B. It is my *particular desire*
that no advertisements of Books be printed at the end of the volume," he wrote
to Biggs and Cottle (EY 308), intent on leaving readers with the impression of
"the unfinished Sheep-fold" that "may be seen / Beside the boisterous brook of
Green-head Gill" (490–91). Although no wholesale repudiation of commercial
print, as in Blake's illuminated manuscripts or, later in the century, William
Morris' fine press editions, Wordsworth's topographical inflections of the

typographical field resist their own quick consumption as well as the codification of feeling and commodification of land. In the context of picturesque publications that encouraged readers to "look and scribble, scribble on and look" ("The Brothers," 8), *Lyrical Ballads* slows the movement of the reader through the book, as it gestures, like a hybrid book-map, toward the patterns that locals make and come to know. Wordsworth's blank verse, in 1800, is a nuanced measure and graphic medium that spaces, and places, print.

Chapter 6

Measuring Distance, Pointing Address

The Textual Geography of the "Poem to Coleridge" and "To W. Wordsworth"

In the previous chapter I discussed Wordsworth's topographical inflections of the typographical field—his passionate spacing of blank verse and exploitation of the long dash in the making of *Lyrical Ballads*. Here I explore another controversial mark of affect, the exclamation point—a mark that focused anxieties about encoding the sounds of passion. My concern is the significance of the mark to the writing and reading of *The Prelude*, a poem that emerged from a literary exchange that depended on absence. It was not so much a poem prompted by the closeness of Wordsworth and Coleridge—as the working title, "the poem to Coleridge," would suggest—but one born of their distance and that forged relationships between selves across temporal and spatial divides by textual, metrical, and vocal devices. These devices, I show, originated in prose and verse sent by mail—in letters that inscribed and sought to overcome distance by using particular forms of address and marks of emphasis: a shared code elaborated on paper rather than in speech. Among these forms of address, the invocation of the "Friend!"—complete with exclamation point—was of particular importance: taken over from the letters, it became a vital part of the poem's formal, thematic, and textual development. It is thus especially unfortunate that the editors of an acclaimed—and still widely studied—standard late twentieth-century edition of the poem chose to remove the exclamation point from this and most other phrases throughout the 1805 poem, obscuring a crucial aspect of the origination in writing—as a textual address—of "the poem to Coleridge."[1]

Apostrophe and address in *The Prelude* have been read as figures for constituting the voice of the poet and overcoming the speechlessness and absence implied by writing. In a compelling reading of their dynamics, Mary Jacobus has shown how apostrophes to nature establish the voice of the poet but at the cost of poetic subject and poetic identity. The fervent, Bacchic outburst of the "glad preamble" defers and even threatens the beginning of the tale while also submerging individual voice within the Orphic "ghostly language of the ancient earth."[2] On the other hand, the addresses to Dorothy, but more so to Coleridge, unify and domesticate Wordsworth's voice, supporting the crucial fiction of an inner colloquy between his present and past selves. It is this inner dialogue that animates the entire poem and gives Wordsworth prophetic self-confidence and vision. "The lyric voice of *The Prelude*," she writes, "is the fiction of the poet talking to himself; the entire poem becomes a self-constituting apostrophe, a 'glad preamble' or necessary interruption to its own beginning which only comes to an end when the poet assumes his prophetic mission, and only becomes prophetic when it finally succeeds in obliterating writing with the unheard or deafening 'voice' of transcendent, disembodied song" (183).

According to Jacobus, address and apostrophe are key figures in Wordsworth's "lyric" fantasy of transcending the materiality of the text; yet, as I argue here, they are deeply embedded in that materiality. As Alan Richardson reminds us, apostrophes to friends in Romantic poetry "reflect a collaborative writing culture in which poems were typically circulated in manuscript or inscribed into familiar letters, often intended . . . for multiple recipients."[3] They also "reflect anxieties raised by the professionalization of poetry, increasingly written for an anonymous, paying readership rather than a circle of patrons and friends, by providing an insulating layer between the poet and the book-buying public" (68). Thus the writing of apostrophe—the inscription of voice in manuscripts—occurred under the pressure of print publication both for Wordsworth and for Coleridge. In "The Nightingale," as Richardson explains, Coleridge's double apostrophe to William and Dorothy provides him "with an internal audience guaranteed to assent to his revisionary views" (68). Yet this "collaborative writing culture," I suggest, is often poorly represented in contemporary editions. The mid-sentence addresses to "my friends!" that punctuate "The Nightingale" typically fall prey to typographical convention, appearing in modern anthologies without their points.[4] So, too, the Norton edition of 1805 *The Prelude*, on which Jacobus relies, elides the majority of the exclamation marks that were diligently inscribed in the manuscripts at a crucial point in their copying. Perhaps the editors omitted the mark on so many occasions

because it shows writing trying too hard to sound like speech—shows it insisting, "embarrassingly, on self-presence and voice."[5] The figure that Culler diag-
nosed as a critical embarrassment—apostrophe—is made more obvious, and
embarrassing, by the typographical signal of voice.[6]

In an essay on punctuation, Theodor Adorno offered a historical explanation for this source of embarrassment, invoking a period when the exclamation
mark appeared less *visibly* on the page. In the early eighteenth-century, before
the elocutionary critique of false "reading tones," the mark called for an "elevation of voice" (see Chapter 5). As its status as a tonal indicator diminished,
Adorno writes, the more it came to look like "an index finger raised in a warning," the more it gained a "definitive physiognomic status."[7] Adorno's claim
that "it is history, far more than meaning or grammatical function, that looks
out at us, rigidified and trembling slightly, from every mark of punctuation"
(92–93) suggests that the exclamation marks that remain in old texts obtrude
upon the eye when the immediate relationship with voice that they once had
ceases. The materiality of writing and typography is disconcertingly fore-
grounded as the mark ceases unproblematically to evoke sound and provoke
feeling.

Wordsworth's description of the cityscape in Book VII of *The Prelude* offers a similar scene of typographical deformity and interpretive disturbance.
He sees "Advertisements, of giant size!," one "fronted with a most imposing
word" (1805, VII: 210, 213). He sees storefronts "like a title-page, / With letters
huge inscribed" and "the word / Invisible" flaming "forth upon [the] Chest!"
of a Sadler's Wells performer (176–77, 309–10). London's language of commerce and spectacle is distinguished by prominent alphabetics and characters.
Words "Press forward . . . on the sight" as does a "Face turn'd up towards us,
strong / In lineaments, and red with overtoil" (211, 216–17). It is not just that
"everything comes to seem like reading matter," as Neil Hertz has suggested.[8]
In a scene of typographical emphasis run amok, a myriad of signs rise beyond
the two-dimensional plane, forcing their way into the sphere of the reader,
where they strive to elicit feeling: "ten thousand" "conspicuous marks . . . /
Look out for admiration" Wordsworth laments, his phrasing signaling the note
of admiration, a contemporary term for the exclamation mark, and the many
such points that mark his text (568, 567, 572). Just as the order of looking is
disturbed, so too are the paths of affective transmission. Instead of coding a
feeling that can "sink" into the mind of the reader (Thomas Sheridan),[9] London's marks "look out" at the reader to be looked at with reader-supplied admiration, wonder, surprise, and interest. Inhuman "marks" seem to gain faces

(the power to look), while human faces lose their markedness. In this urban sea of faces ("face to face, / Face after face" [172–73]), the surface of expression becomes "a mystery!" Sympathy is derailed. The result, for Wordsworth, is not the making of a "forcible impression" but cognitive oppression and mental confusion ("Thus have I look'd, nor ceas'd to look, oppress'd / By thoughts of what, and whither, when and how") (597, 599–600). Signs do not transparently function but conspicuously show, undermining thinking and feeling. For both Wordsworth and Adorno, the mark of this crisis in mediation is the detached and unreadable face: the face "red with overtoil" (217) or the exclamation mark that gains a "definitive physiognomic status."

For Wordsworth the commercial proliferation of signs and types precipitates a crisis because the relationship of writing to feeling no longer seems natural. What he registers in the London book of *The Prelude* as an inscriptional crisis had already been described by critics of print. In his analysis of the problematic of encoding feeing, Sheridan had complained that only a few of the "numberless emotions whereof the human mind is capable" had "peculiar marks belonging to them as their symbols." Among other effects, this defect in written language precluded Britons from developing a "comprehensive and just view of the powers of the mind." Without a "sufficient number of marks to stand as their symbols," Britons could only pretend "to delineate the immense field of mental emotions" and could only fail in their efforts to reform society.[10] Yet Sheridan and others were also wary of the power of signs because "instituted" as opposed to the "natural" signs of the passions—looks, gestures, and tones—fostered artificiality of speech. Tones were the "speech . . . of nature" while facial expressions and gesture constituted nature's "hand-writing."[11] Any scripto- or typographic symbol for a tone expressive of "the passions of man in his animal state; which are implanted in his frame by the hand of nature; and which spontaneously break forth, whenever he is under the influence of any of those passions" would invite the reader to imitate passion without feeling it; "but the cheat will be manifest, and not reach the hearts of the hearers."[12] On the merits of adding new marks to designate the emotions, in order to "reach the hearts" of hearers, John Walker demurred: "Whether a point that indicates passion or emotion, without determining [which] emotion or passion is meant, or if we had points expressive of every passion or emotion, whether this would in common usage more assist or embarrass the elocution of the reader, I shall not attempt at present to decide."[13]

Elocutionists regarded the exclamation mark as a particularly unnatural sign. Its figurality obtruded—and embarrassed—because of its strong association with an elevation of voice, which made the sign emblematic of the false reading tones assigned to punctuation marks by grammarians (see Chapter 5), and because it failed to distinguish between different shades of emotion. Coleridge concurred, writing that it would be "absurd as to imagine that the ? and ! should designate all the moods of passions, that we convey by interrogation or wonder—as the simple question for information—the ironical—the impetuous—the ratiocinative &c—No! this must be left to the understanding of the Reader or Hearer."[14] For Hugh Blair, an additional problem was that, along with "blank lines" and italics, it was a "Typographical Figure of Speech" that was liable to overuse.[15] Although "Exclamation" was a figure of speech "belong[ing] only to stronger emotions of the mind; to surprise, admiration, anger, joy, grief, and the like" (449), it was now a "fashion" among writers "to subjoin points of admiration to sentences" that "contain nothing but simple affirmations, or propositions" (451): "When an author is always calling upon us to enter into transports which he has said nothing to inspire, we are both disgusted an enraged at him. He raises no sympathy, for he gives us . . . words, and not passion; and, of course, can raise no passion, unless that of indignation. Hence, . . . he was not much mistaken, who said, that when, on looking into a book, he found the pages thick bespangled with the point which is called, 'Punctum admirationis,' he judged this to be a sufficient reason for his laying it aside" (450). Passion must be stimulated by language. If repeatedly tacked on in print, the author does not speak to us and raises no sympathy; instead of communicating passion, the book materializes as a thick assemblage of "pages," "words," and "points." Further, an exclamation point without an exclamation (like a smile without a cat) provokes general mistrust, and over time, as Adorno suggests, discredits the sign altogether: "Exclamation points, gestures of authority with which a writer tries to impose an emphasis external to the matter itself, have become intolerable."[16]

For some grammarians, artificiality and overuse of exclamation marks were not an issue. In his 1785 *Essay on Punctuation*, Joseph Robertson promoted the use in prose of the exclamation point that appears so frequently in "the higher poetry, in which all the sentiments and passions of the human mind are usually described with energy and pathos."[17] The chapter on exclamation—"the voice of nature, when she is agitated, amazed, or transported"[18]—offers an exhaustive catalogue of articulations to mark with the point (address, gratulation, invocation, supplication) and the sentiments and passions that it encodes. Supplying literary citations for each, Robertson treats "Expressions of joy, transport, love, admiration"; "Expressions denoting pity or anxiety, an ardent wish, or a pathetic farewell"; "Terror, lamentation, despair"; "Contempt, abhorrence, indignation, threatening, imprecation"; "Vociferation"; "tenderness, love, respect, anger, disdain, etc." (104–7). He also debates the relative merits of flipping the exclamation point upside down to signal irony. In Robertson's hands, then, the mark is not only encompassingly significant but agile.

For Wordsworth, there is a conflict. One reason he is "no adept" at punctuation is because the "business" is overdetermined (EY 289). This conflict is written into the poem, as "Residence in London" reveals, and also onto it, as pointed apostrophes and addressees on "the front / Of this whole Song" (1805, VI: 669–70) everywhere reveal. As I show here, the visibly pointed addresses to the "Friend!" that punctuate *The Prelude* constitute a distinct textual means of marking distance, and perhaps overcoming it, bound up with the Wordsworths' relation to Coleridge. No mere superfluous—and therefore embarrassing—sign, the compound mark of affect (the exclamation and its point) played a formative role in Wordsworth's drafting of what became *The Prelude* and in the conceptualization of autobiography as a bridging, through acts of metrical composition, of temporal distance within the self. At the same time, the exclamatory addresses cannot take the point's correspondence with voice and feeling for granted. Its status as a written mark, for Wordsworth, and later for Coleridge, is both a problem and an opportunity.

Postal Address

The story of the composition of *The Prelude* cannot be told without reference to Coleridge's and Wordsworth's newfound absence from one another, after a year dwelling as neighbors in Somerset, in the fall of 1798. It was while living with Dorothy in Goslar, Germany, days distant from Coleridge, who was studying in Ratzeburg, that Wordsworth drafted the earliest sequences on his boyhood. In November and December, Dorothy copied and mailed some of these sequences to Coleridge, who had been hoping to hear of progress on the philosophical work he had been encouraging Wordsworth to compose—*The Recluse*. By then Wordsworth had completed approximately four hundred lines of what would become *Prelude* Part I.[19] Critics assume that he began Part II back in England, after a several-month hiatus; whenever exactly he recommenced the poem, he did so by addressing it to Coleridge.

Direct address to Coleridge does not appear in the initial draft of *The Prelude*, referred to as MS JJ, which involves two apostrophes to nature and its spirits and a fragmentary, physically "disconnected" coda addressed to a "dearest maiden" (1799, p. 5). In a second stage of composition, Wordsworth extended the conclusion and incorporated the poem's first address to "a loving person,"[20] transforming the prior draft's gentle correction of a maiden's thoughts ("do not deem that these / Are idle sympathies—" [1799, p. 5]) into a wishful plea for understanding approval:

> need I dread from thee
> Harsh judgements if I am so loth to quit
> Those recollected hours that have the charm
> Of visionary things . . . (1799, p. 13)

Stephen Parrish attributes this plea to Wordsworth's need "to justify the self-indulgence of composing these boyhood memories—a concern growing out of anxiety about expectations of him held by [the addressee] who might still be Dorothy, though by now is more probably Coleridge" (1799, p. 13). Wordsworth's next rewriting of the concluding lines, Parrish notes, "speak[s] of 'Reproaches from my former years' and raise[s] the possibility of 'impotent desire,'" suggesting *The Recluse* and "promises made to Coleridge before leaving England" (1799, p. 13). Given this compositional eddying around lack of progress on the proposed philosophical work, how, then, did autobiography proceed and take shape?

In a third stage of composition, Wordsworth drafted the lines on the "spots of time" and again revised the ending, writing now of a "pause," a "doubtful" "lingering," and "a truant heart / Slow & of stationary character" (1799, p. 26). But the lines overleaf (MS 16) mark decision and make progress: here are the words "2nd Part" and the poem's first of many direct addresses to the "Friend":

> 2nd Part
> Friend of my heart & genius we had reach'd
> A small green island which I was well pleased
> To pass not lightly by for though I felt
> Strength unabated yet I seem'd to need
> Thy cheering voice or ere I could pursue
> My voyage, resting else for ever there. (1799, p. 26)

Parrish credits the "firm new start" (p. 26) represented by the direct address and its "dramatic shift of tense" to Wordsworth's hearing of Coleridge's "cheering voice" at Göttingen en route to England in early spring 1799. Oral impetus for poetic "resolve"—the experience of immediacy and presence—is entirely plausible, but it is also by textual echo of letters exchanged between Goslar and Ratzeburg in the winter of 1798–99 that the poem advances, by textual reinscription of a figure of a voice that implies absence and foregrounds mediation. In those letters, emphatic address both measures out and strives to overcome the distance between the friends, prefiguring the trope of retrospective journey that comes ultimately to chart *The Prelude*'s entire progression.

In one of the few surviving Goslar letters from the Wordsworths to Coleridge, dated to 14, 21, or 28 December 1798, Dorothy transcribed lake scenes from William's new "mass of poems" for Coleridge's pleasure and relayed her brother's request that Coleridge "preserve any verses which we have sent you, in fear, that in travelling we may lose the copy."[21] Dorothy's complexly folded and sequenced letter may have been productive as well as preservative, however; for on the "exceptionally large" sheet of laid paper (measuring thirty-four by forty-two centimeters), she set paragraphs of verse from *The Prelude*'s earliest drafts into close textual relation with prose commentary and forthright and affectionate address—the skating scene, the stolen boat episode, and a passage from "Nutting," which Dorothy described as "the conclusion of a poem of which the beginning is not written" (EY 240; 1799, p. 131). "God bless you! dear Coleridge, our very dear friend!," she wrote on the right panel of the back of the sheet (2v), vertically framing one margin of the stolen boat episode, seventeen lines beginning, "And troubled pleasure: not without the voice / Of mountain echoes did my boat move on . . ." (Figure 26).[22] On the left panel of the same side of the sheet—separated by a middle panel addressed "An den Herrn Coleridge / Ratzeburg"—she continued the transcription of the troubling event and subsequent haunting by "unknown forms of being" in two blocks of differently oriented text. These she divided with the request to "preserve" the "copy" as they travel and the first words of her valediction: "farewell! God love you!" As *The Prelude* manuscripts evince, William adopted friendly address as a framing device for the serial boyhood episodes when he recommenced composition. With the confidently loving "Friend of my heart & genius" (1799, p. 26), he inscribed the verse epistle as a form for the poem while establishing and traversing a boundary between textual parts—troped, in the address, as the resumption of a sea voyage after an island hiatus.

Figure 26. "God bless you! dear Coleridge, our very dear friend!" Dorothy and William to Coleridge, the Goslar letter of December 1798, 2v, detail. Reproduced by permission of the Wordsworth Trust, Grasmere.

Can we determine whether the address to the "Friend" emerged from the drift of MS JJ or was borrowed from the outside as an organizational device— from Dorothy and William's letter to Coleridge or indeed from the address to Dorothy at the end of "Tintern Abbey," written the previous summer?[23] Or perhaps the address confounds distinctions of inside and outside, like the letter that Dorothy folds into its own (addressed and postmarked) envelope, and confounds textual and emotional origins, as the plurality of "our very dear friend!" implies. "Friend," of course, also recalls Coleridge's earlier addresses to Robert Southey, Charles Lloyd, Charles Lamb, and his brother George, and his multiple addresses to William and Dorothy in "This Lime-Tree Bower My Prison" and "The Nightingale." In the earliest manuscript of the former, which Coleridge enclosed in a letter to Southey, he singled out the "gentle-hearted" Lamb (line 28) only once, twice invoking at the end of the poem a collective of intimates that included the Wordsworth siblings:

> My Sister & my Friends! when the last Rook
> Beat its straight path along the dusky Air
> Homewards, I bless'd it; deeming, its black wing
> Cross'd, like a speck, the blaze of setting day,
> While ye stood gazing; or when all was still,
> Flew creaking o'er your heads, & had a charm
> For you, my Sister & my Friends! to whom
> No sound is dissonant, which tells of Life!
> (PW, II.i: lines 69–77; p. 484)

With the friendly address, Coleridge not only inscribed affection but loosely mapped it; here he triangulates the space between his friends and himself via the setting sun and traverses that space by a figure of poetry, the rook "Beat[ing] its straight path along the dusky Air." In "The Nightingale," address to the sister and brother seems to mimic the song of the unseen bird, holding the friends in place and detaining them:

> Farewell, O Warbler! till to-morrow eve,
> And you, my friends! farewell, a short farewell!
> We have been loitering long and pleasantly,
> And now for our dear homes.—That strain again!
> (PW, II.i: lines 87–90; p. 682)

Like the recurring strain of the nightingale, iterated address hallows the intimate association and by its periodic or nightly renewal secures it from the lapses of physical separation.

However, in humorous lines that accompanied "The Nightingale" through the mail (to Wordsworth at Alfoxden),[24] Coleridge dropped his elevated figures for poetry—the rook beating its straight path, the nightingale's song—while inscribing, most bathetically, the friends' literal condition of physical separateness:

> In stale blank verse a subject stale
> I send *per post* my *Nightingale*;
> And like an honest bard, dear Wordsworth,
> You'll tell me what you think, my Bird's worth.
>   (PW, I.i: lines 1–4; p. 521)

As "-worth" and "worth" fall dully, extrametrically flat, pulling "Words" and "Bird's" down with them, Coleridge wittily unwings his poetry: neither a bird, nor even the resonant song of a "bard," his writing needs the post to span the distance between the friends. Rather than a "stirring" "harmony" of "skirmish and capricious passagings, / And murmurs musical and swift jug jug / And one low piping sound more sweet than all" (PW, II.i: lines 62, 59–61; p. 681), "stale blank verse in subject stale" passes again over a tried topic, and its exchange for "honest" telling seems unimaginatively prosaic. However comical, Coleridge's metapostal address underlines the spatial and connective energies of his poetic addresses, while also anticipating Wordsworth's interpellation of an addressee to judge of the worthiness of his blank verse ("need I dread from thee / Harsh judgments" [1799 I: 458–89]). The conversational "friends!" is a reflexively textual and geographic figure.

In the letters between Goslar and Ratzeburg, the geography of written address became more salient and crossing the distance between the friends more urgent. Dorothy's letter of December 1798 repeated and renewed the friendly address, while a commentary on the other side of the page anxiously reflected upon the temporal lag between writing and reading, expression and reception: "It is friday evening this letter cannot go till tomorrow. I wonder when it will reach you. One of yours was eleven days upon the road. *You will write by the first post*" (EY 242–43). The postal schedule defers the circulation of the letter, and the contingencies of transmission leave Dorothy to wonder in days the length of its travel. Her striking command that Coleridge "*write by the first post*"—that the reader turn right back into writer—exposes the literal conditions and desires that underlie the rhetoric of immediacy on the verso. The oral figure of address, "God Bless you! dear Coleridge, our very dear friend!," registers the pressure of Dorothy's feeling and will—its dactyls rushing the letter forward and its exclamation marks pointing the desire to contract the distance between the friends.

One of Coleridge's replies, of winter 1798–99, negotiated the intervening miles with full-fledged hexameters and the joint devices of direct address and emphatic pointing.[25] Though not sent by the first post, the letter takes up and enlarges upon Dorothy's metapostal reflections, presenting hexameter as a medium of affective immediacy. In the 1817 *Biographia Literaria*, Coleridge would unflatteringly compare the "tune" of German meters to the "galloping over a paved road in a German stage-waggon without springs" (BL, II: 34), yet during his stay in Germany he experimented with the classical meter recently popularized by Klopstock and Bürger, testing its suitability to another modern accentual language.[26] In the verses sent from Ratzeburg to Goslar by stage wagon, Coleridge instructed the siblings in the proper metrical reception of his letter:

> William, my teacher, my friend! dear William and dear Dorothea!
> Smooth out the folds of my letter, and place it on desk or on table;
> Place it on table or desk; and your right hands loosely half-closing,
> Gently sustain them in air, and extending the digit didactic,
> Rest it a moment on each of the forks of the five-forkèd left hand,
> Twice on the breadth of the thumb, and once on the tip of each
>   finger;
> Read with a nod of the head in a humouring recitativo;
> And, as I live, you will see my hexameters hopping before you.
> This is a galloping measure; a hop, and a trot, and a gallop!
> . . . .
> William, my head and my heart! dear Poet that feelest and thinkest!
> Dorothy, eager of soul, my most affectionate sister!
> Many a mile, O! many a wearisome mile are ye distant,
> Long, long comfortless roads, with no one eye that doth know us.
> O! it is all too far to send to you mockeries idle:
> Yea, and I feel it not right! But O! my friends, my beloved!
>   (PW, I.i: lines 1–9, 15–20; p. 528; also CL, I: 451–52)

Coleridge's hexameters remeasure the "wearisome" miles between Ratzeburg and Goslar. The letter hops, trots, and gallops across them in order to present Coleridge's meters to his friends through acts of digital scansion: "And, as I live, you will see my hexameters hopping before you." As dactyl, in Greek, means "finger," then scanning Coleridge's hexameters with the "digit didactic" would make his sequences of dactyls apparent "as [he] live[s]": not simply as an abstract graphic projection of a meter but as if the siblings' living hands were conduits of Coleridge's vital pulses. And if the taps of their index fingers— twice on the thumb and once "on each of the forks of the five-forkèd left hand"—enact and visualize Coleridge's hexameters, they also point to the poem's multiplying exclamation marks (eighteen in thirty-six lines) and to its play with the metrics of exclamatory address: "William, my teacher, my friend! dear William and dear Dorothea!"; "William, my head and my heart! dear Poet that feelest and thinkest! / Dorothy, eager of soul, my most affectionate sister!" Falling after strong stresses— "friend! dear"; "heart! dear"—and weak— "-thea!"; "thinkest!"; "sister!"—the exclamation marks enforce addresses to brother and sister, with both masculine and feminine endings.

Despite his pretensions to mockery—"O! it is all too far to send to you mockeries idle" (19)—Coleridge thinks seriously here about hexameter as a medium of feeling—both psychological ("But O! my friends, my beloved!" [20]) and physiological:[27]

> Five long hours have I tossed, rheumatic heats, dry and flushing,
> Gnawing behind in my head, and wandering and throbbing about
>   me,
> Busy and tiresome, my friends, as the beat of the boding
>   night-spider.
>   (23–25)

The poet's fevered pulsations throb on in his hexameters, refigured now in the forking legs of the spider, a nightmarish transformation of "the five-forkèd left hand." Metrical, textual, and graphic modes of emphasis index Coleridge to the eyes, hands, and ears, materializing both his "rheumatic heats" and his passion for his friends, even as those readers repeatedly tap out and sound their own names aloud:

> William, my head and my heart! dear William and dear Dorothea!
> You have all in each other; but I am lonely, and want you!
>   (PW, I.i: lines 1–2; p. 528; also CL, I: 451–52)

In calling out to the siblings from Ratzeburg and instructing them in his own oral and metrical projection at Goslar, Coleridge strives, at both ends, to close the gap between writing and reading, expression and reception—tries to bring the friends to a shared point (or a series of shared points) in time and space. This is prosody, and punctuation, at its most playful and plangent.

Intimate Distances

"William, my teacher, my friend! . . . William, my head and my heart!" called a lonely Coleridge. "Friend of my heart & genius," Wordsworth re-called, in a tone of self-possession and with a sense of present sympathy; "we had reach'd / A small green island which I was well pleased / To pass not lightly" (1799, p. 26). With his first address to Coleridge in the manuscripts Wordsworth established a "2nd Part" and a poem in epistolary form, simultaneously extending the poem and giving it shape. Returning thereafter to what was now Part I, he rounded out its close with an address that reflexively acknowledged the shaping effects of sympathetic address: "Nor will it seem to thee, my Friend, so prompt / In sympathy, that I have lengthened out / With fond and feeble tongue a tedious tale . . ." (1799, 1: 447–49).[28] Reflecting on the stream of "lyrical effusions" in MS JJ, Paul Magnuson has argued that "It was not merely Coleridge's sympathetic presence as reader or auditor that shaped the work, it was also the presence of Coleridge's poetry at the beginning of the work."[29] The citation of "Frost at Midnight" and a canceled reference in the closing lines of MS JJ show Wordsworth's recognition of the need to situate his "fragmentary memories" within a signifying context; otherwise they would appear as "isolated moments" lacking unitary form (Magnuson, 206). As the German addresses make clear, however, Coleridge's "presence" is a fiction; in positing Coleridge's ready sympathy, Wordsworth elides Coleridge's loneliness, "the long, long comfortless roads" (18) between them, and Dorothy's wondering the length of days between writing and reception, expression and sympathy. It is not the distance between the friends that concerns Wordsworth here, or the spanning of it with galloping hexameters or beating wings; it is Coleridge's reception of a length of verse that is not the hoped for *Recluse*. His jocular alliteration ("with fond and feeble tongue a tedious tale") is not simply tongue-in-cheek but betrays some apprehension about poetic coherence and Coleridge's approval. Thus as Wordsworth, in his address, spuriously closes the geographical distance between the friends, extension reemerges, transmuted, in the form of poetic length and posits its own legitimacy. Very much on the model of Dorothy's December letter to Coleridge, friendly address gives framing form to the "lyrical effusions" of MS JJ and legitimates the ongoing extension of the poem.

Significantly, Wordsworth's addresses to Coleridge also inscribe autobiographical distance within the self. In an early revision of the opening address of Part II, the conceit of retrospective narrative as a joint sea "voyage" develops into a new figure of geographical and temporal extent—and carries a new confidence. "Friend of my heart & genius we had reach'd / A small green island which I was well pleased / To pass not lightly by" becomes, in the Sockburn manuscript (DC MS 21),

> Thus far my Friend have we retraced the way
> Through which I travelled when I first began
> To love the woods and fields: the passion yet
> Was in its birth sustained as might befall
> By nourishment that came unsought for still.
>   (1799, p. 28)

In rebeginning Part II, Wordsworth shifts the emphasis from a metaphoric seascape and a heroic compositional voyage undertaken with Coleridge to the actual landscapes of the past through which Wordsworth traveled singly as a boy and which now open to view within his memory. His purpose is to "retrace," with Coleridge by his side, his own historical way. The very real roads and geographical distances that separated the friends in Germany yield to an internalized but no less real geography, to a "way" of uncountable miles and days that connects and divides historical versions of the self and its passions.

After the opening address, Wordsworth goes on in the manuscript to discuss "boyish sport" (rowing, picnicking, horseback riding, bowling on a green) that kept him in intimate, though unsought, contact with nature (1799, II: 52). It was after Coleridge's visit to Wordsworth in the Lakes in October 1799 and their three-week walking tour across those very "woods and fields," that Wordsworth articulated the difference between the present and the past as a distance from a passionate origin (1799, pp. 30–31). In a thirty-nine-line extension of the opening address, he emphasized the seasonal measures of his boyhood pleasures: "From week to week from month to month we lived / A round of tumult." He writes of "games / Prolonged in summer," of "revelry" and "uproar" continuing past daylight, and of going to bed, as stars twinkled above, "With weary joints and with a beating mind" (1799, p. 169). The prolongation of passion in the boy's mind—the mind's ongoing "beating" after the day's physical play is over—anticipates adult consciousness, but with a difference. Wordsworth writes,

> A tranquilizing spirit presses now
> On my corporeal frame so wide appears
> The vacancy between me & those days
> Which yet have such self presence in my heart
> That some times when I think of them I seem
> Two consciousnesses, conscious of myself
> And of some other being.
> (1799, p. 169)

The "tranquilizing spirit" brought on by recollection diminishes Wordsworth's sense of a "corporeal frame." The feeling of bodily integrity decreases as recollection both opens to view the "wide" "vacancy" between the present and "those days" and also restimulates the passion they nourished. It is as if Wordsworth, across a long distance, makes a live connection to his boyhood "beating mind"—like the vital metrical connection Coleridge attempted to establish between Ratzeburg and Goslar. It is the powerful "self presence" of "those days"—the boy's "beating mind" within the adult's "heart"—that effects the sense of doubled consciousness, a division or spacing of the self that threatens identity. Although comically ventriloqual, Wordsworth's pronouncing aloud of Coleridge's Ratzeburg address—"William, my head and my heart!"—had interpellated Wordsworth as subject and object of address and partitioned "head" and "heart." Thereafter, in his revision and extensions of the poem, self-fissure becomes a crucial trope; in elaborating his first direct address to Coleridge in the poem, Wordsworth explores the ontological predicament of being in, and beating across, time.

With the elision of the historical spatial distance between the poets, distance emerges within the self (as time and space) as well as between Wordsworth and others. In the valediction at the end of Part II, for instance, Wordsworth firmly closes any geographical distance between himself and Coleridge only to open and explore the emotional distance between men in general. "Thou, my Friend, wast reared / In the great city 'mid far other scenes,

/ But we, by different roads, at length have gained / The self-same bourne"
(1799, II: 496–99). For this reason, he "speak[s]" to Coleridge "unapprehensive
of contempt,"

> The insinuated scoff of coward tongues,
> And all that silent language which so oft
> In conversation betwixt man and man
> Blots from the human countenance all trace
> Of beauty and of love.
>   (1799, II: 500–505)

Wordsworth's portrait of friendship is both allusive and suggestively textual.
Although Coleridge had returned from Germany, toured the Lakes with
Wordsworth, and departed for London by the time these lines were written,
Wordsworth positions the two friends as inhabiting the "self-same bourne." He
renders this "bourne" not as a geographical place but as a shared, and inter-
changeable, poetic language: echoing lines 51–52 of "Frost at Midnight" ("In
the great city, pent 'mid cloisters dim"), "Thou, my Friend, wast reared / In the
great city 'mid far other scenes," enacts a sympathy of oral immediacy and
unmarked citation. The implication is that their dialogue in a shared poetic
language will sustain their intimacy across distances and be its own place.[30]
     Strikingly different is Wordsworth's scenario of "conversation betwixt man
and man," in which the "insinuated scoff of coward tongues" and "silent language" (unspoken fear, hostility, and indifference) divide mind from mind.
Surpassing the anonymity and alienation in Coleridge's "Hexameters"—
"Long, long comfortless roads, with no one eye that doth know us" (18)—face-
to-face encounter is depicted here as tense with uncertainty and unspoken
aggression. The "human countenance" hardens into a surface of strained
reading—a page blotted of "all trace / Of beauty and of love" and thus a sorry
contrast to the intimate "Friend" who sympathetically hears the autobiographical tale. Thus while inscribing as a communicative ideal the immediacy valo-
rized in Coleridge's conversation poems, the passage introduces an implicit
worry about the poem's future reception by a broader public, contrasting by
allusion its literary reception in the marketplace of books and reviewers with
Hartley's reception, imagined in "Frost at Midnight," of "The lovely shapes and
sounds intelligible / Of that eternal language, which thy God / Utters" (PW,
I.i: lines 58–60, p. 456; cf. Magnuson 185–99 on Wordsworth's echoes of the
poem's portraits of intimacy).

Although "Friend" implies intimate oral converse, it repeatedly reveals the written page. Subtending "The Nightingale" and coming to the fore in the German exchange ("Smooth out the folds of my letter, and place it on desk or on table" ["Hexameters," 2]), the page is more markedly delineated in Part II of *The Prelude* when Wordsworth prospectively imagines the reception of his poem by a childhood "Friend / Then passionately loved." "With heart how full," the poet wonders,

> Will he peruse these lines, this page, perhaps
> A blank to other men, for many years
> Have since flowed in between us, and, our minds
> Both silent to each other, at this time
> We live as if those hours had never been.
>   (1799, II: 382–88)

Broadening his reflections upon temporal passage to include another person, Wordsworth construes the lapsed friendship with John Fleming as an influx between them of time—another "wide" "vacancy." Yet where Wordsworth still senses his boyhood "beating mind," a river of silence separates his adult mind from Fleming's. How will the friend who "travelled round" Esthwaite Lake by Wordsworth's side "oft before the hours of school" (II: 379–80) read "these lines, this page"? Will he receive them as affecting blank verses or, perhaps with a broader audience, in affective blankness? Will the page, failing to evoke moving childhood scenes or restimulate past passions, appear "blank"—like a face blotted of "all trace / Of beauty and of love"? With years "between" them, a once passionate "Friend" may become an estranged reader.

This hypothetical scene of reading inverts the metaphorical scene of reading inscribed in Wordsworth's earlier address to Dorothy in "Tintern Abbey":

>   thou art with me, here, upon the banks
> Of this fair river; thou, my dearest Friend,
> My dear, dear Friend, and in thy voice I catch
> The language of my former heart, and read
> My former pleasures in the shooting lights
> Of thy wild eyes. Oh! yet a little while
> May I behold in thee what I was once,
> My dear, dear Sister!
>   (lines 115–22, LB 119)

Standing with Dorothy on the banks of the Wye, Wordsworth can "catch" in her voice the "language of [his] former heart" and "read" in the radiating light of her eyes his "former pleasures." Although Dorothy will play this redemptive, mediating role again in later books of the 1805 *Prelude* (X: 907–20), the comparison shows the post-Goslar poet writing temporal difference as unbridged spatial distance, figuring the passage of time as a stretch of silence between persons and aspects of the self. If friendly address in the German letters strives for immediacy despite, or across, spatial distance, Wordsworth's pointing to "these lines, this page" starkly re-presents that distance. Raising the specter of "blank" vacancy, it puts the burden on writing to revive and renew former feeling and gives the poet leeway to explore those experiences in verse.

Marking for Malta: Outer and Inner Address

Between January and March 1804, when Coleridge was preparing to depart for Malta, Wordsworth extended his "poem to Coleridge" to five books. This version of *The Prelude* "is a product of early 1804," states Duncan Wu, noting its "self-justificatory" tone, "when Coleridge's ill health and imminent departure made completion of *The Recluse* more doubtful than ever."[31] Although no complete manuscript of this state of the poem exists, Wordsworth references a five-book project in several letters of this period, and periodic calculations of his progress suggest its best representation is in MSS WW and W, notebooks that contain drafting toward and fair copy of Books III–V. As we can see in the manuscripts and in Wu's speculative reconstruction of the 1804 poem, Books III and IV maintain the framing addresses to Coleridge; they also develop the trope of the poet's "way." I have "retraced my life / Up to an eminence," Wordsworth states near the start of Book III, warning Coleridge that now "We must descend" into "a populous plain" as he gives his account of roving among throngs of students and idly loitering at Cambridge (Five Book Prelude, III: 167–68; 195, 194). Book IV, which returns Wordsworth to his "native hills" (III: 663) during the summer vacation, finds coherence in Wordsworth's past walks along the "public roads" (IV: 663) and on paths through fields—incidents that illustrate the joint rearing of Wordsworth's imagination by Nature and books (fairy tales, legends, romances, and "glittering verse" [IV: 697]). Book V, which opens with the climactic ascent of Mount Snowdon, describes the "abasement" (IV: 720) and restoration of Wordsworth's imagination. With apostrophes to the "soul of Nature" and "mystery of man" (IV: 202, 332), address to Coleridge falls away, and so too, Reed speculates (*Prelude* 1805, I: pp. 34–38), does the five-book plan, when, toward its end, Wordsworth suggests that he will give an account of his walking journey across the "gorgeous Alps" (V: 267). Sometime between 6 and 12 March, Wordsworth abandoned the five-book project, and by 18 March, he had sent to Coleridge fair copies of most of his short unpublished poems and the first tranche of a newly reorganized version of "the poem to Coleridge," its length as yet undetermined.[32]

As the editors of the Norton *Prelude* note (p. 517), for the Malta text (known as MS M), Wordsworth "set aside for future use" the last book of the five-book poem, divided the fourth book into two, and inserted additions. What they do not observe are changes at the level of punctuation—and thus that William, and Dorothy and Mary, the copyists, added the exclamation mark to "Friend" throughout MS M.[33] It seems that the principal causes of these changes were geographical distance and the shift from oral to written mode of reception that distance entails. Wordsworth had read Part II of the 1799 poem aloud to Coleridge at Grasmere on 4 January 1804—spurring himself, the Norton editors believe, as did Coleridge's Christmastime decision to make the trip, to extend the poem. MS M, by contrast, would be read by Coleridge abroad—and here the page becomes more emphatically an interface for Wordsworth's voice. Consider the Raven's Nest episode: MS V, copied in 1799, shows the insertion of commas sometime between 1801 and 1804 (here indicated in bold):

> Oh, when I have hung
> Above the raven's nest, by knots of grass**·**
> Or half-inch fissures in the slipp'ry rock,
> But ill sustained, and almost, as it seemed,
> Suspended by the blast which blew amain
> Shouldering the naked crag, oh at that time,
> While on the perilous ridge I hung alone,
> With what strange utterance did the loud dry wind
> Blow through my ears, the sky seemed not a sky
> Of earth, and with what motion moved the clouds
>   (1799, p. 233)

Where final punctuation is obscured in MS V, MS U, the variant fair copy, has "clouds!"—signaling the boy's wonder (1799, p. 233). In MS M, however, the exclamatory function of "!" emerges with force:

> Oh! when I have hung
> Above the raven's nest, by knots of grass,
> Or half-inch fissures in the slipp'ry rock
> But ill sustain'd, and almost, as it seem'd,
> Suspended by the blast which blew amain
> Shouldering the naked crag; oh! at that time
> While on the perilous ridge I hung alone,
> With what strange utterance did the loud dry wind
> Blow through my ears! the sky seem'd not a sky
> Of earth, and with what motion moved the clouds!
>   (MS M, f. 137r)

In imitation of the boy's perilous suspension, the sequence of exclamation points keeps the reader's voice cresting across the sentence. The points blow breath and wind ("Oh! . . . oh! . . . ears! . . . clouds!") into the written words, as if lifting the primitive vowels from the page. The acoustic effects of MS M's punctuation support and coincide with the poem's new thematic emphasis on poetic sound: the addition to Book I of the Preamble and post-Preamble, reflexively tracing the poem's own coming into being as utterance (for example, "my own voice chear'd me, and, far more, the mind's / Internal echo of the imperfect sound"; "but the harp / Was soon defrauded, and the banded host / Of harmony dispers'd in straggling sounds, / And lastly utter silence" (MS M, ff. 131r–v)); the addition, in Book IV, of the "froward Brook" passage ("soon as he was box'd / Within ou [sic] garden, found himself at once, / As if by trick insidious and unkind, / Stripp'd of his voice"—which should have been a spur, the adult Wordsworth thinks, "to pen down, / A satire on myself" [MS M, f. 161r]); and the inclusion, in Book V, of the central portion of the dream of the Arab episode, featuring the "Shell"/"Book" that, when held to the ear, makes "articulate sounds, / A loud prophetic blast of harmony, / An Ode, in passion utter'd," and which the Arab/Quixote rushes to preserve beneath the sand in advance of the coming deluge (MS M, f. 171v). It is not unlikely that William, Dorothy, and Mary's busy copying, between January and March, of "all William's smaller Poems" and "the Poem on his Life and the Pedlar" for Coleridge to take on his travels, and their making of a separate copy for themselves under the threat of the loose poems' dispersal and loss, influenced this new emphasis on books which, through their power to sound, "lay / Their sure foundations in the heart of Man" (MS M, f. 173v; cf. EY 448).

With the addition of exclamation points to existing and new addresses to

Coleridge, and the inclusion of the new device of quoted self-address, MS M develops a complex vocal texture. These textual acoustic chambers, moreover, have self-referential and dialogical tendencies, resonating in their reflections on poetic inspiration, composition, subject, and theme. For example, when recalling in the new opening to Book I how passionate utterance collapsed into "utter silence," Wordsworth fills that past silence by quoting himself speaking to himself in the past: " 'Be it so, / It is an injury' said I, 'to this day / To think of any thing but present joy'" (MS M, ff.135r–v). Turning outward, the new address to Coleridge at the end of Book I then performs a strengthening of poetic voice—a climactic resurgence of passionate utterance—while serving as a vehicle for metapoetic comment:

> One end hereby at least hath been attain'd
> My mind has been revived, and if this mood
> Desert me not, I will forthwith bring down,
> Through later years the story of my Life
> The road lies plain before me; 'tis a theme
> Single, and of determined bounds, and hence
> I choose it rather at this time than work
> Of ampler, or more varied argument;
> Where I might be discomfited, and lost;
> And certain hopes are with me, that to Thee
> This labour will be welcome, Honoured Friend!
> (MS M, f. 142r)

For the first time in the manuscripts, Wordsworth markedly differentiates the time of writing and reception—a temporal difference that assumes spatial form in the image of the "road" lying "plain before me . . . Single, and of determined bounds." This figure of thematic organization recalls the metapostal addresses exchanged in Germany, though the "road" neither separates Grasmere from Malta nor must be overcome by verbal and metrical projection. It negatively registers the vast geographic distance now reopening between Coleridge and Wordsworth as a positive freedom for the unfolding "Through later years the story of my Life." Newlyn observes that "Coleridge's departure brings out in Wordsworth a sense of confidence and inner power," quoting this passage from the Norton text of the 1805 *Prelude*.[34] What that text obscures, however, is the crucial addition of exclamation marks to "Friend," depriving it of one of the significant marks carried forward from the Malta manuscript. What is lost by this arbitrary deletion is a stroke that indexes Wordsworth's new confidence and power, as he reinscribes a sign of intimacy that had begun in the conversation poems and continued in the letters sent between Dorothy, William, and Coleridge during the lonely German winter of 1798–99. In MS M, the pointed "Friend!" represents Wordsworth's exploitation of a shared sign by which the three writers historically had inscribed their affection—now shorn, however, of the desire for immediacy of sympathy and serving the sounding out of an individual poetic agenda.

In the books of *The Prelude* that Wordsworth went on to write, Wordsworth distanced Coleridge geographically as well as temporally. In Book VI, he admitted Coleridge's geographical experience into the sphere of address for the first time: no longer a penumbral figure reviewing Wordsworth's past in his thoughts or by his side as he narrates, Coleridge is now an independent wanderer with an independent physical constitution, seeking a restoration of health in the Mediterranean airs. And while Coleridge's trip serves as pretext, in Book VI, for introducing "wanderings of [his] own" (1805, VI: 333), Wordsworth's elaboration of Coleridge's experience, as Newlyn observes (173), advances his articulation of a "private self"—one whom, unlike Coleridge, was fostered by the "sublime and lovely Forms" of nature throughout his early life (1805, XIII: 146). The drawing of distinctions between them comes to a climax in Book X, where Wordsworth worries that Coleridge's stay in Sicily, on his return, threatens to aggravate rather than cure his maladies, for the land offers no hope to "chear the heart in such entire decay" (1805, X: 965). "If for France I have grieved," Wordsworth writes,

> Have been distress'd to think of what she once
> Promised, now is, a far more sober cause
> Thine eyes must see of sorrow, in a Land
> Strew'd with the wreck of loftiest years . . .
>   (1805, X: 954, 957–60)

It is Wordsworth's sympathy-deepening residency in France that makes his sickness after the outbreak of war so acute. But where Wordsworth grounds the resolution of his moral, spiritual, and vocational crisis in a rural geographical history—

> Nature's self, by human love
> Assisted, through the weary labyrinth

Conducted me again to open day,
Revived the feelings of my earlier life,
Gave me that strength, and knowledge full of peace,
Enlarged, and never more to be disturb'd
            (1805, X: 921–26)

—he denies Coleridge the same sure foundation.[35] It is the "airy wretchedness"
of a "mind / Debarr'd from Nature's living images" during childhood that
Wordsworth wants to believe he could have "sooth'd" had they overlapped at
Cambridge (1805, VI: 325, 312–13, 324). Now he can only hope for Coleridge's
restoration in a hopeless situation:

      But indignation works where hope is not
And thou, O Friend! wilt be refresh'd. There is
One great Society alone on earth,
The noble Living, and the noble Dead:
Thy consolation shall be there, and Time
And Nature shall before thee spread in store
Imperishable thoughts, the place itself
Be conscious of thy presence, and the dull
Sirocco air of its degeneracy
Turn as thou mov'st into a healthful breeze
To cherish and invigorate thy frame. (1805, X: 966–76)

So while Wordsworth traces in Books VI–X a similar continental arc for these
"Twins almost in genius and in mind!" (VI: 263), he uses their disparate experiences of nature, from their early lives, to separate them. He states that "the
place itself" will "Be conscious of thy presence" (X: 972–73) and calls on local
spirits to enfold and nurture his friend. Wordsworth never returns Coleridge,
in the poem, to his side: the "Story," he states in Book X, is "destined for thy
ear" (946). Reception and restoration are in the future, and conditional: "a
comfort now, a hope, / One of the dearest which this life can give, / Is mine;
that Thou art near and wilt be soon / Restored to us in renovated health" (XIII:
421–24).

Webs of Address

Coleridge was restored to the Wordsworths in 1806, and although not renovated in health, he was prepared to receive the poem elaborated during his
absence. After listening evening after evening for nearly two weeks to Wordsworth's recitation of *The Prelude*, Coleridge replied in early January 1807 with
"To W. Wordsworth: Lines composed, for the greater part on the Night, on
which he finished the recitation of his Poem (in thirteen Books) concerning
the growth and history of his own Mind." The first of several entries in the
Norton Critical Edition's section on "The Early Reception" of *The Prelude*, the
ode incorporates, in the first strophe, what Reeve Parker has called "an as-
tonishingly deft critical précis of the poem."[36] The précis, however, is just the
first of several responses to Wordsworth's poem that "To W. Wordsworth"
enacts. Its opening triplet of epithets, "O Friend! O Teacher! God's great Gift
to me!" suggests the psychological, critical, and spiritual dimensions of the
reply to come; it also stitches *The Prelude* to its precursors: the blank verse
effusions and meditations of Somerset and the Lakes and the poem-bearing
letters of Germany. If, in its suppression of the pointed "Friend!," the Norton
edition presents a plainer, less emphatic 1805 Wordsworth, it nevertheless offers an effusive Coleridge of 1807, in its printing of a manuscript "which
Coleridge sent to Wordsworth"—"the closest we can come to the poem
Coleridge wrote down just after hearing *The Prelude* read aloud" (Norton 542).
In this text, Coleridge does not merely echo Wordsworth's echoic use of the
sign of friendship ("Friend!"), which he had repeatedly seen in MS M and
heard recited, but grounds in profound and active reception the outward act
of calling-on:

> O Friend! O Teacher! God's great Gift to me!
> Into my heart have I receiv'd that Lay
> More than historic, that prophetic Lay
> Wherein (high theme by Thee first sung aright)
> Of the Foundations and the Building-up
> Of thy own Spirit, thou hast lov'd to tell
> What may be told, to th'understanding mind
> Revealable; and what within the mind
> May rise enkindled. Theme as hard as high!
>   (lines 1–9)[37]

In a climactic opening address, Coleridge declares Wordsworth's redemptive agency only to establish, in the ensuing lines, his own status as worthy receiver of "God's Gift" and of Wordsworth's song of revealed and "enkindled" truth. Coleridge's reception of the "prophetic Lay," the first strophe suggests, is as an active process of analytical imagination: his own mind enkindled by the glossing of subjects, the strophe culminates in a series of exclamations—"An Orphic Tale indeed / A Tale divine of high and passionate Thoughts / To their own music chaunted!" (38–40). Here Coleridge counterpoints the chanting he invokes and answers Wordsworth's expression in Book I of his "favorite aspiration!": his yearning toward "some philosophic Song / Of Truth that cherishes our daily life; / With meditations passionate from deep / Recesses in man's heart, immortal verse / Thoughtfully fitted to the Orphean lyre" (1805, I: 230–35). Wordsworth's song on the "Building-up / Of [his] own spirit," Coleridge suggests, demonstrates his readiness for the more universal song of truth, *The Recluse*.

The second strophe answers Wordsworth's aspirations for "immortal verse" in an exclamatory address that again expands to establish its foundation in Coleridge's experience of reception:

> Ah great Bard!
> Ere yet that last Swell dying aw'd the Air,
> With stedfast ken I view'd thee in the Choir
> Of ever-enduring Men.
>   (40–43)

The address focuses Coleridge's comprehensive view and critical judgment in a vision, sustained to the very edges of sound, of his friend's eternal poetic fame—an image that places Wordsworth in a choir of immortals. Though dated and placed ("Janry, 1807. Cole-orton, near Ashby de la Zouch"), the poem opens to view the "one visible space," outside "Time," from which the "truly Great . . . Shed influence." Wordsworth's fame—and Coleridge's exclamations—lies also in his perception of visual-acoustic transformation:

> Nor less a sacred Roll, than those of old,
> And to be plac'd, as they, with gradual fame
> Among the Archives of mankind, thy Work
> Makes audible a linked Song of Truth,
> Of Truth profound a sweet continuous Song

Not learnt, but native, her own natural notes!
Dear shall it be to every human Heart.
To me how more than dearest!
   (48–55)

Coleridge here registers Wordsworth's ambition, so sharply focused in the
Malta poem, to write a sounding book that lays its "sure foundations in the
heart of Man" (MS M, f. 173v). Surpassing that goal, Wordsworth's codex
unlocks the "Archives of mankind," revealing the essential unity of individual
texts by releasing from their written words "a linked Song of Truth." In this
analysis, Coleridge claims an experience of reception that is at once sensual and
intellectual, of the ear and of the mind, of the mind and of the heart, personal
and exemplary. As he recognizes and celebrates Wordsworth's poetic centrality
(the bard among the choir of great men, the key to the archive), he begins to
establish himself as the poem's most worthy receiver—not because, as *The
Prelude* had declared, to him "The unity of all has been reveal'd" (1805, II: 226),
but because, as the poem's central addresses dramatize, his heart's wounds,
which had previously impeded his reception of Wordsworth's voice, are now
healed by that voice and by the modes of response it elicits from him.

    A cluster of plaintively intimate addresses marks the ode's formal and
psychological center and reflexively points to a history of Coleridge and Wordsworth's "communion." Evoking the experience of being "Scatter'd and whirl'd"
by the currents of Wordsworth's hopes during the early years of their friendship, Coleridge confesses a past failure to respond to Wordsworth's "utterance
of [his] love" (56):

                     thy faithful Hopes,
          Thy Hopes of me, dear Friend! by me unfelt
          Were troubles to me, almost as a Voice
          Familiar once and more than musical
          To one cast forth . . .
             (60–64)

A plaintive address likewise marks the psychological nadir of the third verse
paragraph—"O Friend! too well tho know'st, of what sad years / The long
suppression had benumm'd my soul" (67–69)—which ends with a vision of
Coleridge's corpse strewn with the "Flowers" of all that "Commune with Thee
had open'd out" (79). It is this recognition of a failure to convert into poetry

the fruits of the intimate exchange of 1797–98 that drives the ode's major turn, which is marked in the fourth strophe by self-address renouncing the "Poisons of Self-harm!" (86) ("That way no more!" [82]) and other-address correcting Wordsworth's harmful depictions of Coleridge in *The Prelude*: "Thou too, Friend! / O injure not the memory of that Hour / Of thy communion with my nobler mind / By pity or grief, already felt too long!" [88–91]).

As if actively converting the fruits of the present intimate exchange into poetry (Wordsworth's recitation of his poem to Coleridge; Coleridge's initial lines of reply to Wordsworth), the final strophes offer vivid images of communion and community that renew the former "Hour" of Wordsworth's "communion" with Coleridge's "nobler mind." Whereas Wordsworth had "destined" his story "for thy ear" (Prelude 1805, X: 946), Coleridge answers, in enlarging abstractions, that "Peace is nigh / Where Wisdom's Voice has found a list'ning Heart" (93–94). He also illustrates, in high resolution, his soul's responses to Wordsworth's modulating "strain." "Eve following eve," he writes, "hours" made "more precious, for thy song!,"

> In Silence list'ning, like a devout Child,
> My soul lay passive, by thy various strain
> Driven in surges now, beneath the stars,
> With momentary Stars of my own Birth,
> Fair constelled Foam still darting off
> Into the darkness! now a tranquil Sea
> Outspread and bright, yet swelling to the Moon!
>   (97, 99, 100, 101–7)

This is hearing not with the ear but through it: a sensual rendering of the rhythmical and spiritual dynamics of intimate address. Coleridge does not merely reinscribe the poets' shared textualization of friendship in the ode—replaying the figures and exclamation points that had long been part of their textual intimacy; he radically elaborates address to the "Friend!" by illustrating its interior effects and interpersonal dynamics. In so doing, Coleridge removes Wordsworth from the "one visible space" outside time (the everlasting "Choir") to the "Dear tranquil Time" of the recitation at Coleorton, "when the sweet sense of Home / Becomes most sweet!" (98–99). This form of communion, predicated on the simultaneity of expression and reception, happens in place, in time, and in community.

If "a sudden thought drew [Coleridge] back to the trip to Germany, the three of them alone together," as Kenneth Johnston writes of the image of the waters streaming from the keel of the ship on the crossing to Hamburg, the final strophe firmly closes the distances that had opened between the friends on that trip.[38] Here Coleridge establishes Wordsworth's sphere and incorporates himself within it, closing also the distance that had been left open in "the poem to Coleridge":

> —O Friend! my Comforter! my guide!
> Strong in thyself, and powerful to give strength!
> Thy long sustained Lay finally clos'd
> And thy deep Voice had ceas'd—(yet thou thyself
> Wert still before mine eyes, and round us both
> That happy Vision of beloved Faces!
> All, whom I deepliest love, in one room all!)
>   (108–14)

In stilling Wordsworth before his eyes and surrounding "both" poets with "beloved Faces!," Coleridge assuages both Wordsworth's fear of blank response to the page and his own anxieties about estrangement and inconsequence. In this fantasy of intimate communion, iconically emphasized by parentheses, the poets form two points at the center of love.[39] With this human tableau, suggestive of multiplicity within unity, Coleridge rewrites the close of Wordsworth's lay as a bringing close, as unification of the community and of the person:

> Scarce conscious, and yet conscious of it's Close,
> I sate, my Being blended in one Thought,
> (Thought was it? or aspiration? or Resolve?)
> Absorb'd, yet hanging still upon the sound:
> And when I rose, I found myself in Prayer!
>   (115–19)

While friendly address throughout the ode recalls Coleridge and Dorothy Wordsworth's historic urge for sympathetic immediacy, the final strophes illustrate sympathetic immediacy as well as the aftereffects of auditory reception. With no significant spatial or temporal difference between expression and reception, self-difference dissolves in a harmonizing of "Being." Coleridge inscribes neither a lapse nor a vacancy in the moments after the cessation of

Wordsworth's "Voice" but a resonant pause, punctuated by the rising of his physical body and focusing of his spirit. With this pointed image of prayer in the epode, or stand, Coleridge marks his redemption and his presence in place.

Parker reads the poem as Coleridge's "counter-elegy"—"antiphonal to what he heard in Wordsworth's poem, conceived as though the whelmed poet was answering the verses sung over him by his sorrowing friend."[40] Far from a merely personal expression of pathos, generated by self-interested ambivalence about Wordsworth's tremendous achievement, the "responsive funeral hymn" also engages the emotional and Christian structures of "Lycidas" and by this mediation moves beyond " 'the accidents of individual Life,' " or mere biography, to an "assertion of spiritual being" and recording of Coleridge's "own egotistic and transcendental ideal"—wherein the "One Life" comprehends but does not subsume the individual.[41] "To W. Wordsworth," I have argued, draws also on a history of intimate textual exchange across significant geographical distances. It brings closure to "the poem to Coleridge" by refocusing the emotional and spatial energies of friendly address and by giving them new spiritual point. Although no geographic distance separated the friends when, as the subtitle puts it, "for the greater part on the Night, on which he finished the recitation of his Poem," Coleridge composed "To W. Wordsworth," distance between them remained textually inscribed in *The Prelude*. Recalling the sleepless hours of metrical composition in Ratzeburg, the subtitle produces the image of Coleridge as night-spider, weaving a web of addresses around "All, whom [he] deepliest love[s]" (114). And, as in those epistolary hexameters, Coleridge liberally uses the exclamation point to reinscribe the oral intimacy of the two poets within community. The mark carries sound into the pause of the night after Wordsworth's "Voice had ceas'd" (111) and onto the silence of the page; it makes Coleridge's textual address revert to an oral occasion in which distance between speaker and listener is small enough to be traversed by stress (here, the emphasized enunciation of friendship). The punctuation evokes the state of being within earshot even while acknowledging that this state is no longer one of equality: Coleridge the friend is now an acolyte worshipping in the presence of a prophet, a sea swelling to Wordsworth's moon. He is an inscriber of intimate speech as communion who knows that Wordsworth now uses the exclamation point to acknowledge their distance as much as to overcome it—for Wordsworth has, during the Malta sojourn, found means to relocate distance, and the means of bridging distance, in a dialogue with his own distant past rather than with Coleridge's present.

The Norton *Prelude*: A Plainer, Less Emphatic Language

Given its crucial role in the poem's rhetorical means and historical development, the omission of the exclamation mark from the Norton 1805 poem is
significant. Although the publication of the Cornell *Prelude* has dramatically
altered the critical landscape, the Norton remains the standard parallel-text
edition of the poem. It also continues to advertise the critical significance of
its historical presentation ("to read [all three of the separate forms] together
provides an incomparable chance to observe a great poet composing and re-
composing, throughout a long life, his major work") and to publicize the
"freeing" of the 1850 poem "from the unwarranted alterations made by Wordsworth's literary executors." Alterations to the punctuation of the 1799 and
1805 poems, however, can only be gleaned from a paragraph in the back
matter in which Jonathan Wordsworth decrees the punctuation in the manuscripts "so spasmodic that its absence tells us nothing." Punctuation is "way-
ward" and "mismanaged," he claims, without detailing how it "has been
systemically reconsidered" in the edition.[42] The pointing of the fourteen-book
poem however, follows that of the 1850 first edition, published by Edward
Moxon, which, in the editor's judgment, approximates the author's final
intentions.[43]

Exclamation marks thus make their first pronounced appearance in the
fourteen-book text. Ironically, this facing-page discrepancy makes the Norton
1805 text appear more contemporary while the 1850 text appears embedded in
typographical time and history. With its capitals, double punctuation, and
upright exclamation points, the later version has the look of the Victorian text
that it is. Critics have long leveled the charge that the 1850 text is the more
traditional of the two, citing the political radicalism of the earlier poem and
the institutionalized Christian piety of the later—though historicist rereadings
of the thirteen-book poem have qualified this view.[44] I would add that the
"modern" feel of the Norton 1805 text—and its authority—owes something to
the cleanness of its visual look, as achieved in part by the broad deletion of the
graphic sign of passionate exclamation.

With this cut, the editors minimize the poem's visible symptoms of authorial anxiety and material self-consciousness. For example, by replacing the
comma/exclamation point combination (", perhaps / A blank to other men!")
with a pair of dashes, the Norton text gives the reference to Fleming a look of
cool thoughtfulness:

> With heart how full
> Will he peruse these lines, this page—perhaps
> A blank to other men—for many years
> Have since flowed in between us . . .
>
> (Norton, II: 353–56)

In deleting the mark of vocal passion, the Norton transforms the exclamatory phrase into a considered aside, smoothing the disturbance between the deixical reference to the silent, written lines and the evocation of voice. Wordsworth as a result less apparently exploits exclamation and address to "reach the hearts" of readers. So, too, he less apparently calls out to Coleridge, diminishing the contrast between friendly address and the "silent language" which "In conversation betwixt man and man / Blots from the human countenance all trace / Of beauty and of love" (1805, II: 472, 473–75). MS A reads,

> Thou, my Friend! wert rear'd
> In the great City, 'mid far other scenes;
> But we by different roads at length have gain'd
> The self-same bourne.
>
> (1805, p. 680; II: 466–69)

The modernized Norton 1805 bears no such explicit signs of emphasis:

> Thou, my friend, wert reared
> In the great city, 'mid far other scenes,
> But we by different roads at length have gained
> The self-same bourne.
>
> (Norton, II: 467–70)

The omission quiets the poem's passionate calls, presenting a meditative poet who carries on a colloquy with Coleridge in his mind rather than one who attempts to "speak" (470) to him through the marking of his pages.[45] Not only does this alteration reduce the reflexive tension between the poem's graphic surface and its thematic concern with signs of feeling and typographical emphasis (which come to a head in Book VII);[46] it also effaces textual traces of personal and professional intimacy and the visible affective channel Wordsworth had inscribed in the Malta manuscript. "Farewell! God love you!" Dorothy

had written from Goslar; and William had echoed, at the close of the second
part,

> Fare thee well!
> Health & the quiet of a healthy^{ful} mind
> Attend thee! seeking oft the haunts of men
> But yet more often living with thyself,
> And for thyself, so haply shall thy days
> Be many & a blessing to mankind . . .
>   (1799, p. 216, MS. RV, 13r)

Or, as the Norton text more sternly closes,

> Fare thee well.
> Health and the quiet of a healthful mind
> Attend thee, seeking oft the haunts of men—
> And yet more often living with thyself,
> And for thyself—so haply shall thy days
> Be many, and a blessing to mankind.
>   (Norton, II: 479–84)

Thus in deleting the point, the Norton edition literalizes, or performs, that
very blotting of affective traces that Wordsworth feared and then worked to
overcome. It dismantles a visible system of affective engagement only slowly
adopted in the poem's conceptualization and extension, removing a mark
of the poem's development and its social, geographical, and material
circumstances.

Concerned perhaps that readers would take the point less as a meaningful
mark than as a distracting archaism, less as a part of the language than as, in
Adorno's terms, a "rigidified" infiltrator of the verbal realm, editors succeeded
in distancing the poem from its cultures of inscription—both private and
public. No matter how much the composition of *The Prelude* benefitted from
Coleridge's distance, "Friend!" had situated the blank verse within a particular
social and manuscript culture evolved in the late 1790s, a circuit of feeling and
mutual regard which Coleridge had emphatically narrowed, in his 1807 reply,
to the "beloved Faces" encircling the two friends. In printing that poem with
its numerous points, the Norton volume represents Coleridge as the poet of
volume and passionate, typographical emphasis—the conversational,

sentimental, and effeminate poet to the strong, silent type of Wordsworth—the sublime egotist and prophet of nature. The Norton text also distances the poem from a contentious public culture of print, in which grammarians embraced the affective force of the exclamation mark and elocutionists, skeptically regarding its tonal and temporal associations, encouraged the spacing of feeling.

Chapter 7

Thelwall's Therapoetics

Scanning *The Excursion*

> The old man ceased
> The words he uttered shall not pass away
> Thy had sunk into me, but not as
> > sounds
> To be expressed by visible characters
> For while he spake my spirit had
> > obeyed
> The presence of his eye, my ear had drunk
> The meanings of his voice. He had dis=
> > =coursed
> Like one who in the slow & silent works
> The manifold conclusions of his thought
> Had brooded till Imagination's power
> > c
> Condensed them to a passion whens}e
> > she drew
> Herself, new energies, resistless force
> > —*Ruined Cottage* MS B, 52r, lines 1–12

By the 1860s, Wordsworth's *Excursion* was an examination text in the educational establishments of England. Female students in their second year at the nation's teacher-training colleges had to memorize and recite passages from either the first book of *Paradise Lost* or *The Excursion*: Wordsworth's blank-verse epic was part of a curriculum that aimed to inculcate national character and advance national literacy.[1] However, when the poem was first published in 1814, its claims to represent the best of the national character were controversial: Francis Jeffrey summarily declared, "This will never do," attacking both its subject matter—the exemplary lives of rustics—and its versification.[2] The versification was likewise at issue for John Thelwall, a poet and prosodist who had also suffered under Jeffrey's pen; his response to the blank verse was to scan each and every line of the nine-book poem.

Thelwall's marking of *The Excursion* was the culmination of a dialogue dating from the 1790s, a dialogue second only in importance to our understanding of Wordsworth's views on prosody to that which he shared with Coleridge. Thelwall's ideas about prosody and its representation in print stimulated Wordsworth into some of his most detailed statements about meter and emphasis; they also represented, as Thelwall elaborated them into a physiological system for teaching elocution and for rectifying speech impediments, a materialist reworking of eighteenth-century conceptions of emphasis and a democratic development of the cultural politics of meter announced in the Preface to *Lyrical Ballads*. In Thelwall's eyes—judging from his scansion and annotations—Wordsworth had turned his back on these politics: *The Excursion* embodied a conservative rather than democratic representation of English speech because it symbolically restricted access to the poetry that could best reform the English tongue. In scanning the poem, Thelwall was aiming to return its prosody, which he saw as physiologically founded on bodily rhythms, to ordinary readers who were unable, unassisted, to release it from the lines of blank verse as they appeared on the printed page. Deriving meter from anatomical structure and the laws of motion, and using printed poetry to teach the speaking and reading of English in the lectures he gave across the length and breadth of the nation, Thelwall was demonstrating that the "English rhythmus,"[3] which was best embodied in blank verse, could become a foundational discourse of national identity. He was, in effect, preparing the way for the adoption of Wordsworth's poetry as a set text in the National Schools, an initiative approved by the Schools Inspector Matthew Arnold—another of Wordsworth's critical readers—in an attempt to diffuse a unifying Englishness among the people.[4] These included the sons and daughters of the new manufacturing classes whose vitiated taste for "outrageous stimulation," Wordsworth argued in 1800, threatened to overwhelm the national culture under a tide, as Arnold saw it, of "anarchy."[5]

To understand what was at stake in Thelwall's scansion of *The Excursion* it is necessary to consider their dialogue from the poets' first meeting, in July 1797, which culminated in Thelwall's adoption of the colloquial blank verse that both Wordsworth and Coleridge were then writing. From here I trace Thelwall's gradual elaboration of a physiological prosody and elocutionary pedagogy that privileged blank verse, addressing the poets' correspondence in 1804 to shed light on their diverging ideas about the therapeutic effects of meter within an injurious culture of print. I next read Thelwall's development of his elocutionary anthology into a workbook as a practical, political, and theoretical intervention in a print culture of poetry that contravened universal physical laws. Like the hand scansions of his pupils still visible in the numerous surviving copies of his anthological workbooks, Thelwall's scansion of Wordsworth's epic marks not just a contest over the nature of English meter but also a material and broadly populist correction of Wordsworth's Regency project of "correct[ing]" national despondency by the stimulation of an ultimately spiritual metrical energy.[6]

Somerset Emphases: Blank Verse, Blank Lines

Thelwall's engagement with Wordsworth's poetry began in July 1797, when he visited Coleridge at Nether Stowey and participated in an open-air reading of Wordsworth's manuscript drama *The Borderers*. Writing in a letter to his wife from "All fox Den" on July 18, Thelwall described a ramble "along a wild romantic dell," during which Wordsworth, Coleridge, and he, "a literary & political triumvirate, passed sentence on the productions and characters of the age—burst forth in poetical flights of enthusiasm—& philosophised [their] minds into a state of tranquility."[7] The visit would be significant, in different ways, to each of them.[8] Remembering it in 1841, Wordsworth told Eliza Fenwick that

> Coleridge and [Thelwall] had both been public lecturers: Coleridge mingling with his politics theology; from which the other elocutionist abstained, unless it were for the sake of a sneer. This quondam community of public employment induced Thelwall to visit Coleridge at Nether Stowey where he fell in my way. He really was a man of extraordinary talent, an affectionate husband and a good father. Though brought up in the city on a tailor's board he was truly sensible of the beauty of natural objects. I remember, once

when Coleridge, he, and I were seated together upon the turf on the brink of a stream in the most beautiful part of the most beautiful glen of Alfoxden, Coleridge exclaimed, "This is a place to reconcile one to all the jarrings and conflicts of the wide world,"—"Nay" said Thelwall, to make one forget them altogether.[9]

Coleridge and Thelwall were, as Wordsworth's term "elocutionist" suggests, drawn together by their mutual interest in political rhetoric. Thelwall was the radical whose oratory, attracting large audiences, the government most feared: to quell his influence, it introduced laws banning public meetings.[10] They were also both poets: their conversation had begun in letters; now continued, it concerned politics, philosophy, and religion and hinged on matters of metrical emphasis. As David Fairer and Richard Gravil have shown, Thelwall challenged Coleridge to move away from a poetic style derived from William Lisle Bowles in which it was the "adjectives and weak words" that were emphasized. "*Sore* wounds," "*cold* earth," "*flamy* child!," he wrote incredulously to Coleridge, stating that this "affectation of the Della Crusca school . . . blurs almost every one of your poems."[11] In Thelwall's early notion of public poetry, it was, by contrast, vital to place the "accent" upon the nouns, so that the reader distinctly perceived and gave forcible utterance to weighty and worldly matters. In his *Poems Written in Close Confinement in the Tower and Newgate, Under a Charge of High Treason* (1795), he had relied on the personification of abstractions—"Liberty," "Equality," "Justice"—not only to direct attention to principles and practical concerns, as Fairer has argued, but also to rouse Britain from its "lethargic fetters": to stimulate the "free-born energies" of "Albion's hardy race."[12] These poetic intentions—and typographic and tropological strategies—were likely informed by Thelwall's experience of the "energy" that flowed between orator and audience in the popular political lectures he gave before and continued after his imprisonment and acquittal on treason charges (despite the tightening of Pitt's regime).[13] As Thelwall stated in a 1795 lecture published in his journal *The Tribune*, "In principle, then, not in violence I would have you go forward. In active exertion of mind, not in tumult, I would have you advance. Now is the time to cherish a glowing energy that may rouse into action every nerve and faculty of the mind, and fly from breast to breast like that electric principle which is perhaps the true soul of the physical universe, till the whole mass is quickened, illuminated and informed."[14] As with his own efforts to energize Albion in his prison sonnets and odes, Thelwall's critique of Coleridge's emphasis shows his directing of a cherished elocutionary concept—"emphasis," or "Force or Energy" of voice—to political use.[15] It also reveals his attention to the grammatical and metrical dynamics of printed poetry. His interest in stimulating rational enquiry and vitalizing the body politic was taking a prosodic turn.

Behind the radical politics and emerging prosody was Thelwall's radical theory of life. In January 1793 he had delivered a paper to the Physical Society of Guy's Hospital where he had been attending lectures in medicine and anatomy. Published as *An Essay towards a Definition of Animal Vitality*, the paper directly refuted John Hunter's notion of a "Vital principle being resident in the blood" and indirectly challenged religious orthodoxy by positing a material "vivifying principle." Life—which Thelwall defined as a "state of action"—was not the effect of a divine, immaterial essence, such as an immortal soul or spirit "superadded" to inert matter (as Hunter's theory implied), but was rather the product of a "perfect contact" between "a *specific organization* and a *specific stimulus.*" This stimulus, this "something" of an "equisitely subtle nature," was most likely the "electrical fluid."[16]

Following Nicholas Roe, critics have connected Thelwall's materialist vital principle with his commitment to the free circulation of political information throughout the nation in a time of governmental repression.[17] "The diffusion of a vital principle 'through the organized frame' was . . . essential to both physical and political life," Mary Fairclough observes, adding that the "physiological model Thelwall develops in the *Essay* provides him with a paradigm through which he can claim the sympathetic transmission of political energies as a wholesome rather than a pathological process."[18] Whereas Burke condemned the uncontrollable " 'electrick communication' " of revolutionary discourse and the " 'distemper of the public mind' " it effected,[19] Thelwall likened himself to a human battery or Leyden jar emitting an "electric principle"—"perhaps the true soul of the physical universe"—by which the "whole mass" of assembled listeners "is quickened, illuminated, and informed."[20] In an account of another 1795 lecture, he figured his own spoken sentences as having "darted from breast to breast with electric contagion," uniting individuals into a rational body capable of demanding reform.[21] Thelwall's prison poems and his critique of Coleridge's emphasis, however, signal a development of one of the terms that featured both in rhetorical and physiological discussions—energy. Just as he materialized life by premising it, in 1793, on the contact between a specific organization and the "electrical fluid," Thelwall would materialize the "life" of speech by physiologizing the "energy" of vocal "emphasis." If for Hunter bodily vitality depended upon spirit, and if for Sheridan "emphasis" was the "life and soul of speech," for Thelwall the vitality of speech and the person speaking—and, ultimately, the nation—would depend upon efficient vocalic action: the energetic contraction and release of speech organs in accordance with the universal laws of motion.[22]

It is possible that Thelwall's quasi-materialist strictures on the placement of the emphasis (on the substantives not the "weak words") and Coleridge's passionate defense of his own more subjective and effusive prosody was one of the topics the three poets discussed as they paced the coombs and hills around Alfoxden in July 1797. But, during this visit, Thelwall proved receptive to Coleridge's and Wordsworth's advocacy of a written poetry whose patterns of stress were imitative not of public declamation but of conversational speech.[23] He had come to Somerset, after all, seeking companionship and refuge. His imprisonment (in 1794) and the ban on public meetings had destroyed his career as a radical lecturer and marked him out as an "acquitted felon."[24] This reputation accompanied him wherever he went: he was ostracized by many, while any group of acquaintances among whom he settled found itself under pressure from the authorities. In Somerset, the poets were spied upon by a Home Office agent, and local scandal about Thelwall's presence helped ensure Wordsworth's lease was not renewed. Feeling the heat, Coleridge discouraged Thelwall from taking up residence nearby; Thelwall was left to pursue their shared ideas and communal verse style from a distance. After leaving, he began writing blank verse in Coleridge's and Wordsworth's manner. In contrast to the declaratory, rhyming poems of 1795, his poetry was now "personal and explorative," subtly rhythmic, and pastoral in key.[25]

In the new blank verse, moreover, emphasis was now directly invoked as a mark of friendship and social community, made by the body, and linked with the marking of the material page. In "On leaving the Bottoms of Glocester-shire; where the Author had been entertained by several families with great hospitality. Aug. 12, 1797," Thelwall fondly recalls the "pleasant haunts!" and "cordial intercourse" that will shape his future discourse in some future dwelling: "ah! then the names / Of Norton and of Newcomb—on my tongue, / And hospitable Partridge, not unmark'd / With lengthen'd emphasis, shall frequent dwell." In tension with this loving enunciation of the name is the lengthened silence of the blank line, intimating Thelwall's political anguish and personal grief in the inscription of his reluctance to depart: "———once again, farewell— / Dear Scenes of hospitality and joy!——— . . ."[26] This Coleridgean mark of feeling—a double dash new to Thelwall's poetry but used by Coleridge in his 1796 volume[27]—also featured in other poems written after the encounter. In

"Lines, written at Bridgewater, in Somersetshire, on the 27th of July, 1797; during a long excursion, in quest of a peaceful retreat," Thelwall uses the single and double dash to metrical and affective effect, writing that his

soul

Is sick of public turmoil—ah, most sick
Of the vain effort to redeem a Race
Enslav'd, because degenerate, lost to Hope,
Because to Virtue lost—wrapp'd up in Self,
In sordid avarice, luxurious pomp,
And profligate intemperance——a Race
Fierce without courage; abject, and yet proud;
And most licentious, tho' most far from free.[28] (71–79)

In contrast to the vicious society that he would keep from his infant son's consciousness ("Oh! blest inapprehension!——Let it last"),[29] Thelwall imagines an idyllic social form in which poet-farmers (Coleridge and he) "delve" their "little garden plots" while "Sweet converse" flows:

eager, one propounds,

And listens one, weighing each pregnant word,
And pondering fit reply, that may untwist
The knotty point—perchance of import high——
Of Moral Truth, of Causes Infinite,
Creating Power! . . . ("Lines, written at Bridgewater," 94, 95, 96–101)[30]

In Thelwall's version of the Pantisocratic dream, conversation is a fertilizing activity co-occurring with agriculture. As the diggers talk, "each pregnant word" is received as a potent seed that grows weighty in its "pondering." "Suspending" the working "arm" (95)—a suspension iconically represented in the long blank line—the men pause in their labor, their bodies and minds responding to the stimulus of their speech.

If Thelwall's turn to conversational blank verse was influenced by Coleridge and Wordsworth, his emphases may have influenced them.[31] Wordsworth's instruction to the readers of his first major blank-verse publication that words ought "to be weighed in the balance of feeling" (LB 351) because they "are impregnated with passion" echoes Thelwall's "weighing" of "each pregnant word" and likewise employs the double dash to communicate weight (see

Chapter 5). Thelwall had sent Coleridge his new blank-verse poems from his new home in Llyswen in the autumn of 1797; Coleridge, Dorothy, and William visited him there in August 1798, when Wordsworth was invoking a "motion and a spirit, that impels / All thinking things, all objects of all thought" (LB 101–2). Roe has argued that this animating force in "Tintern Abbey" echoes the language of vital energy that Thelwall had articulated in his *Essay on Animal Vitality*, "showing the extent to which the poetry of Romantic transcendence was dependent upon and articulated the materialist principles of contemporary scientific and medical debate."[32] In fact, we could situate Wordsworth's earlier account of the enlivening of the Discharged Soldier—a scene of "perfect contact" between a *"specific organization* and a *specific stimulus"*—at the intersection of elocutionary-prosodic and physiological debates about vitality.

After the encounter at Llyswen, the poets' paths diverged. Wordsworth and Coleridge went to Germany, where Wordsworth, in preparation for a national epic in the wake of revolutionary disappointment (*The Recluse*), explored the prosodic foundations of his poetic spirit in verse fragments that became the "Poem" on "the growth of [his] own mind" (EY 518). Coleridge, among other projects, wrote hexameters that called for energetic recitation and digital scansion (see Chapter 6). Still in Wales, and also planning a national epic in the wake of revolutionary disappointment, Thelwall stepped beyond Wordsworth's suggestive account of meter and "emphatic language" in the 1800 Preface to *Lyrical Ballads* as he developed a physiological account of prosody that merged his interests in rhetorical stimulation and physical and mental vitality. These common interests, now separately developed, would be topics of debate when the poets met, in person and on paper, on a few occasions between 1803 and 1806. When, in 1814, Wordsworth published *The Excursion* portion of his epic and Thelwall "Scanned" his copy of the book "in metrical cadences + rhythmical clauses,"[33] their ideas on prosody, vitality, and energy, which cross-fertilized in those conversations of 1796–98, crossed once again— this time so as to mark the radical potential of blank-verse reading in postrevolutionary culture.

"The Spirit Was Broken," "Its Spring Was Snapped": Speech as Organic Action

Like Wordsworth in *The Prelude* and Coleridge in "Dejection: an Ode," Thelwall would later write an autobiographical narrative of recovery from a loss of bodily and psychological vitality caused by political and personal disappointments—in his case to explain his discovery of the connection "between Physiological and Elocutionary Science" (HC 14). As he wrote in the 1810 *Letter to Henry Cline*, while studying the prosody of *Paradise Lost* and Dryden's *Aeneid* during his "retirement" at Llyswen, "incongruous impressions" led him to "the detection of those elementary principles, out of which arise—the facilities and harmonies of oral utterance" (HC 3). Reaching back to his studies in medicine and anatomy, Thelwall recalled that a physical law of pulsation and remission regulates all organs, from the legs to the larynx: a "universal principle of action and re-action . . . forms the paramount law of all reiterated or progressive motion, organic or mechanical; from the throb and remission of the heart, to the progress of the quadruped or the reptile, and the sway of the common pendulum" (HC 24). As legs set down and lift up in alternation, so the larynx pulses and releases, dictating the alternation of heavy and light syllables in oral utterance. Syllables that "are absolutely affected to *thesis,* or heavy, [are] pronounced during the pulsative effort of the primary vocal organ" and those that are "determined to *arsis,* or light, [are] pronounced during the remission, or reaction of that organ," he stated.[34] "Organic action" thus determines the production of sound, which proceeds in metrical cadences—temporally equivalent "portions of tuneable sound," "beginning heavy and ending light," but varying in their numbers of syllables.[35] As, for example, | *universe of* | *death* | and also | *Gorgons and* | *Hydras* | (Figure 27).[36] Portions of cadence may also pass in silence, for pauses, as with rhetorical emphasis, count within the measure.[37] Thus, like Joshua Steele, whose signs for *thesis* and *arsis* he borrowed, Thelwall approached speech as a musical science, and he likewise declared duple and triple time the most typical cadences of English. But whereas Steele had attributed the primacy of these time signatures to the abstractions of geometrical proportion ("'may not space of time be analogous to space in geometry; which can only be equally and uniformly divided by quadrilateral or triangular polygons, their multiples, or subduples'"), Thelwall derived the "rhythmical division of musical bars" from "the primary

principles of nature, and the physiological necessities resulting from the organization of vocal beings."[38] "All tribes of voice" speak in cadences, he insisted,
save for the duck, for whom there is "no arsis."[39] *Quack quack quack.*

Yet despite his exciting discovery of "some of the most hidden mysteries
of the Science of Human Speech" (HC 3), and, by inference, the causes and
cures of speech impediment, Thelwall did not at first seek to apply his principle. Instead of acting, resuming the cadence of "universal motion," he found
himself stalled. As he confessed to Cline, new "afflictions" added to existing
"dejection" left his mind "uncollected" and drained of "energy," able neither to
estimate its "new treasure" nor "to make use of it": "The spirit was broken; the
bow had lost its elasticity; it seemed as if its spring was snapped, and it was
never to rebound again" (HC 13). Nonetheless, his "Effusion I," composed
after his daughter Maria's death in November 1799, implied his newfound
understanding:

> —O, my babe!
> Maria! Oh, Maria! thy lov'd name,
> While Nature yet is vocal—while this heart
> To this sad tongue can dictate, thy lov'd name
> The rocks and conscious echoes shall repeat,
> And murmuring Vaga mourn no loss but thine. (117–22)[40]

This passage from the sequence "Paternal Tears" evokes a tellingly psychological and physiological scene of lamentation. The sympathetic mourning of the
Welsh landscape—its repetition of "Maria!"—depends upon the heart's ongoing dictation of the "lov'd name" to the "sad tongue." The lines thus raise the
possibility of both an inner lapse, the heart's inability to "dictate" or the
tongue's inability to respond, and an outward falling off—an unreactive, silent
landscape. In so doing, the poem inscribes breaches of "sympathy" between
mind and body and between body and nature that Thelwall goes to on designate in his scientific writings as the cause of unmelodious speech and
impediment—an "interruption of association" (HC 58) which could only by
repaired by resetting the inner economy of energy expenditure according to
the "universal principle of action and re-action" (HC 24).

One of the most striking passages in the 1810 *Letter to Henry Cline* illustrates the erosion of sympathy between the will and the organs of speech and
expression. Arguing that the majority of speech impediments have a mental or

moral cause, and thus are not "the pure and simple results of organic malcon-formation," Thelwall posits an internal divide:

> —every stammerer, stutterer, throttler, constipator, involuntary con-founder, and unconscious reiterator of the elements of speech . . . is *partially*, and to a certain extent, either idiotic, or deranged: for what but derangement can it be called, to be constantly doing a thousand things that we neither intend to do, nor are conscious of doing? nay, that are the very reverse of all that is in our intention! What, but a species of idiotcy, is it, to be ignorant of the means by which the will is to influence the simplest organs of volition, and (without excuse of palsy, stricture, or organic privation) to be unable to move a lip, a tongue, or a jaw? Or perform the common functions of our species?—to clinch the teeth, when we are bade to open the mouth! and roll the eyes, when we ought to move the lips! (HC 68)

The deeply compassionate portrait turns on a problem of intention: to be "doing a thousand things that we neither intend to do, nor are conscious of doing" is the tragic effect of a hard break between "the will" and the "simplest organs of volition." Rhetorical question, exclamation, and typography amplify the horror of the inability to "move a lip, a tongue, or a jaw." The writing is as emphatic as the scenario is extreme: a prose extrapolation of the disconnection between "heart" and "tongue" that Thelwall had imagined in Effusion I. Where those verses had put the landscape's sympathetic resounding of Maria's name at stake, these lines conjure the loss of the "common functions of our species" and of its common response: sympathetic understanding. They contemplate not neutral inexpression but facial features and vocal organs that betray "proper character" by doing "the very reverse of all that is in our intention!" If emphasis is that "force" or "energy" by which we convey our intention to our listeners, this is a portrait of emphasis undone, or pathological irony.[41]

Fluent and melodious speech, however, demanded not a more conscious application of the will—not a more deliberate direction of energy toward the vocal and enunciative organs—but a restoration of the primary sympathy be-tween mind and body. Thelwall blamed all "harsh, ungraceful, and interrup-tive delivery" on the individual's deviation from the universal principles of motion; likewise he derived "all the customary *impediments of speech*" from "inconsiderate attempts to violate this primary law" of throb and remission (HC 189–90). To put it simply, under- or overwillfulness impaired vocalization. Rehabituation to the natural pattern of pulse and remission would "tranquillize the agitated mind" and "restrain its impetuosity" or "rouse it from its lethargy" and "stimulate its apathy," disciplining the "undisciplined volition" to make judicious its "application" to the vocal organs (HC 58, 189). The "universal principle of action and reaction" thus provided a foundational norm for the expenditure of energy (HC 24). As he stated in an entry for Abraham Rees' *Cyclopædia,* "when the primary organ of cadential or syllabic impulse (the cartilage that surrounds the larynx) has been once contracted for the impulsion of the more energetic note, a re-action of that organ, either silent or accompanied by another note of less energy, must take place before the contractile energy can be renewed."[42]

Indeed, as Thelwall narrates in the letter to Cline, once his mind had been impressed by the melodies of Milton and Dryden, his "mental and moral maladies dissipated" and he "resolved to confront the prejudices of the world," by emerging from retirement to promote and apply his new understanding. The sympathy between "physical perception" and "mental volition" thus reestablished, one key stimulus was required to repair the associations between his volition and the "executive organs" (HC 57, 14, 58).[43] In late 1801 as the Peace of Amiens was being prepared, tranquilizing the "passions of Europe" and freeing "energies" from "brutal contentions" for the "humanizing pursuits of Intellect and Science," stimulus came in the form of an imperative uttered by a friend who had a mind of "communicable energy": " 'Thou,' " he said, " 'must give Lectures on Elocution" (HC 15–16).

In the *Letter to Henry Cline,* Thelwall thus fashions his life story so that his new profession of elocutionist is a renewal of the democratic ideals that had driven his career as a political orator in the 1790s. In the process, he revises his earlier depictions of the vitalizing power of rhetorical "energy." Where he had figured his own sentences as having "darted from breast to breast with electric contagion,"[44] he now offered, as he returned to lecturing in 1801, a "doctrine of physical pulsations and musical proportions"[45] that explained vocalic action as prosodically regulated energy. He presented himself not as an "electrical stimulus," vocally catalyzing a circuit of thought and feeling, but as an analyst of economies of energy—an illuminator of physical and musical laws and a diagnostician of "interruptions of association" within the system. Whereas in 1795, he saw his utterance as the battery producing the charge, he now made not *his* voice but the rhythmus of the "best poets" and prose writers the "stimulus": his lecture audiences would recite poetry and prose and thereby become articulate as they gave tongue to "the English rhythmus." In voicing, they

would "foster those energies which the exigencies of the times may require . . .
extend the intellectual glories, and multiply the resources of Britain!"[46] The
eyes, ears, larynx, and lips were now scenes of political and patriotic action. As
it were, elocutionary practice replicated and elocutionary theory systematized—
but also democratized—the ability Thelwall had formerly identified with the
orator in person: the ability to energize individuals as a group in the cause of
self and national liberation.

Passion, Print, and the "Regular Laws of the Iambic"

Over the next two years, Thelwall lectured extensively throughout the Midlands
and north of England and, in late 1803, he settled with his family in Kendal,
near Grasmere, in hopes of continuing the conversation of Alfoxden and Llyswen in new form. In November Thelwall wrote excitedly to his wife Stella of
visiting Southey and Coleridge in Keswick and of "expatiating and expanding
[his] philosophical principle of pulsation" with Hazlitt, whom he counted with
the two poets as "already among the number of [his] disciples."[47] In December,
he was scheduled to give a course of lectures in Edinburgh, but called them off
after the first night, accusing Francis Jeffrey in a pamphlet, published within the
month, of inciting general mockery of his metrical recitation and of misrepre-
senting Thelwall in his review of the *Poems, Chiefly Written in Retirement*
(1801).[48] Inviting Wordsworth, Coleridge, and Southey to his lectures in Kendal, Thelwall now made common cause with them as fellow victims of Jeffrey's
dismissive response to poetry that challenged literary and social hierarchies (see
Introduction).[49] Only Southey attended a lecture. Wordsworth sent a well-
known letter praising the *Letter to Francis Jeffray* [*sic*] but differentiating his
"own system of metre" (EY 434) from Thelwall's, which could be gleaned from
the body of the pamphlet and from the appendix of detailed lecture outlines.

　　Wordsworth's letter shows that Thelwall had stimulated him to formulate
his thoughts about prosody in more detail than ever before. In response to
Thelwall's derivation of meter from the rhythms of the speaking body, Wordsworth here developed his ideas about meter and passion, first formulated in
the Preface to *Lyrical Ballads*, in terms of pronunciation, identifying a crucial
tension between the "passion of metre" and the "passion of the subject":

　　[Y]our general rule is just that the art of verse should not compell
　　you to read in [tone? some?] emphasis etc that violates the nature

of Prose. But this rule should be taken with limitations for not
to speak of other reasons as long as verse shall have the marked
termination that rhyme gives it, and as long as blank verse shall be
printed in lines, it will be Physically impossible to pronounce the
last words or syllables of the lines with the same indifference, as the
others, i.e. not to give them an intonation of one kind or an other,
or to follow them with a pause, not called out for by the passion of
the subject, but by the passion of metre merely. (EY 434)

Wordsworth's description of his "own system of metre" reflects the late
eighteenth-century loosening of Augustan prosodic doctrine, involving a post-
Sheridan dual endorsement of the regularizing emphases of line endings (the
intonation or pause "called out for" by the "passion of metre") as well as the
enlivening emphases of speech. As he elaborates, using "long" and "short" for
stress and unstress, "1st and 2nd syllables long or short indifferently except
where the Passion of the sense cries out for one in preference 3d 5th 7th 9th
short etc according to the regular laws of the Iambic" (434). Wordsworth's
"Passion of the sense" (or "subject") *cries out* as feeling intonation, a disruptive
countercurrent to the "passion of metre." Though Wordsworth "scarcely" admits any "limits to the dislocation of the verse"—and in another careful litotes,
he "know[s] none that may not be justified by some passion or other" (434)—
the metrical frame, as enforced by printed lines, remains a controlling
feature.

Wordsworth's response to Thelwall entailed a deepening of the arguments
about meter he had previously made in the Preface. There Wordsworth had
explored the psychological uses of metrical regularity. He wrote of meter as a
device employed by poets, and which, like rhyme, gives a "regular and uniform" "distinction" to the words, unlike that "produced" by "poetic diction,"
which is "arbitrary and subject to infinite caprices upon which no calculation
whatever can be made." The pleasure-effects of meter, that is, are calculable
because meters are formal organizations of "passion" separate from the character and whims of the poet: "the metre obeys certain laws, to which the Poet
and Reader both willingly submit because they are certain" (LB 754). They are
also historical forms; the "passion" a meter communicates is subject to no
"interference" save for the extra "pleasure" attached to it by the "concurring
testimony of ages" derived from the meter's association with particular poems
(754). In *Lyrical Ballads* Wordsworth chose to "superadd" the "charm" of meter
to his descriptions of the "great and universal passions of men, the most

general and interesting of their occupations, and the entire world of nature" because of meter's "power" to "give pleasure" over time, "from generation to generation" (LB 754, 755). The passion of meter is impersonal—an effect of its systematic regularity and historicity.

The program of reform that Wordsworth sketches in the Preface—the "improvement of . . . taste" (759) and amelioration of the affections—hinges upon meter's supplementary relationship to diction and story. Because the end of poetry is "to produce excitement in coexistence with an overbalance of pleasure," and because diction, in itself, may over- or underexcite, meter is a crucial resource. In cases of real "danger that the excitement may be carried beyond its proper bounds," "the co-presence of something regular" would enable painful "images and feelings" and "powerful" words to be read with some pleasure. As Wordsworth asserts, meter "cannot but have great efficacy in tempering and restraining the passion by an intertexture of ordinary feeling" (LB 755). On the other hand, if the poet's words are "incommensurate with the passion," meter's "continual and regular impulses of pleasurable surprise" can be recruited to "impart passion to the words, and to effect the complex end which the Poet proposes" (LB 756). Thus just as meter makes available to readers the "deeper passions" conveyed by words or images by tempering their always attendant "painful feeling" with a "complex feeling of delight," so, too, it makes available "important" truths by interesting readers in rude tales they would otherwise overlook (LB 757).

Although Wordsworth refers Thelwall to the passionate intonations of "metre" and "sense," the system he describes is fundamentally nonrhetorical. Despite Wordsworth's keen attention to the "business" of punctuation (EY 289), his accentual-syllabic count of the verse ("3d 5th 7th 9th short") does not account for the accentual effects of pause—that a dash, for instance, could represent a single silent phase of pulsation and remission.[50] So, too, poetry's capacity to reform depends upon its being read, not its being read aloud—and upon the registration, in the mind or psychesoma,[51] of meter's status as the "strict antithesis to Prose" (LB 749). As he states in the Preface, the "perception of similitude in dissimilitude," or uniformity in variety, produces the effect of "pleasure" in the "mind" (756). When in 1804 Thelwall pushes Wordsworth to theorize about the voicing of poetry, his discussion of the "most dislocated line" of his verse that he knows, " 'Impressed on the white road in the same line,' " subordinates aurality and may even imply a nonaural perception of rhythmic disruption. The "passion is att[ached?]" to the words "white road same line" and for the sake of these words, the meter "dislocates"; the "image" excites a "quantity of feeling" in readers; "to those in whom it excites [such? much?] feeling, as in one it will be musical to others not" (EY 434–35). If not silent, the economy of excitement regulated by meter skirts the involvement of voice and ears.

As Wordsworth would have learned from *A Letter to Francis Jeffray* and its appendix of outlines, and possibly also from Coleridge, Southey, or Hazlitt, Thelwall regarded both prose and verse as vocal phenomena organized by "the musical proportion of physical pulsations and remissions."[52] For Thelwall, there was no formal pattern of stress, or "passion," separate from words; syllables, in a stream of speech, had inherent *poise* (heavy or light), and were uttered in cadences of musical proportion. The "sentiments, passions, and images of the mind" were all manifest in the "rhythmus," which was limited only by the "Physical necessity of Action and Reaction, in organic, as in mechanic motion."[53] Thus where Wordsworth found a limiting principle to the "passion of the subject" in the historical phenomenon of "the passion of metre" (EY 434), Thelwall discovered a limit to willful expression in "Physical necessity." Perhaps it was Thelwall's declaration in the outlines of the "Unity of the laws of Elocution and Music" and of the "Fundamental Laws" of "Quantity," "Poise," and "Accent" that prompted Wordsworth's contrary, conservative appeal to the "regular laws of the Iambic"—an insistence on the separation of metrical composition from prose on which his program of aesthetic, moral, and affective improvement depends.[54]

Although the personal correspondence between the two poets lapsed after this exchange, Thelwall's subsequent publications on prosody articulated their differences more clearly; they also identified print culture as an indirect cause of impediment. Whereas Wordsworth had asserted the physical impossibility of pronouncing the ends of printed lines "with the same indifference," and thereby acknowledged print convention's support of "the regular laws of the Iambic," Thelwall launched a critique of print's injurious manipulations of pronunciation and the person, and he developed a program of individual and social reform that hinged on the awakening of the perception of the natural rhythmus concealed in print.

Thelwall's *Selections*: Therapeutic Interactions with Print

As early as 1802, as the extensive "Outline" of his course of lectures shows, Thelwall attributed the "*retarded . . . cultivation of Oral Eloquence, in modern times*" in part to the "Art of Printing" and the "substitution of Graphic, for Oral Instruction."[55] Yet it was after what he referred to as the "Edinburgh Controversy" that he arrived at a key critical conviction: that the print culture of poetry, founded upon erroneous prosodic principles, had obscured the natural rhythmus and dulled prosodic perception. As he had defensively and vividly observed in the *Letter to Jeffray*, because the "*learned critics*" were "deep read in the structure and melodies of language," they unjustly disparaged Thelwall's melodic quantities and qualities: "the organs of the exquisite critics are so delicately susceptible, and their ears so admirably hung—that they positively cannot perceive the difference between the cadences of blank verse and of prose."[56] In an October 1806 letter to the *Monthly Magazine*, Thelwall condemned the "cavil of verbal criticism" directed at Milton and the underlying "system of erroneous mechanism" that perverted the printing and recitation of blank verse, "a system which, in many instances, has even deformed our typography, corrupted our orthography, turned into absolute dissonance some of the most exquisite verses in our language, and caused to be regarded as extremely difficult, to the reader and the reciter, an author, who, considering the sublimity of his ideas, and the vastness of his erudition, is, perhaps, the easiest of all authors who ever wrote" (HC 162, 164). As he elaborated in another letter to the *Monthly*, by discounting the "supernumerary syllables" with which Milton "enriched his lines," pedantic criticism influenced editors and printers to introduce the "most glaring defects of modern typography"—elision, which reduced "a verse of the sweetest euphony to a kind of cluttering cacophony" by constraining the natural action of the vocal organs (HC 172, 171).

Thus the "press" that Thelwall regarded in the *Rights of Nature* (1795) as "that prompt conductor and disseminator of intellect"[57] was also powerfully capable of perverting the production and reception of the "natural rhythmus." In reply to the pedants and printers, Thelwall reprinted a passage of *Paradise Lost*, removing apostrophe and restoring elided syllables to free the verse from the "system of erroneous mechanism"—an extension of Milton's initial radical act of freeing verse from the "troublesome bondage of rhyming."[58] He also contemplated the publication of a complete edition of the poem with "correct orthography" and "accurate punctuation" to assist readers' "perception" of Milton's melody as he composed it—"the spontaneous emanation of the sentiment, the passion, or the image, that glowed in his creative mind"—so as to enable them to give voice to the "free spontaneous flow of oratorical period, which the versification of Milton so transcendantly [*sic*] displays" (HC 165).

That Thelwall did not undertake such an edition reflects the democratic and physiological principles of his evolving pedagogy. Rather than subject Milton to his sole editorial control, he instead expanded the anthology that accompanied his lectures into a workbook. This compendium of extracts was a teaching aid that aimed to show pupils how to perform the oratorical periods that a Milton edition, had he produced one, would have displayed in print. Sold by "all the Booksellers, and by the Door-keepers at the Lecture Room[s]" where he spoke, the *Selections, and Original Articles, Read and Recited in Illustration of Mr. Thelwall's Lectures on the Science and Practice of Elocution* began, in 1802, with outlines and a few short selections, but by 1806 included the outlines, the new "Introductory Discourse," and many additional poems and prose extracts.[59] By 1812, *Illustrations of English Rhythmus: Selections for the Illustration of a Course of Instructions on the Rhythmus and Utterance of the English Language* was clearly marketing itself as a "course" which could be pursued independently of the lectures. It now included both the prosodic manifesto and an illustrative guide that gave the reader the tools to put into practice a system of prosodic scansion and recitation. The *Selections* were now an oratorical textbook and a workbook for a system of elocutionary analysis that would enable readers and speakers, by voicing verse, to master the broader culture of print on their own—to be "mute inglorious Milton[s]" no more.[60]

Thelwall's manifesto set out his own project by a detailed critique of the numerical systems of earlier "prosodaical Tyroes, (Critics, Pedagogues, and Grammarians)."[61] At the heart of this critique was his complaint that reliance upon a system of numerical measure created a climate of typographic and orthographic injury to the English rhythmus that disrupted the economy of energy within the speaker. False "systems of pretended rhythmus" degraded the English heroic line into "five disproportioned and incongruous feet" (iv); they rejected *appoggiatura*—supernumerary or extra syllables that produce "exquisite" variations in a cadence (xlvii)—and they also overlooked the *emphatic cadence*, made of a single protracted syllable beginning heavy and ending light, or a single protracted space of silence, frequently punctuated by a dash (xlvi) (Figure 27). The metrical effect of pause was also a key issue for Thelwall. Whereas the numeric system (accentual-syllabism) discounted them, pauses were critical to Thelwall's metrical proportions; the real quantity of time that pauses occupy, however, was in no way determined by the arbitrary rules of the grammarians but regulated by sense and the temporal signature of the cadence (common or triple time) (iv). These systemic problems were compounded by the terminological imprecisions of the existing criticism: "trifold application of the term *accent*" (to refer to inflection, stress, and quantity) dulled the ear

Of these four kinds, Milton has composed the exquisite rhythmus of the Paradise Lost; using the last sparingly, but with admirable effect; still preserving, by its preponderance, the common cadence as his standard measure; to which, in point of integral quantity, all the others must conform.

" Rocks⌐|caves⌐|lakes⌐|fens⌐|bogs⌐|dens and|shades of|death⌐
" A|universe of| death |ſwhich| God by| curse|
  |Δ ∴ ∴∴| Δ ∴. | | | Δ ∴.

"⌐Cre|ated | evil | — | ſ for | evil| only | good ;|
        |⌐Δ∴.| | Δ ∴.

" Where |all | life | dies |—| death | lives | ſ and | nature | breeds |
" Per|verse, | all | monstrous| —| all pro|digious | things ; |
" A|bominable |ſ in|utterable | ſand | worse |
  | Δ ∴.∴.∴| ∴.| Δ ∴.∴. ∴| ∴.

" Then | fables | yet have | feign'd, or | fear con|ceiv'd |
" — | Gorgons and | Hydras ⌐ and Chi|meras | dire. |"1st edit.
 Δ ∴.| Δ ∴. ∴. | | ∴. ∴.|

The following couplet is, I believe, perfectly unique; for, in thirty years research, I have not found a parallel.

" Thāt tŏ thĕ| hīghth ŏf | thĭs grēat| argŭmēnt|
 Δ ∴. ∴.| Δ ∴. | Δ ∴. | Δ ∴. ∴.|

" I măy ăs|sērt ĕ|tērnāl | prōvĭdĕnce. |"
 Δ ∴. ∴.| Δ ∴.| Δ ∴.| Δ ∴.∴.

Figure 27. The "exquisite rhythmus of the Paradise Lost." John Thelwall, *Selections for the Illustration of a Course of Instructions on the Rhythmus and Utterance of the English Language: with an Introductory Essay on the Application of Rhythmical Science to the Treatments of Impediments, and the Improvement of our National Oratory* (London, 1812), xlviii.

to the essential difference of heavy and light "poise." Further, false prosodic notations "deformed" "pages of illustration."[62]

Thelwall's diagnosis of cultural desensitization resonates with those of Wordsworth and Coleridge. As Wordsworth had asserted in the Preface, a "multitude of causes, unknown to former times, are now acting with a combined force to blunt the discriminating powers of the mind" (LB 746).

Thelwall blamed a culture of "silent study, and silent composition" for the blunting of prosodic perception and constraining of the "organic functions" as well as for the limiting of intellectual and moral faculties (HC 6, 46). Coleridge would later lament in the *Biographia Literaria*, "We have eyes, yet see not, ears that hear not, and hearts that neither feel nor understand" (BL, II: 7). The proposed cure involved, for all three, a renovation of perception made via an engagement with metrical compositions. According to Wordsworth and Coleridge, reading *Lyrical Ballads* rather than "frantic novels and sickly German tragedies" (LB 747) would wipe "the film of familiarity" (BL, II: 7) from the eyes, extend sympathies, and stimulate thought. For Thelwall, reading of this kind could not occur without a *therapoetics*. He trained his pupils to sense "pulsation and remission" in the sounds and silences of cadences: the "renovation of this perception" not only improved "our habits of utterance," by restoring sympathy between mind and body, but extended our sympathy from our "immediate circle of relative connections" to "the sentient universe" and cultivated virtuous action.[63] Restoring "vital perception," however, demanded taking "vital action": Thelwall's pupils would "scan with their ears" as well as "utter with [their] organs."[64] They would realize the text in their bodies—by scanning, scoring, and voicing the English rhythmus, by doing something to and with the typographical page (see HC 179). Thus the renovation of perception and the strengthening of moral feeling entailed not just a transformation in print but in people's interactions with print.

Thelwall's *therapoetics* involved first distancing pupils from the "false" notations of contemporary print culture and habituating them to the symbols for *thesis* and *arsis* that Thelwall had borrowed from Steele.[65] *Thesis* and *arsis* "correspond[ed] with the posing and rising—or accented and unaccented notes of the musician"; aspiring speakers had to apprehend this "fundamental difference in the qualities of the syllables" in their progress toward fluency, broader knowledge, and independence of thought (HC 182, 23). Thelwall featured the glyphic symbols on the title pages of both the *Letter to Henry Cline* and *The Vestibule of Eloquence* as a compound sign for the "instinctive progress from heavy to light" poise.[66] A primary exercise in the workbooks abetted the "association between the technical names, the symbols, and the phaenomena of these alternations."[67] This was not simply a matter of feeling the cadence but of feeling the code. Pupils had to become habituated visually and somatically to the new symbols in order to withstand a typographic culture that alienated them from the natural rhythmus.

It was not simply the public scene of reading that made one adopt a "cadence altogether foreign to [one's] natural manner."[68] Print contributed to this self-difference. When, in his *Introduction to the Art of Reading with Energy and Propriety* (1765), John Rice reformatted selections of *Paradise Lost* by "poetic periods" rather than pentameter lines (see Introduction), he made its organic units of sound and sense more visible and thus more voiceable; he also counteracted the destabilizing appearance of the pentameter. "The Lines drawn up in Rank and File, with a capital Initial at the Head of each, look, formidable, and seem to demand a peculiar Degree of Sound and Energy," he wrote of tragic and epic blank verse. "Hence it is that we see . . . the very Features of the Reader assume a new Form; an Air of consequential Gravity settles on his Brow, his Cheeks swell, and his Lips, forming the *Os magna Sonaturum*, project with all the ridiculous Importance imaginable."[69] Thelwall developed Rice's concerns with the management of "Energy" into a full-fledged physiological and metrical theory. If blank-verse typography could induce overexertion—"a peculiar Degree of Sound and Energy"—and transform the "Reader," *thesis* and *arsis* could reform the reader. Nor would Thelwall have to persuade poets and printers of blank verse to cast off the convention of printing blank verse in ten-syllable lines. If the new symbols were properly internalized, the "mode of movement universally dictated by natural instinct" would temper the volition's application of energy to the organs and manage readers' confrontations with those formidable lines.[70] "Impress the perceptive faculty, clearly and strongly"; "give him a system on which he can see and feel that he may depend . . . and then, with diligence and perseverance, the habit of regular utterance will, progressively, be formed, and the irregular habit will be supplanted" (HC 58–59). Set within the title pages of his books where they initiate the process of rehabilitation, the symbols mark another—and more profound—order of signification. In themselves unvoiceable, they seem the impress of that universal principle of throb and remission.

Surviving copies demonstrate how the *Selections* fulfilled its prescribed function as workbook. For example, a copy now held at the University of Michigan reveals 340 pages heavily scored with bars between cadences, and annotated, in places, with the symbols for *thesis* and *arsis*—marking the heavy poise that fell at the start of the cadence and the light stress or stresses that followed. A copy held at the British Library also shows its verse and prose excerpts scored by an unknown reader's hand for what Thelwall called "cadential reading"—recitation with "attention to the . . . inherent poise and quantities of the syllables, and the number of equal cadences in which they are divisible" (Figure 28).[71] For Thelwall's pupils—those who studied at the school in London, who attended the public lectures with the guinea-edition of the *Selections* in hand, or who

OCCASIONAL ADDRESS,

SPOKEN AT THE THEATRE ROYAL, LIVERPOOL, FOR THE BENEFIT
OF THE CHILDREN OF

MR. PALMER,

Who died upon the Stage, whilst performing the Charac-
ter of the Stranger; having just repeated the empha-
tic Words

" THERE IS ANOTHER, AND A BETTER WORLD !"

ROSCOE.

Ye fairy sprites ! who, oft as fancy calls,
Sport 'midst the precincts of these haunted walls,
Light forms, that float in mirth's tumultuous throng,
With frolic dance, and revelry, and song,
Fold your gay wings !—repress your wonted fire !   5
And, from your favourite seats awhile, retire.
—And thou, whose powers sublime thoughts impart,
Queen of the springs that move the human heart
With change alternate!—at whose magic call,
The swelling tides of passion rise or fall,—   10
Thou too withdraw ;—for, 'midst this lov'd abode,
With step more stern, a mightier power has trod.
—Here, on this spot to every eye confest,
Enrob'd with terrors, stood the kingly guest !
—Here, on this spot, Death wav'd the unerring dart,   15
And struck, his noblest prize,—an honest heart !

What wonderous links the human feelings bind !
How strong the secret sympathies of mind,
As Fancy's pictur'd forms around us move,
We hope or fear,—rejoice,—detest or love !   20

Figure 28. William Roscoe, "Occasional Address, Spoken at the Theatre Royal, Liverpool, For the Benefit of the Children of Mr. Palmer, Who Died upon the Stage, whilst Performing the Character of the Stranger; Having Just Repeated the Emphatic Words, 'There is another, and a Better World!,' " 34. *Selections for the Illustration of a Course of Instructions on the Rhythmus and Utterance of the English Language: with an Introductory Essay on the Application of Rhythmical Science to the Treatments of Impediments, and the Improvement of our National Oratory* (London, 1812), 34. © British Library Board. Reproduced by permission of the British Library.

encountered the sixpence edition in readers' circles, coffeehouses, or pubs—"cadential reading" served the purpose of improving "the oral Language of Englishmen" across the classes.[72] It was to be done "reiteratedly, under the regulation of a time beater,—sometimes solo, and sometimes in chorus," and was to be followed, eventually, by what he called "animated reading": a "recitation . . . trusted to the feeling and perception," free of timer and annotations.[73]

Thelwall presented the *Selections* as democratic and patriotic action: a counteracting in print of the false prosodic systems offensive to the eye and injurious to the tongues of individual speakers and to the progress of "national Elocution."[74] In the long "Introductory Essay on the English Rhythmus," he exercised "the right of diffusing" his principles to effect the "enfranchisement of [his pupils'] fettered organs" (HC 14). In the accompanying anthology he enabled texts, many of which appeared in popular miscellanies, to be apprehended anew through a principle that was true to the workings of the organs. Although the "English rhythmus" organized verse, prose, and all registers of English speech, Thelwall's pedagogy favored verse, for it was the medium in which the rhythmus "appears in its simplest and most perfect state"—and could be "impressed" upon the perceptions of his pupils that had been damaged by grammarians, pedants, and printers.[75] Beside passages of the republican poet Milton, he placed ideologically choice texts of lower register and difficulty, including a "comic illustration" by Allan Ramsay about a boy "in speech so chain'd of tongue" that he struggles to alert his father to a raging fire:

> His pipes set up a hideous roar:
> For Vocal Organs all could play,
> Tho stammering Tongue lethargic lay.
>   His father, when he heard the voice,
> Stept out, an' cried—"What's all this noise?"
> "D'—d'—d'—d'—d'—" strives the Boy;
> But tongue and teeth all pass deny.
> He g'—g'—gapes and glowers about,
> But not a word can tumble out;
> An', be it fire, or be it murder,
> The stranded news can sail no further.
> The father, knowing his defect,
> Yet for the tidings all afret,
> The imprison'd freight from's throat to bring,
>   Roar'd—"Sing ye booby! can't yet sing!"[76]

Ramsay's verses dramatize the effects of singing your speech. Scanned by hand in copies of the *Selections*, they indicate Thelwall's political and ontological deepening of the elocutionary project (Figure 29). While scanning the boy's stammering into cadences worked to "set at large the imprisoned tongue"

He never boggled at a song;
Would trill and carrol, as he went,   15
With strength of voice and heart's content,
And rove, from strain to strain right odly,
Thro pious Hymn and theme ungodly.
    One day his father's kiln he watch'd,
When 'chance the flames the fabric catch'd,   20
And smoke and blaze, their work pursuing,
Threaten'd the Malster's quick undoing.
Off runs the boy, with hasty strides,
To tell his daddy what betides.
At distance—ere he reach'd the door,   25
His pipes set up a hideous roar:
For Vocal Organs all could play,
Tho stammering Tongue lethargic lay.
    His father, when he heard the voice,
Stept out, an' cried—"What's all this noise?"   30
"D'—d'—d'—d'—d—"strives the Boy:
But tongue and teeth all pass deny.
He g'—g'—gapes and glowers about,
But not a word can tumble out;
An', be it fire, or be it murder,   35
The stranded news can sail no further.
The father, knowing his defect,
Yet for the tidings all afret,
The imprison'd freight from's throat to bring,
Roar'd—"Sing ye booby! can't ye sing!"

Figure 29. "The Stammerer; a Comic Illustration. (Altered from Allan Ramsay.)" John Thelwall, *Selections and Original Articles, for Mr. Thelwall's Lectures on the Science and Practice of Elocution: Together with the Introductory Discourse and Outlines* (Birmingham, 1806), 15, detail. Reproduced by permission of the Bodleian Libraries, University of Oxford. Shelfmark 260 e 29, p. 15.

in Ramsay's more limited sense (line 64), this inscriptional action on the printed page also began a more thoroughgoing transformation of the scanner. As Thelwall explained, by repeatedly scanning and reciting, "the Mute, and the convulsive Stammerer" could gain "the free exercise and enjoyment of a faculty, which constitutes the essential attribute of our species" (HC 17). Furthermore, "while under the necessary regulations for the cure of his impediment," he might be "stimulated" to "the cultivation" of a "liberal . . . education," delivering his own speeches and disseminating his own ideas in the process.[77] The strokes on the page thus mark Thelwall's commitment to freedom of speech and thought; they signal the elocutionary actualization of the typographical subject within a universe governed not by god or king but laws of motion and organic action—the physical principle of *thesis* and *arsis*.

Once students had imbibed the principle, they could scan selections of rhyming verse to reveal the "abstract rhythmus" of "inherent poise and quantity," determining the weights and temporal proportions of the syllables and inscribing the cadence bars.[78] They would then graduate to scanning blank verse. While the simpler blanks of Thomson, Young, and Akenside only required a single course of scanning for the "skeleton rhythmus," the drama of Shakespeare and the "lyrical heroics of the 'Paradise Lost'" required scanning a second time for the "vital and more authentic rhythmus, which results from the mingled considerations of sentiment, pause and emphasis" (Figure 30). This involved assigning to grammatical pauses and rhetorical emphases their "just proportion of cadential quantity" and marking additional cadences if necessary.[79] Not merely superadded, pause and emphasis were "inherent parts" of Milton's and Shakespeare's "primitive rhythmus"—the "spontaneous emanation of the sentiment, the passion, or the image, that glowed" in the mind (HC 165). This, then, was the apogee of scanning and recitation: only from the "genuine and perfect blank verse of our language" could "its native genius and capabilities . . . be properly comprehended."[80] Thus if verse was the medium of elocutionary instruction, the blank verse of Shakespeare and Milton was a supermedium, and scanning the numerous extracts in the *Selections* and *Vestibule of Eloquence* was a project of national illustration to make visible on the page "true 'poetic liberty.'"[81]

Thelwall's system was a democratic development of his radical politics in the 1790s. In 1794 his inspiring oratory had energized listeners to campaign for political reform that would return to them their natural rights; now he proposed a method of restoring to readers their natural rhythmus that did not depend upon his inspiring voice. Individuals were now not just listeners or

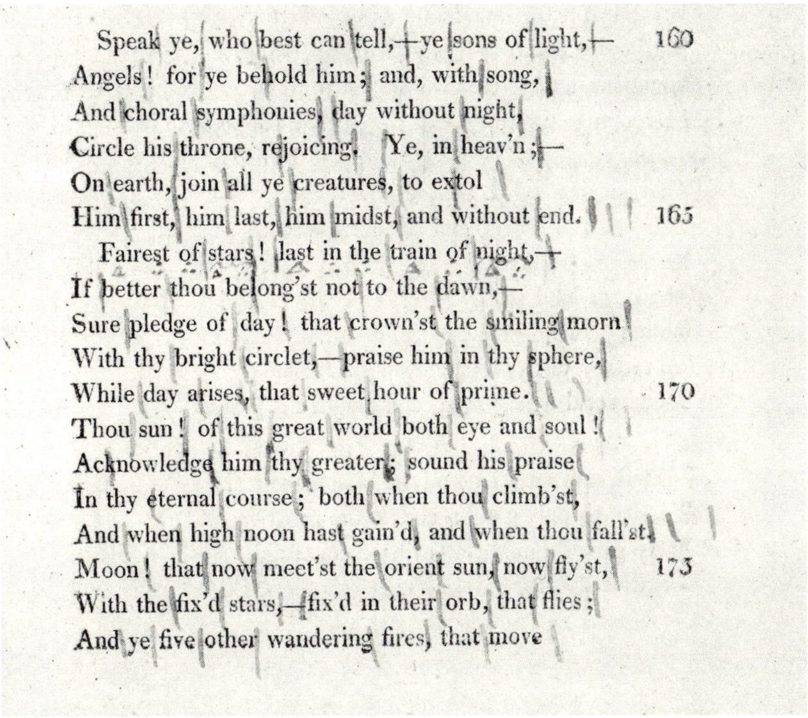

Speak ye, who best can tell,—ye sons of light,—   160
Angels! for ye behold him; and, with song,
And choral symphonies, day without night,
Circle his throne, rejoicing. Ye, in heav'n;—
On earth, join all ye creatures, to extol
Him first, him last, him midst, and without end.   165
    Fairest of stars! last in the train of night,—
If better thou belong'st not to the dawn,—
Sure pledge of day! that crown'st the smiling morn
With thy bright circlet,—praise him in thy sphere,
While day arises, that sweet hour of prime.   170
Thou sun! of this great world both eye and soul!
Acknowledge him thy greater; sound his praise
In thy eternal course; both when thou climb'st,
And when high noon hast gain'd, and when thou fall'st.
Moon! that now meet'st the orient sun, now fly'st,   175
With the fix'd stars,—fix'd in their orb, that flies;
And ye five other wandering fires, that move

Figure 30. John Milton, "The Morning Hymn of Adam and Eve in Paradise."
John Thelwall, *Selections and Original Articles, for Mr. Thelwall's Lectures on
the Science and Practice of Elocution: Together with the Introductory Discourse
and Outlines* (Birmingham, 1806), 39, detail. Reproduced by permission of
the Bodleian Libraries, University of Oxford. Shelfmark 260 e 29, p. 39.

readers but performers and writers: they collectively discovered in themselves,
reciting the verse of the republican Milton, the organic pulses of being that
should vitalize everyone who spoke the English language. And they were empowered to do this, using Thelwall's system, because they were encouraged to
make their own scansion marks on the printed text to enable their recitations.
Enlisted as annotators, his pupils participated in rendering Milton's versification "most harmonious and expressive to the ear"—making appear and making sound the "primitive rhythmus" that finger-counting pedants had
overlooked (HC 160). Scanning and recitation worked transhistorically—it
was not the "spirit" or "soul" that the students of the atheist elocutionist released from the dead letter, but the "feelings and principles of nature under the

influence of which the poet originally wrote" (HC 161): the sentiments, passions, and images of the mind that were expressed as physiological impulses
(vocal, enunciative) at the moment of composition. The students thus not only
empowered themselves politically, physically, and intellectually but also reha-
bilitated the poet whose republican energies had been damaged and defused
by criticism, print, and the "arts" of reading. The strokes across the pages of
the *Selections* thus materialized his pupils' collective moments of sympathy
with a transhistoric pulse. They are marks of the national rhythmus handmade
by its readers—democratic inscriptions mapping temporal and physical configurations of energy.[82]

"Sonorous Cadences": The Subsumption
of Printed Books and Maps in *The Excursion*

Like his inclusion of Southey's verses among his 1812 *Selections*, Thelwall's scansion of *The Excursion* suggests, as would his annotation of *Biographia Literaria*,
a renewal of the lapsed dialogue with his former friends.[83] Like these, it was
also an act of engagement in critical debates about the nature of English meter.
As his formal inscription on the title page of the book indicated, "Scanned
throughout in metrical cadences + rhythmical clauses,"[84] Thelwall sought to
illuminate the poem's versification by his own prosodic system, to lay bare the
metrical principles that he believed organized Wordsworth's verse—contrary
to Wordsworth's own understanding.[85] Milton remained a touchstone: by
scanning the poem, as he had nearly all of *Paradise Lost*, Thelwall was implicitly
measuring Wordsworth's prosody against the "genuine and perfect blank verse
of our language"—the embodiment of "true 'poetic liberty' "—and assessing
what degree of Milton's "rhythmical fire" Wordsworth possessed.[86] The marks
of Wordsworth's "tune" or "rhythmus" thus offer a scan of his "energy" and
"character."[87] But they are not only revelatory of Wordsworth's mind; they also
evidence a physical engagement with the material book—the inscription of a
politics of reading and a *therapoetics* by which Thelwall aided in the elocutionary reception of the epic by his pupils and aimed to strengthen the intellectual
energies and sympathetic virtues of Britons. Kept on Thelwall's private shelves
or at the library at the Institute, the book was listed for sale at its closing in
1820, with the "upwards of 6,000 vols.," in Thelwall's possession—which included "an almost entire collection of English classical poetry, of the elder
poets in particular; . . . with MS annotations on the rhythmatics, pauses,

emphases, and musical quantities."[88] Thelwall is likely to have used material from the poem in class or lecture or set it for his students as an exercise in scanning and recitation.[89] Considering that the fine press quarto (priced at 42 shillings before binding and over 45 shillings bound) was beyond the purchasing power of ordinary readers,[90] and that he considered blank verse the hardest measure to scan, Thelwall's was a significant task of national scansion and democratic development of eighteenth-century efforts to reveal the "genius" of the English language on the printed page.

Scanning the poem was a sign of the regard in which Thelwall held Wordsworth. He "talked of *The Excursion* as containing finer verses than there are in Milton and as being in versification most admirable."[91] This was high praise—for Thelwall termed the measure of "the divine Milton" "rich," "magnificent," and "infinitely diversified, but mathematically perfect."[92] But it is not a sign of unqualified admiration. Indeed, in the margins Thelwall marked several verses as "Prose" or offered otherwise disparaging remarks. Of course in comparing Wordsworth with Milton, Thelwall was responding to Wordsworth's own invitation. *The Excursion* invoked *Paradise Lost* in its Preface, addressing Milton's heavenly muse Urania while announcing a shift in focus from that of Milton's justification of the ways of God to man to the humanist fit between the *"Mind of Man"* and *"the external World"* (*Excursion*, Preface 40, 68). The poem also imagined, in words borrowed from Milton, a *"fit audience . . . though few!,"* as it elaborated a model of textless metrical reception against which Thelwall ranged his project of expanding the audience for blank verse and enfranchising "the fettered organs" (*Excursion*, Preface 23; HC 14). Thus, despite his high praise of the poem, Thelwall's inscription of the book enacted and physically embodied a powerful criticism of it, countering its elitist version of reading with a popular, practical, and intelligible system that functioned by readers' manual marking, and embodied voicing, of a rhythmus founded in anatomical structure and the "laws of physical necessity."[93] This system opposed *The Excursion*'s Christian development of the "one life" vitalism that Wordsworth had shared with Thelwall in the 1790s into a perception of a spiritually energized Nature that traced its power to the first prosodic principle of Heaven.

The Excursion's spiritualization and Christianization of nature is thematized in the poem when the Wanderer, raised in rural poverty, is portrayed as an ideal reader of *Paradise Lost*—one who did not so much read Milton's text as a boy as hear his *"numerous Verse"* in a nature that communicates divine "Impulse and utterance" (Preface 13; *Excursion*, IV: 1164). First, Wordsworth presents the Wanderer's credentials as an interpreter of nature. His imaginative

"intercourse" as a "Herdsman on the lonely mountain tops" is founded on his
early reading of the Bible:

> Oh then how beautiful, how bright appeared
> The written Promise! He had early learned
> To reverence the Volume which displays
> The mystery, the life which cannot die:
> But in the mountains did he feel his faith;
> There did he see the writing;—all things there
> Breathed immortality, revolving life
> And greatness still revolving; infinite;
> There littleness was not; the least of things
> Seemed infinite; and there his spirit shaped
> Her prospects, nor did he believe,—he saw.
> What wonder if his being thus became
> Sublime and comprehensive! Low desires,
> Low thoughts had there no place . . .
>   (*Excursion*, I: 241, 240, 243–56)

Here, nature as the book of God is no mere trope. Prophetic insight into nature's "revolving life" is transferred from the written text at the same time as
the mountains illuminate and breathe life into the dead letter of the Bible:
"There did he see the writing; —all things there / Breathed immortality . . ."
With a "being" and an eye thus spiritualized, the boy surmounts the mechanical processes of reading to gain immediate access to the sublime heights also
of English poetry. Returning once from "a neighbouring town," with the
"Book which most had tempted his desires / While at the Stall he read," he
transcends typography and the page: "Among the hills / He gazed upon that
mighty Orb of Song / The divine Milton" (I: 265–71). The mountains that
convert abstract reverence to embodied revelation ("nor did he believe,—he
saw") likewise convert the printed poem into sound, transforming bookish
desires into worshipful reception. With the apotheosis of Milton as an "Orb
of Song"—like the sun he beheld "Rise up, and bathe the world in light!" (I:
221)—the "writing" of God merges with the song of Milton to create a kind of
Paradise Regained in Westmorland. It follows that the boy nurtured by the
English landscape does not so much read as visually and aurally *absorb* the
energies of the native poet.[94] He is then able to hear "sonorous cadences" in
the universe that he interprets as communications from the divine (IV: 1132).

Having absorbed the republican blank verse into his native vales and sky-scape, Wordsworth establishes the Wanderer as the interpreter and pedagogue of spiritualized nature. The Solitary, and by extension, readers of *The Excursion*, approach it through the Wanderer's commentary. His aim is to restore the Solitary from despondency, a question of renewing the dissipated energies of a man seen, in an echo of the "one life" philosophy of the 1790s, to have lost touch with the animating impulses that are sensed through active, embodied participation in the natural world. The Solitary has lost "Zeal," and with it faith in God and humankind. The disappointment of his political hopes and deaths of his family have caused him to "languidly . . . look / Upon this visible fabric of the World" (III: 202, 969–70), seeing there no "revolving life." Whereas "Fancy, dreaming o'er the map of things" (III: 223) conceives of other regions for the "Soul" to "soar," "far as she can go / Through time or space" (III: 217, 218, 220–21), the Solitary sees no "better sanctuary / From doubt and sorrow, than the senseless grave" (III: 228–29). The image of the map marks the bound-edness of his perspective. Drained of hope, he merely waits for the "current" of his life to reach the "unfathomable gulph, where all is still" (III: 997–98).[95]

It is by finding confluence between his "current" and the "course" of na-ture that the Solitary may be healed. The Wanderer suggests that this is a matter of aural retuning because, if he but acknowledged it, the Solitary al-ready attends to the "sonorous cadences" of the universe. Nature's heavenly impulses impart to his ear

Authentic tidings of invisible things;
Of ebb and flow, and ever-during power
And central peace, subsisting at the heart
Of endless agitation. (IV: 1132, 1138–41)

Healing is to be achieved by a program of physical exertion. By moving his "Frame," he will increase the "Soul's vigour" (IV: 480–81). A daily dose of fell walking will feed the "celestial Spirit" and retune the "distempered nerves" (IV: 1068, 479): "Climb every day, those ramparts; meet the breeze / Upon their tops,—adventurous as a Bee / That from your garden thither soars, to feed / On new-blown heath . . . So, wearied to your Hut shall you return, / And sink at evening into sound repose" (IV: 494–504). This prescription of daily action and nightly reaction, climbing and sinking, recalls Thelwall's principle of pulse and remission that governs all motion in the universe; but whereas for Thelwall this rhythmic principle pervades a purely material universe, for Wordsworth it is a rhythmic energy that originates and ends in divine voice (IV: 1198). "'Nature fails not to provide / Impulse and utterance'" (IV: 1163–64), states the Wanderer:

> "living Things, and Things inanimate,
> Do speak, at Heaven's command, to eye and ear,
> And speak to social Reason's inner sense,
> With inarticulate language." (IV: 1198–1201)

While Nature's speech urges the soul to fellowship with living creatures, it also yields "Far-stretching views into Eternity" (IV: 1183), orienting the soul to the transcendent sphere. In a fit of transport, the Poet-narrator imagines an ecstatic excursion among the mountains and the mists as through this vital universal medium: "'what a joy to roam / An Equal among mightiest Energies,'" adding one's exclamations to "the deafening tumult'" (IV: 531–32, 534).

Retuning oneself to the "ever-during" "ebb and flow" of the universe involves more than just physical exercise. If the Solitary is to open his eye and ear to the "inarticulate language" (IV: 1201) that the Wanderer's biblical and Miltonic interpretation of nature allows him to see and hear, he must give up reading the radical *philosophes* who had inspired Wordsworth and Thelwall in the 1790s, writers whose systems disdain the "Soul, and the transcendent Universe" (IV: 987) and stimulate the reason. He must instead read the "forms of Nature" under the irradiating light of a "power" abiding within "Man's celestial Spirit," a "Virtue" that can give lustre to dark "interpositions," lightening the pains and burdens of existence, soothing disappointment, and also exalting the soul (IV: 842, 1067, 1056). With practice in reading nature not by "human reasoning" but by this "light of love" (IV: 198, 1240)—"an impulse from his soul" and "source of spiritual energy," Johnston notes, that is "called, alternatively, 'virtue,' 'Imagination,' 'the imaginative will,' or the mind's 'excursive power'"[96]—the Solitary will come to recognize the forces of animation throughout the universe ("The spiritual Presences of absent Things" [IV: 1228]). Further, in contemplating the relations between natural forms and man, he will "read" his philanthropic "duties in all forms" (IV: 1235–36). He will emerge from retreat, roused to social action. As Johnston explains, the Wanderer encourages the Solitary to "picture the 'visible fabric of the world' as a veil enabling the imagination to transfigure the accidents of mortal life to moral good."[97] Or, I suggest, for the Solitary's cartographic model of the natural world and of life, the Wanderer aims to substitute a metrical paradigm.

The Pastor's epitaphic tales of Books VI and VII both teach and enact a spiritual, prosodic hermeneutic. He offers up his oral "records" of local individuals at the request of the Wanderer in order to resolve "our doubts" and to teach us " 'To prize the breath we share with human kind; / And look upon the dust of Man with awe' " (V: 656, 658–59). A "Historian" of "grassy heaps" (VII: 1, 31) in the churchyard, he works to interpret the "energy" of the lives they mark (" 'Life, I repeat, is energy of Love / Divine or human; exercised in pain, / In strife, and tribulation . . .' " (V: 1018–20))—and also to put that energy back into circulation through speech. To "Epitomize the life" (V: 652) is to transmit its accent and emphasis. As the Poet's scanning of the graves in the churchyard suggests, the Pastor's series of "Authentic epitaphs" (V: 653) has prosodic implications. The " 'grassy heaps lie amicably close,' " he observes, " 'like surges heaving in the wind / Upon the surface of a mountain pool' "; but why is it, he asks, " 'that yonder we behold / Five graves, and only five, that lie apart, / Unsociable company and sad . . .?' " (VII: 31–33, 35–36). In bringing the five outliers into the "stream" of his "eloquence," the Vicar—exalted above the Welsh bard for his "Strains of power" (VII: 25, 22)— remediates those energies in fluent relation to the community's and land's larger rhythmical patterns of "ebb and flow" (IV: 1139).[98]

The Pastor's story of Oswald foregrounds these spiritual metrical patterns by staging yet another scene of textual absorption into the mountain vales—this time of a topographical map of Europe, which it associates with the stirring of republican passions. The episode attracted the notice of Thelwall, who vertically marked the left margin of the opening paragraphs with a line—those in which the Pastor describes Oswald as a "glorious" youth— beautiful, brilliant, athletic (VII: 746).[99] Though clothed "in simple rustic's garb" and subject to the "impediment of rural cares" (VII: 758–59), "In him revealed a Scholar's genius shone" (VII: 760). A steady-aiming marksman whom "the Fox had learned / To dread" (VII: 768–69), he nonetheless refused to assault the "majesty he loved"—the "wide-ruling Eagle" (VII: 772, 771). It is because Oswald was capable of sympathetically imagining the eagle's perspective (of taking a commanding overview), that he was able to transcend the limited perspective of the valley dweller. When the French tyrant's threats were heard round the nation, Oswald, "like a Chief," roused his fellow stripling shepherds to his nation's defense, leading them "forth / From their shy solitude, to face the world" (VII: 794–96). This was an oratorical leading forth by means of an affective reading of cartographic forms and figures:

"Oft have I marked him, at some leisure hour,
Stretched on the grass or seated in the shade
Among his Fellows, while an ample Map
Before their eyes lay carefully outspread,
From which the gallant Teacher would discourse,
Now pointing this way and now that." (VII: 804–9)

By pointing, in time, to sites of Napoleon's victories, Oswald converts the spatial field into eloquent oratory, rallying his peers against the tyrannical effects of empire. But, significantly, the Pastor does not compare Oswald to any English defender of liberty; neither to the republican patriots of the seventeenth century whom Wordsworth had admired in 1802—Hampden, Sidney, and Milton himself—nor to the radical campaigners of the 1790s—Tooke, Hardy, and Thelwall himself. Instead, he is compared to legendary and biblical figures from foreign lands—William Tell, Gideon, and Joshua. Those "soul-enflamed" resistors of "Idolatry" turn attention from contemporary politics to religion (VII: 837, 838).

The Pastor's portrait excites the Poet-narrator, who responds with a passionate lament about the wasting of bodily and mental "capacities" which is nevertheless so generalized that it is almost impossible to apply it to any particular historical situation or to derive from it any specific political lesson:

"Power to the Oppressors of the world is given,
A might of which they dream not. Oh! the curse,
To be the Awakener of divinest thoughts,
Father and Founder of exalted deeds,
And to whole Nations bound in servile straits
The liberal Donor of capacities
More than heroic! this to be, nor yet
Have sense of one connatural wish, nor yet
Deserve the least return of human thanks;
Winning no recompence, but deadly hate
With pity mixed, astonishment with scorn!"
         (VII: 842–52)

Thelwall was clearly contemptuous of the obfuscatory nature of this exclamation—is the "Awakener of divinest thoughts," divine or human? Is the "Father and Founder of exalted deeds," God the Father, radical philosopher, or the younger Napoleon? In the margin he wrote,

Obscurity out obscur'd!
How far must one dive
for the thought—and
how little is it worth
when found![100]

Presumably Thelwall was bothered by the deflection of critique from the "Oppressors of the world" to the faithless oppressed (who thank their "Awakener" merely with pity and scorn). Nor was he impressed by the moralizing that followed. Rather than engendering political response, the Poet's exclamation leads the Pastor to an equally obscure discussion about the relationship of tyranny and suffering to Providence (VII: 854–67), which Thelwall marked with an X. In its turn this discussion is displaced into eulogy, for it transpires that Oswald, after a vigorous hunt, catches a chill in the river and, twelve days later, dies. "*Oh! most lame and / impotent conclusion!,*" Thelwall wrote in the margin,[101] expressing his frustration with this limitation of the republican potential that Wordsworth had evoked but then foreclosed. Although Oswald sympathizes with the Swiss republic, he does not get to transform those republican sympathies into political action.

In *The Excursion*, the "forms of Nature" (IV: 842) that nurtured "a Scholar's genius" (VII: 760)—that fostered his republican reading and feeling oratory—reabsorb the young man at his funeral. As Oswald's body is received into the earth, and his voice silenced, so too the map of Europe is steadily effaced, replaced by the epitomizing image of Oswald as an embodiment of England—in him "our Country shewed . . . most beautiful" (VII: 872–73)—and second, by a "commanding" overview (VII: 901). Together these topographical visions shift focus, and feeling, from the European theater of war to the insular mountain community, epitomizing and spiritualizing the "spot": " 'And if by chance a Stranger, wandering there' " had " 'looked / Down on this spot, well pleased would he have seen / A glittering Spectacle' " (VII: 900–903) of pallid mourners at the burial service, who

> "started at the tributary peal
> Of instantaneous thunder, which announced
> Through the still air the closing of the Grave;
> And distant mountains echoed with a sound
> Of lamentation, never heard before!" (VII: 908–12)

With the firing of the guns, the martial energies that Oswald's map reading symbolized and stimulated are released and converted. Democratic eloquence is naturalized as the peal echoes in the mountains' "lamentation" (VII: 912) and resonates with mediators and interpreters of nature's inarticulate language. It is also Christianized. Having received these impulses, the Pastor transmits them to the Poet, the Solitary, and the Wanderer, the latter of whom emerges—in the Poet's portrait—as the fittest of the audience. After the Pastor ceased, he

> stood
> Enwrapt,—as if his inward sense perceived
> The prolongation of some still response,
> Sent by the ancient soul of this wide Land,
> The spirit of its mountains and its seas,
> Its cities, temples, fields, its awful power,
> Its rights and virtues—by that Deity
> Descending; and supporting his pure heart
> With patriotic confidence and joy. (VII: 915–23)

The images of deep reception and topographical and temporal extension suggest without circumscribing a circuit of sympathy. Because that circuit transmits the ongoing pulse of the "Land," bringing "patriotic confidence and joy," the death of the "Patriot" (VII: 827) is revealed to be of therapeutic value. The flat, time-bound map is superseded; the liberal "capacities" it organized against Napoleon and the patriotic energies it mediated are revealed to be tributaries of the greater "spirit" of England, the "awful power" that begins and ends in God.

Because the Solitary had concluded the history of his faith's erosion with his own invocation of a map, the Pastor's story of Oswald is a fitting correction. The figure of the map had marked the dominance of reason, his habit of reading with the "Dull and inanimate" eye (IV: 1251) instead of by the "light of love" (IV: 1240). Book VII's replacement of map reading with a sensing of the "Land" stages a movement beyond the morbid passions toward commune with the "Soul of Things" (IV: 1261) and a consciousness of immortality. Commune is a matter of being in harmony with the rhythms of nature—an implicitly prosodical fitting of the mind of man and nature by a sensing of "glad impulse" (IX: 34). Miltonic and, by extension, Wordsworthian blank verse is the epitome of this harmony, a grammar in which the rhythms of English and England are best matched and mediated. The story of Oswald and the Wanderer's response to the story thus model the poem's central aim—the conversion, via blank verse, of "mortal life to moral good."[102]

Maps, Meter, and the Rematerialization of Blank Verse

The map figures significantly in both Wordsworth's and Thelwall's projects, as an image of patriotic feeling and national unity—so does meter, as a means of shaping readers into a national community of English speakers. The map and meter, in fact, intersect in the work of both writers: the map emerging as a visual and verbal grammar that can be read, aloud, in time, organizing and communicating patriotic energy; meter emerging as a spatial and visual patterning of energy, symbolic of national cohesion and strength. How the map is made metrical—and meter made mappical—is illuminated by Thelwall's scansion of *The Excursion* as he set out a contrasting vision of nationhood.

The relationship in *The Excursion* between the map, eloquent speech, and the rhythms of blank verse is also present in Thelwall's writing. In fact, Thelwall's invocation of national maps symbolizes his commitment to a practice of reading blank verse as a mode of stimulating national energy and independence. He makes the invocation in the "Oration on the Influence of Animated Elocution in Awakening Martial Enthusiasm" (1810) when he associates eloquence with "democratical states." The "glories of Rome" expired "with her elocutionary energy," he warns, while the eloquence of Thebes and Attica "rendered them invincible":

> And what was this Athens—so boundless in the Chart of
> Intellect?—
> "Filling so vast a space in Learning's eye!"
> Search for her, in another Map. Let the Geographer delineate
> the magnitude of this unrivalled Sovereign of the World of Mind,
> and compare her proportions, in the general Portraiture of Nations.
> "What little body, with a mighty heart!"
> The whole territory of Attica, would scarcely rival, in roods and
> perches, the individual district of Yorkshire; and for extent, population, and Commerce,—the Town and Port of Liverpool, might be
> the Athens after which we enquire.[103]

Thelwall's hypothetical "Chart of Intellect" transposes ancient Athens' great magnitude of "energy" and "character"[104] onto a contemporary national map, transforming Yorkshire and Liverpool into places for the rekindling of a "glowing energy" that once burned brightly.[105] This cartographic figuring of eloquence, I suggest, spatializes the metrical inscriptions he promoted. Like the marks in *The Excursion*, the strokes of English rhythmus made by students in Yorkshire, Liverpool, and elsewhere encode their striving toward that prosodically regulated energy that the "animation of an elocutionary system of education" was calculated to produce.[106] We may thus read those metrical marks mapically as the material traces of a "mighty heart"[107] in progress: a Britain "vital with expressive eloquence," in harmonious sympathy with itself and "universal Nature."[108] Read cartographically, the marks of the national rhythmus, felt and voiced by individual speakers, suggest a collective projection of national eloquence—patriotic patternings of energy in language.

Thelwall's cartographic figuring of a nation unified by an animating physiological prosody was timely. English Romantic cartography aimed for the depiction of a vital nation, and this could best be achieved, it was argued, through organic rather than abstract "portraiture" of hills. A map that was both correct and impressive, one that communicated clearly and stirred the feelings, depicted the character of the nation as embodied in its natural morphology through nonnumerical, artistic techniques of shading. As Arnold's celebration of the hachuring of Ordnance Survey maps suggests, this aesthetic and ideological argument lent itself to conceptions of the map as a spatial document perused in time, and perhaps, as with Oswald's map and Thelwall's *Selections*, both traced with the finger and translated into speech. With Oswald, Wordsworth brings cartography and elocution into convergence; and his depiction of Oswald's perusal and articulation of the map registers not merely the prosodical methodology of the eighteenth- and nineteenth-century "arts of reading"—elocutionists' insistence on the marking of emphasis—but also Thelwall's manual textual approach (Figure 31). Oswald rouses republican energies through his act of digital scansion, "pointing this way and now that" and then along the mighty Danube that " 'winds from realm to realm;— / And, like a serpent, shows his glittering back, / Bespotted with innumerable isles' " (VII: 809, 812–14). Tracing these mundane "spots," Oswald is aroused:

> Thence—along a tract
> Of livelier interest to his hopes and fears
> His finger moved, distinguishing the spots

> Where wide-spread conflict then most fiercely raged;
> Nor left unstigmatized those fatal Fields
> On which the Sons of mighty Germany
> Were taught a base submission.—"Here behold
> A nobler race, the Switzers, and their Land;
> Vales deeper far than these of ours, huge woods,
> And mountains white with everlasting snow!" (VII: 816–25)

Oswald's finger moves from flashpoint to flashpoint in concert with this voice, leaving no site of tyrannical subordination "unstigmatized," marking out, with greater emphasis, the sublime mountains of Switzerland and thus amplifying

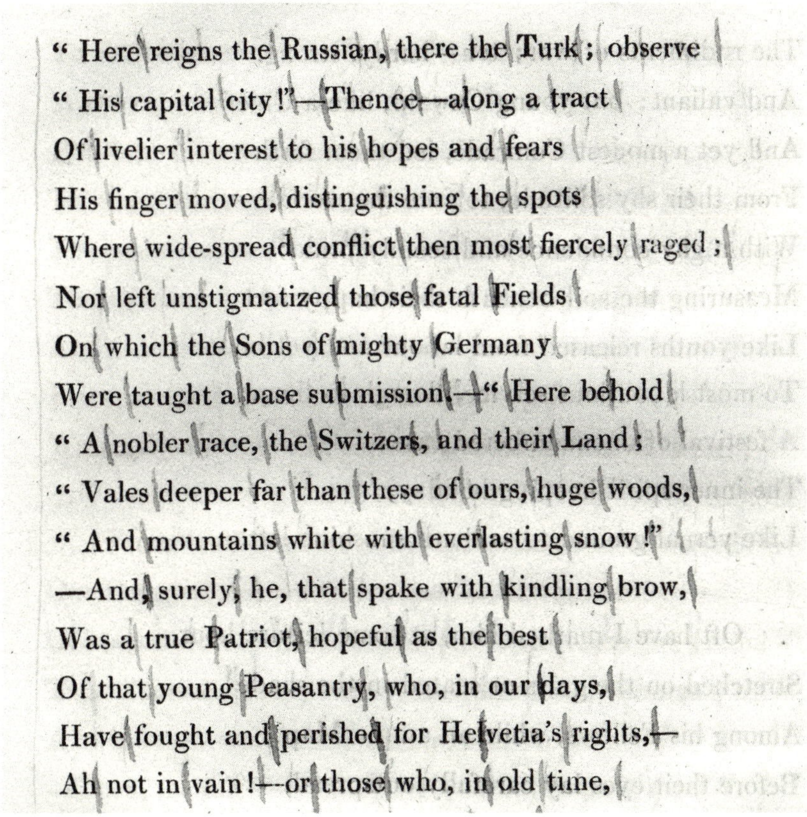
" Here reigns the Russian, there the Turk; observe
" His capital city!"—Thence—along a tract
Of livelier interest to his hopes and fears
His finger moved, distinguishing the spots
Where wide-spread conflict then most fiercely raged;
Nor left unstigmatized those fatal Fields
On which the Sons of mighty Germany
Were taught a base submission.—" Here behold
" A nobler race, the Switzers, and their Land;
" Vales deeper far than these of ours, huge woods,
" And mountains white with everlasting snow!"
—And, surely, he, that spake with kindling brow,
Was a true Patriot, hopeful as the best
Of that young Peasantry, who, in our days,
Have fought and perished for Helvetia's rights,—
Ah not in vain!—or those who, in old time,

Figure 31. "Thence—along a tract . . ." Wordsworth, *The Excursion*, "Scanned in metrical cadences + rhythmical clauses, by John Thelwall" (London, 1814), 346, detail. By kind permission of Paul F. Betz.

the patriotic sympathy evoked by the English fells. With Oswald's topographical exclamation (" 'Here behold . . . !' "), Romantic cartography's representation of uplands converges with, and politicizes, literary culture's inscription of vocal passion.

Yet, as I have shown, the passionate energies communicated by this enlightening topographical eloquence are absorbed into those fells at Oswald's death and remediated, by the "soul of this wide Land" (VII: 918), as a divine pulse that does not agitate but soothes the feelings. Further, Wordsworth shows that "patriotic confidence and joy" (VII: 923) are generated and sustained by the ecclesiastical organization of the English landscape. The governing topographical image of "The Church-Yard Among the Mountains" (the title of Books VI and VII) redefines enlightenment as spiritual and traditional. Oswald's topographical map, and the stirring discourse of transitory contentions it makes available, is superseded by the Poet's apostrophe and prayer that represents England as an expansive unity of nature, "Church," and "State" (VI: 8, 6):

> —And, O, ye swelling hills, and spacious plains!
> Besprent from shore to shore with steeple-towers,
> And spires whose "silent finger points to Heaven;"
> Nor wanting, at wide intervals, the bulk
> Of ancient Minster, lifted above the cloud
> Of the dense air, which town or city breeds
> To intercept the sun's glad beams—may ne'er
> That true succession fail of English Hearts,
> That can perceive, not less than heretofore
> Our Ancestors did feelingly perceive,
> What in those holy Structures ye possess
> Of ornamental interest, and the charm
> Of pious sentiment diffused afar,
> And human charity, and social love. (VI: 17–30)

Spots of light pattern this visualization. Whereas Oswald's pointing illuminated "spots" where human conflict "raged," the spires sprinkled across England constitute a spiritual digital scansion: pointing silently "to Heaven," they emphasize human passion's subordination to the eternal. Never too widely dispersed, these admonitory fingers distribute faith, love, and charity in spatial zones or parishes, organizing national space and punctuating it with feeling (a geographical Burkean vision comparable to that of the *Ecclesiastical Sonnets*). Unlike the Ordnance Survey's arbitrary plotting of the nation by triangulation points (see Figure 15), to which this passage alludes, Wordsworth's "steeple-towers" and "ancient Minster[s]" mark out an organic spiritual topography; they "intercept" the light of Heaven in the form of the "sun's glad beams," diffusing feeling at unquantified "intervals."[109]

This ecclesiastical spatial organization is suggestively metrical. The Church has marked the land by what constitutes a spiritual prosody: a loosely regular but repeating pointing of the landscape through a time span of centuries. Because these "holy Structures" have stimulated and sustained, from generation to generation, a complex of feeling blending aesthetic "interest" with the "charm / Of pious sentiment," "human charity, and social love" (VI: 28–30), their addition to the landscape is like the superaddition to "natural description" of meter, which Wordsworth characterized in the Preface as a spellbinding or entrancing "charm" (LB 754). Like the ancient minsters, meter is a historic form—a recurrence of impulse that has the power to both stimulate and restrain passion. Praying for their protection from "bigot zeal" (VI: 35) and for the "true succession" of spiritual feeling within "English Hearts" (VI: 24), the Poet promotes a mode of traditional, national feeling that, governed by the impulses of Heavenly energy, is not "outrageous stimulation" but "regular and uniform" (LB 746–47). By contrast, the local youths encouraged to war by Oswald march to a more terrestrial and transitory beat, "Measuring the soil beneath their happy feet," the "inner spirit keeping holiday" (VII: 798, 802). The implication is that the country will become strong, in the post-revolutionary era, not by the power of a good military map, based on a mathematical survey that fixes all the "material points" of the nation,[110] but by Wordsworth's song: his emphases and cadences, loosely governed by the "regular laws of the Iambic" (EY 434), can attune readers to the spiritual energy that courses through the land and is transmitted by its churches and best speakers. As in post-1814 revisions to *The Prelude* (e.g., "point marked out by heaven" [1850, VI: 754]), the map emerges as an anti-model for the poem, which figures eloquence as the momentary projection of an ideal image of the world. As his wife says of the Wanderer,

"How pure his spirit! in what vivid hues
His mind gives back the various forms of things,
Caught in their fairest, happiest attitude!

While he is speaking I have power to see
Even as he sees; but when his voice hath ceased,
Then, with a sigh I sometimes feel, as now,
That combinations so serene and bright,
Like those reflected in yon quiet Pool,
Cannot be lasting in a world like ours . . ."
                    (*Excursion*, IX: 465–73)

Thelwall's maps lead in a different direction. If in *The Excursion*, cartography leads to a historical and geographical prosody that is ecclesiastical before it is spiritual, in *The Hope of Albion*, Thelwall's epic on the origins of the nation's constitutional civil and religious freedoms, the map articulates the rhythms of democracy. Book IV, published in the Institute workbook *The Vestibule of Eloquence*, opens with Edwin's tracing of map of England on a wall, determining not to flee but to "take [his] stand" to defend the land from tyranny.[111] This tracing of a map, like Oswald's, organizes patriotic energy into eloquence; in Thelwall's poem, however, the tracing of the map leads ultimately to eloquent action—to Edwin's "battle of words" against his nemesis Edelfrid and to debate at the witenagemot, the "proto-democratic Saxon council much idealized by reformers of the 1790s."[112] Thelwall's poem puts the map—traced by finger and eye, articulated as oratory—at the origin of the collective debate that founds English democracy and law, and within the workbooks that sustain and reinvigorate those debates.[113] His scansion of Oswald's passionate mapreading in Wordsworth's poem works to release the rhythmus from the printed page and to cultivate voice, patriotism, and nobility among Britons beyond the English fells.

Thelwall and Wordsworth both use the map as a device that has the power to energize: to arouse patriotic feeling and delineate national unity (against the threat of oppression). They show that it has to be articulated for this power to work—its spatial patterns have to be transformed into the temporal rhythms of lively English speech. Its marks then become measures. But if the two writers have this *cartoprosody* in common, their cultural politics are opposed. Thelwall imagines the transformation of marks to measures as occurring through elocutionary pedagogy and democratic debate, in the nation of commercial towns and cities. Wordsworth subsumes the map, the secular-textual marking system, and converts its republican into vital energies that he invests in nature, in traditional institutions (the spatial prosody of "holy Structures" [VI: 27]), and in the words of priestly interpreters (Pastor, Wanderer, Poet) through whom readers must approach it. Wordsworth's naturalization of printed Miltonic blank verse is another manifestation of this elitism.

The "'philosophic song,'" Johnston states of *The Recluse*, "was squarely addressed to the proposition that the mental energy released by the French Revolution should not dissipate in cynicism."[114] The "basic rhetorical structure and contract" of *The Excursion*, he writes, is "meant to displace the Solitary's disillusionment into the larger context of natural cycles of life and death"; the "failure of political ideals or any other 'paths of glory' are not corrected or criticized but subsumed into larger universal rhythms."[115] It is by engaging contemporary notions of metrical scansion and elocutionary energy, and by subsuming printed texts that organize political and prosodic practices, that Wordsworth inscribes those "larger universal rhythms." Thus the Wanderer's fundamental question—the question posed by the whole poem—contains its own answer. He asks,

> "But how acquire
> The inward principle, that gives effect
> To outward argument; the passive will
> Meek to admit; the active energy,
> Strong and unbounded to embrace, and firm
> To keep and cherish? How shall Man unite
> A self-forgetting tenderness of heart
> And earth-despising dignity of soul?
> Wise in that union, and without it blind!"
>   (V: 572–80)

But those terms—"inward principle," "passive will," "active energy"—have already been deeply associated with the "sonorous cadences" (IV: 1132) of the poem, its mediation of the universal "ebb and flow" (IV: 1139). It is by reading Wordsworth's blank verse—a "Song" that strives to efface its own textual condition—that "Man" may "unite" in "commune with the invisible world, / And hear the mighty stream of tendency" (IX: 87–88). By contrast, Thelwall aims to make legible and perceptible, through a stepped program of metrical marking and recitation, the "universal principle of action and reaction" (HC 24) that enables universal sympathy. Thelwall's revelation of this underlying principle that moves Wordsworth's blank verse—his division of the pentameter into varying numbers of cadences, and his incorporation of dashes, exclamation marks, and line endings into cadences (Figure 31)—plays out a critical debate about the nature of English meter as a debate about access and the intermedial crossing of blank verse from print into speech.

In the "Essay, Supplementary to the Preface," Wordsworth stated that he wished his poems to extend the "domain of sensibility, for the delight, the honour, and the benefit of human nature" (*W Prose*, III: 84). In *The Excursion*, the Wanderer, himself sensitive to the "prolongation of some still response" (VII: 917), and the Poet-narrator who tracks his deep perception, would seem to extend sympathetic capacity to the reader. But this circuit remains available only to those well enough educated to be able to read the periods of *The Excursion*. Thelwall's marking of the text aimed to extend this circuit although he did not agree with Wordsworth's suggestion that, while cycling through nature and man, it begins and ends in "Heaven's command" (IV: 1199). In effect, his marking was both a *therapoetics* and a *politiscansion*—deeply patriotic and national in impulse, committed to releasing the English rhythmus from print into the bodies and voices of the people—those who had not been nurtured, like the Wanderer, in the "remotest vales" (VII: 784), and thus had neither heard on the mountain slopes Milton's divine "Orb or Song" nor "scanned" the "laws of light" in the "rainbow hues" of the waterfall's mists (I: 317, 322). What had England done for "blank"-eyed child laborers and the "tens of thousands uninformed" (VIII: 414, 435), asks the Solitary (channelling Thelwall)—those who, as infants, had never "puzzl[ed] through a Primer, line by line"? (VIII: 418). His question prompts the Wanderer's call for national education and the diffusion of learning to the British colonies around the globe:

> "Oh for the coming of that glorious time
> When, prizing knowledge as her noblest wealth
> And best protection, this Imperial Realm,
> While she exacts allegiance, shall admit
> An obligation, on her part, to *teach*
> Them who are born to serve her and obey;
> Binding herself by Statute to secure
> For all the Children whom her soil maintains
> The rudiments of Letters, and to inform
> The mind with moral and religious truth,
> Both understood and practised,—so that none,
> However destitute, be left to droop
> By timely culture unsustained . . ." (IX: 292–304)

Thelwall does not await the coming of "that glorious time" of national education. In seeking to make blank verse available to ordinary readers, his scansion anticipates it and its derivation of cultural authority from the recitation of national poems like Wordsworth's. His relentless inscription of— insistence on—the material *Excursion* graphically recalls the historic difficulties of blank-verse reading and the tradition, since Samuel Say's essay "On the Numbers of Paradise Lost" (1745) of re-presenting and reprinting the meter to illuminate its melodies and measures and enable its voicing. His copy counters Wordsworth's subsumption of maps and poems into nature and mystification of reading and meter: "*my Song / With star-like virtue . . . may shine; / Shedding benignant influence*" (*Excursion*, Preface: 88–90). Instead Thelwall puts literacy and elocution at the center of liberal education, as a route to engagement in the print public sphere. With his London school, his lectures, tours, and workbooks, he offered the disenfranchised access to Milton and Wordsworth, and he offered the possibility, beyond the rural arena, of integration with social community and "universal Nature."[116] By scanning *The Excursion,* he aimed to redeem its blank verse from the Tory conservatism that it registers and to recover within it the democratic and organic poetics of the Alfoxden and Llyswen conversations: the "plainer and more emphatic language" that had become, in places, philosophically obscure and devoutly epitaphic. His is a Wordsworthian program—prosodic, physiological, moral, intellectual—that returns Wordsworth's story of spiritual and ontological restoration to a democratic program of liberation and human development.

Notes

INTRODUCTION

1. Jeffrey, review of Robert Southey, *Thalaba the Destroyer*, *Edinburgh Review*, I (October 1802): 63–83.

2. Gillray's July 1798 cartoon in the *Anti-Jacobin Review and Magazine*. On Jacobin meter see Ernest Bernhardt-Kabisch, " 'When Klopstock England Defied': Coleridge, Southey, and the German/English Hexameter," *Comparative Literature*, 55.2 (Spring 2003): 137–40.

3. Jeffrey, review, 72. *Thalaba the Destroyer*, ed. Tim Fulford, vol. III of *Robert Southey: Poetical Works 1793–1810*, 5 vols. (London: Pickering and Chatto, 2004), 3.

4. *Thalaba the Destroyer*, 3.

5. *Selections for the Illustration of a Course of Instruction on the Rhythmus and Utterance of the English Language* (London, 1812), 145.

6. Thomas Sheridan, *A Rhetorical Grammar of the English Language Calculated for the Purposes of Teaching Propriety of Pronunciation, and Justness of Delivery, in that Tongue, by the Organs of Speech* (1781; facs. rpt. Menston, Yorks.: Scolar Press, 1969), xvi.

7. Review of *Thalaba the Destroyer*, *British Critic*, 18 (September 1802): 309–10.

8. For Wordsworth's letter see EY 430.

9. Thelwall annotation to the title page of his copy of *The Excursion* (London, 1814), by kind permission of Paul F. Betz.

10. In his *Augustan Measures: Restoration and Eighteenth-Century Writings on Prosody and Metre* (Aldershot: Ashgate, 2002), 12–14, 98, 14, Richard Bradford observes that Johnson's criticism was offered initially by John Dryden who called blank verse *prose mesurée*. For further discussion of the animus against blank verse see Peter McDonald, *Sound Intentions: The Workings of Rhyme in Nineteenth Century Poetry* (Oxford: Oxford University Press, 2012). Late in the century Richard Payne Knight repeated the charge of "measured prose" in *The Progress of Civil Society* (London, 1796), III: 522–24.

11. For discussion of the perceived relationship between prosodic and moral regulation, see Paul Fussell, *Theory of Prosody in Eighteenth-Century England* (New London: Connecticut College, 1954).

12. John Rice, *An Introduction to the Art of Reading with Energy and Propriety* (London, 1765), 177.

13. Richard Roe, *The Elements of English Metre, Both in Prose and Verse, Illustrated, Under a Variety of Examples, by the Analogous Proportions of Annexed Lines, and by Other Occasional Marks* (London, 1801), 1, 2, 7, 3. On equivalence and equal-time theories of prosody, see Fussell, *Theory of Prosody*, 101–63.

14. See Bradford, *Augustan Measures*, 130–31.

15. First published in Edinburgh, 1841, and reissued in 22 editions by the end of the nineteenth century. Here I cite the Edinburgh, 1842 edition, page 4.

16. The phrase is reported by Henry Crabb Robinson in a letter of 12 September 1857; cited in Brennan O'Donnell, *The Passion of Meter: A Study of Wordsworth's Metrical Art* (Kent, Ohio: Kent State University Press, 1995), 206.

17. *Black's Picturesque Guide to the English Lakes , Including an Essay on the Geology of the District by John Phillips, FRS, GL, Late Professor of Geology and Mineralogy in the University of Dublin* (Edinburgh, 1850), 82. Subsequent references are cited in parenthesis in the text from this edition, unless otherwise stated.

18. Cited in O'Donnell, *The Passion of Meter*, 272.

19. Thelwall, *Selections*, x; HC 161.

20. For example, Sally Bushell, *Text as Process: Creative Composition in Wordsworth, Tennyson, and Dickinson* (Charlottesville: University Press of Virginia, 2009).

21. See, for example, "Revision as Form: Wordsworth's Drowned Man," in Susan J. Wolfson, *Formal Charges: The Shaping of Poetry in British Romanticism* (Stanford: Stanford University Press, 1997), and Andrew Bennett, *Wordsworth Writing* (Cambridge: Cambridge University Press, 2007). Also, Jonathan Wordsworth, *William Wordsworth: The Borders of Vision* (Oxford: Oxford University Press, 1984) and Kenneth R. Johnston, *Wordsworth and "The Recluse"* (New Haven: Yale University Press, 1984). Romantic poets' revisions and their significance are also discussed in Jack Stillinger, *Multiple Authorship and the Myth of Solitary Genius* (Oxford: Oxford University Press, 1991) and *Coleridge and Textual Instability: The Multiple Versions of the Major Poems* (Oxford: Oxford University Press, 1994).

22. Maureen N. McLane, *Balladeering, Minstrelsy, and the Making of British Romantic Poetry* (Cambridge: Cambridge University Press, 2008), 14, 225–40. See also Michael Baron, *Language and Relationship in Wordsworth's Writing* (London: Longman, 1995), 235–51, and J. H. Prynne, *Field Notes: The Solitary Reaper and Others* (London: Barque Press, 2007). On "mediality"—"the general condition within which, under certain circumstances, something like 'poetry' or 'literature' can take place"—see David E. Wellbery, foreword to Friedrich A. Kittler, *Discourse Networks, 1800/1900*, trans. Michael Metteer with Chris Cullens (Stanford: Stanford University Press, 1992), xiii. See also Celeste Langan and Maureen N. McLane, "The Medium of Romantic Poetry" in *The Cambridge Companion to British Romantic Poetry*, ed. David Chandler and Maureen N. McLane (Cambridge: Cambridge University Press, 2008), 239–62.

23. McLane, *Balladeering*, 234.

24. Joshua Steele, *An Essay Towards Establishing the Melody and Measure of Speech to be Expressed and Perpetuated by Peculiar Symbols* (1775; facs. rpt. Menston, Yorks.: Scolar Press, 1969), 8.

25. John B. Bender and Michael Marrinan, *The Culture of Diagram* (Stanford: Stanford University Press, 2010).

26. John Addington Symonds, *Blank Verse* (London: John C. Nimmo, 1895), 16.

27. For George Saintsbury (*A History of English Prosody from the Twelfth Century to the Present Day*, 3 vols. [London: Macmillan, 1906–10]), Shakespearean and Miltonic blank verse exhibits "the astonishing and almost miraculous powers of the English blend" of prosody, which incorporates the "discipline of classical and early modern regularity, and the life of ancient English freedom" (III: 512; I: 376). Easthope, *Poetry as Discourse* (London: Methuen, 1983), 53. Celeste Langan, *Romantic Vagrancy: Wordsworth and the Simulation of Freedom* (Cambridge:

Cambridge University Press, 1995); Marshall McLuhan, *The Gutenberg Galaxy: The Making of Typographic Man* (Toronto: University of Toronto Press, 1962).

28. Symonds, *Blank Verse,* 71–72; Saintsbury, *A History of English Prosody,* I: 316. "A type and symbol of our national literary spirit," Symonds continues, blank verse is "uncontrolled by precedent or rule, inclined to extravagance, yet reaching perfection at intervals by an inner force and *vivida vis* of native inspiration" (72).

29. Review of Wordsworth, *The Excursion; Edinburgh Review,* 24 (November 1814): 1–4 (1).

30. Hugh Blair, *Lectures on Rhetoric and Belles Lettres,* 3rd ed., 3 vols. (London, 1787), I: 221.

31. Blair, *Lectures on Rhetoric and Belles Lettres,* I: 220.

32. Christopher Ricks, "Wordsworth: 'A Pure Organic Pleasure from the Lines,'" *Essays in Criticism: A Quarterly Journal of Literary Criticism,* 21 (1971): 1–32 (6–7).

33. The historical approach to national meter inaugurated by Edwin Guest, *A History of English Rhythms,* 2 vols. (London: W. Pickering, 1838), T. S. Omond, *A Study of Metre* (London: Grant Richards, 1903), and Saintsbury, *A History of English Prosody.* Genealogy continues to inform approaches to blank verse by, for example, O'Donnell, *The Passion of Meter,* Henry Weinfield, *The Blank-Verse Tradition from Milton to Stevens: Freethinking and the Crisis of Modernity* (Cambridge: Cambridge University Press, 2012), and Robert Burns Shaw, *Blank Verse: A Guide to Its History and Use* (Athens: Ohio University Press, 2007).

34. E.g. Derek Attridge, *The Rhythms of English Poetry* (London: Longman, 1982). Attridge's scheme is applied to Wordsworth by O'Donnell, *The Passion of Meter.*

35. Benedict Anderson, *Imagined Communities: Reflections on the Origin and Spread of Nationalism* (London: Verso, 1991).

36. Notable exceptions include Richard Helgerson, *Forms of Nationhood: The Elizabethan Writing of England* (Chicago: University of Chicago Press, 1992) and Tom Conley, *The Self-Made Map: Cartographic Writing in Early Modern France* (Minneapolis: University of Minnesota Press, 1996).

37. Joseph Priestley, *A Description of a Chart of Biography; with a Catalogue of All the Names Inserted in It, and the Dates Annexed to Them* (London, 1790), quoted in Roe, *The Elements of English Metre,* title page. My book thus closely examines a moment in the "history of communication theory" described by John Guillory (in "Enlightening Mediation," *This is Enlightenment,* ed. Clifford Siskin and William Warner [Chicago: University of Chicago Press, 2010], 37–63). On Locke's *Essay on Human Understanding,* he writes: "Communication by signs (words) compensates for the absolute (because unmeasurable) distance between one mind and another. That distance, which is not exactly physical, is nonetheless conflated in the history of communication theory with the physical distance between bodies in space. Every communication can be seen as a telecommunication, and conversely long-distance communication as a figure for the inherent difficulty of communication" (46).

38. William Gilpin, *Observations . . . on Several Parts of England: Particularly the Mountains and Lakes of Cumberland, and Westmoreland* (London, 1786), I: xix.

39. Wordsworth's prose description of the Lake country was retitled several times, as *A Topographical Description of the Country of the Lakes in the North of England* (1820), *A Description of the Scenery of the Lakes in the North of England* (1822 and 1823), and *A Guide through the District of the Lakes, in the North of England, with a Description of the Scenery, etc. For the Use of Tourists and Residents* (1835). The shorthand title *Guide to the Lakes* derives from Hudson and Nicholson's 1842 republishing of the 1835 text in an expanded volume (*A Complete Guide to the Lakes, Comprising Minute Directions for the Tourist, with Mr. Wordsworth's Description of the Scenery of the Country . . .*).

40. For a different approach to Wordsworth's lexicon see Hugh Sykes Davies, *Wordsworth and the Worth of Words* (Cambridge: Cambridge University Press, 1986).

41. On the Survey's history see W. A. Seymour (ed.), *A History of the Ordnance Survey* (Folkestone: Dawson, 1980), and Rachel Hewitt, *Map of a Nation: A Biography of the Ordnance Survey* (London: Granta, 2010).

42. Michael Wiley, *Romantic Geography: Wordsworth and Anglo-European Space* (Basingstoke: Palgrave Macmillan, 1998); James Garrett, *Wordsworth and the Writing of the Nation* (Aldershot: Ashgate, 2008).

43. Edward R. Tufte, *Envisioning Information* (Cheshire, CT: Graphics Press, 1990), 12. Tufte borrows the idea of "flatland" from A. Square [Edwin A. Abbott], *Flatland: A Romance of Many Dimensions* (London, 1884).

44. E.g. Paul De Man, "Hypogram and Inscription," in *The Resistance to Theory* (Minneapolis: University of Minnesota Press, 1986), 32. See also Jonathan Culler, "Apostrophe," *Diacritics,* 7.4 (Winter, 1977): 59–69.

45. Virginia Jackson, *Dickinson's Misery: A Theory of Lyric Reading* (Princeton: Princeton University Press, 2005).

46. *The Prelude: 1799, 1805, 1850,* ed. Jonathan Wordsworth, M. H. Abrams, and Stephen Gill (New York: W. W. Norton, 1979), 525. The text of the 1805 poem is based on MS A (DC MS 52).

47. Marjorie Levinson, *Wordsworth's Great Period Poems* (Cambridge: Cambridge University Press, 1986) and *The Romantic Fragment Poem: A Critique of a Form* (Chapel Hill: University of North Carolina Press, 1986); Adela Pinch, *Strange Fits of Passion: Epistemologies of Emotion, Hume to Austen* (Stanford: Stanford University Press, 1996). Yopie Prins, *Victorian Sappho* (Princeton: Princeton University Press, 1999); Jackson, *Dickinson's Misery.* I take the phrase from Wolfson, *Formal Charges,* 14.

48. Bennett, *Wordsworth Writing,* 5; Bushell, *Text as Process: Creative Composition in Wordsworth, Tennyson and Dickinson* (Charlottesville: University of Virginia Press, 2009).

49. Paul Keen, *The Crisis of Literature in the 1790s: Print Culture and the Public Sphere* (Cambridge: Cambridge University Press, 1999); William St. Clair, *The Reading Nation in the Romantic Period* (Cambridge: Cambridge University Press, 2004); Adrian Johns, *The Nature of the Book: Print and Knowledge in the Making* (Chicago: University of Chicago Press, 1998); Leah Price, *How to Do Things with Books in Victorian Britain* (Princeton: Princeton University Press, 2012); Tom Mole, *Byron's Romantic Celebrity: Industrial Culture and the Hermeneutics of Intimacy* (Basingstoke: Palgrave Macmillan, 2007); Nicholas Mason, *Literary Advertising and the Shaping of British Romanticism* (Baltimore: Johns Hopkins University Press, 2013); Heather Jackson, *Romantic Readers: The Evidence of Marginalia* (New Haven: Yale University Press, 2005); Deidre Shauna Lynch, T*he Economy of Character: Novels, Market Culture, and the Business of Inner Meaning* (Chicago: University of Chicago Press, 1998).

50. Janine Barchas, *Graphic Design, Print Culture, and the Eighteenth-Century Novel* (Cambridge: Cambridge University Press, 2003); Andrew Piper, *Dreaming in Books: The Making of the Bibliographic Imagination in the Romantic Age* (Chicago: University of Chicago Press, 2009).

51. Jerome McGann, *Black Riders: The Visible Language of Modernism* (Princeton: Princeton University Press, 1993), 21.

52. Jerome J. McGann, *A Critique of Modern Textual Criticism* (Chicago: University of Chicago Press, 1983).

53. Yopie Prins, "Historical Poetics, Dysprosody, and the Science of English Verse," in "New Lyric Studies," *PMLA,* 123.1 (January 2008): 229–34; Simon Jarvis, *Wordsworth's Philosophic Song*

(Cambridge: Cambridge University Press, 2007), "Prosody as Cognition," *Critical Quarterly,* 40.4 (1998): 3–15, and "What Is Historical Poetics?" in *Theory Aside,* ed. Jason Potts and Daniel Stout (Durham: Duke University Press, 2014), 97–116. Other historical approaches include Jason Rudy, *Electric Meters: Victorian Physiological Poetics* (Athens: Ohio University Press, 2009) and Jason Hall, *Meter Matters: Verse Cultures of the Long Nineteenth Century* (Athens: Ohio University Press, 2011).

54. O'Donnell, *The Passion of Meter,* 181.

55. O'Donnell, *The Passion of Meter,* 11; Ricks, "Wordsworth: 'A Pure Organic Pleasure from the Lines'"; Hollander, *Rhyme's Reason: A Guide to English Verse* (New Haven: Yale University Press, 1981).

56. Eric Griffiths, *The Printed Voice of Victorian Poetry* (Oxford: Oxford University Press, 1989); Yopie Prins, "Victorian Meters," *The Cambridge Companion to Victorian Poetry*, ed. Joseph Bristow (Cambridge: Cambridge University Press, 2000), 89–113.

57. John Hollander, *Vision and Resonance: Two Senses of Poetic Form*, 2nd ed., (New Haven: Yale University Press, 1985), 95–101.

58. Yopie Prins, "Metrical Translation: Nineteenth-Century Homers and the Hexameter Mania," in *Nation, Language and the Ethics of Translation*, ed. Sandra Bermann and Michael Wood (Princeton: Princeton University Press, 2005), 229–56; Catherine Robson, *Heart Beats: Everyday Life and the Memorized Poem* (Princeton: Princeton University Press, 2012); Meredith Martin, *The Rise and Fall of Meter: Poetry and English National Culture, 1860–1930* (Princeton: Princeton University Press, 2012).

59. For discussion of this issue in Saintsbury's *History of English Prosody*, see Martin, *The Rise and Fall of Meter*, 79–108.

60. Celeste Langan, "Understanding Media in 1805: Audiovisual Hallucination in *The Lay of the Last Minstrel,*" *Studies in Romanticism* 40.1 (Spring 2001): 52, 53.

61. Elfenbein, *Romanticism and the Rise of English* (Stanford: Stanford University Press, 2009), 108–43, and especially 137–38.

62. Simonsen, *Wordsworth and Word-Preserving Arts: Typographic Inscription, Ekphrasis and Posterity in the Later Work* (Basingstoke: Palgrave Macmillan, 2007).

CHAPTER I

1. On the role of cartography in the consolidation of "India," see Matthew Edney, *Mapping an Empire: The Geographical Construction of British India, 1765–1843* (Chicago: University of Chicago Press, 1990).

2. Geoffrey H. Hartman, "Wordsworth, Inscriptions, and Romantic Nature Poetry," in *Beyond Formalism: Literary Essays 1958–1970* (New Haven: Yale University Press, 1970), 208. Further references to this text will be denoted parenthetically.

3. See Cynthia Chase, "Monument and Inscription: Wordsworth's 'Rude Embryo' and the Remaining of History," in Kenneth R. Johnston, Gilbert Chaitin, Karen Hanson, and Herbert Marks (eds.), *Romantic Revolutions: Criticism and Theory* (Bloomington: Indiana University Press, 1990), 50–77 (55).

4. Crosthwaite published "An Accurate Map of the Matchless Lake of Derwent" first in 1783; he followed it with six more, issuing them together as *Seven Maps of the Lakes* in 1794, 1800, 1809 and 1819 (London: published and sold by Peter Crosthwaite, the Author, at his Museum in Keswick).

5. For bibliographic details, see above in note 39 to the Introduction; *W Prose*, II: 123–49.

6. (London, 1755).

7. George Pearch (London, 1768) reprinted 1770, 1775, 1783. Both Brown's text and part of Dalton's poem appeared as addenda to editions of Thomas West, *A Guide to the Lakes, in Cumberland, Westmorland, and Lancashire. By the author of The Antiquities of Furness* (London, 1780) from 1780 onward. Wordsworth also quoted Brown's poem in his *Guide to the Lakes*. Just as verse was incorporated within and added to the ends of prose tours, prose tours were appended to verse; the 1775 *Poems of Mr. Gray*, for instance, included as an appendix Thomas Gray's journal. See Peter Bicknell, *The Picturesque Scenery of the Lake District, 1752–1855: A Bibliographic Study* (Winchester: St Paul's Bibliographies, 1990), 2–3. In 1820, Wordsworth published his *Description of the Scenery of the Lakes* with *Vaudracour and Julia*, excerpted from *The Prelude* manuscript, and his *Duddon Sonnets*.

8. Gilpin's *Observations, Relative to Picturesque Beauty, Made in the Year 1772, on Several Parts of England; Particularly the Mountains, and Lakes of Cumberland, and Westmoreland*, 2 vols. (London, 1786) derives from his eight-volume manuscript *Tour through England; more particularly the mountainous parts of Cumberland, and Westmorland. . . .* Here I quote *Observations*, I: xix.

9. Gilpin's *Observations* contains thirty illustrations: one line drawing of antique vases, one line-diagram of hill forms, and twenty-five views. The remaining three illustrations are sketch-plans of the Lakes—simple outlines of Ullswater, Windermere, and Derwentwater, not to scale.

10. William Hutchinson, *An Excursion to the Lakes, in Westmoreland and Cumberland, August 1773* (London, 1774), 61, citing Mason, *The English Garden* (1772–82), Book I, lines 212–15. I retain original punctuation to demonstrate the visual effects of verse citations.

11. Citing Thomson, *Summer*, from *The Seasons* (1726–1730), lines 590–606.

12. Malcolm Andrews, *The Search for the Picturesque, Landscape, Aesthetics and Tourism in Britain, 1760–1800* (Stanford: Stanford University Press, 1989), 76.

13. On the problem of closure in blank verse, see Barbara Herrnstein Smith, *Poetic Closure: A Study of How Poems End* (Chicago: University of Chicago Press, 1968), 78–84.

14. On the serial logic of the eighteenth-century tour, see Alan Liu, *Wordsworth: A Sense of History* (Stanford: Stanford University Press, 1989), 5–7.

15. Samuel Johnson, "Milton," *Lives of the English Poets*, ed. George Birkbeck Hill, vol. I (Oxford: Clarendon Press, 1905), 192–93.

16. Considering the "ascendancy of accentualism" in British poetry after 1770, Paul Fussell posits a prior "deafness" to "the element of stress in English"—a "disinclination or pure inability to recognize the force of accent" (Fussell, *Theory of Prosody in Eighteenth-Century England* [New London: Connecticut College, 1954], 153).

17. See Richard Bradford, *Augustan Measures: Restoration and Eighteenth-Century Writings on Prosody and Metre* (Aldershot: Ashgate, 2002), 130–31. Coward and Mason quoted in Bradford, 131.

18. Citing William Mason's *English Garden*, Book I, lines 169–71.

19. Citing *Night Thoughts* (1742–45), Night IV, lines 80–88. The excerpt runs eight more lines.

20. *Night Thoughts*, Night II, line 572.

21. Hutchinson, *An Excursion to the Lakes*, 67, quoting *English Garden*, Book I, lines 358–59.

22. John Housman, *A Topographical Description of Cumberland, Westmoreland, Lancashire, and a Part of the West Riding of Yorkshire; Comprehending, First, A General Introductory View. Secondly, A more detailed account of each County; . . . Thirdly, A Tour through the most interesting*

Parts of the District (Carlisle: Francis Jollie, 1800), 152, citing Hutchinson's *Excursion*, which is citing Milton, *Paradise Lost*, Book IV, lines 606–9.

23. John Mason, cited in Bradford, *Augustan Measures*, 131.

24. For Wordsworth's "perfect Republic of Shepherds and Agriculturists," the "almost visionary mountain republic,'" see his *Guide through the District of the Lakes* in *W Prose*, II: 206–7.

25. The lines continued to appear in the introduction's later reformulations as *A Guide to the Lakes*.

26. Quoted in Stuart Curran, *Poetic Form and British Romanticism* (Oxford: Oxford University Press, 1986), 40.

27. Gilpin, *Observations*, I: 122, quoting William Mason, *Caractacus* (1759), Act I, scene i, lines 13–15.

28. Gilpin, *Observations*, I: 122–23, quoting John Milton, *Paradise Lost*, Book XI, lines 417–20.

29. The bibliographic history of the text that began as the introduction to Wilkinson's *Select Views* is given above in note 39 to the Introduction.

30. In his guidebook, Wordsworth introduces high-magnification views with such phrases as "Among minuter recommendations will be noticed" (*W Prose*, II: 182).

31. In *The Poetical Works of William Wordsworth* (London: Longman, Rees, Orme, Brown, and Green, 1827), II, 51–52 the lines were titled "Water-Fowl." In an interesting inversion, Wordsworth quotes a prose line from the 1823 *Guide to the Lakes* as a headnote to the poem, marking now the prose as an extract: " 'Let me be allowed the aid of verse to describe the evolutions which these visitants sometimes perform, on a fine day towards the close of winter.'—Extract from the Author's Book on the Lakes."

32. On other examples of this culture, including the annuals and the reviews, see Lee Erickson, *The Economy of Literary Form: English Literature and the Industrialization of Publishing, 1800–1850* (Baltimore: Johns Hopkins University Press, 1996), 28.

33. Books primarily of interest to antiquarians are an exception; for example, Thomas West's *The Antiquities of Furness* (London, 1774) contained a *Map of the Liberty of Furness in the County of Lancaster*, scaled at one inch to two miles.

34. See Bicknell, *The Picturesque Scenery of the Lake District*, 26 for Young's *Six Months Tour* (London, 1770); 27 for Hutchinson's *Excursion* (London, 1774); 31 for Thomas Gray, whose widely circulated journal of his 1769 tour of the Lakes was first published, also mapless, in 1775 as part of *The Poems of Mr. Gray. To which are prefixed memoirs of his life and writings by W. Mason, M.A.* (York, 1775).

35. West, *A Guide to the Lakes . . . in Cumberland, Westmorland and Lancashire* (London, 1784), viii.

36. Bicknell, *The Picturesque Scenery of the Lake District*, 13–15.

37. Bicknell, *The Picturesque Scenery of the Lake District*, 7, 13.

38. Bicknell, *The Picturesque Scenery of the Lake District*, 71. At one inch to two miles, the map was more detailed than West's one-quarter inch to the mile.

39. Bicknell, *The Picturesque Scenery of the Lake District*, 13–14.

40. In incorporating prose annotations on the map, Crosthwaite was developing a practice that had begun to feature on the county maps of the mid-eighteenth century. For example, a marginal note in Emmanuel Bowen's 1765 map of Cumberland and Westmorland reads, "Winander Mere *is reckon'd the largest Lake in England, / and affords great plenty of Fish, which belong to Ap- / plethwaite in Winander Mere Parish. All the Isles of / this Lake (or Holmes as they are

call'd) are parts / of the county of Westmorland." In *The Royal English Atlas: Eighteenth Century County Maps of England and Wales; by Emanuel Bowen and Thomas Kitchin,* ed. J. B. Harley and Donald Hodgson (Newton Abbot: David and Charles, 1971).

41. Alan Hankinson, *The Regatta Men* (Milnthorpe: Cicerone Press, 1988), 8.

42. For more detail, see the museum handbill reproduced in William Rollinson's Introduction to *A Series of Accurate Maps of the Principal Lakes of Cumberland, Westmorland and Lancashire . . . First Surveyed and Planned Between 1783 and 1794 by Peter Crosthwaite* (Newcastle-on-Tyne: Frank Graham, 1968).

43. Quoted in Hankinson, *The Regatta Men,* 10.

44. Crosthwaite's handbill, Rollinson, Introduction to *A Series of Accurate Maps.*

45. Rollinson deduces that they were "very popular," Introduction to *A Series of Accurate Maps.* Crosthwaite's maps sold for one shilling and six pence each; the set for nine shillings.

46. David Wilson, "Peter Crosthwaite (1735–1808): Museum Owner, Mapmaker, and Inventor," in *Keswick Characters,* vol. II, ed. Elizabeth Foot and Patricia Howell (Carlisle: Bookcase, 2007), 28.

47. The first phrase appears in the 1792 handbill for the museum, reproduced in Rollinson's Introduction to *A Series of Accurate Maps.*

48. Within the lake boundaries, numerals indicate lake depths; arrows show the flow of water currents, and a compass rose indicates cardinal directions. Outside the lake boundary, pictographs (signs that resemble what they denote) mark villages and towns, rectangular blocks represent properties, and crosses signal churches. Different forms of line mark roads and parks; names indicate fields and woods.

49. Thomas West, *A Guide to the Lakes . . . in Cumberland, Westmorland and Lancashire* (London, 1778), 24.

50. Peter Crosthwaite, "Keswick and the Cumberland Lakes" (London, after 1819). The maps that I reproduce and analyze belong to a made-up volume held by the William L. Clements Library at the University of Michigan, Ann Arbor. The volume, stamped "Edensor Inn, Near Chatsworth," contains six maps (Pocklington Island is missing). Henceforth, references to individual maps in this volume will be denoted parenthetically.

51. On the maps, the three stanzas of iambic hexameter are concluded by a single line of iambic heptameter.

52. England, Wales, and Scotland.

53. A Renaissance emblem typically comprises verbal and pictorial elements: the *inscriptio* (title, headline) and *pictura* (image), and sometimes also a *subscriptio* (a discursive caption, usually in verse). For a discussion, see James Elkins, "Emblemata," *The Domain of Images* (Ithaca: Cornell, 1999), 195–211.

54. Although the punctuation of the quoted passage—the articulation of language—is considerable (e.g., *"the Scale Force, (a Water Fall,) in one day, by the help of the Chaise, and a Boat"*), the map fails to indicate where those "2 miles" are to be divided into "3 intervals of time." This disjunction points both to the map's drive to mark and measure and to its insufficiency as a navigational device.

55. On Crosthwaite's inventions, see Rollinson, Introduction to a *Series of Accurate Maps.* Rollinson is quoting from an anonymous preface to the 1863 edition of Crosthwaite's *Series of Accurate Maps.*

56. *"Here lie the Splendid Spoils of Mountain Floods"* points *"Here,"* to the *"Fertile Plains,"* and *"yon,"* to the *"Stupendous Chasms,"* claiming that the former is the spoil of the latter by the forces of floods over time.

57. The Derwent map is the only one of the series that advances beyond pictorial representation of peaks (the inset profile) to show them cartographically, employing the new European method of depicting peaks in plan view (as if from directly above).

58. Crosthwaite added these lines in 1809. See Rollinson, Introduction to *A Series of Accurate Maps*, and s.v. "Derwentwater."

59. On the rising popularity of walking, see, for example, Robin Jarvis, *Romantic Writing and Pedestrian Travel* (New York: Palgrave Macmillan, 1998), 9–19.

60. Wordsworth's map was scaled at 1¾ inch to 10 miles. Otley's *Map of the District of the Lakes* was issued in a handy portable format and was also included in Otley's guidebook and William Green's *Tourist's New Guide* of 1819. Otley's appellation *"District of the Lakes"* precedes the first recorded use of the term "Lake District." According to *A Dictionary of Lake District Place-Names* (ed. Diana Whaley [English Place Name Society: University of Nottingham: Nottingham, 2006]), the Lake District was first so called in the 1829 Parson & White *Gazetteer*.

61. *Black's Picturesque Guide to the English Lakes with a copious itinerary; a map, and four charts of the Lake District; and engraved views of the scenery* (Edinburgh, 1842), 4.

62. The terms appear in the two-page preface to the 1842 edition (v–vi). For a discussion of the development of the Lake District as Wordsworthian country in *Black's* and other Victorian guidebooks, see Saeko Yoshikawa, *William Wordsworth and the Invention of Tourism, 1820–1900* (Farnham: Ashgate, 2014).

63. On the sophistication of the visual representations of geology, see Martin S. Rudwick, "The Emergence of a Visual Language for Geological Science, 1760–1840," *History of Science*, 14 (1976), 149–95. The fifth edition is entitled *Black's Picturesque Guide to the Lakes, Including an Essay on the Geology of the District by John Phillips, FRS, GL, Late Professor of Geology and Mineralogy in the University of Dublin.*

64. The 1853 edition concludes with "Memoranda for Botanists," listing scientific names, locations, and periods of flowering.

65. *Black's Picturesque Guide to the English Lakes, Including an Essay on the Geology of the District by John Phillips,* 2nd ed. (Edinburgh, 1844), v.

66. Misquoting *Excursion*, III: 55–56. By condensing and reformatting information conveyed in the lengthy prose sections of the guide, the itinerary better suits the experience of the carriage and foot-traveler. *Black's* itinerary recalls John Ogilby's innovative strip-road maps from his *Britannia* (1675): a 300-page volume showing narrow strips (depicted as scrolls) of continuous post road between towns in England and Wales. John Cary modernized Ogilby's strip maps in his 1790 road-book, *Survey of the High Roads from London . . .* , indicating properties and arrays of lines from positions on the road "to shew the points of sight from where the Houses are seen." Quoted in Catherine Delano-Smith and Roger J. P. Kain, *English Maps: A History* (Toronto: University of Toronto Press, 1999), 170.

67. Hartman, "Wordsworth, Inscriptions, and Romantic Nature Poetry," 229.

CHAPTER 2

1. For estimates of distance, see Donald E. Hayden, *Wordsworth's Walking Tour of 1790* (Tulsa, OK: University of Tulsa Press, 1983), 116–19.

2. Although Geoffrey H. Hartman, following Wordsworth, dates the Ravine of Gondo passage to 1799 (*Wordsworth's Poetry, 1787–1814* [New Haven: Yale University Press, 1964], 45),

early 1804 is now recognized as the composition date for this passage and all of Book VI (1805, pp. 11–39).

3. For a bibliographical list of the six principal sources, see Max Wildi, "Wordsworth and the Simplon Pass I," *English Studies*, 40 (1959): 226. See also Hayden, *Wordsworth's Walking Tour*, 3–6.

4. For a reading of the focal position of the Simplon episode in the critical discourse on *The Prelude*, see David Ferris, "History, Wordsworth and the Simplon Pass," *Studies in Romanticism*, 30 (1991): 391–438. For treatments of the episode since Hartman's *Wordsworth's Poetry, 1787*, see, for example, M. H. Abrams, *Natural Supernaturalism: Tradition and Revolution in Romantic Literature* (New York: Norton, 1973), 448–53; Thomas Weiskel, *The Romantic Sublime: Studies in the Structure and Psychology of Transcendence* (Baltimore: Johns Hopkins University Press, 1976), 195–204; Mary Jacobus, *Romanticism, Writing, and Sexual Difference* (Oxford: Clarendon Press, 1989), 3–32; and Alan Liu, *Wordsworth: The Sense of History* (Stanford: Stanford University Press, 1989), 3–31.

5. Raymond Havens, *"The Prelude": A Commentary*, vol. II of *The Mind of a Poet* (Baltimore: Johns Hopkins University Press, 1941), 420–23.

6. Hayden, *Wordsworth's Walking Tour*, 4–6 passim. Wildi, "Wordsworth and the Simplon Pass I," 227.

7. Michael Wiley, *Romantic Geography: Wordsworth and Anglo-European Space* (New York: St. Martin's Press, 1998), 16.

8. William to Dorothy Wordsworth, 6 and 16 September 1790, EY 32. Subsequent references to this letter are cited parenthetically in the text by page number.

9. Liu, in *Wordsworth: The Sense of History*, 9, remarks but dismisses one reference to limited "room" as an instance of the inexpressibility topos, linking it with other "clichés of circumvention."

10. Dorothy Wordsworth to Jane Pollard, 6 October 1790, EY 39.

11. Liu, *Wordsworth: The Sense of History*, 11–12, 4–5.

12. Liu, *Wordsworth: The Sense of History*, 6–7.

13. As Hayden notes (*Wordsworth's Walking Tour*, 108), Wordsworth acknowledges in *Descriptive Sketches* his indebtedness to the observations appended to Ramond de Carbonnière's French translation of *Travels in Switzerland*, which included Coxe's map.

14. William Coxe, *Travels in Switzerland. In a Series of Letters to William Melmoth, Esq.*, 3 vols. (London: 1789).

15. Liu, *Wordsworth: The Sense of History*, 11.

16. A crucial distinction between Wiley's work and my own is Wiley's interest in the way in which blank spaces on maps could make it possible for Wordsworth to spatialize imagination. I am interested in the highly mapped area of Simplon Pass and the way in which graphic complexity and confusion inform Wordsworth's discourse of mind and nature. Wiley interprets the apostrophe to the imagination as a "geographical blanking" (*Romantic Geography*, 15)—even though, as I will show, this site was thoroughly mapped and in strikingly different ways in this period.

17. Homann Heirs, *Vallesia Superior* (Nuremberg: 1768).

18. In *Cartographic Relief Presentation* (Berlin: Walter de Gruyter, 1982), 3, Eduard Imhof writes, "Earlier maps gave the misleading impression of ubiquitous level ground and valley floors, devoid of any landforms, lying between isolate mountain symbols, the shapes of valleys and gently undulating ground not being shown."

19. Guillaume Henri Dufour, *Topographische Karte der Schweiz . . . Ingenieure unter der Aufsicht des Generals G. H. Dufour* (Berne, 1833–63).

20. Samuel Dunn, *Switzerland Divided into Thirteen Cantons with their Subjects and their Allies . . .* , 1786, in Dunn's *A New Atlas of the Mundane System . . . with a general introduction to Geography and Cosmography* (London: 1788).

21. In his *Cartographic Relief Presentation*, 8, Imhof notes that the "wholesale transition from side and oblique views of mountains to the planimetric form for complete coverage of Switzerland took place in the maps of the Napoleonic military topographer Bacler d'Albe just before 1800, and in the so-called 'Meyer Atlas.'"

22. On the technique of layering and separation, see Edward R. Tufte, *Envisioning Information* (Cheshire, CT: Graphics Press, 1990), 53–66.

23. Imhof, *Cartographic Relief Presentation*, 10–11.

24. P. D. A. Harvey discusses the problem of showing rivers and roads on hills in both picture maps and scale maps. *The History of Topographical Maps: Symbols, Pictures, and Surveys* (London: Thames and Hudson, 1980), 181–83.

25. Captain C. A. Chauchard, *Carte de la Partie Septentrionale de l'Italie* (Paris: 1791).

26. Louis Albert Guislain, Baron de Bacler d'Albe, *Carte Générale du Théâtre de la Guerre en Italie et dans les Alpes* (Paris: 1802).

27. I thank Denise Riley for suggesting the term *cartospection* to me.

28. *Quintilian's Institutes of Oratory, or Education of an Orator,* trans. Rev. John Selby Watson, M.A., 2 vols. (London: George Bell and Sons, 1903), II: 163–64.

29. As Reed notes (1805, 182), Wordsworth quotes James Thomson, "The Castle of Indolence," I: 128.

30. "Imagination slept, / And yet not utterly" (III: 260–61).

31. "Ode, Intimations of Immortality from Recollections of Early Childhood," in *Poems, in Two Volumes, and Other Poems, 1800–1807,* ed. Jared Curtis (Ithaca: Cornell University Press, 1983), p. 274, lines 91, 93–94.

32. Jacobus writes, in *Romanticism, Writing, and Sexual Difference*, regarding the diagrams, that the "historically unmoored subject can take comfort from the Newtonian scheme of overarching order and proportion" (79).

33. Hartman, *Wordsworth's Poetry*, 240–41.

34. Weiskel suggests that the episode of the unwitting crossing is a screen memory Wordsworth uses to forestall and repress a more traumatic encounter with the order of Eternity at Gondo Gorge (*Romantic Sublime*, 202).

35. "Regarded as a digressive form, a sort of interruption, excess or redundancy, apostrophe in *The Prelude* becomes the signal instance of the rupture of the temporal scheme of memory by the time of writing—a radical discontinuity which ruptures the illusion of sequentiality and insists, embarrassingly, on self-presence and voice; insists too that invocation itself may be more important than what is invoked," Mary Jacobus, "Apostrophe and Lyric Voice in *The Prelude*," in *William Wordsworth's "The Prelude,"* ed. and intro. Harold Bloom (New York: Chelsea House, 1986), 149. Wordsworth's self-address in the Simplon episode, which I read as a special form of apostrophe, suggests that he presents himself in an integrated circuit of speaking and hearing. A distinction emerges between the trope of *hypotyposis* ("behold a map"), which positions Wordsworth in time and place, and the placeless immediacy, or point, of self-address.

36. The "mind" (1805, VI: 542) appears as "soul" in MS D (1850, p. 711; I: 610).

37. For dating of later manuscripts (MSS D and E), see 1850, pp. 6–9.

38. 1850, VI: 581. See also 1850, pp. 11 and 711. This change is retained in further revisions of the poem, including those of 1838–39, and appears in the first print edition of the poem in 1850.

39. 1850, VI: 643–44. This change does not appear in MS D, but is recorded by the editor as appearing as a correction in Wordsworth's hand to MS E, which would date the revision to 1838–39, or after (p. 131, note 643–44; and pp. 6–9, 25–26).

40. 1850, VI: 588. See 1850, p. 129, notes 587–96.

41. 1850, I: 16–18 read, "should the chosen guide / Be nothing better than a wandering cloud, / I cannot miss my way."

42. Wordsworth would contemplate how the pure relations of geometry "could become / Herein a leader to the human mind" (1805, VI: 146–47).

43. 1850, VI: 752–54. A facsimile of the MS D page appears on 1850, p. 728.

44. What the editor, Mark Reed calls C-stage revision. See notes 505–6 on p. 669 of 1805, II. A facsimile of MS A (DC MS 52) 134r appears in 1805, I: p. 820.

45. Suggestively, but not significantly, the deletion lines tangle into a dark mass reminiscent of Romantic-era cartographic renderings of the Pass.

46. *Track* is defined in *OED* as "the mark, or series of marks, left by the passage of anything" (I.1.a). So, too, *trace* is understood as "the track made by the passage of any person or thing, whether beaten by feet or indicated in any other way" (5.a). However, the cartographic references in *Prelude* Book VI and the practices of map-line tracing associated with its epistolary antecedents foreground the representational implications of "[?line] / Traced out mockingly" and the class of textual meanings attached to the word "trace."

47. *OED*, s.v. "trace," *v.*1, 3.9, 10.

48. *Wordsworth's Poetry*, 39.

49. The poem in revision also shares with the map the use of typography to signal geographical significance. Sometime between 1824 and 1832, after the Wordsworths' return trip to the Alps, the copyist of MS D (either William or Mary) called for the rare resetting of an entire clause in italics (by underlining it in the manuscript): "*that we had crossed the Alps*" (1850, VI: 592). Italics dictate a slowing of reading, as per the understanding of the day, emphasizing here the geographical knowledge gleaned from the Peasant and the ensuing full stop. Brought to the aid of "human speech," typography intensifies the affective-epistemological turn at this point in the text (1850, VI: 593–95).

50. The 1850 text has "The only track now visible was one / That from the Streamlet's farther bank, held forth / Conspicuous invitation to ascend / A lofty mountain" (VI: 580–83).

51. Abrams, *Natural Supernaturalism*, 284–85.

52. Abrams, *Natural Supernaturalism*, 285, citing 1850, I: 639–41.

53. 1850, VI: 754.

54. 1850, VIII: 451–53.

CHAPTER 3

1. On cartography's excitement of the cultural imagination in the early nineteenth century, see Rachel Hewitt, *Map of a Nation: A Biography of the Ordinance Survey* (London: Granta, 2010), 202–12.

2. William Wordsworth, "View from the Top of Black Comb," line 5, *Shorter Poems, 1807–1820*, ed. Carl H. Ketcham (Ithaca: Cornell University Press, 1989), 99.

3. Matthew Edney, *Mapping an Empire: The Geographical Construction of British India, 1765–1843* (Chicago: University of Chicago Press, 1990), 325. See also 24–25 and 53–54.

4. See Catherine Delano-Smith and Roger J. P. Kain, *English Maps: A History* (Toronto: University of Toronto Press, 1999), 81.

5. W. A. Seymour explains that the Royal Society "implicitly" supported "surveying done with scientific objectives" (2). *A History of the Ordnance Survey*, ed. W. A. Seymour (Folkestone, UK: Dawson, 1980).

6. Seymour, *History of the Ordnance Survey*, 14.

7. Seymour, *History of the Ordnance Survey*, 4.

8. Seymour, *History of the Ordnance Survey*, 46.

9. Quoted in Tim Owen and Elaine Pilbeam, *Ordnance Survey: Map Makers to Britain Since 1791* (Southampton: Ordnance Survey, 1992), 11.

10. Edney, *Mapping an Empire*, 19.

11. Owen and Pilbeam, *Ordnance Survey: Map Makers*, 7.

12. For description of early methods of the topographical survey, see Seymour, *History of the Ordnance Survey*, 59–60.

13. Edney, *Mapping an Empire*, 21.

14. Quoted in Seymour, *History of the Ordnance Survey*, 7.

15. Hewitt, *Map of a Nation*, 106, 206.

16. Delano-Smith and Kain, *English Maps: A History*, 82.

17. Seymour, *History of the Ordnance Survey*, 49.

18. Delano-Smith and Kain, *English Maps: A History*, 90. See also J. B. Harley and R. R. Oliver, introductory essay to *Northern England and the Isle of Man, Old Series Ordnance Survey Maps of England and Wales*, vol. VIII, ed. Harry Margary (Lympne Castle, Kent : H. Margary, 1991), xxii.

19. Stations were marked by wooden pipes set into the ground and, after 1791, with stones. Seymour, *History of the Ordnance Survey*, 29; 38. Delano-Smith and Kain, *English Maps: A History*, 99.

20. Helen M. Wallis and Arthur H. Robinson, *Cartographical Innovations: An International Handbook of Mapping Terms to 1900.* (Tring: Map Collector Publications [1982] in association with the International Cartographic Association, 1987), "Hachures," 218.

21. Wallis and Robinson, *Cartographical Innovations*, "Point Symbol," 235.

22. P. D. A. Harvey, *The History of Topographical Maps: Symbols, Pictures, and Surveys* (London: Thames and Hudson, 1980), 183. Alan G. Hodgkiss, *Discovering Antique Maps* (Princes Risborough, UK: Shire, 1996), 13.

23. Hodgkiss, *Discovering Antique Maps*, 43.

24. Comparable to French revolutionary rationalization of space. See Hewitt, *Map of a Nation*, 106–8.

25. See Joel Gascoyne's nine-sheet *Map of the County of Cornwall newly Surveyed* (1699) which represents towns "ichnographically" (in plan). In Delano-Smith and Kain, *English Maps: A History*, 86–87.

26. Line 9. See *Poems, in Two Volumes and Other Poems*, ed. Jared Curtis (Ithaca: Cornell University Press, 1983), 207–8.

27. *The Ruined Cottage and The Pedlar*, ed. James Butler (Ithaca: Cornell University Press, 1979), *The Pedlar* MS E, lines 143–46, p. 394.

28. Christopher Ricks, "Wordsworth: 'A Pure Organic Pleasure from the Lines,'" *Essays in Criticism*, 21 (1971), 1–32; Susan Wolfson, *Romantic Interactions: Social Being and the Turns of Literary Action* (Baltimore: Johns Hopkins University Press, 2010), 144.

29. *Wordsworth's Poetry, 1787–1814* (New Haven: Yale University Press, 1964), 211.

30. Lee M. Johnson, *Wordsworth's Metaphysical Verse: Geometry, Nature and Form* (Toronto: University of Toronto Press, 1982). On the poet's use of "geometrical thought" as "the rational keystone of a belief in a principle of immortality," see 3.

31. Hartman, *Wordsworth's Poetry*, 33.

32. Hartman reads "images of liquid light" as part of the "imagery of continuous revelation in Wordsworth" (*The Unmediated Vision: An Interpretation of Wordsworth, Hopkins, Rilke, and Valéry* [New Haven: Yale University Press, 1954], 31, 30).

33. *Unmediated Vision*, 17–21.

34. On the "relationships between an individual's participation in time and his completed poetic self's reliance on timeless geometrical patterns," see Johnson, *Wordsworth's Metaphysical Verse*, 67–122 (68).

35. For a similar linkage between fishing line and the poet's verse lines, see Wolfson, *Romantic Interactions*, 144.

36. The sense of grammatical repair derives from the reinstatement of hypotaxis following five lines linked and divided by the coordinating conjunction.

37. The parallel lines of mountains, Wordsworth wrote in his fragment on "The Sublime and the Beautiful," produce sublime effects by suggesting the infinite and eternal. *W Prose*, II: 357.

38. Parrish relies for his reading text on MSS U and V; here he imports the first line from MS V.

39. The "varied line is that alone in which complete beauty is found." Edmund Burke, *A Philosophical Enquiry into the Origin of Our Ideas of the Sublime and the Beautiful*, ed. Adam Phillips (Oxford: Oxford University Press, 1990), 105.

40. OED, s.v., *lineament*, (1): "A line; also, a delineation, diagram, outline, sketch; *pl.* outlines, designs. lit. and fig."; and (Obs. 3): "In narrower sense, a portion of the face viewed with respect to its outline; a feature."

41. Ricks, "Wordsworth: 'A Pure Organic Pleasure,'" 6–7.

42. Dorothy Wordsworth to Jane Pollard, 6 October 1790, EY 39.

43. See Jonathan Arac's compelling reading of this revision in "Bounding Lines: *The Prelude* and Critical Revision," *Boundary*, 7 (1979), 31–48.

44. For example, see Hewitt, *Map of a Nation*, 201–6.

45. On nature inscriptions and the convention of the *genius loci* (spirit of the place), see Geoffrey Hartman, "Wordsworth, Inscriptions, and Romantic Nature Poetry," in *Beyond Formalism: Literary Essays 1958–1970* (New Haven: Yale University Press, 1970), 211–13. See also Chapter 1.

46. The principal text I will use is reading text 2 of the poem, the first published text, as appears in *Shorter Poems, 1807–1820*, 97–98 (lines 10, 1–6).

47. Hartman, *Beyond Formalism*, 222.

48. *The Fenwick Notes of William Wordsworth*, ed. Jared Curtis (London: Bristol Classical Press, 1993), 29.

49. DC MS 80, 28v, in *Shorter Poems, 1807–1820*, p. 337.

50. *Poems by William Wordsworth*, 2 vols. (London: Longman, Hurst, Rees, Orme, and Brown, 1815), II: p. 286, lines 23–24.

51. *The Poetical Works of William Wordsworth*, 6 vols. (London: Edward Moxon, 1836–37), III: 281, 22–24.

52. On county maps, see 311 n. 40.

53. *Poems by William Wordsworth*, II: p. 286.

54. In his *Romantic Geography: Wordsworth and Anglo-European Space* (New York: Palgrave Macmillan, 1998), 160, Michael Wiley asserts that Wordsworth assumes the perspective of Colonel Mudge and reconciles himself to the project of mathematically delineating the nation. The poem's philosophical stance, I suggest, is more complex and less resolved.

55. I take the text from its first publication in *Poems by William Wordsworth* (1815), I: 305–6. It is reproduced in Wordsworth, *Shorter Poems, 1807–1820*.

56. Wiley, *Romantic Geography*, 166.

57. Wordsworth reconciles his "natural, home-centered, pastoral-idyllic geography" with the Trigonometrical Survey's "nationalistic-militaristic model of the land," which was a "necessary to safeguard whatever remained" of the former (Wiley, *Romantic Geography*, 162).

58. Wiley, *Romantic Geography*, 163.

59. Wordsworth also associates mountain lines with motion in the mind in his fragment "The Sublime and the Beautiful," in *W Prose*, II: 352.

60. *The Poetical Works of William Wordsworth*, 4 vols. (London: Longman, Rees, Orme, Brown, Evans, & Longman, 1832), II: p. 11, lines 23–25.

61. See MS photographs and transcriptions, *Shorter Poems, 1807–1820*, 341–51.

62. DC MS 80, 28r, in *Shorter Poems, 1807–1820*, 341.

63. *The Miscellaneous Poems of William Wordsworth*, 4 vols. (London: Longman, Hurst, Rees, Orme and Brown, 1820), II: p. 128, lines 23–28.

64. On the political implication of the shepherd's view of Ireland, see James M. Garrett, *Wordsworth and the Writing of the Nation* (Aldershot: Ashgate, 2008), 74.

65. "Preface" to the 1815 *Poems of William Wordsworth. W Prose*, III: 33.

66. "Preface" to the 1815 *Poems of William Wordsworth. W Prose*, III: 36.

67. *The Fenwick Notes of William Wordsworth*, 29.

68. See Delano-Smith and Kain, *English Maps: A History*, on the enlargement of scale in English maps and also late eighteenth-century attempts to depict slope more naturalistically (81–91). See also Yolande Jones, "Aspects of Relief Portrayal on 19th Century British Military Maps," *Cartographic Journal*, 11 (1974): 19–33, and Harvey, *History of Topographical Maps*, 181–83. Although lacking in detail, Emmanuel Bowen and Thomas Kitchin's *A New Map of the Counties of Cumberland and Westmoreland Divided into their Respective Wards* (approximately four miles to one inch) indicates upland in plan view (London, 1760).

69. On Roy's late eighteenth-century experimentation with the barometer for measuring height (called leveling), see Seymour, *History of the Ordnance Survey*, 13. A device introduced in the period called the clinometer could estimate slope angles (the dip) and heights, but in itself did not offer a way to measure and render entire forms. Jones implies that it is unclear how much these were used by Ordnance surveyors ("Aspects of Relief," 21).

70. Some methods involved the precise quantifying of hachures. Jones, "Aspects of Relief," 20; Dawson quoted in Jones, "Aspects of Relief," 21.

71. On the Ordnance Survey as a training ground and on Robert Dawson's "natural history principle" of drawing, see Jones, "Aspects of Relief," 21–27, and also see Seymour, *History of the Ordnance Survey*, 50–53.

72. Harley and Oliver report the impression of slope can be "confused"; one Ordnance official found contours "clear in the upland but confused in the lowland area of the sheet" (*Northern England and the Isle of Man*, xiii).

73. Major General Sir James Carmichael-Smyth, *Memoir upon the Topographical System of Colonel Van Gorkum* (London, 1828), 1, cf. 8 and 2.

74. Carmichael-Smyth, *Memoir upon the Topographical System*, 53. Carmichael-Smyth

promoted a mode of ascertaining slope by treating it as a hypotenuse of a right-angled triangle. His revision of a recent Dutch method regulated hachures by assigning particular thicknesses and lengths of line—called "normals"—to particular angles of slope, whose precise degree could be assessed by reference to a published scale (1; 20).

75. For the most detailed history of the introduction of contours to the topographical maps of Great Britain, Ireland, and Scotland, see Harley and Oliver, *Northern England and the Isle of Man*, vii–xxvi.

76. Eduard Imhof makes clear the distinction: "In contrast to contours, shading and shadow tones can never express the forms of features with metric accuracy, since they possess only visual character. In the depiction of forms this method of surface tone gradation is far superior to the network of contour lines, as it can reveal individual shapes and the complete form at one and the same time. Shading and shadow tones, therefore, are effective additions to contours in many maps, transforming the metric framework into a continuous surface. On the other hand, they can be used alone, without contours." Imhof, *Cartographic Relief Presentation*, ed. H. J. Steward (Berlin: Walter de Gruyter, 1982), 159.

77. Harley and Oliver explain that the committee's reason for convening was to determine the scale at which Scotland would be mapped; with the display of contoured map 91 SE at the Great Exhibition, however, the committee's debate focused on modes of relief depiction (*Northern England and the Isle of Man*, xii).

78. Lieutenant Colonel Dawson to Sir C. Trevelyan, *Correspondence on Contouring and Hill Delineation*, No. 3, Parliamentary Papers. Accounts and Papers (7) 1854, 349.

79. Dawson to Trevelyan, 349.

80. Map 91 SE, in its second incarnation, appeared with hachure lines drawn in the office from a base grid of contour lines. This practice, which began in the 1840s, was discontinued in 1854.

81. Dawson to Trevelyan, 349.

82. Dawson to Trevelyan, 349.

83. Robert Dawson, "Thoughts on Plan-Drawing, with Particular Reference to the Representation of the Physical Forms of Ground in Topographical Maps," *Correspondence on Contouring and Hill Delineation*. Parliamentary Papers. Accounts and Papers (7) 1854, 362.

84. *The Works of John Ruskin*, ed. E. T. Cook and Alexander Wedderburn, 39 vols. (London: George Allen, 1903–1912), vol. III *Modern Painters*, 307. In the earliest volumes of *Modern Painters*, used by Dawson, Ruskin's engagement with landscape was thoroughly Wordsworthian. Each volume began with an epigraph from *The Excursion*; Ruskin also quoted "Tintern Abbey" to demonstrate how the artist is "to hold to the unpenetrated forest and the unfurrowed hill" (III, *Modern Painters*, 628). Several other quotations from Wordsworth's poetry exemplified "the intense penetrative depth of Wordsworth" (V, *Modern Painters*, 330). For his part, Wordsworth praised Ruskin for having "given abundant proof how closely he has observed and how deeply he has reflected" in *Modern Painters. The Letters of William and Dorothy Wordsworth, The Later Years, Part IV, 1840–53*, ed. Ernest de Selincourt, rev. Alan G. Hill (Oxford: Oxford University Press, 1988), 780–81.

85. Robert Dawson, "Thoughts on Plan-Drawing," 360, 363.

86. Robert Dawson, "Thoughts on Plan-Drawing," 359, 361.

87. Lt. Col. Dawson to Trevelyan, 352, 354.

88. Lt. Col. Dawson to Trevelyan, 354.

89. Lt. Col. Dawson to Trevelyan, 350.

90. Robert Dawson, "Thoughts on Plan-Drawing," 360, 361.

91. Robert Dawson, "Thoughts on Plan-Drawing," 361.

92. Qtd. in Jones, "Aspects of Relief," 20.

93. Robert Dawson, "Thoughts on Plan-Drawing," 359.

94. Robert Dawson, "Thoughts on Plan-Drawing," 359, 361.

95. Robert Dawson, "Thoughts on Plan-Drawing," 359, 363, citing *Modern Painters, The Works of John Ruskin*, III: 161.

96. Robert Dawson, "Thoughts on Plan-Drawing," 359.

97. Lt. Col. Dawson to Trevelyan, 350, 354.

98. Lt. Col. Dawson to Trevelyan, 359.

99. Thomas Arnold cited in Lt. Col. Dawson to Trevelyan, 359.

100. Robert Dawson, "Thoughts on Plan-Drawing," 363.

101. Robert Dawson, "Thoughts on Plan-Drawing," 363, citing *Modern Painters, The Works of John Ruskin*, III: 468.

102. Quoted in Harley and Oliver, *Northern England and the Isle of Man*, xvi.

103. Robert Dawson, "Thoughts on Plan-Drawing," 363, citing Ruskin, *Modern Painters, The Works of John Ruskin*, III: 262.

104. Matthew Arnold, "Ordnance Maps," *Democratic Education*, vol. II, ed. R. H. Super (Ann Arbor: University of Michigan, 1962), 253.

105. Arnold, *Democratic Education*, 253.

106. Arnold, *Democratic Education*, 253. Though appearing to reduce the symbolic content of maps to shading and names, Arnold merely opposes these cartographic elements to criticize the Ordnance Survey's inattention to shading. Arnold's opposition points to the Ordnance Survey's increasing prioritization of names over and against hachuring and their valorization of legibility over and against expressivity.

107. Arnold, *Democratic Education*, 255–56.

108. As Seymour explains, Roy did take the representation of relief seriously, and he criticized the late eighteenth-century mapmakers for their seeming disregard to a matter he deemed crucial for military not aesthetic reasons (*History of the Ordnance Survey*, 7).

109. Carmichael-Smyth, *Memoir upon the Topographical System*, 53.

110. Arnold, *Democratic Education*, 253.

111. Arnold's letter literalizes Benedict Anderson's understanding of the nation as an imaginary community: community that exists by virtue of its opportunity to imagine the national form into being. *Imagined Communities: Reflections on the Origin and Spread of Nationalism* (London: Verso, 1983).

112. Robert Dawson, "Thoughts on Plan-Drawing," 363.

113. Arnold, "Memorial Verses," *Poetical Works of Matthew Arnold* (New York: A. L. Burt, 1900), 273–74. Arnold's poems are all cited from this edition.

INTERCHAPTER

1. Martin J. S. Rudwick, "The Emergence of a Visual Language for Geological Science, 1760–1840," *History of Science*, 14 (1976): 149–95 (151).

2. J. B. Harley, *The New Nature of Maps: Essays in the History of Cartography* (Baltimore: Johns Hopkins University Press, 2002), 54.

3. William Kenrick's 1773 *Dictionary*, incorporated a rhetorical grammar in which the *Elements of Speech in general and those of the English Tongue in particular are analyzed; and the Rudiments of Articulation, Pronunciation, and Prosody intelligibly displayed.*

4. Sheridan, *Lectures on the Art of Reading, First Part, Containing the Art of Reading Prose* (London, 1775), 146. See also Sheridan, *A Course of Lectures on Elocution* (London, 1798), 32.

5. See John Thelwall, *Illustrations of English Rhythmus: Selections for the Illustration of a Course of Instructions on the Rhythmus and Utterance of the English Language* (London, 1812).

6. Paul Fussell, *Theory of Prosody in Eighteenth-Century England* (Hamden, CT: Archon Books, 1966), 80, 134.

7. Say, *Poems on Several Occasions and Two Critical Essays* (London, 1745), 104.

8. *Poems on Several Occasions*, 174, 172, 173.

9. Fussell, *Theory of Prosody*, 153.

10. Thomas Sheridan, *A Course of Lectures on Elocution*, 154.

11. Sheridan, *A Course of Lectures on Elocution*, 155–57.

12. Sheridan, *Lectures on the Art of Reading, Second Part, Containing the Art of Reading Verse* (London, 1775), 387.

13. Walker, *Elements of Elocution: Being the Substance of a Course of Lectures on the Art of Reading*, 2 vols. (London, 1781) I: 139.

14. R. C. Alston, editorial headnote to Joshua Steele, *Essay Towards Establishing the Melody and Measure of Speech to Be Expressed and Perpetuated by Peculiar Symbols* (1775; facs. rpt. Menston, Yorks.: Scolar Press, 1969).

15. Steele, *An Essay Towards Establishing the Melody and Measure of Speech*, 17.

16. Steele, *An Essay Towards Establishing the Melody and Measure of Speech*, 4–5.

17. Michael Maittaire, *The English Grammar: Or, an Essay on the Art of Grammar, Applied to and Exemplified in the English Tongue* (1712; facs. rpt. Menston Yorks.: Scolar Press, 1967), 193.

18. Steele, *An Essay Towards Establishing the Melody and Measure of Speech*, 5.

19. Sheridan, *A Course of Lectures on Elocution*, 184.

20. William Cockin, *The Art of Delivering Language* (1775; facs. rpt. Menston, Yorks.: Scolar Press, 1969), 82.

21. Catherine Delano-Smith and Roger J. P. Kain, *English Maps: A History* (Toronto: University of Toronto Press, 1999), 89.

22. Steele dedicated his *Essay* to the Royal Society ("Instituted for the Improvement of Natural Knowledge") as well as to the "Society for the Encouragement of the Arts," usually referred to as the Society of Arts.

23. Steele, *An Essay Towards Establishing the Melody and Measure of Speech*, 17. Steele refers to the chromatico-diatonic scale.

24. Steele, *An Essay Towards Establishing the Melody and Measure of Speech*, 5.

25. Only in the 1830s did spot heights begin to appear on Ordnance Survey topographical maps.

26. John Denham, "Cooper's Hill," *Poems and Translations; with the Sophy, a Tragedy*, 5th ed. (London, 1709), lines 40, 160, 42, 43–44. (The remediated couplet represents lines 191–92.) As Steele's emphasis is the "rhythmus of quantity" in this example, not "melody," he illustrates the cadences and the temporal quantities of thesis, arsis, and rests.

27. On the construction of the speech of Ireland and Scotland as provincial dialects of a "standard" English spoken in London, see Lynda Mugglestone, *Talking Proper: The Rise of Accent as Social Symbol* (Oxford: Oxford University Press, 2007), 44–47.

28. Steele, *An Essay Towards Establishing the Melody and Measure of Speech*, 11; Walker, *Elements of Elocution*, 121.

29. The lines on the abolition movement remain but are slightly changed: after the C-stage

revision, no political "contention" but the "first memorable onset" of abolition stirs the air (1850, X: 247).

30. "Day after day, up early and down late, / From vale to vale, from hill to hill we went" (1805, VI: 431–32).

31. "On the Morning of Christ's Nativity," commemorating the moment when "That glorious Form, that Light insufferable" "chose with us a darksome house of mortal clay," lines 9, 14.

CHAPTER 4

1. Thomas Sheridan, *Lectures on the Art of Reading, First Part, Containing the Art of Reading Prose* (London, 1775), 146–47.

2. W. J. B. Owen, *Wordsworth as Critic* (Toronto: University of Toronto Press, 1969). Owen's goal is not to historicize forcible communication but to draw out the naturalism of the Preface: the "attempt to define a permanent rhetoric is for Wordsworth a means of aligning poetry with nature, of giving it, as far as possible, a form as 'steady' and as 'perennial' as that of the mountain" (8, 5).

3. Hans Aarslef, "Wordsworth, Language, and Romanticism," in his *From Locke to Saussure: Essays on the Study of Language and Intellectual History* (Minneapolis: University of Minnesota Press, 1982), 372–81. On Wordsworth's adaptation to autobiography of the primitive encounter at the core of Enlightenment speculative histories of language, see Alan Bewell, *Wordsworth and the Enlightenment: Nature, Man, and Society in the Experimental Poetry* (New Haven: Yale University Press, 1989), 71–213. See also James K. Chandler, *Wordsworth's Second Nature: A Study of the Poetry and Politics* (Chicago: University of Chicago Press, 1984), 216–34.

4. Alan Richardson, *British Romanticism and the Science of Mind* (Cambridge: Cambridge University Press, 2005), 75.

5. *British Romanticism and the Science of Mind*, 77, 81.

6. Notable exceptions include Andrew Elfenbein, *Romanticism and the Rise of English* (Stanford: Stanford University Press, 2009) and Lucy Newlyn, *Reading, Writing, and Romanticism: The Anxiety of Reception* (Oxford: Oxford University Press, 2000).

7. MS A of *The Ruined Cottage*, composed between March and 4–7 June 1797, and containing the tale of Margaret and her husband. See *The Ruined Cottage and The Pedlar*, ed. James Butler (Ithaca: Cornell University Press, 1979), 79–87.

8. MS B (DC MS 17), the first complete manuscript of *The Ruined Cottage*. See *The Ruined Cottage and The Pedlar*, 46. Editors surmise that the Alfoxden Notebook contained work on the introduction to *The Ruined Cottage*, which itself included the brief history of the Pedlar, and that these lines contributed to lines 1–147 of MS B (13). For the dating of the passage, see 13 and 18–21.

9. Only two pages (50v and 6r) of the Discharged Soldier are extant in MS 14 (the Alfoxden Notebook). Letters on stubs 3, 4, and 5, however, indicate that the pages "once contained a version" of lines 1–102 of the passage.

10. On the earliest versions of the then untitled poem, in the Alfoxden and Christabel Notebooks and MS Verse 18A, see Beth Darlington, "Two Early Texts: *A Night-Piece* and *The Discharged Soldier*," in *Bicentenary Wordsworth Studies in Memory of John Alban Finch*, ed. Jonathan Wordsworth, Ephim Fogel, and Beth Darlington (Ithaca: Cornell University Press, 1970), 425–48. My citations of the poem, however, are from the version presented in LB 278–82.

11. Celeste Langan, *Romantic Vagrancy: Wordsworth and the Simulation of Freedom* (Cambridge: Cambridge University Press, 1995), 189–200.

12. Milestones were a feature of the eighteenth-century roads built by the army in Scotland and India to facilitate the movement of troops and so quell uprisings. On milestones as "measure" of "the vastness of empire" and of the "infinite expansion of capital," see Langan, *Romantic Vagrancy*, 223–24.

13. Samuel Johnson, *A Dictionary of the English Language* (London, 1755). Compare the *OED* definition of emphatic: (1989) s.v. "emphatic." "Of language, modes of statement or representation; also of tones, gesture, etc. Forcibly expressive."

14. *OED* (1989), s.v. "emphasis," see sense 6.

15. Murray Cohen, *Sensible Words: Linguistic Practice in England, 1640–1785* (Baltimore: John Hopkins University Press, 1977), 79.

16. Joseph Priestley, *The Rudiments of English Grammar Adapted to the Use of Schools; with Examples of English Composition* (London, 1761; facs. rpt. Menston, Yorks.: Scolar Press, 1969), 50.

17. John Herries, *Elements of Speech* (London, 1773), 217.

18. Herries, *Elements of Speech*, 217.

19. *Quintilian's Institutes of Oratory, or Education of an Orator*, trans. Rev. John Selby Watson (London: George Bell and Sons, 1903), II: 106, 107.

20. Heinrich Lausberg, *Handbook of Literary Rhetoric: A Foundation for Literary Study*, ed. David E. Orton and R. Dean Anderson (Leiden: Brill, 1998), 262–63.

21. Lausberg differentiates figures of speech and thought: "*figurae elocutionis* have to do with linguistic concretization itself (changed precisely by the *figurae*), *figurae sententiae* on the other hand go beyond the realm of *elocutio* and have to do with the conception of ideas" (273).

22. *Quintilian's Institutes of Oratory*, II: 155, 170.

23. Lausberg, *Handbook of Literary Rhetoric*, 396.

24. George Puttenham, *The Arte of English Poesie*, ed. Edward Arber (London, 1869), 155, 194.

25. *OED* (1989) s.v. "emphasis," see sense 2.

26. Wilbur S. Howell, *Eighteenth-Century British Logic and Rhetoric* (Princeton: Princeton University Press, 1971), 243.

27. *OED* (1989) s.v. "emphasize": "To impart emphasis to (anything); to lay stress upon (a word or phrase in speaking); to add force to (speech, arguments, actions, etc.); to lay stress upon, bring into special prominence (a fact, idea, feature in a representation, etc.)."

28. Thomas Sheridan, *A Rhetorical Grammar of the English Language: Calculated Solely for the Purposes of Teaching Propriety of Pronunciation, and Justness of Delivery, in That Tongue, by the Organs of Speech* (London, 1781; facs. rpt. Menston, Yorks.: Scolar Press, 1969), 159.

29. John Locke, *An Essay Concerning Human Understanding*, in *The Works of John Locke*, 3 vols. (London: John Churchill, 1714), I: 238.

30. Vivian Salmon, "English Punctuation Theory 1500–1800," *Anglia: Zeitschrift fur Englische Philologie*, 106.3–4 (1988), 285–314 (306); Michael Maittaire, *The English Grammar: Or, an Essay on the Art of Grammar, Applied to and Exemplified in the English Tongue* (1712; facs. rpt. Menston, Yorks.: Scolar Press, 1967), 200–201.

31. Maittaire, *The English Grammar*, 201–2.

32. Accent diverged from its standard placement in a word only under the condition of "plain Opposition" in a sentence. Watts, *The Art of Reading and Writing English, or The*

Chief-Principles and Rules of Pronouncing our Mother-Tongue, both in Prose and Verse; with a Variety of Instructions for True Spelling (1721; facs. rpt. Menston, Yorks.: Scolar Press, 1972), 56–57.

33. Watts, *The Art of Reading*, 57. This work was repeatedly printed from 1721 to at least 1783 on both sides of the Atlantic.

34. Watts, *Art of Reading*, 59. Salmon observes Watts' primacy in this recognition ("English Punctuation Theory 1500–1800," 307).

35. Lindley Murray, *English Grammar* (1795; facs. rpt. Menston, Yorks.: Scolar Press, 1968), 155.

36. Murray, *English Grammar*, 154. Although Robert Lowth does not treat emphasis in his 1762 *English Grammar*, Murray does (1795), demonstrating the influence of the elocutionary movement on the teaching of grammar.

37. Cohen, *Sensible Words*, 119.

38. Locke, *An Essay Concerning Human Understanding* in *The Works of John Locke*, I; 182.

39. See, Aeschylus, *Persians*, 518, and Euripides, *Bacchae*, 22. My gratitude to Timothy Bahti for clarification of the early Greek senses and for the examples.

40. Sheridan, *A Course of Lectures on Elocution* (London, 1798), 110.

41. Watts, *Art of Reading*, 59; Matthew Arnold, "Ordnance Maps," *Democratic Education*, vol. II, ed. R. H. Super (Ann Arbor: University of Michigan Press, 1962), 253.

42. Sheridan, *A Course of Lectures on Elocution*, 129.

43. Sheridan, *A Rhetorical Grammar*, xvi.

44. Sheridan, *A Course of Lectures on Elocution*, 164, 165.

45. Sheridan, *A Course of Lectures on Elocution*, 186.

46. Sheridan, *A Course of Lectures on Elocution*, 132, 125.

47. Samuel Say, *Poems on Several Occasions, and Two Critical Essays* (London, 1745), 98.

48. John Rice, *An Introduction to the Art of Reading with Energy and Propriety* (London, 1765), 353, 195.

49. Sheridan, *The Art of Speaking*, 7th ed. (London, 1792), 11.

50. Sheridan, *A Course of Lectures on Elocution*, 130.

51. Sheridan, *A Course of Lectures on Elocution*, 120. Sheridan suggests that "gross errours" in the pronunciation of the church service both amount to and incite the commission of sins.

52. Sheridan, *A Course of Lectures on Elocution*, 129.

53. Howell, *Eighteenth-Century British Logic and Rhetoric*, 240. Sheridan, *A Rhetorical Grammar*, xviii.

54. Sheridan, *British Education* (Dublin, 1756), 202.

55. Sheridan, *A Course of Lectures on Elocution*, 69, 128–29.

56. John Walker, *A Rhetorical Grammar, or Course of Lessons in Elocution* (1785; facs. rpt. Menston, Yorks.: Scolar Press, 1971), 99.

57. John Walker, *A Critical Pronouncing Dictionary* (1791; facs. rpt. Menston, Yorks.: Scolar Press, 1968), vii.

58. *Quintilian's Institutes of Oratory*, II: 355.

59. Herries, *Elements of Speech*, 218.

60. Sheridan, *A Course of Lectures on Elocution*, 129.

61. Sheridan, *A Course of Lectures on Elocution*, 128. As Paula McDowell has argued, "literate groups' ideas about oral forms and practices developed in an especially close dialectical relationship with ideas about print (especially print commerce)" ("Mediating Media Past and Present: Toward a Genealogy of 'Print Culture' and 'Oral Tradition,'" in *This Is Enlightenment*, ed. Clifford Siskin and William Warner [Chicago: University of Chicago Press, 2010], 246).

62. Sheridan, *Lectures on the Art of Reading, First Part,* 181–82.

63. Sheridan, *Lectures on the Art of Reading, First Part,* 286, 297–98.

64. Sheridan, *Lectures on the Art of Reading, Second Part, Containing the Art of Reading Verse* (London, 1775), 387, 389.

65. Walker, *Rhetorical Grammar,* 111.

66. Elfenbein, *Romanticism and the Rise of English,* 114.

67. Walker, *Rhetorical Grammar,* 100, 112.

68. Walker, *Rhetorical Grammar,* 114–19. For Walker's theory of inflexion, see the Interchapter.

69. Rather than value his advice to "avoid artificiality and to keep to [a] natural manner of delivery," some of the instructors Sheridan inspired "valued instead his idea that rules could be devised to enable ordained teachers in the art of arousing passions by a system of fixed tones and gestures." Howell, *Eighteenth-Century British Logic and Rhetoric,* 243. Sheridan, *Lectures on the Art of Reading, First Part,* 153.

70. Enfield, *The Speaker: or, Miscellaneous Pieces, Selected from the Best English Writers* (London, 1782), xviii.

71. Cockin, *The Art of Delivering Written Language, or, An Essay on Reading: in Which the Subject is Treated Philosophically as well as with a View to Practice* (London, 1775), 41, 44–52.

72. Cockin, *The Art of Delivering Written Language,* 149–50.

73. These are the only extant manuscript lines of Dorothy's Alfoxden journal, parts of which were first published by William Knight in 1889. Pamela Woof disputes their common attribution to Dorothy, observing that vocabulary and syntax "point rather to W[illiam]" as the base author. *The Grasmere and Alfoxden Journals,* ed. Pamela Woof (Oxford: World's Classics, 2008), 274.

74. When the "moon burst through the invisible veil which enveloped her," Dorothy records, "the shadows of the oaks blackened, and their lines became more strongly marked." When a "white thin cloud" again covers the moon, the "sky is flat, unmarked by distances;" the dog "makes a strange, uncouth howl." Dorothy Wordsworth, *The Grasmere and Alfoxden Journals,* 142.

75. *The Grasmere and Alfoxden Journals,* 142.

76. The Wordsworths were writing forward from the first leaf and backward from the last leaf in the notebook. The Payne Knight quotation appears on 49v. See LB 715–16. Butler and Green omit Dorothy's "Dr."

77. See my discussion of Johnson and the heroic measure in Chapter 1.

78. Richard Payne Knight, *The Progress of Civil Society* (London, 1796). He also credited the "roughness" of English diction for giving "Impressive sense and energy" to poetry (it "stamps, in sound less flowing and refined, / Each thought and image strongly on the mind" (III: 522–24).

79. Hugh Blair, *Lectures on Rhetoric and Belles Lettres,* 3rd ed., 3 vols. (London, 1787), II: 438.

80. On Wordsworth and Quintilian see Brad Sullivan, *Wordsworth and the Composition of Knowledge: Refiguring Relationships Among Minds, Worlds, and Words* (New York: Peter Lang, 2000). See also Roger N. Murray, *Wordsworth's Style: Figures and Themes in the "Lyrical Ballads" of 1800* (Lincoln: University of Nebraska Press, 1967), 37 note 3.

81. *Quintilian's Institutes of Oratory,* II: 155.

82. James Burgh, *The Art of Speaking, in Two Parts,* 2nd ed. (Dublin, 1763), title page. On *The Speaker,* see Dorothy Wordsworth, *The Grasmere and Alfoxden Journals,* 85–86.

83. Langan, *Romantic Vagrancy,* suggests that Wordsworth's aesthetic drive to present the self as autonomous (aesthetically, politically) depends upon a staged encounter with the

vagabond-double. Wordsworth's is a strategy of reduction and displacement, refusing to engage fully with the vagrant, resulting from aesthetic drive.

84. Langan, *Romantic Vagrancy*, 177.

85. Newlyn, *Coleridge, Wordsworth and the Language of Allusion* (Oxford: Clarendon Press, 1986), 30; Geoffrey H. Hartman, *Wordsworth's Poetry 1787–1814* (New Haven: Yale University Press, 1964), 12. And according to Bewell, "we can see the Discharged Soldier as a figure of superseded fictions, a belated version of the Dantesque and Miltonic sublime." Bewell, *Wordsworth and the Enlightenment*, 91.

86. Watts, *Art of Reading*, 59.

87. Sheridan, *A Course of Lectures on Elocution*, 215. Peter De Bolla notes the importance of coordinating gestures, looks, and vocal tones. (*The Discourse of the Sublime: Readings in History, Aesthetics and the Subject* [London: Basil Blackwell, 1989], 179).

88. Enfield, *The Speaker*, xv.

89. Burgh, *The Art of Speaking*, 16.

90. *The Art of Speaking*, 16.

91. Peter De Bolla explains, "The text must become internalized, thereby turning the dead letter into living speech. . . . The exterior textual matter is assimilated within the interior sentiments of the mind of the orator, who then expresses the combined text/internal sentiment" in the appropriate manner." *Discourse of the Sublime*, 167.

92. Sheridan, *A Course of Lectures on Elocution*, 115.

93. Burgh, *The Art of Speaking*, 12.

94. Blair, *Lectures on Rhetoric and Belles Lettres*, II: 448–49.

95. Burgh, *The Art of Speaking*, 12. Compare Sheridan, *A Course of Lectures on Elocution*, 128–29.

96. De Bolla, *Discourse of the Sublime*, 231.

97. On the soldier's alienation and its social causes, see discussions by, among others, Alan Bewell, *Romanticism and Colonial Disease* (Baltimore: Johns Hopkins University Press, 1999); Gary Harrison, *Wordsworth's Vagrant Muse: Poetry, Poverty and Power* (Detroit: Wayne State University Press, 1994); Langan, *Romantic Vagrancy*; and David Simpson, *Wordsworth's Historical Imagination: The Poetry of Displacement* (New York: Methuen, 1987).

98. De Bolla, *Discourse of the Sublime*, 159.

99. On the allusion to Dante's *selva oscura* and the way in which the "journey takes on the symbolical resonances of a classical catabasis," see Bewell, *Wordsworth and the Enlightenment*, 88.

100. Herries, *Elements of Speech*, 218.

101. Sheridan, *A Course of Lectures on Elocution*, 186, 32.

102. Herries, *Elements of Speech*, 218.

103. Paul D. Sheats has argued that the soldier redeems Wordsworth from the solipsism he enjoyed at the start of the passage. Sheats, *The Making of Wordsworth's Poetry, 1785–1798* (Cambridge MA: Harvard University Press, 1973). For an alternative reading, see Lucy Newlyn, *Coleridge, Wordsworth and the Language of Allusion*, 29.

104. According to Alan Bewell, "the episode thus incorporates an idea of literary history that justifies the notion of a poetry of everyday life. For the 'man' that speaks in Wordsworth's poetry to appear, 'a man speaking to men,' he had first to pass through the sublime underworld of a fear-enchanted past, whose vestigial traces and echoes can still be found in dreams and the fictions of romance." Bewell, *Wordsworth and the Enlightenment*, 91.

105. Burgh, *The Art of Speaking*, 16.

106. Sheridan, *A Course of Lectures on Elocution*, 129.

107. See, for example, Langan, *Romantic Vagrancy*, 19–20.

108. Langan, *Romantic Vagrancy*, 164, 200. See also 171–75.

109. Say, *Poems on Several Occasions*, 142.

110. Payne Knight, *Progress of Civil Society*, III: 530.

111. Payne Knight, *Progress of Civil Society*, quoted in the Alfoxden Notebook (LB 715–16).

112. Sheridan, *A Course of Lectures on Elocution*, 156.

113. Sheridan, *A Course of Lectures on Elocution*, 132.

114. Sheridan, *A Course of Lectures on Elocution*, 109.

115. I offer this not as a definitive but possible voicing of the line. A four-beat alternative, "The *gravita*tion and the *fili*al *bond*," is also possible. Both readings expose the limitations of the foot-based system of scansion promoted by George Saintsbury in his *History of English Prosody: From the 12th Century to the Present Day* (London: Macmillan, 1906–10), and point up the dependency of metrical description on performance. For an application of Derek Attridge's more nuanced system (*The Rhythms of English Poetry* [London: Longman, 1982]), see Brennan O'Donnell, *The Passion of Meter: A Study of Wordsworth's Metrical Art* (Kent, Ohio: Kent State University Press, 1995).

116. Sheridan, *Lectures on the Art of Reading, First Part*, 148.

117. See the discussions of activity and energy in the vitalist philosophy of Joseph Priestley and his followers in H. W. Piper, *The Active Universe: Pantheism and the Concept of Imagination in the English Romantic Poets* (London: Athlone Press, 1962). The elocutionary conception of emphasis here resonates with what Paul de Man calls the "face-making," "totalizing power of language." *The Rhetoric of Romanticism* (New York: Columbia University Press, 1984), 91.

118. Sheridan, *Lectures on the Art of Reading, First Part*, 301.

119. Sheridan, *A Course of Lectures on Elocution*, 129.

120. In a letter to John Thelwall concerning, among other matters, his "system of metre" in blank verse, Wordsworth stated that "any dislocation of the verse" (disruption of the "Iambic") may be "justified by some passion or the other." Mid-January 1804, EY 434. See Chapter 7.

121. Herries, *Elements of Speech*, 218.

122. For a reading of the way in which Wordsworth rewrites his origin in the mother so as to identify himself as the origin of motion and e-motion, see Cathy Caruth, *Empirical Truths and Critical Fictions: Locke, Wordsworth, Kant, Freud* (Baltimore: Johns Hopkins University Press, 1991), 48–57.

123. Sheridan, *Lectures on the Art of Reading, Second Part*, 248. As he explains, the strong stress on the first syllable in the line produces an "uncommon cesura" and has a "striking" effect.

124. Sheridan, *A Rhetorical Grammar*, xvii.

125. Langan, *Romantic Vagrancy*, 195.

126. Blair, *Lectures on Rhetoric and Belles Lettres*, I: 451, 297.

127. Blair, *Lectures on Rhetoric and Belles Lettres*, I: 285, 298, 452.

128. Longinus, "On Sublimity," in *Classical Literary Criticism*, ed. D. A. Russell and Michael Winterbottom (Oxford: Oxford University Press, 1989), 164. *Quintilian's Institute of Oratory*, II: 171.

129. The babe illustrates, then, the early, more propositional lines from Goslar: "There is an active principle alive in all things," a "Spirit that knows no insulated spot, / No chasm, no solitude, —from link to link / It circulates, the soul of all the worlds" (LB 309).

130. Blair, *Lectures on Rhetoric and Belles Lettres*, I: 451.

131. Maittaire lists epanalepsis (the repetition of a word at the beginning and end of a sentence) among the "Figures or Schemes," which "alter not the signification, but enlighten and

enliven the Composure of the Words, either by an Emphatical Simple or Compounded repetition, or by a Passionate Argumentative Persuasion and Confirmation." *The English Grammar,* 221.

132. Lausberg, *Handbook of Literary Rhetoric,* 396.

CHAPTER 5

1. Thomas Sheridan, *Lectures on the Art of Reading, First Part, Containing the Art of Reading Prose* (London, 1775), 146.

2. Line 65: *The Ruined Cottage and The Pedlar,* ed. *James Butler* (Ithaca: Cornell University Press, 1979).

3. Lucy Newlyn, *Reading, Writing, and Romanticism: The Anxiety of Reception* (Oxford: Oxford University Press, 2000), 92, 98. For another treatment of Wordsworth's publication anxiety, see Andrew Franta, *Romanticism and the Rise of the Mass Public* (Cambridge: Cambridge University Press, 2007).

4. For example, John Rice, *An Introduction to the Art of Reading with Energy and Propriety* (London, 1765), 195.

5. M. B. Parkes, *Pause and Effect: An Introduction to the History of Punctuation in the West* (Aldershot: Scolar Press, 1992), 49.

6. Vivian Salmon, "English Punctuation Theory 1500–1800," *Anglia: Zeitschrift für Englische Philologie,* 106: 3–4 (1988): 306.

7. Henry Dixon, *The English Instructor* (1728; facs. rept. Menston, Yorks.: Scolar Press, 1967), 105.

8. Michael Maittaire, *The English Grammar: Or, an Essay on the Art of Grammar, Applied to and Exemplified in the English Tongue* (1712; facs. rpt. Menston, Yorks.: Scolar Press, 1967), 193.

9. John Mason, *An Essay on Elocution and Pronunciation* (1748; facs. rpt. Menston, Yorks.: Scolar Press, 1968), 20.

10. Mason, *An Essay on Elocution and Pronunciation,* 21.

11. Mason, *An Essay on Elocution and Pronunciation,* 23.

12. See 307, n. 37.

13. Thomas Sheridan, *A Rhetorical Grammar of the English Language: Calculated Solely for the Purpose of Teaching Propriety of Pronunciation, and Justness of Delivery, in That Tongue, by the Organs of Speech* (1781; facs. rpt. Menston, Yorks.: Scolar Press, 1969), 103.

14. Sheridan, *Rhetorical Grammar,* 89, 130, 168, 108, 104, 105, 109.

15. Sheridan rejected grammarians' basing of punctuation on the quantitative system of rests in music. Thomas Sheridan, *A Complete Dictionary of the English Language, Both With Regard to Sound and Meaning: One Main Object of Which is, To Establish a Plain and Permanent Standard of Pronunciation; To Which is Prefixed a Prosodial Grammar,* 2nd ed. (London, 1789), xliv.

16. Sheridan, *Prosodial Grammar,* in *A Complete Dictionary,* xliv, lxxv.

17. Sheridan, *Prosodial Grammar,* xlvi.

18. Thomas Sheridan, *A Course of Lectures on Elocution* (London, 1798), 137.

19. Sheridan, *Rhetorical Grammar,* 104, 113.

20. William Cockin, *The Art of Delivering Written Language* (1775; facs. rpt. Menston, Yorks.: Scolar Press, 1969), 99.

21. Walker, *Elements of Elocution,* (1781; facs. rpt. Menston, Yorks.: Scolar Press, 1969), I: 111.

22. Locke, *An Essay Concerning Human Understanding,* ed. Kenneth P. Winkler (Indianapolis: Hackett, 1996), 33.

23. Abbé Batteaux, quoted in John Rice, *An Introduction to the Art of Reading with Energy and Propriety* (London, 1765), 238.

24. On the history of ellipsis marks, including the dash (but not the "blank line"), see Anne C. Henry, "The Re-mark-able Rise of '. . .': Reading Ellipsis Marks in Literary Texts," *Ma(r)king the Text: The Presentation of Meaning on the Literary Page*, ed. Joe Bray, Miriam Handley, and Anne C. Henry (Aldershot: Ashgate, 2000), 120–43. On their use in the novel, see Janine Borchas, *Graphic Design, Print Culture, and the Eighteenth-Century Novel* (Cambridge: Cambridge University Press, 2003). See also Andrew Piper's argument that, along with asterisks, floral ornament, and "blank, black, and marbled pages" in *Tristram Shandy*, dashes highlighted the inexpressible, indecent, unthinkable, or forgotten, and the silent or suspenseful passage of time. Piper, *Dreaming in Books: The Making of the Bibliographic Imagination in the Romantic Age* (Chicago: University of Chicago Press, 2009), 183.

25. Robert Lowth, *A Short Introduction to English Grammar, with Critical Notes* (London, 1762), 154–72.

26. Robertson, *An Essay on Punctuation* (1785; facs. rpt. Menston, Yorks.: Scolar Press, 1969), 29. In his examples of the use of the dash to mark "an unexpected turn in the sentiment; or a sort of epigrammatic point," Robertson uses both the short and long forms of the dash (132).

27. Walker, *Elements of Elocution*, I: 63.

28. Walker, *Elements of Elocution*, I: 106.

29. I cite the manuscript letter now held by the Beinecke Library, Yale University (*MS Vault Shelves Wordsworth—Lyrical Ballads).

30. See, for example, Lucy Newlyn, *William and Dorothy Wordsworth: All in Each Other* (Oxford: Oxford University Press, 2013) and Susan Wolfson, *Romantic Interactions: Social Being and the Turns of Literary Action* (Baltimore: Johns Hopkins University Press, 2010), 166–78, 179–207.

31. Assessing Davy's involvement in the corrections, James Butler and Karen Green observe that there is "no way of knowing whether this initial sheet of poems went to [Davy] or directly to Biggs and Cottle," given that a note directs the letter to the printers "'In case of Mr D—'s absence'" (LB 124). Moreover, the ink of the corrections "is indistinguishable from Grasmere work" and the number of corrections on the sheet is no greater than that on subsequent sheets sent directly to the printers. We know for certain that Wordsworth was actively involved in correcting the copy at Grasmere. In her journal spanning this period, Dorothy frequently mentions her brother's "altering" of his poems, and part of her entry for October 1, 1800, "we corrected the last sheet," suggests a regular and ongoing practice. Dorothy Wordsworth, *The Grasmere Journals*, ed. Pamela Woof (Oxford: Oxford University Press, 1991), 29, 23. Cornelius H. Patton, "Important Coleridge and Wordsworth Manuscripts Acquired by Yale," *Yale University Library Gazette*, 9.2 (1934): 42–45. Given Wordsworth's supervision of verbal and nonverbal elements throughout the copy, the Cornell editors can only hedge on the matter of Davy's involvement (LB 124).

32. First drafted in the *Prelude* lines of DC MS 19 (MS JJ), excerpted in a letter to Coleridge, reworked in DC MS 15, copied separately by William and Dorothy in DC MS 16, and copied again by Dorothy, "There was a Boy" is increasingly punctuated. Still, DC MS 29, Dorothy's fair copy of the poem, is significantly less punctuated than MS 1800 (the printer's copy), which adds twenty-two commas, among other signs, nineteen more than are in William's fair copy, DC MS 16.

33. Commas new to MS 1800 are in boldface here; commas apparently added to the copy in correction follow "sometimes" and "Listening."

34. Cornell *Lyrical Ballads* editors Butler and Green read the dash in Dorothy's fair copy (DC MS 29) also as double (LB 408). This is possible; it is more definitively double in MS 1800.

35. As I discuss below, two appear in "The Female Vagrant," bracketing one phrase.

36. Of authors admired by Wordsworth, two stand out for their use of the long, 2-em dash: Laurence Sterne, who uses them throughout the much admired *Tristram Shandy*, and Charlotte Smith. Wordsworth subscribed to, and gave to his daughter Dora, his copy of *Elegiac Sonnets with additional sonnets and other poems* (5th ed., London, 1789), which is pervaded by 2-em dashes. Duncan Wu, *Wordsworth's Reading, 1770–1799* (Cambridge: Cambridge University Press, 1993), 127–28.

37. Sheridan, *A Course of Lectures on Elocution*, 137.

38. Sheridan, *A Course of Lectures on Elocution*, 137–38.

39. Geoffrey H. Hartman emphasized that the significance of "the voice of mountain torrents" and "the visible scene" are not available to the boy: he has a "presentiment" of death that is only known, reflected upon, by the Wordsworthian "I" in the second verse paragraph. Commenting on Paul De Man's several readings of this passage, Timothy Bahti links the boy's unconsciousness of death to the imagery of phenomenal reflection and to the insubstantiality of linguistic trope. Like the figure of chiasmus (which reflects and reverses), the reflection of the "uncertain heaven" on the surface of the "steady lake" can be spotted on the page but not "read," that is, interpreted. See Geoffrey Hartman, *Wordsworth's Poetry 1787–1814* (New Haven: Yale University Press, 1971), 19–22; Timothy Bahti, "The Unimaginable Touch of Tropes," *Diacritics*, 25.4 (1995), 39–58.

40. Sheridan, *Prosodial Grammar*, xlvii.

41. Frances Ferguson, *Wordsworth: Language as Counter-Spirit* (New Haven: Yale University Press, 1977), 166–70.

42. Sheridan, *A Course of Lectures on Elocution*, 137, 138.

43. In "The Female Vagrant," lines 265, 266–67, 270; LB 58.

44. Ferguson, *Wordsworth: Language as Counter-Spirit*, 167.

45. Robertson, *An Essay on Punctuation*, 131.

46. For discussion of the history, and amendments to the notes in later editions, see also David Duff, "Paratextual Dilemmas: Wordsworth's 'The Brothers' and the Problems of Generic Labelling," *Romanticism*, 6.2 (2000): 234–61.

47. On the paratexts used by Romantic poets to bridge the perceived distance between author and audience, see Andrew Elfenbein, *Romanticism and the Rise of English* (Stanford: Stanford University Press, 2009), 110.

48. John Walker gave the colon double the time of the semicolon (*A Rhetorical Grammar* [London, 1785], 32). My analysis is based on the manuscript letters that Wordsworth sent to Davy and printers Biggs and Cottle (Beinecke Rare Book and Manuscript Library, Yale University: *MS. Vault Shelves Wordsworth—Lyrical Ballads, Folders 1–13). These manuscripts, designated MS 1800 in LB, are used for the Reading Text of "The Brothers" in LB.

49. For "sink" more deeply, see Sheridan, *A Course of Lectures on Elocution*, 128.

50. Susan J. Wolfson, *The Questioning Presence: Wordsworth, Keats, and the Interrogative Mode in Romantic Poetry* (Ithaca: Cornell University Press, 1986), 83–84.

51. The first dash is introduced in the printer's copy; the semicolon and final dash are introduced as corrections to the printer's copy (MS 1800). In a deflection and deferral of the truth, Leonard here points to a grave that he recognizes as his grandfather's.

52. Compare LB 392–402.

53. DC MS 174. See LB, p. 415.

54. The LB Reading Text reverts to DC MS 174's more visually dramatic final punctuation of "headlong—" (397), which is obscured by the margin of MS 1800. The printed text of 1800 shows "head-long" (see *Lyrical Ballads, with Other Poems*, 2 vols. [London: T. N. Longman and O. Rees, 1800], II, 43; also LB note for line 397 on p. 158).

55. See Anne-Lise François, *Open Secrets: The Literature of Uncounted Experience* (Stanford: Stanford University Press, 2008), 7–9.

56. The remainder of the verse ("The Priest here ended—") begins the next verse paragraph and is thus printed on the next line, aligned vertically with the end of the line above. Because the line is hypermetrical and also ends with an em dash, the 2-em dash after "hung" in the manuscript pushes Wordsworth's line to the limits of his printers' paper. (See *Lyrical Ballads, with Other Poems* [1800], II, 44). MS 1800 shows 2-em dashes also at lines 220, 263, 282, and 312; these appear in print in 1800 as em dashes.

57. The lines correspond to LB Reading Text, lines 343–51.

58. On Wordsworth's not reading proofs, see the editors' introduction to LB 127. The 1800 printed text of "The Brothers" is indeed more heavily punctuated; changes include the addition of five exclamation marks, two dashes, and quotation marks to indicate the direct speech of the Priest in the opening narrative.

59. The mark also heralds changes to the poem in the edition of 1802, in which "the publisher imposed consistent house styling." Textual presentation became more of a negotiation, insofar as Wordsworth "saw (and sometimes altered) these changes before their publication in 1802" (LB 127). The 1802 edition also raised new tensions for Wordsworth. Because in 1800 the printers had departed from the manuscript copy numerous times and egregiously omitted fifteen lines from "Michael," Wordsworth's concerns about the "business" of punctuation were now complicated by the business of negotiating with printers at a distance. On the major omission of fifteen lines from "Michael" and other printing errors, see J. E. Wells, "*Lyrical Ballads*, 1800: Cancel Leaves," *PMLA*, 53 (1938): 220–22.

60. Andrew Bennett, *Wordsworth Writing* (Cambridge: Cambridge University Press, 2007), 78–100.

61. Dorothy's fair copy of the poem, found in DC MS 16, is untitled. According to Butler and Green, no surviving documents indicate that the Contents title "originated with Wordsworth" (LB 211). That the poem is an inscription is the clear implication of the title given only in the Contents of editions from 1800 to 1820, "Lines written on a Tablet in a School," but is not otherwise a necessary inference. Wordsworth listed the poem by other names in editions after 1820.

62. In 1815, Wordsworth classified "Lines written on a Tablet in a School" as a Poem Proceeding from Sentiment and Reflection, not as an Inscription.

63. On the convention of the plea for reverence, see Geoffrey H. Hartman, "Wordsworth, Inscriptions and Romantic Nature Poetry," in *From Sensibility to Romanticism: Essays Presented to Frederick A. Pottle*, ed. Frederick W. Hilles and Harold Bloom (London: Oxford University Press, 1965), 389–414.

64. This charged image of abjection (and reduction of the human to a stagnant and immobile nature) gains force by an allusion to *King Lear*, which puts the dead Matthew on a level with Poor Tom who drinks "the green mantle of the standing pool" (III. iv).

65. Without developing the typographic implications, Bennett states, "the manual force of inscription takes on a special significance in such poems, poems in which the graphics or graphology of poetry, in which a certain graphopoesis, is contemplated and emphasized." *Wordsworth's Writing*, 81.

66. The Preface to *Lyrical Ballads* was probably composed between 29 June and 27 Sept 1800 (LB 740).

67. On the relation to discourses of discovery and coastal naming (Captain Cook), see Michael Wiley, *Romantic Geography* (New York: St. Martin's Press, 1998), 81–106, and Carol Bolton, *Writing the Empire: Robert Southey and Romantic Colonialism* (London: Pickering and Chatto, 2007), 95–109.

68. For reproduction of MS page, see LB 733.

69. Marjorie Levinson, *Wordsworth's Great Period Poems* (Cambridge: Cambridge University Press, 1986), 59.

70. The bibliographic implication of the "sheep-fold" also appears in "Inscription For the House (an Outhouse) on the Island at Grasmere," lines 9-13, where Wordsworth contrasts the homely masonry of the sheep-fold with the architectural plans of classical buildings displayed in "red Morocco folio." See LB 182–83.

71. For the dating see Stephen Parrish, *The Art of Lyrical Ballads* (Cambridge, MA: Harvard University Press, 1973), 151, 149–54.

72. Although the Cornell reading text, which is based on MS 1800, does not record this, the manuscript clearly shows a 2-em dash at the start of the line (LB 389). Evidently, while correcting the comma at the end of the previous line to a period (which Cornell does record in the list of nonverbal variants), Davy or the printer also changed the 2-em dash to an em dash.

73. Brennan O'Donnell, *The Passion of Meter: A Study of Wordsworth's Metrical Art* (Kent OH: Kent State University Press, 1995), 182.

74. Qtd. in Parrish, *The Art of Lyrical Ballads*, 183.

75. See Parrish, *The Art of Lyrical Ballads*, 183–84. In his letter to Fox, Wordsworth quoted from Quintilian (*Institutio Oratoria*, X. vii. 15; Loeb) claims that he would use as the epigraph for the 1802 and 1805 editions: "It is feeling and force of imagination that make us eloquent. It is for this reason that even the uneducated have no difficulty in finding words to express their meaning, if only they are stirred by some strong emotion" (qtd. in LB 377–78).

76. O'Donnell, *The Passion of Meter*, 179–80. Lines encompassed "dramatic, narrative, philosophical, autobiographical, descriptive, and lyric genres" (180).

77. There are 2,843 lines in volume II. I thank Michael Gamer for confirming my calculations.

78. See O'Donnell's sensitive demonstration of Wordsworth's variety of blank-verse voices in *The Passion of Meter*, 179–237; and on the double negative structure throughout "Tintern Abbey," see Elfenbein, *The Rise of English*, 53–54.

79. On the presentation of the surface for visual imagination see Elaine Scarry, "Imagining Flowers: Perceptual Mimesis (Particularly Delphinium)," *Representations*, 57 (Winter 1997): 90–115.

80. The semicolon in line 53 is added for the 1802 edition but included in the LB Reading Text.

CHAPTER 6

1. A rare exception is the opening invocation of the breeze (1805, line 5). *The Prelude: 1799, 1805, 1850*, ed. Jonathan Wordsworth, M. H. Abrams, and Stephen Gill (New York: W. W. Norton, 1979). Henceforth cited as Norton. This edition remains in print and is advertised by the publisher as one of "the essential texts for studying this author" in the new edition of *Wordsworth's*

Poetry and Prose, ed. Nicholas Halmi (New York: W. W. Norton, 2013). In the *Prelude* text that Halmi prints, the exclamation marks, silently omitted in 1979, are returned to the 1805 poem. On "the poem to Coleridge," see Norton, ix.

2. Mary Jacobus, *Romanticism, Writing and Sexual Difference: Essays on* The Prelude (Oxford: Clarendon Press, 1989), 176–77.

3. Alan Richardson, *The Neural Sublime: Cognitive Theories and Romantic Texts* (Baltimore: Johns Hopkins University Press, 2010), 68. For a Bakhtinian reading of Wordsworthian apostrophe, particularly in *Lyrical Ballads*, see Michael Mackovski, *Dialogue and Literature: Apostrophe, Auditors, and the Collapse of Romantic Discourse* (New York: Oxford University Press, 1994).

4. See, for example, *Romanticism, An Anthology*, ed. Duncan Wu, 4th ed. (Oxford: Wiley Blackwell, 2012), p. 363, lines 88, 110.

5. Jacobus, *Romanticism, Writing and Sexual Difference*, 166.

6. Jonathan Culler's reference to *apostrophe* as embarrassing put the figure, along with *prosopopoeia*, emphasized by Paul de Man, at the center of discussion of lyric. Culler, "Apostrophe," *Diacritics*, 7.4 (1977): 59–69.

7. Theodor W. Adorno, *Notes to Literature*, vol. I, trans. Shierry Weber Nicholsen (New York: Columbia University Press, 1991), 90.

8. Wordsworth's "red" should be punningly read—read "with overtoil." In an influential reading, Neil Hertz drew attention to the figuration of the cityscape as a visual surface that threatens to erode the difference between reading and seeing and thereby to disable Wordsworth's writing of autobiography. "The Notion of Blockage in the Literature of the Sublime," *The End of the Line: Essays on Psychoanalysis and the Sublime* (New York: Columbia University Press, 1985), 56–60, quotation on 57.

9. Thomas Sheridan, *A Rhetorical Grammar of the English Language: Calculated Solely for the Purposes of Teaching Propriety of Pronunciation, and Justness of Delivery, in That Tongue, by the Organs of Speech* (London: 1781; reprint Menston, Yorks.: Scolar Press, 1969), 128.

10. Thomas Sheridan, *A Course of Lectures on Elocution* (London, 1798), xv.

11. Sheridan, *A Course of Lectures on Elocution*, 186.

12. Thomas Sheridan, *A Complete Dictionary of the English Language, Both With Regard to Sound and Meaning: One Main Object of Which is, To Establish a Plain and Permanent Standard of Pronunciation; To Which is Prefixed a Prosodial Grammar*, 2nd ed. (London, 1789), xlvi.

13. John Walker, *Elements of Elocution*, vol. 1 (1781; facs. rpt. Menston, Yorks.: Scolar Press, 1969), 319.

14. [Notebook Draft of an Essay on Punctuation], *The Complete Poems of Samuel Taylor Coleridge*, ed. William Keach (London: Penguin, 1997), 422.

15. Hugh Blair, *Lectures on Rhetoric and Belles Lettres*, 3rd ed., 3 vols. (London, 1787), I: 451.

16. Adorno, *Notes to Literature*, I: 93.

17. Joseph Robertson, *An Essay on Punctuation* (1785; facs. rpt. Menston, Yorks.: Scolar Press, 1969), 103.

18. Robertson, *An Essay on Punctuation*, 103, quoting "Introduction to the Study of Polite Literature."

19. MS JJ, DC MS 19; DC MS 15; DC MS 16. See Stephen Parrish's Introduction to *The Prelude 1798–1799* (1799), pp. 3–36.

20. Lines reconstructed from textual stubs in a second notebook, MS 15, with help from MS U. Parrish notes that they are "evidently fresh composition, and they introduce a new element into main body of the poem. Here for the first time is a loving person addressed" (1799, p. 13).

21. Dorothy and William to Coleridge, letter of December 1798, sent at the time

Wordsworth was finishing the completion of MS JJ (EY 239, 243). Although Dorothy's earlier letter to Coleridge, which contained the lines "There was a boy" (from MS JJ) and which he acknowledged in a letter of 10 December, does not survive, we do have Coleridge's reply (CL, I: 452).

22. Although De Selincourt and Shaver do not record a final exclamation mark (EY 243), the manuscript letter clearly shows a dark exclamation mark ("our very dear friend!") sloped just like three in the valediction that they do record. Still, the final punctuation may be William's. Parrish writes, "After transcription, Dorothy or William went over the text and added or altered some of the punctuation" (1799, p. 131).

23. "For thou art with me, here, upon the banks / Of this fair river; thou, my dearest Friend, / My dear, dear Friend, and in thy voice I catch / The language of my former heart . . ." (lines 115–18, LB 119).

24. A letter of 10 May 1798, CL, I: 406.

25. Coleridge did not date the letter. Ernest H. Coleridge dates the letter to "winter 1798–99" and Griggs conjectures "Early Dec 1798" (CL, I: 450–53). Others have suggested early February.

26. Leading him to understand that "as in English & German we form our harmony from tone not quantity—or perhaps our quantity depends upon the Intonation" (qtd. in Ernest Bernhardt-Kabisch, " 'When Klopstock England Defied': Coleridge, Southey, and the German/ English Hexameter," *Comparative Literature*, 55.2 (Spring 2003): 130–63 (143). On Coleridge's experimentation see 130–51.

27. On hexameters, Coleridge, and debates about the most appropriate national meter, see Yopie Prins, "Metrical Translation: Nineteenth-Century Homers and the Hexameter Mania," in *Nation, Language and the Ethics of Translation*, ed. Sandra Bermann and Michael Wood (Princeton: Princeton University Press, 2005), 229–56.

28. Inserted, evidence suggests, sometime after the opening of Part II. The lines first appear in the fair copies of the 1798–1799 text, MSS U and V.

29. Paul Magnuson, *Coleridge and Wordsworth: A Lyrical Dialogue* (Princeton: Princeton University Press, 1988), 206.

30. On the deceptive use of "friendly quotation," see Lucy Newlyn, *Coleridge, Wordsworth and the Language of Allusion* (Oxford: Clarendon Press, 1986), 145–46, 167–71.

31. *The Five Book Prelude*, ed. Duncan Wu (Oxford: Blackwell, 1997), p. 10. Henceforth cited as Five Book Prelude.

32. Reed notes that by 18 March "the family had sent off to Coleridge, in parts, the manuscript now known as MS M (DC MS 44), with its copies of almost 'all William's smaller poems' " (1805, I: p. 11).

33. See, for instance, "Thus far, My Friend! have we, though leaving much / Unvisited . . ." (MS M, f. 143r).

34. Newlyn, *Coleridge and Wordsworth*, 172.

35. Newlyn, *Coleridge and Wordsworth*, 175–76.

36. Parker, "Wordsworth's Whelming Tide: Coleridge and the Art of Analogy," in *Forms of Lyric: Selected Papers from the English Institute*, ed. Reuben A. Brower (New York: Columbia University Press, 1970), 75–102 (89).

37. I take the 1807 text from the Norton Prelude as the only widely available printing of the manuscript text of 1807 which was given to Wordsworth. Cf. PW, II. ii, pp. 1028–36.

38. Kenneth R. Johnston, *The Hidden Wordsworth: Poet, Lover, Rebel, Spy* (New York: W. W. Norton, 1998), 833.

39. On Coleridge's iconic exploitation of parentheses, see John Lennard, *But I Digress: The Exploitation of Parentheses in English Printed Verse* (Oxford: Clarendon Press, 1991), 127–36.

40. Parker, "Wordsworth's Whelming Tide," 80.

41. Parker, "Wordsworth's Whelming Tide," 77, 102. Parker quotes Coleridge's letter to Wordsworth of 30 May 1815, CL, IV: 570–76.

42. Wordsworth, "The Texts: History and Presentation," Norton, 511.

43. "The Texts: History and Presentation," Norton, 525.

44. See, for example, Alan Liu, *Wordsworth: The Sense of History* (Stanford: Stanford University Press, 1989), James K. Chandler, *Wordsworth's Second Nature: A Study of the Poetry and Politics* (Chicago: University of Chicago Press, 1984), and Celeste Langan, *Romantic Vagrancy: Wordsworth and the Simulation of Freedom* (Cambridge: Cambridge University Press, 1995).

45. Although Jonathan Wordsworth retains the spelling of the base manuscript throughout the 1799 poem, he alters the spelling of the preterit throughout the 1805 text, choosing " 'to mark the occasional "éd" that requires a stress' rather than 'to preserve apostrophe "d" for the many that don't.' " On the destruction of this "evidence of William Wordsworth's preferred practice," see Donald H. Reiman, "Cornell Wordsworth, Norton *Prelude*," in *Romantic Texts and Contexts* (Columbia: University of Missouri Press, 1988), 152. Reiman also critiques the Norton's alteration of the 1799 and 1805 poems' punctuation and capitalization.

46. The Norton edition differentiates the poet as a user of language from the inscriptional surfaces of London. In Book VII, "Advertisements, of giant size!" and the "Delusion bold!" of Jack the Giant-killer's "Coat of Darkness" are shorn of their exclamation points; "the word / Invisible flames forth upon his Chest!" not only loses its exclamation point but also acquires capitals, indicating a preference for visual emphasis over emphasis of vocal phrasing: "the word / INVISIBLE flames forth upon his chest" (1805, VII: 210, 308, 304, 309–10, cf. Norton, VII: 210, 308, 304, 309–10).

CHAPTER 7

Epigraph: *Ruined Cottage* MS B, *The Ruined Cottage and The Pedlar*, ed. James Butler (Ithaca: Cornell University Press, 1979), 52r, lines 1–12, p. 275.

1. As J. P. Ward shows in " 'Came from Yon Fountain': Wordsworth's Influence on Victorian Educators," *Victorian Studies*, 29 (1986), 405–36 (420) citing the educational journal *Papers for the Schoolmaster* which printed the Regional Training Board examination papers. See also Catherine Robson, *Heart Beats: Everyday Life and the Memorized Poem* (Princeton: Princeton University Press, 2012), 50, citing Ian Michael, *The Teaching of English: From the Sixteenth Century to 1870* (Cambridge: Cambridge University Press, 2005) and showing passages from *Excursion* Book I were set for learning and recitation in women's training colleges.

2. Jeffrey, review of *The Excursion*; *Edinburgh Review*, 24 (November 1814): 1–4.

3. From the title of Thelwall's *Illustrations of English Rhythmus: Selections for the illustration of a Course of Instructions on the Rhythmus and Utterance of the English Language* (London, 1812).

4. On Matthew Arnold's efforts to have Wordsworth's poems adopted in the education system, so as to use their "beauty" to counteract "anarchy," see Ward, " 'Came from Yon Fountain'," 434.

5. Wordsworth, Preface to *Lyrical Ballads* (LB 746–7); Arnold, *Culture and Anarchy* (London, 1869).

6. From the title of Book IV, "Despondency Corrected."

7. John Thelwall to Susan Thelwall ("Stella"), 18 July 1797. In Damian Walford Davies, *Presences that Disturb: Models of Romantic Identity in the Literature and Culture of the 1790s* (Cardiff: University of Wales Press, 2002), 296.

8. See Nicholas Roe, "John Thelwall and the West Country: The Road to Nether Stowey Revisited," in *John Thelwall: Critical Reassessments*, ed. Yasmin Solomonescu, *Romantic Circles Praxis.* Accessed 28 June 2012. http://www.rc.umd.edu/praxis/thelwall/HTML/praxis.2011.roe.html. See also Judith Thompson, "An Autumnal Blast, a Killing Frost: Coleridge's Poetic Conversation with John Thelwall," *Studies in Romanticism*, 36.3 (1997): 427–56.

9. *The Fenwick Notes of William Wordsworth. A Revised Electronic Edition*, ed. Jared Curtis (Bristol: Bristol Classical Press, 1993; rev. ed. Tirril, Penrith, 2007), 45.

10. See E. P. Thompson, "Hunting the Jacobin Fox," *The Romantics in a Revolutionary Age,* ed. Dorothy Thompson (New York: New Press, 1997), 156–217; Nicholas Roe, *The Politics of Nature: William Wordsworth and Some Contemporaries,* 2nd ed. (Basingstoke: Palgrave, 2002), 13–24; Michael Scrivener, *Seditious Allegories: John Thelwall and Jacobin Writing* (University Park: Pennsylvania State University Press, 2001), 3; *John Thelwall: Radical Romantic and Acquitted Felon,* ed. Steve Poole (London: Pickering and Chatto, 2009), 165ff. For a different reading of the passage of the Two Acts, see Johnston, *Unusual Suspects: Pitt's Reign of Alarm and the Lost Generation of the 1790s* (Oxford: Oxford University Press, 2013), 26.

11. See David Fairer, *Organising Poetry: The Coleridge Circle, 1790–1798* (Oxford: Oxford University Press, 2009), 239–44, from which quotations of these letters are drawn. Richard Gravil, "The Somerset Sound; or, the Darling Child of Speech," *The Coleridge Bulletin: The Journal of the Friends of Coleridge*, NS 26 (2005), 18–21.

12. I quote from "Sonnet III To Luxury," 6, "Ode. II," 53–4, and "Sonnet V. The Source of Slavery," 2, 5, 6. On Thelwall's "directness of speech," refusal of the subjective, and commitment to "principles of honesty and truth" through personification, see Fairer, *Organising Poetry*, 237–38.

13. See Johnston, *Unusual Suspects*, 25–32.

14. From a lecture of 6 November 1795, printed in *The Tribune*, 47. In *The Politics of English Jacobinism: the Writings of John Thelwall,* ed. Gregory Claeys (University Park: Pennsylvania State University Press, 1995), 316.

15. John Rice, *An Introduction to the Art of Reading with Energy and Propriety* (London, 1765), 138.

16. *An Essay towards a Definition of Animal Vitality: Read at the Theatre, Guy's Hospital, January 26, 1793; in which several of the opinions of the celebrated John Hunter are examined and controverted* (London, 1793), 39, 41. On the literary and ideological ramifications of Thelwall's materialist theory of vitality over the four decades of his career, see Yasmin Solomonescu, *John Thelwall and the Materialist Imagination* (New York: Palgrave Macmillan, 2014).

17. Roe suggests "that it was Thelwall's scientific speculations, as much as his politics, which brought the charge of treason in 1794": *Politics of Nature*, 92. See also Fairer, *Organising Poetry*, 236. So, too, Noel Jackson reads the poetry of 1798–1801 as suggesting a force in language akin to the "electrical fluid" that stimulates passion in listeners. Noel Jackson, *Science and Sensation in Romantic Poetry* (Cambridge: Cambridge University Press, 2008), 54.

18. Mary Fairclough, *The Romantic Crowd: Sympathy, Controversy and Print Culture* (Cambridge: Cambridge University Press, 2013), 109.

19. Quoted in Jackson, *Science and Sensation in Romantic Poetry*, 47, 45.

20. From a lecture of 6 November 1795, printed in *The Tribune*, 47. In *The Politics of English Jacobinism: the Writings of John Thelwall*, 316.

21. Qtd. in Mrs. Cecil (Boyle) Thelwall, *The Life of John Thelwall* (London, 1837), 347. See Molly Desjardins, "Thelwall and Association," para. 12, in *John Thelwall: Critical Reassessments*. Accessed 28 June 2014. http://www.rc.umd.edu/praxis/thelwall/HTML/praxis.2011.desjardins. html. See also Hazlitt's description, probably of Thelwall: " 'The most dashing orator I ever heard is the flattest writer I ever read. In speaking, he was like a volcano vomiting out lava; in writing, he is like a volcano burnt out. . . . The lightning of national indignation flashed from his eye; the working of the popular mind were seen labouring in his bosom . . . but . . . read one of these very popular and electrical effusions . . . and you would not believe it to be the same!' " (qtd. in Thompson, *The Romantics in a Revolutionary Age*, 158).

22. Thomas Sheridan, *A Course of Lectures on Elocution* (London, 1798), 129. See also Hugh Blair: "On the right management of the Emphasis depend the whole life and spirit of every Discourse." *Lectures on Rhetoric and Belles Lettres*, II: 438.

23. See Fairer, *Organising Poetry*, 236–59.

24. A label given him by Secretary of State for War, William Windham: see *John Thelwall: Radical Romantic and Acquitted Felon*, ed. Steve Poole (London: Pickering and Chatto, 2009), 1–11.

25. Fairer, *Organising Poetry*, 255. On this poetry of retirement and the Llyswen period, see Yasmin Solomonescu, "Mute Records and Blank Legends: John Thelwall's 'Paternal Tears,' " *Romanticism*, 16.2 (2010), 152–63, and Judith Thompson, *John Thelwall in the Wordsworth Circle: The Silenced Partner* (Basingstoke: Palgrave, 2012), 125–60.

26. "On leaving the Bottoms of Glocestershire; where the Author had been entertained by several families with great hospitality. Aug. 12, 1797." *Poems, Chiefly Written in Retirement* (Hereford, 1801), 138–39.

27. It makes no appearance in *Poems Written in Close Confinement*.

28. *Poems, Chiefly Written in Retirement*, 129.

29. "To the Infant Hampden," *Poems, Chiefly Written in Retirement*, 141.

30. *Poems, Chiefly Written in Retirement*, 130.

31. On the reciprocal influence, see Roe, *The Politics of Nature*, 96–119; Walford Davies, *Presences that Disturb*, 193–240. In the *Silenced Partner*, 53–56, Judith Thompson argues that Coleridge's "Frost at Midnight" responds to Thelwall's "To the Infant Hampden." See also Gravil, "Somerset Sound." Thelwall's use of the 2-em dash perhaps also influenced Wordsworth's use of the mark in *Lyrical Ballads* (1800).

32. See Roe, *Politics of Nature*, 93–95, quotation on 95.

33. Thelwall's inscription of his copy of *The Excursion* (London, 1814), by kind permission of Paul F. Betz.

34. *Selections for the Illustration of a Course of Instruction on the Rhythmus and Utterance of the English Language* (London, 1812), 73. Henceforth cited as *Selections*.

35. *Selections*, xliv.

36. Syllables vary from none to five (five usually reserved for prose, the most "base" of feet). Pacing changes according to the number of syllables.

37. Thelwall defines "emphasis" as the "superadding to the customary energy of the poise or heavy syllable" a species of time, inflexion, or extra "emphatic force." s.v. Emphasis, Abraham Rees, *The Cyclopædia; or, Universal Dictionary of Arts, Sciences, and Literature* (London, 1819). The volume in which this entry appeared was first published in 1809.

38. Steele quoted in *Selections*, i–ii. In an 1806 letter on "Pulsation and Remission"

published in the *Monthly Magazine* and reprinted in the *Letter to Henry Cline*, Thelwall claimed to have independently arrived at his ideas. HC 177–79.

39. *Selections*, v–vi.

40. "Effusion I" of the verse sequence "Paternal Tears" in *Poems, Chiefly Written in Retirement*, 149.

41. Cf. Celeste Langan, "Pathologies of Communication from Coleridge to Schreber," *South Atlantic Quarterly*, 102 (2003): 117–52.

42. Rees, *The Cyclopædia*. The volume in which this essay appeared was first published in 1809.

43. Cf. *Selections*, lviii.

44. Qtd. in *The Life of John Thelwall*, 347.

45. John Thelwall, *A Letter to Francis Jeffray on Certain Calumnies and Misrepresentations in the Edinburgh Review; the Conduct of Certain Individuals, on the night of Mr. Thelwall's Probationary Lecture, at Bernard's Rooms, Edinburgh . . . With an appendix, containing Outlines of a course of lectures on the science and practice of elocution* (Edinburgh, 1804), 95.

46. John Thelwall, *Concluding Address to a Course of Lectures at Huddersfield*, 12, in *A Letter to Francis Jeffray*. Elocution worked "to give energy to every other pursuit of genius and intellect." *The Vestibule of Eloquence* (London, 1810), 54.

47. The letter text is given in Walford Davies, *Presences that Disturb*, 18.

48. Thelwall, *Letter to Jeffray*, see especially 69–72.

49. On Thelwall in Kendal, see Judith Thompson, *Silenced Partner*, 17.

50. Thelwall refers to "Accent of Punctuation" in his outline of "Part I" of "Lecture the Twelfth." *Letter to Jeffray*, "Outline," 8.

51. On poetry as a "metrical medium, transmitting . . . surges of pressure to the psychesoma," see Maureen N. McLane, *Balladeering, Minstrelsy, and the Making of British Romantic Poetry* (Cambridge: Cambridge University Press, 2008), 241.

52. Thelwall, *Letter to Jeffray*, 109.

53. Thelwall, *Letter to Jeffray*, "Errata," n.p.

54. *Selections*, lxix.

55. *Selections, and Original Articles* (1802), 3.

56. Thelwall, *Letter to Jeffray*, 68–69.

57. Thelwall, *The Rights of Nature Against the Usurpations of Establishments* (Norwich, 1796), 75.

58. *Letter to Henry Cline*, 165, 164.

59. *Selections and Original Articles, for Mr. Thelwall's Lectures on the Science and Practice of Elocution; Together with the Introductory Discourse and Outlines* (Birmingham, 1806).

60. Thomas Gray, "Elegy in a Country Churchyard," line 59.

61. *Selections*, iii.

62. "Introductory Essay," *Selections* (1806), iv.

63. *Selections*, xi, 30.

64. *Selections*, iv.

65. *Selections*, iv.

66. *Selections*, v.

67. *Selections*, xl.

68. According to Hugh Blair, "When one mounts a Pulpit, or rises in Public Assembly, one assumes a new, studied tone, and a cadence altogether foreign to [one's] natural manner." *Lectures on Rhetoric and Belles Lettres*, 3rd ed., 3 vols. (London, 1787), II: 448.

69. Rice, *An Introduction to the Art of Reading with Energy and Propriety* (London, 1765), 16.
70. *Selections*, v.
71. *Selections*, 40.
72. *Vestibule of Eloquence*, 1.
73. *Selections*, 40, 44.
74. *Selections*, 1.
75. *Selections*, 34.
76. *Selections and Original Articles* (Birmingham, 1806), page 15, lines 13, 26–40.
77. "Historical and Oratorical Society at Mr. Thelwall's Institution," *Monthly Magazine*, 28 (1809): 152–57 (154). Cited in Judy Duchan, *A History of Speech-Language Pathology: John Thelwall, A Nineteenth-Century British Elocutionist 1764–1834*. Online resource. Accessed 28 June 2012. http://www.acsu.buffalo.edu/~duchan/new_history/thelwall/politics_practice.html
78. *Selections*, xxi.
79. *Selections*, x, see also xxi.
80. *Selections*, xvi–xvii.
81. *Selections*, xix; see also xv, xviii.
82. In her contextualization of Thelwall's program with respect to the early nineteenth-century British Lyceum movement (a "nationwide system of adult education which was unified in its mandate to advance a democratic tradition of interdisciplinary education" [148]), Tara-Lynn Fleming reads the *Selections* "not only as cultural sites of learning" and sociability that cut across the classes, but as "material expressions of the lyceum institution" (159): Tara-Lynn Fleming, "Tracing the Textual Reverberation: The Role of Thelwall's Elocutionary Selections in the British Lyceum." In *Radical Romantic and Acquitted Felon*, 147–60.
83. Building upon E. P. Thompson's comparison of the figure of the Solitary and the disappointed revolutionary who retreated from public life to the Wye valley (E. P. Thompson, *The Romantics: England in a Revolutionary Age*, 196–201), Judith Thompson argues that by scanning *The Excursion* Thelwall wrote himself back into a conversation with Wordsworth and Coleridge from which he had been excluded and inscribed himself into a literary history that would go on to erase him. *The Silenced Partner*, 255–73.
84. Thelwall's inscription of his copy of *The Excursion* (London, 1814), by kind permission of Paul F. Betz. By rhythmical clauses, Thelwall seems to mean balanced groupings of cadences, divided from each other by "*grammatical pauses, emphases, and caesurae.*" Rhythmus "*consists in an arrangement of cadences, or metrical feet, in clauses more or less distinguishable by the ear.*" Verse "*is constituted of a regular succession of like cadences, or of a limited variety of cadence, divided . . . into obviously proportioned clauses; so as to present sensible responses, at proportioned intervals, to the ear*" (*Selections*, lv–lvi). Prose is "perpetually varying, not only in the length of clauses, and the recurrence of emphases, but thro' all the practicable varieties of cadence" (xv).
85. My interpretation of Thelwall's act of scansion should be compared with Richard Gravil, "Mr Thelwall's Ear; or, hearing *The Excursion*," in *Grasmere 2011: Selected Papers from the Wordsworth Summer Conference*, ed. Richard Gravil (Humanities e-books, 2012), 189–203.
86. *Selections*, xxii, xix, xxiii.
87. *Selections*, xvii.
88. From an announcement in *The Times*, 17 April 1820. Qtd. in Roe, "Lives of John Thelwall: Another View of the 'Jacobin Fox,' " in *John Thelwall: Radical Romantic and Acquitted Felon*, 13–24 (20). *The Excursion* is listed as item number 203 in *A Catalogue of the Genuine Library of Valuable Books, Maps in Cases, Busts, Pair of Globes, Medals and Coins, and Miscellaneous Effects of*

John Thelwall, Esq. . . . Which will be Sold by Auction by Mr. Armstrong. I am grateful to Patty O'Boyle for sharing this reference with me.

89. Judith Thompson, *Silenced Partner*, 264.

90. William St. Clair considers the poem "for its length, perhaps the most expensive work of literature ever published in England." He adds, "For the price of *The Excursion* in quarto, a reader in Salisbury could have bought over a hundred fat pigs," *The Reading Nation in the Romantic Period* (Cambridge: Cambridge University Press, 2004), 201–2.

91. Entry of 15 February 1815, *Diary, Reminiscences and Correspondence of Henry Crabb Robinson*, 3 vols. (London, 1869), I: 473.

92. *Selections*, 23.

93. In Thelwall's *Selections* and *Vestibule of Eloquence*, Judith Thompson states, poetry becomes "a site of sociable conversation and education" (*Silenced Partner*, 264). Sally Bushell argues that *The Excursion* models a form of active reception that brings the solitary reader into a position of a discursive community with other minds and achieves by proxy the restoration of the Solitary. Bushell, *Re-reading* The Excursion*: Narrative, Response and the Wordsworthian Dramatic Voice* (Aldershot: Ashgate, 2002).

94. The boy applies this mode of natural, pleasurable assimilation to geometry books. By clothing "the nakedness of austere truth" in nature's "hues," "forms," and the "spirit of her forms," he delights in learning: "her simplest laws, / His triangles—they were the stars of heaven, / The silent stars!" (I: 290, 288, 289, 292–4).

95. Similarly, the image of a river running into a sea on a map, in the contemporary "Essay upon Epitaphs," is used to counterpoint the sense of a "receptacle without bounds or dimensions," the sense of a powerful feeder of "the perpetual current"—the sense, that is, of "immortality" (*W Prose*, II: 51).

96. Kenneth R. Johnston, *Wordsworth and* The Recluse (New Haven: Yale University Press, 1984), 274.

97. Johnston, *Wordsworth and* The Recluse, 273.

98. To Kevis Goodman, the therapeutic value of the stories lies in their seriality: their spacing out of accidents and of death, slowly across time, acts as a retroactive counter to the Solitary's past trauma. Goodman, *Georgic Modernity and British Romanticism: Poetry and the Mediation of History* (Cambridge: Cambridge University Press, 2004), 106–43.

99. On Thelwall's sidebars and other notations, see Judith Thompson, *Silenced Partner*, 271–72.

100. *The Excursion* (London, 1814). By kind permission of Paul F. Betz.

101. *The Excursion* (London, 1814). By kind permission of Paul F. Betz.

102. Johnston, *Wordsworth and* The Recluse, 273.

103. "Oration," *Vestibule of Eloquence*, 45–46.

104. *Vestibule of Eloquence*, 44.

105. From a lecture of 6 November 1795, printed in *The Tribune*, 47. In *The Politics of English Jacobinism: the Writings of John Thelwall*, 316. As Catherine Packham writes, in the 1790s Thelwall identified this "energy" with "reason"—an "animating force" that he differentiated from enthusiasm. Packham, *Eighteenth-Century Vitalism: Bodies, Culture, Politics* (Basingstoke: Palgrave Macmillan, 2012), 133.

106. *Vestibule of Eloquence*, 44.

107. *Vestibule of Eloquence*, 46.

108. *The Trident of Albion . . . To Which Is Prefixed, an Introductory Discourse on the Nature and Objects of Elocutionary Science* (Liverpool, 1805), 24, 23.

109. On Wordsworth's visit to Ireland during the Ordnance Survey of that country (1829), his growing interest in triangulation, and possible repercussions for revisions to *The Prelude*, see Rachel Hewitt, *Map of a Nation: A Biography of the Ordnance Survey* (London: Granta, 2010), 262-63.

110. William Roy quoted in Seymour, *History of the Ordnance Survey*, 7.

111. *Vestibule of Eloquence*, 122.

112. Thompson, *Silenced Partner*, 262, 263.

113. Parts of Thelwall's incomplete poem, published in *The Vestibule of Eloquence*, were read and recited at Thelwall's Institute and heard at his lectures.

114. Johnston, *Wordsworth and* The Recluse, 313.

115. Johnston, "Wordsworth's *Excursion*: Route and Destination," *Wordsworth Circle*, 45.2 (2014): 106–13 (110).

116. *Vestibule of Eloquence*, 23.

Index

220–21, 224–25, 332n.65; locodescriptive poetry, 24; lyric, 13, 16, 24–25, 33, 34–36, 37, 53, 74, 227; measured prose (*prose mesurée*), 4, 30, 162–63, 305n.10; ode, 1, 70, 246, 250–55, 263, 268; print inscriptions, 207; rhyme, 1–2, 4, 10–11, 29–30, 34, 132, 158–60, 162–63, 265, 272–73, 276, 284; sonnet, 21, 34, 49, 193, 263, 299; verse epistle, 233. See also meter

politiscansion, 131, 302–3

Pollard, Jane, 58, 59, 60, 61, 78

Pope, Alexander: *An Essay on Man*, "Epistle IV," 134 (fig.); "Prologue to *Cato*," 158–59

Price, Leah, 19

Priestley, Joseph: *Rudiments of English Grammar* (1761), 151

Prins, Yopie, 18, 20, 335n.27

prosodic notations. See marks of speech

punctuation: blank line or double dash, 16, 20, 184, 186, 189–90, 192, 195, 196, 202–205, 204 (fig.), 215, 221–23, 224, 226, 230, 265–67, 331n.34, 331n.36, 332n.56, 333n.72, 338n.31; "business" of, 190–91, 231, 274; colon, 187, 191, 331n.48; comma, 187, 190, 191, 245, 256–57, 330n.32, 330n.33, 333n.72; dash, 109–11, 176, 184, 188–91, 200, 202, 211, 221–23, 256, 274, 277, 297 (fig.), 301–302, 330n.24, 330n.26, 332n.56; double paragraph, 186; double punctuation, 256; ellipsis, 330n.24; exclamation mark, 17, 131, 136, 176, 184, 185–87, 189, 191, 192, 200, 206, 226–31, 237–39, 245–48, 251, 253, 255, 256–59, 270, 290, 297 (fig.), 298, 301, 332n.58, 333n.1, 335n.22, 336n.46; full stop or period, 157, 182, 185–86, 187, 190–91, 200, 202, 316n.49, 333n.72; hyphen, 191; interspace, 215; notes, 141, 185, 228; overdetermination of, 231; paragraph breaks, 184, 185, 186, 189, 190–91, 196, 215, 216, 217; parenthesis or brackets, 14, 110–11, 185, 200, 254, 336n.39; *punctum admirationis* or point of admiration, 186, 228, 230; question mark or point of interrogation, 77–78, 136, 141, 176, 186, 191, 230; semicolon, 185, 187, 191, 200 , 331n.51, 333n.80; spoken punctuation, 152–53; vacant line, 186–87, 189; wondering point, 136, 185–86

Puttenham, George, 152

Quintilian, 69, 163, 177; *Institutes of Oratory*, 151–52, 333n.75

Radcliffe, Ann, 50

Ramsay, Allan: "On Wit," 282–84, 283 (fig.)

Ratzeburg, 231, 233–39, 241, 255

Reed, Mark, 77, 245

Rees, Abraham: *The Cyclopædia; or, Universal Dictionary of Arts, Sciences, and Literature*, 271

Rees, Owen, 219

Rhine, river, 57

Rhone, river, 58

Rice, John, 4, 155; *Introduction to the Art of Reading with Energy and Propriety* (1765), 280

Richardson, Alan, 146, 227

Richardson, Samuel, 188

Ricks, Christopher, 20, 93, 100

Riley, Denise, 315n.27

Robertson, Joseph: *Essay on Punctuation* (1785), 188–89, 230–31

Robson, Catherine, 20

Roe, Nicholas, 264, 267

Roe, Richard, 4

Roscoe, William: "Occasional Address," 281 (fig.)

Rousseau, Jean Jacques, 146

Roy, William, 86, 87, 88, 91–92, 96, 117, 124, 128, 319n.70, 321n.109

Ruden, 62, 65, 67 (fig.)

Rudwick, Martin J. S., 129

Ruskin, John, 119, 122, 123, 126, 320n.85

St. Herbert's Island, 30

St. Jacob, 62 (fig.), 64, 65, 66 (fig.), 67 (fig.)

Saintsbury, George, 12, 20, 306n.27; *History of English Prosody* (1906–10), 10, 328n.115

Salisbury, 341n.90

Savoy, 56

Say, Samuel, 4, 132, 144, 155, 170; "On the Harmony, Variety, and Power of Numbers, whether in Prose or Verse," 132; "On the Numbers of Paradise Lost," 132, 303; *Poems on Several Occasions, and Two Critical Essays* (1745), 132; "Remarks on the Scripture Sense of Preaching," 132

Scale Force, 44, 312n.54

Scale Hill, 6, 44

scansion. See meter

Schaffhouse, 57

Scotland, 6, 86, 107, 108, 110, 113, 116, 146, 148, 320n.78, 324n.12

Scots, 141, 146, 322n.26

Acknowledgments

Many people have shaped this book. I wish to thank Marjorie Levinson, Adela Pinch, and Yopie Prins for giving it lift and emphasis, and Karl Eric Longstreth for unrolling the maps. I am grateful for the readings, conversations, and comments of Eyal Amiran, Timothy Bahti, Ian Balfour, Thora Brylowe, Kieran Cannon, Hannah Carlson, and Matthew H. Edney; Kalli Federhofer, Anne-Lise François, Michael Gamer, Stephen Gill, Nicholas Halmi, Meredith Martin, and Dahlia Porter; Sarah Riggs, Zak Sitter, Yasmin Solomonescu, Rei Terada, Judith Thompson, Yofi Tirosh, and Valerie Traub. They have all made their mark. The opportunity, in the midst of this project, to write collaboratively on European print culture with an impressive group of scholars led by Andrew Piper, Tom Mole, and Jon Sachs was enlightening and a pleasure. The generosity of Paul F. Betz, Jeff Cowton, Fitz Gitler, and Jerry Singerman—with needful texts, technology, and time—has been critical, as has the camaraderie of colleagues at Cincinnati, including Beth Ash, Don Bogen, Jana Braziel, John Drury, Jenn Glaser, Jon Kamholtz, Laura Micciche, Arnie Miller, Maura O'Connor, Lee Person, Jay Twomey, Gary Weissman, Barbara Wenner, and Elissa Yancey. Tim Fulford has helped to land the typographical plane.

Research and writing were supported by the University of Michigan Institute for the Humanities, the Mellon Foundation, and the Charles Phelps Taft Research Center at the University of Cincinnati. Parts of Chapters 1, 2, 3, and 5 were derived from the following articles: "*Prose Mesurée* in the Lakes Tour and Guide: Quoting and Recalibrating English Blank Verse," *European Romantic Review* 20.2 (2009), 227–36; "The Map at the Limits of His Paper: A Cartographic Reading of *The Prelude*, Book 6," *Studies in Romanticism* 49.3 (2010), 375–404; "Topographical Measures: Wordsworth's and Crosthwaite's Lines on the Lake District," *Romanticism* 16.1 (2010), 72–93; "Measuring Distance, Pointing Address: The Textual Geography of the 'Poem to Coleridge' and 'To

W. Wordsworth,'" *Romanticism and Victorianism on the Net* 61 (November 12, 2013). I thank the editors as well as the Trustees of Boston University and Edinburgh University Press.

I am grateful to the following individuals and institutions for permission to reproduce images from their collections: Paul F. Betz; the Bodleian Libraries, University of Oxford; the Trustees of the British Museum; the Board of the British Library; the John Hay Library, Brown University Library; the William L. Clements Library and the Map Library, University of Michigan; the Lionel Pincus and Princess Firyal Map Division, The New York Public Library, Astor, Lenox and Tilden Foundations; the Wordsworth Trust, Grasmere; the Beinecke Rare Book and Manuscript Library, Yale University.